OLD JEWISH FOLK MUSIC

Moshe Beregovski (1892–1961)
(Courtesy of Eleanor Gordon Mlotek)

OLD JEWISH FOLK MUSIC

The Collections and Writings of
MOSHE BEREGOVSKI

edited and translated by
MARK SLOBIN

University of Pennsylvania Press · Philadelphia · 1982

Publications of the American Folklore Society
New Series
General Editor, Marta Weigle
Volume 6

The music and texts on pp. 45–242 are reproduced by permission of YIVO Institute for Jewish Research and are taken from the original copy of M. Beregovski, *Jidišer Muzik-Folklor, Band I* (Moskve: Meluxišer Muzik-Farlag, 1934), which is in the YIVO Library.

This work was published with the support of the Haney Foundation.

Designed by Adrianne Onderdonk Dudden

ISBN 0–8122–7833–X (cloth)
0–8122–1126–X (paper)

LC No. 81–43526

Printed in the United States of America

*This volume is dedicated to all
the scholars and musicians of Jewish Eastern Europe
who perished under Hitler and Stalin.*

CONTENTS

ILLUSTRATIONS

Plates

Map

PREFACE

This volume is meant to speak to two audiences. One is composed of ethnomusicologists, folklorists, and specialists in Jewish studies. For them, this anthology of songs and writings is meant to fill the deplorable gap left by the scanty scholarly literature on the folklore and folk music of Eastern European Jews. The other audience consists of nonspecialists who, it is hoped, will make practical use of the patrimony of songs and tunes included herein. The available popular collections of songs and dance tunes of the "Yiddish" tradition do little justice to the breadth and depth of folk creativity in what is loosely called "The Old Country," and the arrangements often overshadow the music.

Most Jewish-Americans see Eastern Europe as a cultural monolith. The present volume is part of an effort by the current generation of Jewish studies specialists to break down such stereotypes as are offered by, say, *Fiddler on the Roof* by offering new perspectives on a complex, lively, and tangled culture that extended from the Baltic to the Black Sea across a thousand years of history. Some of us also feel a need to reach across the abyss of the Holocaust to retrieve important primary sources, such as Beregovski's works, which have lain dormant all too long.

I would like to acknowledge with heartfelt thanks the assistance of the staff of the YIVO Institute for Jewish Research, the bastion of contemporary scholarship on Eastern European Jewish culture and its major storehouse. Eleanor Gordon Mlotek was kind enough to make available her encyclopedic knowledge of the Yiddish song. Lucjan Dobroszycki and Marek Web provided valuable archival materials and suggestions. Warmest thanks are due to Barbara Kirshenblatt-Gimblett for encouraging my dream of an English-language Beregovski edition. On the linguistic side, I acknowledge a debt to Mordko Nachtajler for helping with the Yiddish, and Greta Nachtailer Slobin for assistance with Russian. This project was aided in part by research funds and sabbatical time from Wesleyan University.

Mark Slobin
Middletown, Connecticut
May 1981

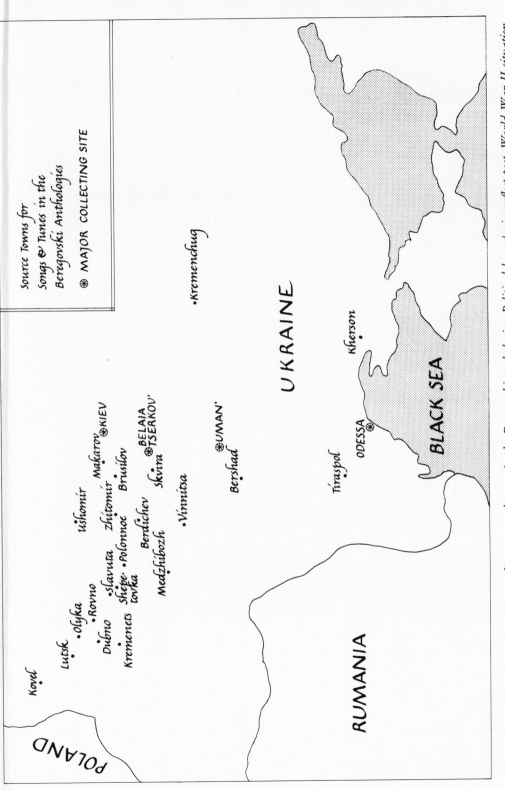

Map of the Ukraine. Source towns for songs and tunes in the Beregovski anthologies. Political boundaries reflect post–World War II situation, all locales now being in the Ukrainian SSR.

NOTE ON TRANSLITERATION
AND TRANSLATION

Transliteration

Beregovski used the Soviet system for transliteration of Yiddish in the song texts of his anthologies, as opposed to the now generally accepted YIVO system of romanization in standard post–World War II Western sources (see Uriel Weinreich's standard *Modern English-Yiddish/Yiddish-English Dictionary* [New York: YIVO and McGraw-Hill, 1968]). In addition, Beregovski had to transliterate Yiddish names into the Cyrillic alphabet when publishing in Russian. As a result, it is difficult to use a single system throughout the present edition. The following rules prevail:

1. Beregovski's song texts and citation of Yiddish terms in the texts of essays have been kept in the Soviet system.

2. The YIVO system is used for bibliography so as to facilitate locating the sources in Western libraries.

3. The YIVO system is used for Yiddish proper names.

4. The Library of Congress system of transliteration is used for Russian proper names (e.g., Belaia Tserkov').

Soviet Romanization of Yiddish

A few of the Soviet equivalents may confuse the reader used to other systems (equivalents from Weinreich 1968).

x = *ch* (YIVO *kh*) as in German *ach*
š = *sh* as in *shoot*
c = *ts*
č = *ch* as in *chin* (YIVO *tsh*)
oj = *oy,* shorter than in *boy* (YIVO *oy*)
aj = *i* as in *fine* (YIVO *ay*)
ej = *ey* as in *grey* (YIVO *ey*)

Translation of Song Texts

The general intention of the translation of the song texts is to convey a colloquial manner of speech. No attempt has been made to imitate the meter and rhyme of the original and punctuation has been kept to a minimum to avoid interpretation. The Yiddish interjections *ax,* and *oj vej* have been kept partly for local color and partly because "ah" and "Oh, woe" seem out of place. A few words here and there remain somewhat obscure; Beregovski himself seemed to guess at meanings at times, as indicated by footnoted comments. It is of course difficult to reconstruct the vernacular of early twentieth-century Ukrainian Yiddish with complete reliability, though it is hoped that basic errors have been avoided. The responsibility for errors as well as for the occasional, inevitable inconsistencies in transliteration is completely mine.

INTRODUCTION

MARK SLOBIN

The study of Eastern European Jewish folklore was beginning to bear major scholarly fruit when the Holocaust put an end to the archives, many of the researchers, and of course to the culture being studied. While the impact was most tragic on those who perished, such as S. Z. Pipe, whose promising studies of Jewish folk music have been reissued in Israel (Pipe 1972), scholars who survived also had their activity cut off. Moshe Beregovski (1892–1961) lived to see the destruction of his patient research and the musicians he cherished and ultimately to find himself the victim of postwar Stalinist persecution. Unable to publish the results of a decade of fieldwork and writing, he was imprisoned for several years until 1955. Freed only on medical grounds, he managed to witness his rehabilitation (Braun 1978:106). It is a tribute to his reputation within the Soviet Union that two posthumous works were published (1962, 1973, both included in the present volume), and it seems time to bring his writings and song anthologies to public attention outside the Soviet Union. Recent information hints at a parallel revival in the USSR with the possibility of a forthcoming re-issue of Beregovski's works.

Moshe Beregovski was the son of a teacher at the Kiev Jewish Music School who also taught and recited sacred texts. He managed to combine composition studies under Shteinberg and Yavorsky at the Kiev and Leningrad conservatories with important ethnomusicological work in the field expeditions of the late 1910s. In 1919 he became the founder and director of a music section of the Jewish Culture League in Kiev, which closed in 1920. Subsequent biographical details vary in different accounts of Beregovski's life. According to the *Encyclopaedia Judaica* (1971:600), he was head of the ethnomusicological section of the Institute of Jewish Proletarian Culture of the Ukrainian Academy of Sciences from 1930 until it ended in 1948. A more detailed chronology is quoted by Braun (1978) from a manuscript autobiography of Beregovski recently brought to Israel by Aron Vinkovetski, who worked at the Beregovski archive in Leningrad. This source states that Beregovski was head of the Folk Music

Division from 1928 to 1936, but was then at the Folklore Department of the Kiev Conservatory, becoming director of the Folk Music Section of the Institute of Literature's Department of Jewish Culture under the Ukrainian Academy of Sciences from 1941 to 1949. Beregovski was awarded a doctorate for his work on Jewish folk instrumental music in 1944. It is interesting that the latest thorough essay on Soviet-Yiddish folklore study (Mlotek 1978) gives slightly different dates for stages of Beregovski's life; his career, set in a period of turbulence, remains somewhat resistant to documentation.

Whatever the exact dates and positions of Beregovski's career, his accomplishments are clear enough. By 1946 his collection at the Ukrainian Academy of Sciences consisted of at least seven thousand items of music, and he had written much of his projected five-volume study of Eastern European Jewish folk music. What percentage of the archival material survived World War II is unclear. A certain amount is housed at the Institute of Theater, Music, and Cinema in Leningrad. Conversations with emigrés who are familiar with that institute lead me to believe that only a small amount of material remains; perhaps future Soviet publications will clarify the matter.

More important than this account of the ephemeral quantitative aspect of Beregovski's work is its qualitative side, which can be summarized in a single statement: Beregovski is a major but forgotten ethnomusicologist of Eastern Europe. A brief survey of the works included in the present volume will help to amplify this assertion. The song anthologies presented here represent our chief corpus of accurately notated songs in Yiddish from oral tradition; there is not even a close runner-up. The first important publication of Yiddish folk songs (Ginzburg-Marek 1901) presented texts only—not a single tune was included. Furthermore, the songs were sent in from urban enthusiasts, not written down from oral sources. The next major collection (Cahan 1912) was indeed gathered directly from singers, but Cahan sang his own versions, learned by ear, to the cantor and popular song arranger Henry Rusotto, who then notated them. This is far from the norm for ethnomusicologically acceptable transcription. And so it goes. Beregovski's notations are meticulously detailed and annotated, and they hold up against the highest standards of his day and our own.

As for the three essays published here, each stakes a claim in a territory that remains as yet unmapped. The essay and questionnaire on folk instrumental music give us direct insight into Beregovski's methodology and his broad knowledge of the subject and have no parallels. Even the sidelight of the piece, a brief discussion of the traditional Jewish folk dance, is pathbreaking. In our own time there has been a significant revival of the old-time Jewish instrumental dance band; some of the revivalists have even read Beregovski. Yet only very recently (e.g., Friedland 1981) has anyone taken up the question of reconstructing the basic dance steps that go with the tunes.

Like the instrumental music essay, the essay on Jewish-Ukrainian musical interaction stands alone as a monument to a scholarly road that has not been properly pursued. There is an implicit basic philosophy of fieldwork that has only just begun to be accepted within the field of Jewish folklore studies: seeing the Jews as part of a rich interethnic musical network within a given region. In the early 1970s, Barbara Kirshenblatt-Gimblett adopted this policy in designing the YIVO Jewish Folksong Project. One of the project's basic principles was to collect not just "pure Jewish" songs from immigrant informants, but their entire repertoire, in whatever language (e.g., Ukrainian, Polish, English).

Beregovski's essay on musical symbolism was also considerably ahead of its time and is perhaps only now capable of producing an adequate response. It strongly influenced my own thinking (Slobin 1980) as a way of focusing on the question of where to locate musical ethnic boundaries, since the tonal structures Beregovski describes are not unique to the Jews, but are understood as being quintessentially Jewish.

Aside from the value of Beregovski's work, we must pause to consider its context in his own time, a period full of turmoil, trepidation, and terror for Soviet Jewry and its scholars. Anxiety forms the basic context: imagine being a Jew working for the Ukrainian Academy of Sciences in the 1930s, aware of the looming shadow of Hitler and the immediate danger of Stalinist purges. Under these conditions, it is amazing that Beregovski was able calmly to plan research expeditions and transcribe songs. It is equally surprising that he managed to publish the earlier works translated here. The second volume of his projected five-volume edition of Yiddish folk songs was set into print, title page and all, in 1938—but not published. Miraculously, the author's own set of proofs, marginal corrections and all, was discovered at the YIVO Institute for Jewish Research in New York in 1981, its path from author to archive unknown. Holding this unique copy of Volume Two in one's hands, it is not possible to question deeply the sometimes bombastic nature of Beregovski's rhetoric (see the controversial introduction to his Volume One, pp. 19–42, below). We can only be grateful for what we have: it is a voice which calls from a lost world.

Nevertheless, the reader needs some guide through the thicket of prose of that 1934 introduction. What is Beregovski attacking so vehemently and why? How can we assess his polemics? It is not within the scope of the present volume to offer an authoritative evaluation of the historical and scholarly context of Beregovski's work, nor, in some sense, do I think it entirely ethical to do so, given the historical conditions cited above. It is nearly impossible for us to gauge the pressure under which the man worked and how it shaped his output. What will be essayed here is an outline of two quite divergent recent explorations of the subject (Slotnick 1976; Mlotek 1978), with my own additional perspective as a third point of view.

In a survey of Soviet Jewish folkloristics, Susan Slotnick (1976) argues for the forceful originality of the work of the period she discusses. Like Beregovski, she sees the studies of his time as standing in sharp contrast to what is called the *folksgayst* ("spirit of the people") approach of earlier decades:

The Soviet Yiddish scholars began by criticizing previous students of Yiddish folklore (such as Y. L. Kahan, Sh. An-ski) for their "romantic nationalism" and adherence to the nineteenth century concept of the *folksgayst*. . . . The "folk" was considered to be backward, illiterate, rural —essentially non-modern; . . . an ethnic group was considered homogeneous with respect to their "folk-soul." . . . Students of Yiddish folklore, for example, dealt with what they considered "typical" and specific to the Jews, and thus emphasized the *shtetl* (which they saw as relatively autonomous from coterritorial non-Jewish society) rather than studying the "assimilating" urban elements. . . . This also explains the emphasis on Hasidism and on the archaic in folklore (Slotnick 1976:2).

As opposed to this older school, Slotnick portrays the radically different view of Beregovski's generation:

In the Soviet framework, the "folk" is defined primarily in economic terms. They are urban, industrial and revolutionary, rather than rural, non-modern and conservative. The Soviet folklorists repudiate the previous nationalism and stress instead the international unity of the working classes. . . . They emphasized the role of the individual and of social forces in the creation and transmission of folklore, and considered it to be both an agent and an indication of change (Slotnick 1976:3–4).

Although she is an American, Slotnick tends to agree with the Soviet views she cites, concluding her study with the following characterization of Soviet Jewish folklore studies:

The work of . . . Goldberg, Dobrushin, Skuditski, Viner and Beregovski is rarely accorded the importance it deserves, as the turning point from a primitive, romantic interest in folklore to the dynamic, socially-oriented discipline that we associate with the best traditions of contemporary folklore scholarship (1976:11).

Mlotek's 1978 article "Soviet-Yiddish Folklore Scholarship" is a precisely aimed attack on Slotnick's stance. As a major scholar of Yiddish folklore, Mlotek draws on a deep knowledge of the historiography of the Yiddish song. Her main thrust is at the presumed originality of the Soviet approach. She refutes Slotnick's (and, implicitly, Beregovski's) claims point for point by showing that pre-Soviet Jewish scholarship was indeed interested in the contribution of the individual, in the class basis of folk song, and in the cross-ethnic significance of folklore. On the other hand, Mlotek also points out inconsistencies in the Soviet scholars' own work, finding in certain aspects of Beregovski's contributions the "failings" he attributes to his predecessors. Mlotek also takes into account the extreme hardship under which the Soviet Jewish folklorists worked and the possibility that their writings were deformed as a result.

It is my job not to take sides in this argument but to present a third plane of perspective on a complex issue. Both Slotnick and Mlotek follow a traditional line of argument in Jewish studies, one which is extremely limiting: they assume a closed world of Jewish scholarship. This world may be subject to outside pressure, but it exists in a certain ethnic vacuum. Slotnick and Mlotek essentially debate the relative novelty and intrinsic merit of the Soviet Jewish folklorists purely as if they were members of a single lineage of Jewish origin. However, some light can be shed on the nature of Beregovski's work by appealing to a more general scholarly context in which he worked: Eastern European folklore studies. After all, Beregovski was trained in Russian conservatories and worked in the Ukrainian Academy of Sciences. He was part of a large scholarly enterprise that focused on the collection, notation, and study of the folk musics of peoples of his part of the world, an international endeavor. Some of the attributes of his work reflect long-standing regional traditions. For example, every history of folklore mentions that, as early as the mid-nineteenth century, Russian folklorists pioneered in realizing the importance of the individual as shaper of oral tradition, as opposed to the "communal" emphasis of Western European scholars. By looking at the broader scholarly context, we may be able to bypass the extreme close-up of the Jewish studies situation.

Perhaps Beregovski can best be put into context through a brief comparison with the career and work of Klement Vasil'evich Kvitka (1880–

1953), another neglected, important ethnomusicologist of the region. Kvitka, a Ukrainian, worked in the Ukrainian Academy of Sciences from 1920 to 1933. He was the founder and de facto director of the Cabinet of Musical Ethnography, the ethnomusicological wing of the Academy. His basic writings, on the topic of Slavic folk music, were done between 1923 and 1930, just before Beregovski began his own work (for a biography, see Ivanenko 1973). Beregovski cites Kvitka twice in the materials included in the present volume; I will attempt to outline the impact the older man may have had on Beregovski. Kvitka underwent the common period of eclipse of Soviet scholars during the Stalinist era and has recently been acknowledged through a two-volume reprint of his writings (Kvitka 1971, 1973a).

Three basic factors link Kvitka's work directly to the writings of Beregovski: (1) a strong interest in the research methodology of fieldwork; (2) a strong emphasis on the accuracy of contextualization of sound recording and the accuracy of transcription; (3) a decided bias toward the study of the interrelatedness of ethnic folk musics. These preferences will become clear to the reader who peruses Beregovski's works in the present volume; here we will touch on Kvitka's approach, point by point, as background for comparison.

1. In 1924 (Kvitka 1973b), Kvitka published a program for researching folksingers and instrumental musicians which serves as a direct predecessor to Beregovski's own study and which Beregovski cites. It consists of an introduction and a long series of specific questions to ask local informants. Sample passages show Kvitka's interest in interethnic musical contact, including his awareness of a Jewish contribution to the local music culture:

Do musicians of other ethnic groups travel, or have traveled in villages, namely Rumanians, Italians, Czechs, Slovaks, Gypsies, Jews. . . . Were Rumanian melodies also included in their repertoire? . . . Did the local population willingly listen to songs in foreign languages? . . .

Who mostly plays the cimbalom in a given locale: locals, Gypsies, Rumanian or Hungarian Gypsies, Jews, Armenians or others? . . . Is there a feeling that Ukrainians learned to play the cimbalom from other peoples? . . .

If in a given place one finds fiddlers of both local and outside origin, is it considered that the former play better and, consequently, are better paid? What strata of the population invite these musicians? Did the local fiddlers learn from fiddlers of foreign origin, and are memories or tales preserved about how in olden times the peasants learned to play the fiddle from foreigners or in the cities, or in the earlier lords' orchestras? (Kvitka 1973a:16–25)

Kvitka's effect on Beregovski can be seen in many of the latter's own questions (e.g., questions 52–55 of his 1937 survey, pp. 545–46 here). Another noteworthy aspect of the Kvitka passages just quoted is their strong interest in matters of social organization of music, mentioning even class-related matters. When Beregovski delves into such questions it is with an overlay of Marxist rhetoric, leading observers like Slotnick to conclude that his works fall into the "hard-line" period of the 1930s. Yet detached from their tone and specific vocabulary, Beregovski's views do not seem that far from the pre-"hard-line" Kvitka of 1924. My point here is that one way of looking at the thorny prose of Soviet musicologists is to see not what they say but what they do.

2. In an essay (Kvitka 1973a:30–37) toward the end of his career (the date is uncertain), Kvitka pointedly addresses the question of the transcription of folk music. He undertakes a long critique of poor-quality publications, saying they have impeded the progress of ethnomusicology. He states that transcription is not "automatic" work, that it involves prior analytical decisions and must include "performance practice, circumstances, and an explanation of the place the work occupies in the folk way of life" (Kvitka 1973a:37). This emphasis on performance context not only sounds quite up-to-date, but also resonates with Beregovski's approach. Beregovski paid a good deal of attention to the careful noting down of the age and occupation of informants, and to their performance practice. Most interesting here are observations in the introduction to the unpublished 1938 volume recently unearthed at YIVO. For example, he quotes informants' accounts of how recruit songs were actually sung in the army (in call-response fashion, at night). At another point, he distinguishes groupings of traditional singers, contrasting those who stretch out songs with heavy ornamentation, "permeated with dramatics" from those who are of intelligentsia origin. The latter, he says, have not a "direct" but a "literary" connection to the songs and treat their own personal versions as "authentic" and others as "crippled"; they never vary the song (Beregovski 1938:13–15).

3. We have already seen how, in his questionnaire on instrumental folk music, Kvitka stressed interethnic relationships. In a provocative essay on ethnomusicological research (Kvitka 1925:3–27), he states his credo:

The national character of the music of a given ethnic group in comparison to that of others which are geographically and culturally close cannot be portrayed as totally original, with elements belonging exclusively to the given group; there may not be such traits, or they may occupy an insignificant place. National music can be characterized by the relative strength of those elements which also make up the music of other peoples, but in a different configuration and in a different relationship. . . . One and the same melody can have a quite different character in the performance of different peoples thanks to differences in timbre and expression such that the untrained listener will not even notice them (Kvitka 1973b:10–11).

This was a remarkably forward-looking point of view for 1925, even considering world ethnomusicology as a whole. Indeed, Kvitka was aware of the early published works of major outside scholars such as Béla Bartók and finds reason to criticize them on methodological grounds, as Beregovski did in his introduction to the unpublished 1938 volume. What is important to stress here is that attitudes toward cross-ethnic musical interchange and the nature of musical ethnicity in Beregovski need not stem from the Soviet nationalities policy of the 1930s (as observed by Soifer 1978:5), but can be seen as descending through a scholarly genealogy within Beregovski's own institution, the Ukrainian Academy of Sciences, where they continued to remain in force at least as late as Kolessa's 1932 article on cross-ethnic musical influence in the Carpathian region (Kolessa 1932).

I am not trying to establish Beregovski as a camp follower of Kvitka. What is being advanced is a perspective on his work which sees Beregovski in the context of general ethnomusicology, not just of Jewish studies. Above and beyond the specifics of Beregovski's printed positions and the conjectures about his intellectual and biographical development, he must stand before us quite simply as a significant but neglected ethnomusicologist of his day whose subject matter was the folk music of the Eastern European Jews.

Works Cited

Beregovski, M.
    1938   *Yidishe folkslider*, vol. 2 (unpublished).
    1978   *Jews and Jewish Elements in Soviet Music*. Tel Aviv: Israel Music Publications.
Cahan, Y. L.
    1912   *Yidishe folkslider mit melodies, oys dem folksmoyl gezamlt*. 2 vols. New York and Warsaw: Internatsyonale Bibliotek Farlag.
Encyclopaedia Judaica
    1971   "Beregovski," in *Encyclopaedia Judaica* p. 600. Jerusalem: Keter.
Friedland, Lee-Ellen
    1981   "A Step Toward Movement Notation: The Case of a 'Freylekh' as Danced in the Ukraine, 1900–1915." *Jewish Folklore & Ethnology Newsletter* 5, nos. 1–2:30–32.

Ginzburg, S. M., and Marek, P. S.
1901   *Evreiskie narodnye pesni v Rossii.* St. Petersburg: Voskhod.
Ivanenko, B. G.
1973   "Materialy k biografii K. V. Kvitka." In *K. V. Kvitka: Izbrannye Trudy,* vol. 2, ed. P. Bogatyrev, pp. 346–59. Moscow: Sovetskii kompozitor.
Kolessa, Filaret
1932   "Karpatskii tsikl narodnikh pisen." In *Sbornik praci I. Sjezdu slovanskych filologu v Praze 1929,* part 2, pp. 93–114.
Kvitka, K. V.
1971   *K. Kvitka: Izbrannye trudy v dvukh tomakh,* ed. P. Bogatyrev, vol. 1. Moscow: Sovetskii Kompozitor.
1973a   "O kritike zapisei proizvedenii narodnogo muzykal'nogo tvorchestva." In ibid., vol. 2, pp. 30–37.
1973b   "Professional'nye narodnye pevtsy i muzykanty na Ukraine. In ibid., pp. 279–324.
1973c   "Vstupitel'nye zamechaniia k muzykal'no-etnograficheskim issledovaniiam." In ibid., pp. 3–26.
Mlotek, E. G.
1978   "Soviet-Yiddish Folklore Scholarship." *Musica Judaica* 2, no. 1: 73–90.
Pipe, S. Z.
1972   *Yiddish Folksongs from Galicia: The Folklorization of David Edelshtat's Song 'Der Arbeter'; Letters,* ed. Dov Noy and Meir Noy. Folklore Research Center Studies 2. Jerusalem: Hebrew University.
Slobin, Mark
1980   "The Evolution of a Musical Symbol in Yiddish Culture." In *Studies in Jewish Folklore,* ed. F. Talmage, pp. 313–30. Cambridge, Mass.: Association for Jewish Studies.
Slotnick, Susan
1976   "The Contributions of the Soviet Yiddish Folklorists." *Working Papers in Yiddish and East European Jewish Studies* 20. New York: YIVO Institute for Jewish Research.
Soifer, Paul
1978   "Soviet Jewish Folkloristics and Ethnography: An Institutional History, 1918–1948." *Working Papers in Yiddish and East European Jewish Studies* 30. New York: YIVO Institute for Jewish Research.

Members of the Presidium of the Institute of Jewish Proletarian Culture of the Ukrainian Academy of Sciences, October 1934. Beregovski is seated in the first row, second from left. (Courtesy of YIVO Institute for Jewish Research)

Sh. An-ski (in armchair, center), author and pioneer collector of Eastern European Jewish folklore, in Lutsk with members of the local branch of the Jewish Literary Association, ca. 1910. (Courtesy of YIVO Institute for Jewish Research)

Scenes of early folklore collecting: (a) A young man transcribing his grandfather's memoirs, Brailov, n.d. (b) Z. Kiselhof recording folk songs during the An-ski ethnographic expedition of 1912–14. Some of the resulting items are included in Beregovski's anthologies. (Courtesy of YIVO Institute for Jewish Research)

Scenes from Kremeniets, site of songs in the Beregovski anthologies: (a) children playing in a courtyard. Photo from the An-ski expedition of 1912–14. (b) Jewish students in a trade school, 1929. The bulk of Beregovski's 1934 anthology consists of songs of workers and revolutionary movements, and many songs stem from such industrial settings. These were composed and/or circulated by young Jewish students and workers, beginning around the turn of the century, when the older, small-town way of life gave way to a more urbanized one. (Courtesy of YIVO Institute for Jewish Research)

View of Lutsk, 1920s. Photo by Alter Kacyzne. Kacyzne, a writer, also took some of the finest photographs of pre-Holocaust Eastern Europe. Here we see a typical small city with signs of reconstruction after World War I-era destruction. Beregovski's anthologies rely on folk singers from many such small cities, but most of his songs come from large towns and cities. (Courtesy YIVO Institute for Jewish Research)

An elderly couple on a balcony over their butcher shop, Rovno, 1920s. Photo by Menachem Kipnis. Kipnis, an important folk song collector, here captures the generation from whom the An-ski expedition gathered the major early collection of folk songs in Yiddish (1912–14), and whom Beregovski tapped still later in the 1930s. (Courtesy YIVO Institute for Jewish Research)

Jewish klezmer band. Poland, late nineteenth century. The figure on the far right in black is the badxn, *the wedding entertainer. (Courtesy YIVO Institute for Jewish research)*

A non-Jewish band in the Polesie region, 1930s. Photo by S. Obrebski, Polish ethnographer. (Courtesy of the Archives of the University of Massachusetts at Amherst)

PART ONE

~⚘~

FOLK SONGS AND INSTRUMENTAL TUNES

1

JEWISH FOLK MUSIC
(1934)

Introduction

The striving of the bourgeoisie to distract the working masses from participation in the revolutionary struggle against capitalism can be seen in the "ethnographism" and "folklorism"[1] of the imperialist epoch, that is, in the exaggerated practical and creative interest and fidelity to ethnography and folklore, in the curious "panethnographism" and in the striving to introduce ethnographic and folkloric "bases" in politics, journalism, art, and literature.

The Jewish bourgeoisie introduced the problem of national regeneration as a counterweight to the social struggle of the proletariat, which had already taken on organized form in the 1890s in Russia. The ideologues of Jewish bourgeoisie turned to ethnography and folklorism as a means to effect "national regeneration, national consciousness, and unification," as a means to "cement" and "strengthen" the national organism without class differences. In Jewish musical and oral folklore, the bourgeois ideologues sought, and found, an extensive "national spirit," a "crystal-pure folk soul," and "the past greatness of our unfortunate people," that people which "looks toward the future and awaits better days, the happy days of its national liberation and regeneration on the soil of its old greatness"

Originally published as *Evreiiski muzykal'nyi fol'klor*, vol. 1 (Moscow: Gosmuzizdat, 1934).

1. The terms are M. Viner's. See his 1932:11. In the present work I follow the conceptions of Viner in questions of folklorism and folkloristics.

(Vints 1898:2). Using similar reactionary, hollow, and sentimental banalities, the bourgeois folklorists, composers, and musicians (such as Leo Vints, S. Ginzburg, P. Marek, L. Saminsky, S. An-ski, N. Prilutski, and many others) sought to veil the true social roots of the bourgeois ideologues' interest in ethnographism and folklorism. These were to play an especially important role in relationship to the petit bourgeoisie, for whom they would serve as an opiate in the period of sharpening class struggle, when they began to feel the shakiness of their position and a yearning for "the good old days" with their ethnographic way of life, for the "idyllic" and "patriarchal" life. The bourgeoisie sought to abstract the fledgling petit bourgeois masses to its side in the class struggle through ethnographism and folklorism and to distract the proletariat from class struggle.

The forces of reaction and nationalism always strived, and continue to strive, to use the "distinctiveness" and "specificity" of national culture as means to weaken and lull the movement of the oppressed and exploited within the country and as a political, imperialist means against other peoples. National specificity leads the bourgeoisie to its nationalistic chauvinist track. In such situations the bourgeoisie unwillingly reveals its class interests, while appearing to speak in the name of the entire nation. Nationalist ideology dictated the need for Jewish bourgeois composers to make a "pan-Jewish," "pan-national" musical art from Jewish folk melodies. But willy-nilly the Jewish bourgeois composers finally had to note, while trying to concretize their aims, that there is nothing uniform about so-called folk music in all its parts and that the content, themes, and musical means of expression of various classes, strata, and groups of a single society are not identical.

The bourgeois composer or researcher is unwilling to view musical (or any other) folklore in its historical development. He fixes the musico-folkloric situation at a given time and tries to find in it an "eternal, ethnic, classless treasurehouse" which expresses the national essence of the people and which seems to exist outside space and time. From such prejudices arises the attempt to create a definitive national musical grammar, to find the eternal national specificity, which will be obligatory once and for all for the composer of the given nationality.

However, historical change in the expressive means of a musical language does not proceed simultaneously in all segments of a given folk art. Alongside whatever portrays the new, we find in musical (as in oral) folklore remnants of the recent and distant past, and sometimes even survivals, recycled traces of old, long forgotten social situations. To articulate new social conditions and a new ideology, or for new expressive demands, one uses those means of the tradition which suit a particular goal and which conform to the demands of social expressiveness. Along with the reworking of the old, new expressive means are created. Folklore is not something ossified, not an art made once and for all according to some eternal, unchanging, metaphysical "national spirit" or "eternal national soul." The national specificity of folk music is a historically developed national form which reflects specific social and economic content.

As noted above, musical practice forces the contemporary bourgeois composer and musician to note that not all the "riches" of folk music are useful for the national "mission," so he must choose those musical means of expression which best answer the demands of the class whose ideology is reflected in his "national" art and for whose interests he must influence other classes through his art.[2]

In the early twentieth century the musical activity of Jewish composers took two directions in connection with Jewish folk music: the petit bourgeois liberal-populist trend (Engel, Kiselhof, et al.) and the bourgeois clerical-Zionist trend (Saminsky, Idelsohn, et al.). To the extent that both trends agree on many questions, it is hard to distinguish clearly the two orientations on the basis of musical problems and artistic ideology. The clerical-Zionist trend is marked by the combativeness and resoluteness of its judgments and initiatives, whereas the liberal-populist trend is distinguished by the shakiness of its position and by its conciliatory nature, which employs the tactic of "let's have it our way and your way."

The point of divergence of these two trends was the evaluation of and relationship to so-called secular folklore. The "democracy" of the liberal-populist trend expressed itself in the fact that its representatives (especially Engel and Kiselhof) conceded the "national" and artistic value of secular folklore (i.e., daily life, domestic, love songs, lullabies, and other songs in Yiddish) and not just of religious songs in Hebrew. On the other hand,

---

2. N. Briusov (1930) writes: "The composers of 'cultural music' long ago *raised the price* (stress mine—M.B.) of these artless (= folk—M.B.) songs. They took them as raw material and put them in their works, 'arranged', as prefabricated (!)" Briusov seems to think that the understanding or misunderstanding of the "price" of folk music is the sole reason that composers in given periods turn their attention to folk music and "arrange" it in their compositions, whereas other composers are completely uninterested in folklore, or even hold it in contempt. Briusov does not seem to suspect the social roots of this occurrence. However, it is hard to hide the social roots, in terms of both the composer's relationship to folklore and the choice he makes from all of folk music. Speaking of the social roots of this choice, we mean the general ideological tendency of the composer, and not each actual instance. Of course, in using a particular melody the composer chooses according to the actual artistic task at hand.

the clerical-Zionists (Saminsky and especially Idelsohn) insisted that Jewish secular folklore is a product of the Diaspora and so cannot have ethnic value. Not arising on "sacred soil," it consists of a mass of "obvious foreign layers, borrowed from Eastern music, Polish dances, etc." (Saminsky 1915:27) or, as Sabaneiev concisely paraphrases the thought, Jewish secular folklore is a "Yiddish musical jargon" (Sabaneiev 1924; for more on this ultra-reactionary brochure where Sabaneiev lays out Saminsky's theory in "high style," see below.)

The zealous adherents and preservers of the liturgical musical tradition condemned Jewish secular folklore to death and did not want to believe that this useless "Yiddish musical jargon" lay at the basis of Jewish "national music culture." The only Jewish music worthy of "regeneration," according to the clerical-Zionists, was the "lofty liturgical melody" and the "most rare and noble examples of religious music" of ancient Hebrew melody in which the sensitive nationalistic ear of Saminsky detected echoes of the "conquerer nation."

Engel and Kiselhof agreed with Saminsky that Jewish religious music was actually higher in national and artistic terms than secular folklore. In order to raise the value of the latter, they tried to demonstrate that secular folklore is permeated with religious elements. Both, according to them, are worthy of being the basis of Jewish national music. The clerical-Zionists sharply criticized the national and artistic significance of secular folklore. (Cf. the discussion between Engel and Saminsky [1915, 1916] and Kiselhof 1911).

Even Engel was able to show the absurdity of the views, and the entire "theory" of Saminsky of the "mass of clearly foreign layers" in Jewish secular folklore and the chemical purity of the "lofty liturgical melody," although Engel, as we have seen, did not differ sharply from Saminsky in his evaluation of religious music. This ultra-reactionary and extremely absurd "theory" could only be taken on faith in extreme arch-nationalistic circles. Engel showed that Saminsky only worked with common phrases taken from songs selected at random. After a superficial and fleeting survey of Jewish wedding songs, for example, Saminsky comes to the entirely unexpected and unsubstantiated conclusion that these melodies are influenced by "all sorts of gavottes and bourrées of the period of Bach and Handel." In the *redlax* (dances) of Lithuanian Jews, Saminsky, with his "comparative" method, discovers the influence of Polish dances and so on. Saminsky gets rid of all the problems he touches (e.g., ethnic specificity, borrowing) by means of nationalist chatter and lyric outpourings. He did not even need to do a detailed and circumstantial analysis of folk music. On his own admission he could not be "academically comfortable in questions of the ordinary (?!) types of our melodies." The gaze of this most national hero is attracted only to the loftiest and purest (Saminsky was always attracted to superlatives) examples of Jewish music, which he finds not by analysis but by some sort of super-national intuition.

Engel himself did not stray far from the deeply reactionary point of view of Saminsky, recognizing the special value of religious and religio-daily-life music, but he could not agree with the dogmatism of the clerical-Zionists in relation to secular folklore. Engel asks Saminsky (Engel 1915:17): "You yourself must know all of this quite well as a long-time researcher in the difficult and under-studied field of Jewish music. How then can one explain your cruel condemnation of Jewish songs of daily-life? One would like to think there is some misunderstanding here."

However, there was no misunderstanding with Saminsky. The most elementary truth was foreign to Saminsky, according to which a musical language, like all living languages, changes under the impact of economic, social, political, and cultural causes. He did not want to know this basic fact: even in those far-off times, when what he considers the only worthy Jewish music was "born," music was influenced by the neighboring music cultures of the time, exactly as the contemporary music of any people feels "foreign" influence.

Saminsky and those of his school did not want to see this, since they looked at the question from the bourgeois clerical-Zionist point of view. With a single stroke of the pen, Saminsky wiped out the whole history of the Jews in Europe in the last thousand years and made an artificial jump from the late biblical period to a "new" Jewish music of the bourgeois Jewish salon. Bourgeois salon music with a biblical pedigree was undoubtedly more suitable and more imposing than the musical craft of the shtetl artisan or, to be sure, than the art of the Jewish proletariat, which evoked unpleasant associations and shocked the capitalist "believer." While the wavering liberal-populist nationalists (e.g., Engel and Kiselhof), as a result of their wavering class ideology, seemed to search for a compromise between secular and religious folklore, the Jewish bourgeoisie was not interested in the folklore of the Jewish working masses; indeed, it was necessary to discredit and belittle that folklore in the eyes of the "national" composers. The remnants of liturgical and religious music, applied in a "contemporary" way, could serve the class of oppressors better and more faithfully than secular folklore. Religious music was better suited to correspond to ideology in distracting certain strata of Jewish workers from social struggle and keeping them in thrall to the exalted national "mission" of the Chosen People.

A. Z. Idelsohn took on the role of the "calm academic" researcher of Jewish folk music with true professorial, scholarly resolve. The collecting and scholarly work of this venerable "scholar" is remarkably ample. He published a multivolume collection of Jewish folk music (naturally, exclusively of a religious and semireligious character) and a whole series of books and studies on questions of Jewish music. Idelsohn's conceptions can be summarized as follows. At the "exile" of the Jews from the "Holy Land," the fragments of the Jewish people carried "Jewish music" with them into the lands of exile. The task of Idelsohn and of other bourgeois nationalist researchers is to find the true, authentic, ancient Jewish music preserved since biblical times and to renew it and establish it in our days. To this end he collected the music of Jews of various lands to find what was "common" in this music, what was preserved from the biblical Golden Age, and which music represented the quintessence of a true, independent Jewish music. Doubting the authenticity and originality of these ancient fragments, Idelsohn avers: "The musical wellsprings rise up from the soul of the nation. The soul is eternal and does not change its nature. From this it is clear that Jews could not replace their semitic-Oriental music with another music."[3]

Saminsky, Idelsohn, and the others set themselves the same task: to find the high, "pan-Israeli" proto-music and, on the basis of this proto-music which only they know, to build a new Jewish musical art. They seek to demonstrate the unity and commonality of a worldwide (naturally, classless) Jewish nation through jointly held "authentic" national-cultural treasures. All these reactionary bourgeois views serve the general class goals of the bourgeiosie.

In L. Sabaneiev's "The Jewish National School in Music" (Sabaneiev 1924), we find an attempt to restore the old nationalistic theories of Saminsky and Idelsohn. Basically, Sabaneiev retells, in a wordy and high-flung style, the "theories" and "findings" of Saminsky. His book mobilizes all the tools of idealistic, nationalistic, and reactionary-bourgeois theory. Here we also find a "racial type of music," the "artistic realization of its (i.e., Jewish) musical essence (!)," "national florescence," and so on and so forth. In terms of the question that interests us, the evaluation of secular folklore and religious music, Sabaneiev announces that "Jewish daily life music with its layers of the Aryan (!) and Iranian (!) type and with its clear

3. For more on Idelsohn, see Beregovski 1932.

Europeanization of style also relates to the magnificently ornamental liturgical melody (and to its tributary [?], the expected new art of the Jews)
as the "jargon" (!) created on Galician (?) and German soil [= Yiddish
language—M.S.] relates to the monumental and mighty Hebrew language" (Sabaneiev 1924:18).

Bourgeois-Zionist conceptions protrude from every one of Sabaneiev's sentences. Although Sabaneiev is not a Jew, he has internalized the
relationship of the Zionists to the "jargon" they hate and no doubt has
learned from them the remarkable evidence of the arising of Yiddish on
"Galician-German soil."

Saminsky, Idelsohn, their philo-semitic colleague Sabaneiev, and a
whole host of petit-bourgeois musicians on their coattails—all these de-
vout ideologues of the Jewish bourgeoisie did not basically prove what
they hoped to prove. They showed that their approach to Jewish secular
folklore and religious music was far from "objective," far from purely
"scientific-theoretical," as the bourgeois scholars loved to assert, but was
undoubtedly tendentious. They tried to choose elements of the folk-
musical heritage which to a great extent correspond to the class whose
ideology they reflect and whom they serve with all their musical activity.

Musical interchange among peoples does not of course occur in order
to offend the preservers and exponents of a national musical tradition.
Ethnic specificity in folk music, as in all manifestations of a national culture, is only a historically given form of expression, a determined social
content. In the end, as the content changes, so does the form of expression.
Among the older means of expression, those elements survive that are
most suitable to the new demands and their corresponding new ideology.
Parallel to those internal new means of expression are those taken from
the "external sound" environment. Naturally these borrowings are not
mechanical. Not everything that "resonates" in the environment is simply
adopted and remains as "foreign matter." The borrowings enter the repertoire transformed, in accordance with the ideology of the social stratum
that borrows. Finally, not all strata and groups with folkloric demands
borrow the same external elements. Each group tends to adopt what is
"consonant" with its new content.[4] By confirming the fact of significant
outside influence on Jewish folk music and considering it a natural and
general occurrence, we are in no way denigrating the better ethnic forms

4. For example, if one examines the influence of Ukrainian folk music on Jewish folk
music, it is easy to notice that elements of the folklore of certain social strata penetrated into
religious and Hasidic tunes, while other strata influenced the secular songs of Jewish artisans.

and original style of Jewish folk music. As in the folklore of other peoples, in Jewish folk music "foreign" elements are not simply mechanically interspersed but are transformed in accordance with ethnic forms in the given historical situation, constituting a reflection of the social psychology and ideological striving of those strata of Jews who relate to the given folklore.

For the exploited and oppressed classes, strata, and groups, their artistic folklore has, at certain stages of their development, social functions analogous to the "official" art of the ruling classes. In saying this we do not wish to restrict the role and significance of the exploited classes for literature and art in general, or the specific relationship of the ruling classes to folklore. We only want to emphasize that folklore is characterized by being largely an art of the exploited and repressed classes. However, just as we cannot consider literature, music, or graphic art as a single monolithic art of all literate classes, strata, and groups without differentiation, so we cannot indiscriminately consider folklore to be a unique art of all the lower classes. The peasant folklore of a single people, for example, must be distinguished by class according to the internal social differentiation. By studying and arranging folk music materials only as a national cross-section, we are hiding the class distinctions in the data. Of course, one cannot identify the ideology reflected in given works of folklore with those social groups who are the producers and users of that folklore. The ideological action of folklore is not limited to the principal class milieu in which it originates and circulates. Not all folklore current among certain strata of workers, or even created by these strata, reflects the ideology of the working class. We can also detect the traces of outside influence.

Often folklore can be created by and even circulate among the ruling classes. The function of folklore in these classes is quite different from its function among the oppressed and exploited. For the latter, folklore is often the only available means of artistic expression. For example, it is clear that the greater part of Russian peasantry up to the end of the nineteenth century could not in fact use the "official" literature and art due to the weak spread of literacy in czarist Russia. Folklore tendencies in "cultured" art often (though by no means always) correspond to the striving of the upper classes to work on the lower classes and approach them. Often this inclination to folklore (among the ruling classes) is followed in given periods and situations for reactionary goals, but sometimes an inclination to folklore can be seen as progressive. Only a concrete approach can tell, with careful assessment of a specific historical situation.

The class leanings of the bourgeois folklorists appears not only in their research work but also in the very collecting of folklore materials. The bourgeois folklorists cannot remain only "objective," detached collectors of folklore materials "in general"; they deliberately ignored, for example, working-class, and especially revolutionary, creations. The "national spirit," the conception of the definite "originality" of folk art, cannot be reconciled with the "lackey" (according to An-ski) *chastushka* [a late nineteenth-century popular Russian song genre—M.S.], with the factory song or particularly with clearly revolutionary works.

During certain periods, folklore reflected powerful, creative, progressive moments of striving, hope, protest, and rebellion of social groups and strata. This included the progressive and revolutionary (in its day, particularly during the English and even the French revolutions) bourgeoisie, the serf or "free" small peasantry, and sometimes, though significantly more rarely, the revolutionary proletariat. On the other hand, it must be said that this folklore reflects the backwardness, limitations, national stagnation, and age-old rot which overspread the oppressed masses as a result of the enslavement, inhuman exploitation, poverty, horrible living conditions, and spiritual darkness in which they were kept by the exploiting classes (cf. Viner 1932:90).

The reactionary bourgeois and petit bourgeois folklorists would rather turn to precisely those backward elements of folklore and ignore the progressive and revolutionary part of folklore. If for one reason or another they could no longer muzzle the revolutionary folklore, then they talked about "distortion of folklore" or the "contamination of folk songs." The Jewish bourgeois musicologists and composers who were engaged in tapping the "pure gold" of true national music from the "mines" of folklore not only did not gather the songs of Jewish workers and revolutionary songs, but often acted as if they doubted the very existence of such songs. The only exception in the Jewish petit bourgeois camp is the collector Sh. Leman, who in 1921 published the first anthology of Jewish workers' and revolutionary songs of the 1905 period (Leman 1921).

S. An-ski touched on the question of workers' and revolutionary creativity very little. He had to admit that "the folk song commented not just on personal experiences but also on well-known social movements" (An-ski 1909:56). It would seem, then, that An-ski would have had to admit to the natural reaction of folklore to new "social movements." But An-ski, in love with the "ancient national song" and relishing the most primitive survivals of Jewish life, could not be objective about new creativity. "Since the 1880s," he writes, "when a ferment of ideas began to penetrate even into the national circle, a new folk song was born, very far from the earlier type in form and content. The old, mostly naive-poetic, tender, and sad songs were replaced by limp (!), untalented (!) doggerel, reminiscent of Russian factory and lackey (!) chastushki."[5] It bothered him that along with the old, authentic Hasidic songs (i.e., the "true, folk creation"), vulgar "anti-Hasidic" songs were sung (An-ski 1909:56). It seems that not only are new revolutionary songs "limp, untalented doggerel," but also that folk songs which dare to make fun of the Hasidim must be vulgar, without exception. This characterization of "new" creation, this deeply reactionary, aesthetic-narrow-minded scorn of the social democrat An-ski toward the "limp and untalented doggerel" of the workers and the proletariat does not demand any particular explanation. In his extensive activity in collecting Jewish folklore (special expeditions of 1912–14 and later), An-ski mainly collected "authentic Hasidic" religious folklore and items connected to backward superstitions and only isolated examples of the hundreds of revolutionary and socialist songs.

The Yiddishist bourgeois folklorist Y. L. Cahan expressed himself more extensively on the topic of Jewish workers' and revolutionary folklore. In his extensive review of Leman's *Arbayt un frayhayt,* Cahan refrained from calling the songs in the anthology "folk songs" on the basis that (1) the content of the majority of songs was clearly revolutionary and (2) they represent reworkings of texts of older folk songs. According to him, these are *zersungene* (deteriorated) social songs of known and anonymous authors (Cahan 1926:141). In refusing to call these songs "folk," Cahan means to say that they have no artistic value since they have been created for the purpose of agitation. The term "non-folk" in the mouths of this type of folklorist represents the highest degree of scorn toward the material cited.

Naturally workers' and revolutionary folklore is not the same as "traditional" folklore (about which, more below). But the Cahans and An-skis relate pejoratively to workers' and revolutionary songs not because they are dissimilar to traditional folklore, but precisely because these songs are revolutionary. Folklorists of this type seek naiveté, modesty, and other virtues of "crystal-pure folk soul" in folklore. Mass gatherings, strikes, freedom, prison, arrest, exile, police, exploiters—all these new words and new concepts that infiltrate the working revolutionary creativity grate on

5. The "repentant" social democrat An-ski, seeking to escape his "revolutionary" sins through ultra-nationalistic ethnographic and folklore activity, cut out not only revolutionary creativity but also everything else that touched the "basis" of Jewish tradition.

the ears of these honorable folklorists.[6] Were Cahan more consistent in his demands on folklore, he would have also ruled out of bounds all the old folklore items which in their own way reacted to the social and political occurrences of their time. Jewish folklore reflected the social and antireligious mood of certain social strata, "enlightenment" tendencies, protest against the Jewish communal structure and its rules, the relationship to political events, and so on. On close examination, it is easy to ascertain that these folklore items reflect the relationship of various social groups to given circumstances and events.

Revolutionary folklore is not the same as the older, "traditional" folklore; furthermore, its development must go beyond the bounds of folklore. Revolutionary folklore is a transitional stage from folklore to revolutionary literature, and precisely therein lies its great value. The "ethnographic" way of life gradually vanishes in proportion to the growth of the capitalist form of production, with its attraction of the masses to factories, plants, and mines. "Capitalism," writes Lenin (1925:35–36) "replaces the dense backward, sedentary, and savage Russian or Ukrainian peasant with a lively proletarian, whose conditions of life break the specific national narrowness of the Russian or Ukrainian."

Since the second half of the nineteenth century, that is, the period of rapid development of capitalism in Russia, Russian ethnographers and folklorists (like those of Western Europe in relationship to their region) have confirmed the fact of the dying out and disappearance of the "ethnographic" way of life and of traditional folklore. With the disintegration and vanishing of the economic basis of the "ethnographic" way of life, it vanishes along with its folklore.

We can sometimes observe the development of revolutionary folklore in capitalistically underdeveloped countries among a proletariat that is revolutionary within the bounds of cultural backwardness. To a considerable extent the workers' attempt at a highly developed "literary" creativity is hindered by systematic material and cultural oppression, which lowers the level of the workers, by continuous inhuman persecution and repression, and by the underground nature of the revolutionary movement. In these cases, revolutionary folklore belongs to the appropriate circles of agitation. Here folklore is converted into revolutionary art, and all forms of art, all styles and genres which lead toward revolutionary goals in the

---

6. The folklorist E. V. Barsov complains that it makes a respectable person ashamed to hear songs "composed at factories and places of work" (Barsov 1903:1). Incidentally, the entry on Barsov in the *Great Russian Encyclopaedia* (vol. 4, p. 1784) makes no mention of his reactionary ideology.

given situation and circumstances, are progressive and revolutionary. But in this case it is the last folklore, since it already serves the revolution, which annihilates every basis for a further development of folklore.

The changes introduced by the October Revolution in social relationships have simply hastened the process of the dying-out of folklore. The development of cultural forms in life and art that were systematically held down by repression and backwardness has been liberated from the bonds of the putrid capitalist structure. The oral tradition of the oppressed classes and strata is gradually being edged out by the new proletarian art. The proletariat, as a whole, is taking giant steps toward "literary" creativity.[7] The general tendency toward the disappearance of folklore (both oral and musical) is not changed by the fact that musical literacy comes after general literacy; the question is only the length of time. We already have significant penetration of the songs of proletarian composers into the mass repertoire, the systematic growth of tours by visiting workers' concert groups, and so on. If there is still mainly more or less passive "listening," we can also already see the rudiments of active and creative participation of broader masses in immediate musical work. All this does not decrease or diminish the importance of the collection and study of works of folklore, especially of those aspects of folklore which have been so carefully ignored by the bourgeois and nationalistic folklorists, and also the collection and study of folklore arrangements in the new proletarian "written" music while these arrangements still have a place.

Having established the fact of the disappearance of traditional "ethnographicity" and folklore, and seeing the inevitability of this disappearance, the reactionary folklorists could not relate calmly to this phenomenon. They agitate and aim toward artificially holding back the process of the inevitable dying-out and vanishing of traditional "ethnographicity" and folklore-ness.

There are cases in which, under the influence of reactionary nationalistic agitation, even antique, long-forgotten ethnographic customs have been revived. According to Professor K. V. Kvitka, in 1916–20 in the city of Gadiach, under the influence of counterrevolutionary circles, the custom of the *koliada,* (winter carols) which had long since disappeared from practice, was revived) (Kvitka 1922:236). This is just one episode of a whole system of ethnographism and folklorism carried on by Ukrainian

---

7. Cf. Viner 1932: chap. 7. Comrade Viner notes that this development is not in contradiction with the fact that some peoples of the U.S.S.R. may continue to develop folklore for some time. "For the dialectic, these facts do not overshadow a proper evaluation of the actual tendencies of development" (ibid., note to p. 70).

bourgeois and reactionary-nationalistic circles in literature, politics of language, painting, music, and so on. It is worth remembering the "national"
costumes of the armies of Petliura and the hetmans [during the Civil War
period—M.S.].

Jewish workers' and revolutionary folk songs can be divided into two
categories: (1) songs created before the arising of an organized workers'
movement and (2) songs created under the immediate impact of an organized revolutionary workers' movement and reflecting its various stages.

Songs of the first group reflect the preproletarian psychology of Jewish
workers, the psychology of the hired artisan or small craftsman, not united
with his comrades for a common struggle, not seeing his class enemy
clearly enough, and not yet recognizing the inevitability and the means of
class struggle. In these songs, passive complaining, tears, and groans
predominate; at times we still find an appeal to God. The songs of the
second group—revolutionary songs—reflect class psychology, recognizing its possibilities, optimism, and belief that the future belongs to it.
Struggle with attendant sacrifices and difficulties are unavoidable. But the
worker, recognizing himself as a part of the great proletarian family,
knows that these sacrifices are necessary and not in vain. In cases of arrest,
exile, and persecution, he can manfully comfort and hearten the weeping
relatives with the fact that "some day people will envy you your children,
since they suffer, poor folk, for the whole people" (see no. 39). He is
deeply convinced that "the people" will triumph.

We can date the origin of the revolutionary songs to the 1890s. It is
considerably harder to date the origin of the songs of the first group.
According to specific traits found in these songs, one can place them in
the second half of the nineteenth century, and in part to an even earlier
period. However, similar songs were created by more backward groups
of workers even after the arising of the organized workers' movement.

The most common type of Jewish worker of the late nineteenth century was in a small shop where, outside the boss, there were one or two
hired artisans. In order to hold his own against the ever-growing competi-
tion of factory work, the boss resorted to inhuman exploitation of his
workers. The workers' day lasted from twelve to twenty hours (especially
before holidays), with only short breaks. In addition to this exploitation,
there was a patriarchal relationship between the boss and the worker. In
most cases the worker lived and boarded with the boss. The boss himself,
and sometimes members of his family, worked from morning to night.
The worker thought himself only temporarily obliged to work for hire and

dreamed of soon becoming the boss of such a shop himself. All this dulled and restrained the development of class consciousness among hired Jewish artisans. The female worker who entered a shop in the 1880s had even fewer possibilities for developing her class-consciousness. In the early stages the only escape, the only possibility of avoiding the inhumanly difficult work, was to collect a dowry and get married, so her husband could take her away from work.

The class-consciousness of Jewish workers grew with the development of industrial capitalism on the one hand and the organization and growth of a workers' movement on the other. Workers went from passive complaining, lamenting their "dark days," to organizing revolutionary actions and struggling for a new life; this situation was reflected in songs we have put into the second group.[8]

There are usually four genres of Jewish workers' and revolutionary songs: lyric, balladlike, satiric, and hymnlike.

According to manner of performance, we can divide these songs into two groups: solo and choral. To the solo group largely belong the lyric and balladlike, and some satiric songs; the choral group primarily includes the hymn songs and some satiric songs. The former are primarily performed solo and do not musically suit choral performance. The latter are meant largely for collective mass performance. In the text content as well the "individual" and collective beginning, there is a characteristic moment (among other such moments) separating prerevolutionary from revolutionary songs. According to their music, the choral songs, that is, those meant for collective singing, were as cited above partly satirical and mostly hymnlike songs. The narratives of the lyric and balladlike songs very often speak for the collective, in the name of "sisters and brothers," but in fact the narrator (more accurately, the musical performer) of these songs is a single person, who seems to be standing with his song before an invisible collective or who is remembering and reliving his (and the collective's) participation in a revolutionary action.

As opposed to the peasant or the unskilled village worker, Jewish workers over the last centuries (until the twentieth century) usually were not involved in the typical collective types of work (e.g., construction, transport of building materials, and other heavy things, hauling barges, joint plowing). It is worth noting that in Jewish folk song we never find songs with a refrain or call consisting of meaningless shouts and the

---

8. The classification and general characterization of Jewish workers' and revolutionary songs given above is taken from Skuditski n.d.

accompanying collective work songs. The crafts and jobs in which Jewish workers usually engaged demanded an individual tempo of work. This corresponds to the fact that the traditional Jewish folk song is not only monophonic but usually unsuitable for collective performance. The more widespread traditional Jewish folk songs were usually performed by a single folksinger and very often with greater or lesser deviation and variation. The stimulus and need for adjusting one's musical performance to another singer, or the stimulus as a result of collective work, were lacking at this time among Jewish workers.

We do not think that the monophonic, solo quality of traditional Jewish folk songs depends completely on the forms of work. This question is quite complex, and demands a special, comprehensive investigation. However, we must remember that traditional Jewish folklore was principally (though not exclusively) performed at work, and this in some way must reflect on the song itself. The Jewish worker of the late nineteenth century most often sang only at work. After a hard working day lasting, as stated above, from twelve to twenty hours, there was neither time nor occasion for singing. The number of songs in the repertoire of the Jewish artisan and apprentice is very great, and many contemporary eyewitnesses confirm the fact that people often sang at work. The conditions of work themselves—the primitive technology of the shop, work until late at night, or the whole night before holidays—called for singing as a means of enlivening, brightening up, and reviving attention at work.

In my own work of collecting folk musical materials, I have encountered singers who sang with some tension if they were not accompanied by the familiar work processes. They freed themselves from this tension only when they began to make the gestures they were accustomed to make at their work. During our folklore expeditions I often tried to bring together small groups of singers who knew one another and saw one another often or who had worked together for long periods of time, for joint performance of some song they knew. I did this to clarify the ability of Jewish folksingers to perform their song repertoire chorally. I achieved no positive results: each sang the given song slightly differently, and it was hard for him to accustom himself to the other singers.[9]

The lyric and balladlike and some satiric songs of the revolutionary type were able to use the musical tradition of the Jewish folk song to a

---

9. This relates only to the performance of traditional Jewish folk songs. It was easier for this sort of improvised choir to sing more or less successfully well-known Ukrainian songs (e.g., the very popular "Oy u poli verba riasna").

considerable extent. These genres, usually performed solo, could find some congenial means of expression in the traditional folklore. The satirical revolutionary songs largely use the devices of contrast and parody, as did the older satirical songs. Parodying the synagogue and religious melody, the satirical song did this with particular sharpness and expressivity (see nos. 4 and 9 in Leman 1921, and no. 21 in the present anthology). One can also find the solo introduction and choral verse in the satiric song (see Leman no. 11, our no. 20).

The genre of revolutionary hymns and marches ran into a problem that was basically new to Jewish secular folklore.[10] This genre required new musical means of expression (for Jewish folklore), new melodic and rhythmic usages and forms, since these songs, reflecting a new ideology, served as the organizing moment for the whole collective during mass meetings, demonstrations, and all other mass occasions and had to be performed by the whole collective. Until the rise of the workers' revolutionary folklore, the song-march did not exist in Jewish folklore (not counting the religious, partly Hasidic song, which belonged to the enemy ideological sphere and tradition), since the song-march had no function in Jewish life. The folk song-march could only arise with the beginning of the workers' movement, with the development and growth of collective performance which had to organize the marchers or arouse revolutionary fervor and activity among demonstrators.

This new folklore genre of revolutionary hymns and marches could not borrow its means of expression from the solo folklore song. On the other hand, the primarily religious and Hasidic choral folk song could not, and in fact did not, become the source for the musical expressive means of this new folklore genre. The social existence and function of the religious and Hasidic song were alien and inimical to the revolutionary song, and the workers consciously turned away from this source. The heroic folk song-hymn and song-march sought expressive means from another musical tradition.

The path of creating a new style, in particular a choral one, was difficult not only for Jewish folk music. Failures, and even outright fiascoes, are unavoidable along this path. Thus, for example, a melody like that of the so-called old Jewish workers' "Švue" (a solemn oath, written in 1895–96, our nos. 60–61) is made through combining three melodies. The first is taken from the first part of the Russian church hymn "Kol' slaven," the

10. In traditional folklore, some Hasidic songs and dances (almost always limited to males and, except for rare cases, sung in unison) were sung chorally, as were a few compositions of synagogue music.

second is a popular German song (the same melody used during the first years of the Revolution for the Pioneers' song "Vpered zare navstrechu"), and the third is a typical galop from the repertoire of bandstand orchestras. These melodies, unknown to the Jewish listener and unfamiliar in Jewish circles, did not attract the workers or call forth the associations with which the melodies were connected. Jewish workers' folklore used the solemn character of these melodies, which did not evoke any religious or reactionary associations at all among the Jewish workers.[11]

It should be noted that the heroic song-hymns were sung monophonically by Jewish workers. Polyphony in this song would have expressed the choral origin of the melody. Only melodies were borrowed; the tune of the hymn "Kol' slaven" does not have the intonations characteristic of Russian church singing. Aside from the fact that the folklore period of the Jewish revolutionary song was short and that the heroic song could not receive appropriate and full development, and notwithstanding the fact of such unsuccessful borrowings as the "Švue" cited above, Jewish revolutionary folklore succeeded in posing, and in some cases resolving, the problem of the heroic genre.

In the workers' songs of the first group (prerevolutionary) the borrowings were largely from the repertoire of the bourgeois and petit-bourgeois strata. In the lyric and balladlike genres we have a whole series of songs which represent reworkings of individual types, like the "cruel" and "sentimental" romances* (e.g., nos. 10, 11, 12 are reworkings of the romance "Karie glazki," and nos. 32, 33 of "Ne plach' ty, Marusia"; such borrowings can also be found in traditional Jewish folklore). In the heroic song-hymn we see the influence of general revolutionary repertoire (e.g., "Dubinushka"), which was spread among workers' circles in the 1905 period, and we find almost no influences from the bourgeois, sentimental "sound environment." In the heroic genre of song-hymns, we meet for the first time (in Jewish secular folklore) a lively rhythm and the confident stride of the masses. Notwithstanding the predominance of the minor mode in these songs, they generally express solemnity and exaltation. In its day, the Jewish folk-revolutionary song had an enormous revolutionary significance among Jewish workers' circles.

When Jewish workers took their first revolutionary steps they created

11. Incidentally, the textual content of the German song cited above is the nationalist-reactionary "Andreas Hofer-Lied von Julius Mosen, komponiert von Leopold Knebelsberger." There the music is given. The author of the book says that the composer, L. Knebelsberger, was born September 14, 1814. He was the director of a wandering troupe of singers. According to some information, this same tune has been adapted as a fascist song in recent years in Germany.

[*The romans is the Russian parlor song—M.S.]

revolutionary songs, which helped organizing the working class in its struggle for a new world and a new life, alongside the work of agitation and creating proclamations, brochures, newspapers, leaflets, and so on. These songs spread quickly and were sung everywhere by Jewish workers. The contemporary outlines of Jewish revolutionary song included much of the heroic struggle which that song accompanied, and in it were reflected the mood and experiences of the revolutionary struggle of the workers. For us these songs sound like important, cherished documents of the heroic struggle, of strikes, demonstrations, exile, prison, difficult defeats, and new victories, and for us they serve as a resounding call to the new battle and to new victories.

In general, folk music has great significance for us as an artistic heritage. To ignore folk music is to ignore the musical way of life and the musical expression of the oppressed and exploited classes, who in those times could not yet reach a "literary" art and for whom folklore was the only available means of artistic expression. That part of folklore which reflects protest and the mood of rebellion and revolution of the oppressed classes is particularly valuable. Revolutionary folklore materials have enormous significance for the beginning period of proletarian art, but they also have great importance for the history of the revolutionary movement.

Can folk music be used for contemporary Soviet art?

We can use traditional musical folklore to the extent that we can use any musical tradition, or any musical heritage of the past, that is, through socialist reworking and dialectic resolution. Revolutionary folklore is of particular importance. In revolutionary folk songs we are dealing with the precursors of proletarian art and even (in the highest achievements of the revolutionary song) with the beginning of the period of proletarian musical art.

The present anthology consists of four divisions: (I) Workers' and revolutionary songs; (II) songs about artisans; (III) songs about family and daily life; and (IV) songs about soldiering and war.

We have placed greatest stress on the workers' and revolutionary songs (83 out of 140 items) and have divided them into five categories: (1) songs of work, exploitation, and poverty; (2) songs about strikes; (3) songs of struggle and victims; (4) revolutionary hymns and songs; and (5) melodies to the revolutionary songs of early Jewish proletarian poets (Vintshevsky, Edelshtat, and others).

The revolutionary folklore of workers, especially in its beginning stages of development, grows from traditional folklore. In order to illustrate more clearly what was newly introduced by the revolutionary song into Jewish folk music, we thought it necessary to include examples of other categories of folklore, such as songs about family and daily life and songs about soldiering and war. We have already noted that up to the present there has been only one published anthology of Jewish workers' and revolutionary songs, that of Leman, which includes seventy-three items, of which fifty-six are given with melodies. Leman collected his materials in Poland. In his anthology we have very few songs collected in the Ukraine and even fewer from Belorussia. Even our anthology does not exhaust the totality of Jewish workers' and revolutionary repertoire. It is the result of the first and by far not systematic attempt to collect this type of material, mainly from among Jewish workers in the Ukraine (unfortunately we have not included the materials transcribed from Belorussian Jewish workers). We might hope that the present anthology, not being exhaustive, will serve as the impetus for further collecting and study of the material.

The selection of songs and their arrangement was done purely on the basis of the text. Most of the songs are published here for the first time. An insignificant portion consists of variants of previously published songs. To date, the melodies to songs about soldiering and war have been published in only insignificant numbers (as individual items). The texts of these songs have been published in considerably greater numbers. All the melodies of this category are published for the first time.

The melodies to the poems of Vintshevsky, Edelshtat, et al. we considered worth placing in a special group. Naturally, they cannot be grouped with the folk repertoire according to text, although some of these songs produced numerous folk variants. The musical component presents a whole series of typical indications of folklorization, such as the anonymity of the melodies, spread exclusively by the oral tradition, and the characteristic melodic variation typical of oral tradition.[12] The folk variants of these songs would not lose their folklore significance even if the musical originals of the songs had been published; however, we do not know of a single anthology or separate publication of old Jewish revolutionary literary

12. There is evidence that the melodies were not specially created for these texts but that old melodies were adapted to the texts after their publication. In his memoirs (Vintshevsky 1926) Vintshevsky tells how, for example, someone adapted a Jewish melody to his poem "Ir lempele, lamternele" (which we have not succeeded in transcribing), and soon the song became popular (ibid., p. 231). Similarly, other old Jewish tunes were adapted to other poems of Vintshevsky (ibid., pp. 236, 246).

songs where music was included. Unfortunately, to date we have been able to transcribe only a small number of these songs. This amount does not even begin to serve as a full listing of literary revolutionary songs of Jewish workers, as we have been able to establish on the basis of various sources. Through continuing the general collecting of Jewish folk musical materials, we hope to fill that gap.

Four-fifths of all the items in the present anthology (112 out of 140) have been transcribed from cylinders of the *phonoteque* of the Cabinet of Folk Music of the Ethnographic Section of the Institute of Jewish Proletarian Culture of the Ukrainian Academy of Sciences (Kiev). Hoping to have the transcription as exact and as faithful as possible, I myself supervised the transcription several times and checked a significant portion of the transcriptions along with an associate of the Cabinet, S. Shnayder. In addition, we took every opportunity to have other musicians check the transcriptions. We did not have a chance to use a special tonometric apparatus to measure the absolute pitch of individual sounds. We noted only those pitches for which we could confirm by ear that they were slightly above or below the corresponding notes of our musical system. This in no way reduces the need to carry out an exact measurement of at least a few songs with appropriate equipment. By ear, it may seem that the raisings of pitch of various songs in the anthology are accidental. The lowerings somehow seem less accidental. When repeating a given musical phrase, the performer often sings a minor second above the tonic instead of a major second. But the performer tries to lower somewhat even this minor second.

It sometimes happens that the performer is not immediately at home in the appropriate scale and the first musical phrase or half-phrase is performed a bit tentatively, from which one gets the impression that this phrase is performed in another scale. For example in no. 49 we hear B and E instead of B-flat and E-flat. But already in the second phrase the performer settles into the minor mode and we no longer hear the B and E, but always B-flat and E-flat. We have something similar in no. 130 (compare this song to the similarly constructed nos. 126 and 127). In these situations, we have given the pitch appropriate to the given scale. (For similar cases of the tentative performer for the first phrase, see Lineva 1905:252.)

We have indicated the tempo with metronome markings. Through the aid of the metronome, we were able to more or less precisely indicate the tempo in those songs (or parts of songs) in which the performer sings more or less evenly. Most of the singers appearing in the present anthology usually accelerate the tempo toward the second half of the song. This is probably because, sitting before the recording apparatus, the singer begins in a slower than usual tempo. Only toward the middle of the song is the singer's usual tempo for the song established. Often the accelerando continues up to the end of the song. Significant changes in tempo also occur at the second singing. For example, the tempo may go from 63 to 92 for the second performance, from 56 to 80, and so on. The dynamic level is usually in a range between forte and mezzo forte. Rarely do we meet more diverse dynamic nuances. (Here we have in mind cases when the folksinger sings for someone else and not for himself or herself.)

The range of the voice is usually from A–B of the small octave to F^2–G^2 (men's voices an octave lower). One singer (age 46, a harness-maker from a village near Odessa; see no. 128) sang in a high falsetto, reminiscent of a boy's soprano. In terms of performance practice, it is possible to extrapolate the following characteristic traits. (1) Very frequent glissandi: There are glissandi from lower pitches to higher; these glissandi lend the song, especially in a moderate or slow tempo, a certain connected quality, sometimes even a certain "viscousness" of the musical structure. These are common devices. (2) Sometimes the last note of a musical phrase descends (seems to slip) a fourth down, and sometimes down to a note of indeterminate pitch. (3) The voice is open, often shrill and sharp (most often among mezzo-sopranos and altos). Male voices (usually of the high tenor type) often have a guttural or nasal shading. (4) One often meets intonations similar to sighs or sobs; typical examples can be found in nos. 27, 55, 130.

All the songs of the present anthology have been transcribed into one tonality, G. Jewish folksingers do not always perform their songs to the same basic pitch, so we felt it unnecessary to give these songs in the original tonality (i.e., the tonality in which the song is sung). Transposing all the songs to one tonal level makes the transcriptions more accessible to a broad circle of readers and facilitates the study and classification of folk music materials according to musical elements. Of our 140 songs, the tonality of G is not completely comfortable for five or six songs where there are pitches that are too high (up to B^2). All identical or similar musical phrases, melodic lines, cadences, and so on, have the same graphic indication, so the similarities, as well as the differences, of identical or similar structures are more easily noticeable. In the Lists of Informants, we indicate the original tonality. Songs with melodies made up of two or more independent melodies are transposed according to the first melody. The remaining melodies are given in the tonality required by the modulatory plan of the song.

A few words about the transcription of the texts are in order. We did not set ourselves the goal of an absolutely precise phonetic transcription of texts, but we also did not want to avoid phonetic transcription completely. It is more like a phonetic transcription of the text as sung than as it would be in ordinary speech. Sometimes one finds elements of another dialect which have come into the language along with the song. These elements are found much more rarely in the ordinary speech of the given dialect. The influence of literary language can be found on the pronunciation of some words due to printed and copied-out texts. Usually the transcriptions of texts done by slightly literate singers is closer to their dialect than to the literary language. Sometimes supplementary syllables are added while singing. If there are more pitches than words in a phrase, the singer adds a suitable number of syllables. Usually they add such interjections as *oy* and *oy vey.*

When one cannot add such interjections (e.g., in mid-word), the singer puts in vowels almost never heard in ordinary speech, such as "ine" for *un* or *in, cigenejmene* for *cugenumen,* and *blijet upegijejisn* for *blut opgisn.* Sometimes, albeit rarely, they put in altogether foreign syllables (usually *vo, vu*), for example, *povolicie (policie)* and *juvurn (jorn).* We have not found any closed *e*'s. Elided words, like *hocax* for *hot zix* or *zetus* for *zet dos,* are written divided, in order to facilitate reading the text underlay. We paid no attention to specific pronunciation of consonants. The titles of songs (first line or half-line of text) are given in the literary language. In the fifth group of workers' songs (to texts of Vintshevsky et al.) we used the usual titles as given in the collected works of the authors in question (Vintshevsky 1924, 1927; Fefer and Fininberg 1931; *Mut* 1920). The texts (not in underlay) are given in literary language, preserving the dialect characteristics only in cases where it is necessary for the rhyme. We could not include all the variants to the songs given. Of 140 items, 100 are "basic" and 40 are variants of given songs. Variants are not given in full; only the more characteristic verses were included. Often while repeating a musical phrase the singer takes a different note; in those cases we have placed the note stems on different sides of the note head. The bibliography for melodies and texts is exclusively from Jewish folklore anthologies.

We collected most of the songs dated 1928–31 in Kiev, Odessa, Belaia Tserkov', Uman', and Skvir. We transcribed twenty-one of the items from the materials of the *phonoteque* of the former Jewish Historic-Ethnographic Society (Leningrad), transferred to our Cabinet in February 1930 (nos. 2, 17, 19, 27, 37, 42, 45, 63, 78, 82, 90, 93, 96, 102, 104, 110, 112, 113, 115, 121). The annotations on performers and place of recording in the

List of Informants are taken off the cylinder cases; we have no other sources. In cases where there are no annotations, we indicate male voice or female voice. We gave the date of recording as 1912–14 for want of better evidence, as the main work of the An-ski expedition ("Society for Jewish Music," whose materials make up the *phonoteque* of the Historic-Ethnographic Society in Leningrad) falls in those years. We put the tempo markings and pitch level of the songs from this *phonoteque* in parentheses, because the phonograph on which the recordings were made and played back had no speed indicator and it is therefore impossible to reproduce the songs exactly in the tempo (or pitch level) at which they were re-corded. Usually while using such equipment a pitch pipe was used to tune the phonograph for playback, but the Leningrad *phonoteque* did not use this system. In each case we chose a tempo and pitch level that corresponded to what we knew to be common practice through our work on Jewish folk music for the given song and performer. We also use parenthetical annota-tions of tempo for songs transcribed by ear or sent to us by correspond-ents.

No. 85 was transcribed from a cylinder in the *phonoteque* of Joel Engel. The Engel collection consists of twenty-nine cylinders transcribed in 1912 during Engel's folk music expedition in Volynia and was transferred to the Cabinet along with the An-ski collection in February 1930. No. 71 is taken from Engel's archive. Engel's archive, consisting of twelve folders with unpublished essays, music manuscripts, letters, documents, concert pro-grams, photographs, and so on (about three hundred items), was put into order and given to the Cabinet in 1929 by the widow of the composer, A. K. Engel. In his manuscript Engel did not write out the whole text of the first verse; we completed it according to the published text of Vint-shevsky.

Six songs were transcribed by B. Gutianskii (nos. 8, 95, 97, 98, 100, 106), and three (nos. 50, 94, 131) by I. Khabenskii. M. Shpolianskii of Belaia Tserkov' sent us one song (no. 58). S. Shnayder transcribed nos. 3, 9, 13, 14, 19, 38, and 39 under my supervision.

Z. Skuditski did the bibliographical annotations to most of the texts and transcribed the texts of L. Bresler and several other singers. A. Gursh-tein and the poet D. Gofshtein took part in the editing of the translation of the Yiddish texts into Russian.

I must express my gratitude to V. O. Khar'kov, M. S. Pekelis, I. A. Margolina, and M. F. Geilig for suggestions on several songs. I am grateful to N. I. Shtif, director of the philological sector of the Institute of Jewish

Proletarian Culture for advice and suggestions on the transcription of Yiddish texts. I owe many valuable suggestions to the director of the Cabinet of Musical Ethnography of the Ukrainian Academy of Sciences, Professor K. V. Kvitka, and would like to express my gratitude here.

I would also like to acknowledge the many comrades in Kiev and other cities who sang their songs for us, and all those who, with comradely readiness, helped us in our collecting work both in Kiev and on our expeditions. I must particularly note the participation of the Jewish oral folklore collector Sh. Kupershmid (Belaia Tserkov'). Thanks to his initiative and active participation, our first folk music expedition to Belaia Tserkov' (May and June 1929) took place. Comrade Kupershmid transcribed the texts of all the songs that I recorded there. Without the help of these comrades our work of collecting folk music would have been much more difficult, and at times impossible.

I owe a great deal to M. F. Viner, whose advice and suggestions I always used in setting up the plan of the present anthology. He also kindly took on the general editing of the anthology; for all this he has my deepest gratitude.

Kiev

August 1932

Songs

Key to Symbols Used in Transcription

‿ Slightly shorter than notated

⁀ Slightly longer than notated

↑ Slightly higher (less than a half step) than the corresponding tempered pitch

↓ Slightly lower than the corresponding tempered pitch

⌒   Glissando

⹁⸳⸳₈ Performed an octave higher

₈⹁⸳⸳ Performed an octave lower

∽   A not completely clear ornament

⹌   A sound of indeterminate pitch

We have included in brackets individual notes or whole phrases when we were not sure of their notation (e.g., the sound or phrase was sung extremely quietly). We have also used brackets for phrases which were not achieved on the recording (usually at the ends of songs) for which we have taken phrases from previous stanzas.

I. WORKERS' SONGS

Songs About Work, Exploitation, and Poverty

1. Sver un biter vi der tojt

fyn _ cter di tejg, se mir by _ ter di jur oj

♩ = 92

y _ le tuug vynč ix mir dejm to _ o _ ojt.

Parlando

3. Oj, ix kim a _ rajn yn _ der _ fri yn štei mix a _ vek bamba _ le _

♩ — 88

bu _ es ojf der tir, bamba.le bu _ es ojf den tir yn

♩ = 100

sme je nox nyt ojs re _ dn kajn hoje x vort, ix hob dox

moj _ re er zol nyt up _ zu _ gn mir yn

♩ = 88

zol nyt ci _ ne.men a cvej.tn af majn o _ o _ ort, ix

hob doxe moj _ re er zol nyt upe _ zu _ gn mir yn

zol nyt ci _ ne.men a cvej.tn af majn o ort

2. Jx štej dox uf gancfri

Jx štej dox if ganc tri, ix zec mix cymge _ nej, yn

har _ cn yz far _ try _ knt yn x'vyl a gle _ zl tej.

Oje vist yn vej yz cy maj _ ne jin _ ge ju _ rn k

vus ix byn tyn drhe _ jem a _ rojs ge _ fu _ rn.

3. Ajn šnej, mame

Ajn šnej, ma me, aj šnej, my _ ter, an šnej mame, myt ajn

re _ gn, an šnej ma me, myt ajn re _ gn. Yn majn ma me hot mix

ojs _ ge _ xo _ vet, oj, tyn dejm šnaj _ ders vej _ gn,

yn dy ma _ me hot mix ojs ge _ xo _ vet, oj far dejm šnaj _ ders

vej _ gn. 2. Der šnajder šelt yn ba _ grubt, yn me

myz dus a _ les cy _ laj _ du   me myz dus a _ les cy_

laj _ dn,   yn majn ma _ me hot   mix ojs _ ge _ xo _ vet   oj,

fyn dejm šnaj _ ders   vej _ gn.   3. Az ix ким halb

zекs a _ zej _ ger, oj, zugt der šnaj _ der s'yz   git,   e,

zugt der šnaj _ der s'yz   git,   yn   az ix ким, oj

cen my _ nyt špe _ ter   capt er mir   maj _ ne blyt.

4. A šnej, mame

A šnej, ma _ me, a šnej, mu _ ter, a šnej mit   a

re _ gn,   a šnej mit   a   re _ gn.   Oj, du host mix

ojs _ ge _ xo _ vet fun dem šnaj _ ders ve _ gn, fun dem šnaj _ ders vegn.

5 Tog azojvi naxt

6. Jn drojsn gist a regn

Yn droj_sn gist a re_gn yn droj_sn gist a re_gn

yn se ši_it a snej, a šnej, yn se ši_it a

šnej, a šnej. A _ zoj zo_nen a _vek_ge_gajn_gen

a _le maj_ne jin_ge ju rn zy_ cn_dik šten_dyk bam ge_

nej, bam ge_nej. A _nej, bam ge_nej. 2. Tug a_zoj vi naxt,

naxt a_zoj_vi tug, ke_sej_der myt der nu_dl nor ge_

što_xn. Oj, di go_ot, di vejst dox, oj, dem e_mes, az

maj_ne bej_ner zo_nen mir ce_bro_xn. bro_xn. 3. Ce_

bro_xn zo_nen maj_ne bej_ner vej_sn vejs nyt kej_ner nor ejn got a_

lejn, a_lejn, nor ejn got a lejn, a lejn... [nit farendikt.]

7. Bin ix mir a nejterкe

Byn ix mir a nej_ter_кe, di лu-dl af majn far-meг, ix

darf zix sojn nyt zor gn far mor-ge-dy-кe teг jx

darf zix mer nyt zor-gn, se yz mir nyt кajn nojt, ix

кon zix mir far-di_nen af majn šty-кe_le brojt.

8. Ba di mašinen

Ba di ma-ši-nen ajn-ge_boj-gn žic ix, ma-me-ňu, dajn

ein_ciк кind, aj, je_der bejn_de_le ce _ nojf-ge _coj-gn

fun der ar_bet ver ix šir nit blind. Kajn i_be_ri_кe za_xn zix

nit far-gi _ nen, vajl di кop_кe кumt on ze_jer šver, un

ba_der_baj hob ix mir in_zi_ nen, az mir heL_fn hot nit ver

9. Oj, in fabriκ zic ix ajngebojgn

♩=126

Oj, yn fa - brik zyc ix ajn - ge - boj - gn

'na - zej zyc ix, an u - remkind, oj, maj - ne gly - der ce -

nojf - ge - coj - gn, az fyn majn ar - bet ver ix šir nyt blynd. 2. Ce -

nojf - ge - ny - men, oj, o - le koj - xes, a , vek ge - le - jegt

ojf a zajt, yn majn mo - jex vert mir ojs - ge - try - knt, az

cy 'na šy - dex yz šojn nyte vajt 3. [- - - - - - - - - - - -

- - - - - - - - - - - - - - -] est er no - dn,

trinkt dus blyt. Oj, fyn majn lej - bn vel ix

zajn ce - fri - dn, ix vel nox hu - bn an an - tyk.

10. Oj, ba majn arbet tu ix zicn

Oj, ba majn ar‿bet ti ixe zy‿cn, oj, ajn‿ge‿boj‿
gn, ix u‿reme kynd, oj, je‿dere bejn‿de‿le ce‿
nojf‿ge‿coje‿gn, az fyn majn ar‿bete ver ix
šir nyt blynd, šir nyt blynd. 2.Oj, x'ho' ge‿kloj‿bn a' kop‿ke
cy naj kop‿ke vajl di kop‿ke, zi kymt un šver. Oj,
vy‿der hejb ix zix un cy ba‿re‿xe‿nen, az
cy kajn šy‿dax yz šojn ojx nyt va‿ajt, aj, ojx nyt vajt.

11. Ba majn mašindl tu ix zicn

Ba majn ma‿šyn‿dl ti ixe zy‿cn un‿ge‿hoj‿gn, ix
u‿rem kynd. Je‿dn bejn‿de‿le ce‿nojf‿ge‿coj‿gn yn

fyn majn ar_bet ver.ix šir nyt blynd. Oj, je _dn
bejnde_le ce _ nojf_ge_coje-gn yn fyn majnarbetver ix
šir nyte blynd. 2.A _ zoj dy kop_kehobix ce _ nojf_ge_kloj.
_bn, oj, a _ vekgelejgthobixzi ojf a zajt. Oj, majnmo_jaxvert
mir ce_fa_ln yn cy kajn ši_dax yz šojn ojxe nyt vajt.

12. Ba majn mašindele tu ix zicn

Ba majn ma_šyn_de_le ti ix zy_cn un_ge_boj-
gn, ajn u _ rem kynd, yn jej_der bejn_de_ le ce_
nejf_ge_coj _ gn, yn fyn majn ar _ bet ver ix
šir nyteblynd, yn jej_der bejnde_le ce _ nejfge_coj-
gn yn fynmajnar_bet ver ix šir nyte blynd.

13. A gance vox

14. A gance vox

A gon-ce vox, a gon-ce vox zyc ix af der

kol- ke, dem ej- nem tuge šo- bes far-

kem ix zix di pol- ke. Far- kem ix zix di

pol-ke un lejg mir ojs di hur, ix ti a kik yn

špi-ge- le ny- tu cy mir kajn pur. 2. Ix gei a-rois yn

droj-sn, ix gej a-rajn yn štib, majn mo- me tit mix

šel- tn: „zolst hu- bn a- zel- xe vel- tn." Ax

cu- rese ńe-pri- jat- host, se maxt mir nyt ojs, a-

bi majn ko- tike zugt mir: „ax, ty ńe bes- po- kojs"

15. A gance vox horevet zi

A gan_ce vox ho_re_vet zi bam šnaj_der ojf der

kol_ke. Se kimt der fraj_tyk far_naxt vert zi fyn der

ar_bet vol _ ne, zi vašt cex ojs dem kop, zi fran

zirt zix un dejm čub, zi us_pe_jet nyt e_sn dy

lok_šn myt der jux, az zi šojn yn štib ny_tu. 2.Zi

xapt dus roj_te ša_le_xl far ym_pet ojf eju o_jer. Zi

hot kajn cajt nyt myt kej_nem cy_rej_dn, vajl der

šej_ner vart bam to _ jer. Zi gejt myt im a_rym byz

cve_lf a zej_ger af_der_naxt yn af mor_gn na_

zna_čet zi im yn tanc_klas af a zej _ ger axt. 3.Myt

fi _ rn a _ zoj _ ne vel _ tn   Di gejst a _ rim my tn

šej _ nem byz cve _ lf a zej _ ger ba _ naxt,   ix der

ken dox šojn yn dir,   'stim na _ zna _ čet af mor _ gn af der _

naxt!" 5. Vi   zi der _ hert a   xo _ se _ ne   ba ir

xa ver tos a frajn _ tl,   ojf der xo _ se _ ne

myz zi gejn, zi myz dox xa _ pn a ten cl.   Der

šej _ ner yz ras _ pa _ ra di _ tel   yn   zi taṇet no _ xn

kla _ ang   yn af   mor _ gn ba _ rajst er   zi,   kymt

zi   yn   a   ce _ ry _ se _ nem pal _ to.

16.Oj ix hob šojn nit kajn kojex

Oj, ix hob šojnnyt kajn koj _ jax ba majn ar_bet ajn _

cy _ zy_je _ en,   yn majn mo_me zugt,az zi   zyt dus

nyt a _ ro_jes,oje   vej,.   oj, di hob af mir raxe_

mu _ nes, yn di   ver far mir a   xu _ sn,   oj, di

nem mix fynder vis_ter   fab_ry_ke   a _ rojs.   2.Oj, v'a_

zoj zol   exe   dix fyn der fab_ry_ke   a_rojs_ ne _

men, az ix hob an el _ te _ re šve _ ster fyn

mir,   oje vej. Oj, az got vet mir hel _ fn, az majn

šve_ster vet a   ko _ le ve _ rn, oje,   xo_se_ne

ju_bn oje   vel ix   far dir. Oj, az   dir. 3.Oj, a

vis _ tn sof, oje, zol dajn mo _ me

ju _ bn, yn af i _ re fis zol zi nyt ke _ nene

gejn af der velt. Oj, a _ za sko _ re po _ mešč, vus er

furt a _ rim y _ ber der gon _ cer velt, er vet zi

ne _ men un klej _ der, oj, yn un a kop _ ke gelt. 4. Oj, vus

hos _ te, lu _ be _ le, cy šel _ tn majn movo _ men, di

šelst majn mo _ men yz glax a _ zoj _ vi mir, oje

vej. Ot 'es _ te ze _ jene, lu be _ ñu, az der xa _

rak _ ter vet zix ba ir ba _ tn, vest nox

zajn a _ mul ba ir dy un _ ge _ lejeg _ te šnir.

17. Ix hob šojn nit kajn kojex

Ix hob šojn nyt kajn ko _ jax, oj e, ba majn

ar _ bet cy zy _ en, oj, n'af majn pu _ nym zejt

kej _ ner nyt a _ rojs, oj, n'af majn pu _ nym zejt

kej _ ner nyt a _ rojs, oj, hob šojn raxe _

mu _ nes yr v'er far mir a xu _ sn, fyn der vis _ ter ar _ bete

nem mex šojen a _ rojs. Oj, rojs. 2. ix volt šojn far dier,

oj, ___ a xu _ sn ge _ vo _ rn, a xu _ sn vej _ rn

[verst dox]nyšt a _ lejn, a xu _ sn vej _ rn [verstdox]nyšt a _

lejn, oj, ix byn a jin _ ge _ le myt ej _ ge _ ne ge _

dajn _ ken, az ix ba _ re _ xn, cy ix darf cym pry _ zyv

štejn. Oj, ix вуп a jin‿ge‿le myt ej‿ge‿ne ge‿

daju‿ken, az ix ва‿re‿xn, az x'darf cym pry‿zyv štejn.

18. Oj, undzere jorelex gejen undz avek

Oj, hyndze‿re ju‿ra lax ge‿jen yndza‿ve‿ek

myt hyc yne my‿ji‿jit ro‿jax, oj, oj. Git nor

a‿kik vi a jid fyn zex‿cyk ju‿er, er hot šojn, oj.

mejn fyn indz ko‿jax, ko‿jax. 2. A‿zoj‿vi a miji‿ji!,

vus ži ar‿вet ke‿sej‿der, hot zi ва got an up‿

štand, oj, oj. Ša‿вes far‿naxt, vi me

zejt nox nyt kajn šte‿rn mir hal‿tnšojndus fa‿jer ynder

hant, hant. 3. Oj, zy‿mer yn di hy‿en, yn

vyn_ter yn di kel _ tn, oj, saj ba _ tug yn saj ba_

na _ axt, oje, oj. Far_ šol_tn zol ve_ rn der _ do _ zy_ker

.menč, vus er hot dus be_ke_raj ojs_ge_traxt Far traxt

19. Oj, undzere kojxes, oj, gejen undz ojs -

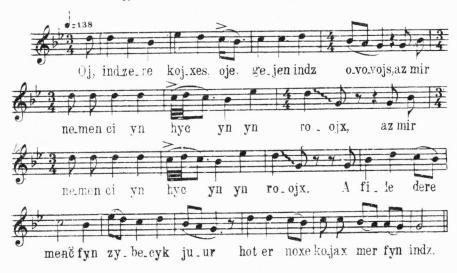

Oj, ind_ze_re koj_xes. oje. ge_jen indz o_vo_vojs, az mir

ne_men ci yn hyc yn yn ro _ ojx, az mir

ne_men ci yn hyc yn yn ro_ojx. A fi _ le dere

menč fyn zy_ be_ cyk ju _ ur hot er noxe ko_jax mer fyn indz.

20. Di baleboste gejt arajn

Di ba_le_bo _ ste gejt a _ rajn, hop du _ naj, du _ naj,

xev _ re, xev _ re, štil zol zajn, hop du _ naj, du _ naj.

21. Di madam Rabinovič gejt arajn

Parlando

Di ma_dam Ra_bi _no _vič gejt a_rajn 'my_tn plu _še_nem

♩=140

sak,my_tn fe_je_nem kol_ner mejnt, az zi dy kli_ge. Dy

gan_ce ra_bo_če zugt, a' ziz for _ mal_ne me _ ši _ ge oj,

hy _ le, kap_en, vus darf_ste zor_gn, vus darf_ste zor_gn

vus se vet žajn mor_gn, hy_le, kap_en, dir fejlt

o _ les, yn hy _ le, kap_en, freje _ le_xer do_les.

22. Di mašines klapn

(♩=116 –120)

Di ma _ ši _ nes kla· _ pn, di re_der, zej dre_jen

zix, in fab _ ri _ ke za raš mit a ge _ vald.

Oj, vej, nemt zix ce _ no _ ojf, šve_ster un bri _ der,

no _ mir a _ le ba_fra _ jen und _zer land.

КЛ 1296

23. In drojsn iz fincter

24 Viazoj zol ix nit mekane zajn

mor_gn zeks-dem zej _ ger ba'_ darf ix šojn y.n

man_ster-ska _je zan, az man-ster-ka _je zan.

3. Dy ma _ šy _ nes klo _ pn, dy aj _ zns, zej

ča _ dn.yn stib yz ajn rojex yn s'yz hejs, der

k.op vert ojs-ge_dart,dy oj_gn ve_rn tin _ kl

nor fyn ho _ re _va_ne yn fyn švejs, der

kop vert ojs_ge _ dart yn di oj_gn tin _ kl

nor fyn ho _ re _va _ ne yn fyn švejs.

25. Ir, balebatim, ir, merder.

Ir, ba_le_ba_tym, ir, mer — der, vus capt ir fyn dem

ar_be_tu_rer dus blyt. Jr mejnt, az di mal_xu_me vet ajx

gly — kn, ir mejnt, se vet ajx tu_myd zajn git? Se

zol a — fi_le dy_ne_rn yn bly — en, se

meg a _fi_le yn_ter_gejn dy velt, _____ axt šu yn

tug veln mir zy____ en, dus y_be_ry_ke vet ajx ko_stn

1. gelt, 2. gelt. Mir ho_bn y_le ju_rn ge_

ho_re_vet, byz mir ho_bn dy svo_bo_de der _ lebt, yn

Кл. 1296

ye _ ter yz dox un _ ge _ ki _ men Pet _ lu _ rov _ ces yn

vy _ ln dy svo _ bo _ de ce _ ryk, nor mir ve _ ln

ge _ jen byz dem bly _ yt, mir ne _ men dy svo

_ bo _ de ce _ ryk. Mir ve _ ln ge _ jen byz dem

bly _ yt, mi _ rn ne _ men dy svo _ bo _ de ce _ ryk.

26. Arbet der snajder a gance vox

1. Ar _ bet der šnaj _ der a gan _ ce vox, far _ dint er a
2. Far _ a _ ju _ rn nyt hajnt ge _ daxt ho _ hn mir ge _

gi _ ln myt a lox. Ot a _ zej nejet a šnaj _ der
ar _ bet a gan _ ce naxt.

Ot a _ zej klopt er ci, ot a _ zej nejet a šnaj _ der
t'a _ zej t'a _ zej

ot a _ zej klopt er ci. 3. Jn _ dzer strućke hot un _ ge _ maxt mir

ar _ be _ tn šojn mer nyt fyn axt byz axt. Ot a _ zej

и.а.z.v.
и. т.д.

27. Musju Maxovski, vos capt ir mir majn blut

(♩=116)

Mu_sju Ma_xov_ski, vus capt ir mir majn blyt,

a_le men_čn lozt ir ar_be_tn mir ej_nem, oj,

nyt. Mir ve_ln ax ba_fej_ln [. . . . .] mir

ve_ln ax ojs_bre_nen myt o_lin a_je_re oj_gn. 2. A_

zoj hot er zax un_ge_hej_bn ka_čen vi a fajl fyn bojgn:

„Oj, ge_va___ald, men_čn, ix hob šen nyt kajn oj_gn." A_

zoj ho_bn zax un_ge_ri_fn a_le myt ajn mul: „A_

des yz dox ajn groj_se štut, vi s'yz du ajn go_špy_tul."

28. Lipson iz a balebos

♩=104

Lip_son yz a ba_le_bos nor m'et im far der

4. Ra_bi_no_vič myt Lip_so_nen ho_bn zix ge_maxt ejn

hant, zej ho_bn if_ge_klept ob_jav_lē_ñes af der

vant, draj_syk kop_kes ojf dem toj_znt gib ix dem na_rod, yn

az zej vy_ln nyt ne_men 'e_ln zej gejn af„čor_ny

xod." Draj_syk kop_kes af dem toj_znt git er dem na_rod, yn

az zej vy_ln nyt ne_men 'e_ln zej gejn af„čor_ny xod."

5. Pa_pi_ros_ni_ces, kar_don_šči_kes ho_bn zix ge_maxt ejn

hant, zej ho_bn if_ge_klept ob_jav_lē_ñes af der vant, fercyk

ru_bl dem xoj_deš vyl der na_rod, yn az ir vet nyt

ge_bn ve_ln mir gejn„pa_rad_ny xod." Fer_cyk

gejn „pa_rad_ny xod." 6. Lip_son yz dox

dyrx_ge_gajn, dus kvy_tl y _ ber_ge_lejnt,   er hot

y _ ber_ge_ lejnt, er hot o_koršt nyt ge_vejnt,   fyn

zynt er yze   ba _ le _ bus, ge _hert het er dos nyt,

di par_šy _ ve mejd_lax, zej   ca _ pn im dus blyt.

29. A gut morgn ajx, Rabinovič.

♩ = 152

A git mor_gn ajx, Ra_bi_no_vič, a git jur ajx, Jo_sl

Lip_son, vus hert zix ba ajx yn fa _ brik? - Ba   mir   yn fa_

brik yz ajn bu_re myt ajn stač _ ke, dy   ar_be_ tu_rer

zi_xn ba mir   glyk. Ba   glyk. 2. Oj,   ar_be_tn vus

vej_ny_ker yn sxi_res vus mez, dus 'et men ba mir nyt ojs_

fi _ rn,   ot   'el   ix a _ rajn_fi _ rn dem fin_yn_

spek_ter myt žan_dar_me_ske   vet men ajx šojn y_le   a _ re_

sti_rn.   Ot sti_rn.3.Der fin_yn_spek_ter myt žan_dar_me_ske

dre_jen zix a_rvm: „myt dy ar_be_tu_rer kon men gur_nyt

ma_xn,   git zej šojn up,   oj,   a_les,vus zej trebe_yen,

mejn kajn za_ba _ stov_kes nyt ma_xn.   Git zej šojn up,   oj

a_les vus zej tre_be_ven mejn kajn za_ba_stov_kes nyt ma_xn."

30. A gut morgn dir, Mojške

(♩ = 108)

A gut mor _ gn dir,Mojš_ke, a gut jor, Jo_ sł

Lip son, vos hert zix e _ pes ba dir   in fa _ brik? –

Ba mir in fa_brik   iz a   l'a_rem mit a

stač _ ke; di ar _ be _ ter zu _ xn ba mir glik.

31. A gut morgn dir, Avremele

„A git mor-gn dir, Av_re_me_le, a git jur dir e,
Me_jer_vus hert zix ba dir yn fa _ bryk?"- „Ba mir yn fa_
bryk yz a bunt myt a stač _ ke, ar_ be_tu_rer
zi_xn ba mir glyk. 2.Ar_ be_tn vus vej_ny_ker yn
gelt vus me_rer, zej ve_ln dox ba mir nyt ejs_
fi_rn. On gejt dox balda_rajn der žan_dar_me ske polkov nik
vet er zej o_le a_re _ sti_rn. 3. A _ zoj_vi der žan_
dar_me_ske yz a_rajn_ge_ki_men: „myt kyn ra _ bo _ če
ke_nen mir gur_nyt ma_xn.. Jr git zej dy na _ bav _ ke yn
axt šu yn tug ar_be_tn ve_ln zej kajn sta_čkes nyt ma_xn..

4. Da _ løj   di   ku _ la _ kn yn   na _ gaj _ kes yn   ko _

za _ kn, dy tre be _ va _ ne ve _ ln mir øjs _ fi _ rn..

32. Af maloarnautske un puškinske

♩ = 92

Af   ma _ lo _ ar _ na _ ut _ ske yn puš _ kin _ ske, ba Po _

po _ vu yn fa _ bryk   hot zax un _ ge _ hej _ bn

ze _ jer a grej _ sar bynt. Der bynt yz ge _ ve _ zn

i _ ber a na _ bov _ ke,   to _ mer vet ir yndznyt gi _ bn veln mir

♩ = 104

ma _ xn a za _ ba _ stov _ ke. 2. Cen e kop _ kes a _ fn toj _ znt

yz dox nyt kajn sax,   git yndz di na _ bov _ ke a _ nyt

ge _ jen mir af glax,   git yndz di _ na _ bov _ ke   vet ir ma _ xn

be _ ser.   to _ mer vet ir yndz _ nyt gi _ bn, git yndz up di

pe - ser. 3.Gor-do - vy - je, nad-zi - ra - te - li na

fa - bri-ku pri-šli, pod-na - li na-gaj - ki i

krik-nu-li: „žy-dy! sad-te na ra-bo - tu, ja vam go-vo-

ru, jes-li vy ne sa-de-te v'tur-mu po-sa-žu.

23. Der bunt iz gevorn iber a nabavкe

Der bunt yz ge-vo-rn y-ber a na-bay-ke,

m'hot nyt gi - volt gi - bn yz ge - vo rn a za - ba-

stov-ke.2.Ba Lan-des-ma-nen-yn fa - bry-ke z'ge-vo-rn a ge-

ri-der, dort ho-bn zix ce-bun-te-vet di šve ster yn

bri-der. Zej ho-bn zix ge-bun-te-vet, se ge-vo-rn a

ge-šrej, s'a-ra-jn ge-gajn po-li - ci-je: „po-li-ci-je da-loj!"

♩=112

3. Po _ li _ ci _ je za _ rajn ge _ gajn hot men ge _ ge _ bn a ge _

šrej: „za _ be _ ri _ te vot e _ ti bun _ tov _ šči _ ki

tol _ ko po _ sko _ rej." _ „Hert nor ojs, Krom _ berg, ir

vet es nyt ojs fi _ rn, in _ dze _ re ra _ bo _ če vet men

nyt a re _ sti _ rn." 4. A _ zej ho _ bn mir six ojs _ ge _ zect

y _ le ojf di ty _ šr, a _ zoj hot men ge _ ge _ bn

Fyš _ ki _ nen cy vy _ sn. Yn Fyškinyz a rajnge _ ki _ men:

„Vustit ir du š tejn, ver se vyl na _ tav _ kese megzixgeina hejm."

5. Fyš _ kin hot ge _ mejnt, az er vet ma _ xn be _ ser, mir

ho _ bn ge _ ge _ bn a ge _ šrej: „git indzup di pe _ ser."

Oj, mu _ sje Fyš _ kin, ix ken es nyt far _ štejn,

34. In ale gasn vi me geijt *)

pu_šet, bri_der, un fan_ta_zje, maxt a za_by_

stov_ke. Ty dy ra la la la la, ta ra ra la la la

la, ta ra ra la la la la ta ra la la la la.

2. A šna_der_mej_dl ojs_ge_blejxt, zi kymta_hejmnyt ce_

fri_dn, zi šrajt:„ge_nig šojnzajn a knext fyf_cn šo cym

ji_dn." Vi lang yz zi ge_ven a pro_ste ge_

vejnt_le_xe mo_dist_ke, a cynd gejt zi dy

hur ce_flox_tn, a py_skl vi an ar_tist_ke, zi

šyt myt ver_ter gur un šir, a gon_ce fi_lo_zof_ke, zi

šrajt:„di ar_bet lejgt a_vek yn e maxt a za_ba_

stov ke." Ty_dy ra la la la la la ta ra ra la la la

la ta ra ra la la la la, ta ra la la la la.

3. A jin.ger.man, a yn.ty.li gent, er redt zix vej.nyk ge.

šly.fn, cym šraj.bn hot er cvej gil.der.ne hent yn

ly.pe.lax ojf šru.fn, kin.stlaxredt er ru.syš git,

ji dyš nyt kajn vort, oj, lon.ge hur myt

švar.ce von.cn. a kop.cn per.vy sort, er git zix a

štel tar ajn ka.sir yn maxta sa.man.di.rov.ke,(?) far.

nenit dy ka.se byz dem šir yn maxt a za by.

stov ke. Ty dy ra la la la la ta ra ra la la la

la, ta ra ra la la la la la la la la la la.

5. Dort šrajta da.me cy ir man, zi darf hu.bngelt af klej.der,

se vet ki_men dy gol_de_ne cajt cy fu_rn yn dy

va_re_me bej_der, er yz dox ir trejf paskidne,zi

rift im un: „do_xla_če, di zolst a_fi_le dem

tojt ba_ky_men darf ix hu_bn a da_če. Di

zolst a_fi_le Springen ca_pom, ba_dar ix hu_bn ma_

jov_ke, ojs_špi_ln vel ix min_ha_stam fyn

in_dzere za_ba_stov_ke." Ty_dy ra la la la la ta

ra la la la la ta ra ra la la la la ta ra la la la la.

35. Jn ale gasn vi me gejt

Yn a_le ga_sn vi me gejt hert men za_ba_stovkes,

jin glax mejdlax kind yn kejt, me redt šojn fyn pri_bav_kes, yn

84

a-le ga-sn tit men šrajen: „Bri-der, lomir lej-bn fraj, ge -

nig šojn, brider, bor-gn yn la-jen yn ho - re - ven ge-traj,

az der šlexter bor-že, er zejgt indz vi ajn pjavke, ge -

nig šojn, brider, un fan-ta-zje ma - xn za - ba-stov-ke."

2. Ajn šnaj-der mej-dl un-ge-blejxt-zi kymt a hejm ce

fri - dn, zi redt di ver-ter gur un šrek

fer-en šu-ey rej-dn, vi - lang yz zi ge - veje - zn a

pro-ste ge-vi - se mo-dist-ké, ject gejt zi dy

hur ce - lozt, ajn e pys-kl a - nar-xist-ke, zi

redt di ver-ter gur un šrek fyn der na-sov-ke, fyn

a-jer ar-bet maxt an ek yn ejnkol za - ba-stov-ke.

3. Šrajt ajn da_me, vej iz ir, ir tox_ter yz me_ši_ge,   zi

hot cy_tun myt pek pa_pir yn iz dermyt ajn kli_ge.   To_

va_riš_čes, oj, šir a šire   loj_ter loj myt bry _ ln,

ki_men zej šojn dy _ ln.   „Oj   vej, majn tox_ter,   di

byst šojn greb_lax dav_ke,   štra _ da _ jest šojn draj

fer _ tl   jur   ce _ lib   der   za _ ba_stov_ke.“

33. Vi me gejt un vi me štejt hert men zabastovke

Vi me gejt yn vi me štejt, oj, hert men e za_ba_stov_ke,

al_te men_ěn, kyn dyn e kejt, zej   vy_ln ajn na_bav_ke,

al_te men_ěn kyn dyn kejt, zej   vy_ln lej_bn traj,   ge_

nig cy_ la _ jen yn cy bor_gn yn ar_be_tn ge_traj.

2. Dort krigtzix a man myt zajne vajb, zi šrajtaf im:„dyxe-
l'a_če,   di   megst a_fi_le dem tojt ba_ky_men,
šrajt zi, ix vyl a da če.   Ajne da_cě, da_cě vyl ix
cy_der_ci po_prav_ke, zi krejn̄kt Šojn̄,oj,drajfer_tl jur fyn der
eršter za_ba_stov_ke.   Oj, vi me gejt yn vi me štejt
hert men za_ba_stov_ke,   al_te men_ěn, kyn̄d yn kejt, zej
vy_ln ajn na_bav_ke,   al_te men_ěn, kyn̄dyn kejt, zej
vy_ln lej_bn fraj,   ge_nig cy bor_gn
yn̄ cy la_jen yn   ar_be_tn ge_traj.
Ej_ner zugt:„lejg a_vek e, lejg a vek dy ar_bet," der,
cvejter zugt:„lejg a_vek, a_nyt ver_sti ge_harget," der

dry _ ter zugt: „łejg a _ vek, vus ar _ bet _ sti far

a _ le, n lejg a _ vek dajn arbet yn gej šojncy dajnka _ le."

37. Jn ale gasn vi me gejt

Yn a _ le ga sn vi me gejt e hertmen za _ ba _

stov _ kes, ji nglax, mejliax, kyndyn kejt, zej re _ dn fyn par _

bav _ kes, ge _ nig šen, oj, cy bor _ gn cy la _ jen

hu _ bn lej _ bn fraj, yn di ar _ bete varft a _ vek yn

are _ be _ tn ge _ traj, yn di ar _ bete varft a _ vek yn

ar _ be _ tn ge _ traj. Ge nig šen, oj, dem

šlex _ ın bur _ žuj ajx cy zej _ gn vi a plav _ ke,

un fan _ ta _ zje, bri _ der yn mąxt a za _ ba _ stov _ ke.

38. Vi mir hobn zix ale sobirajet

Vi mir ho_bn zix a_le sa_bi _ ra_ jet Sa_ka_

vie_kes šil yz ge_vej_zn far yndz šmul yn ver se

hot ge_ge_bn po_vo_li _ cje cy _ vej _ sn der zol

lej _ gn yn Kiev yn go_ špy _ tul. 2. Vi der u_

rad _ nik yz nor yn šil a_rajn_ge _ ki _ men, a_

zej ho_bn mir zix far _ ny_men myt im kri_gn, se baldyn

šil a_rajn_ge_ki_men ko _ za_kn myt žin _ da _ rn

yn m'hot indz un_ge_hej _ bn, oj, a _ le a_ res_ti _ rn.

3. Vi me hot indz, oj, a _ le a _ re_stirt cvej a

39. Oj vej, švester un brider

zo_nen ge_ven y_le myt a_mul yn ver se hot ge-

ge_bn po_li_cje cy_vy_sn der zol foj_ln yn

Kievyn go_spy tul. Oj, yn tul. 3. Afe

mor_gn yz cy n'indz der pry_stev ci_ge_fu_rn. Mir

ho_bn zax myt im e_pes far_krigt mir krigt a_

zej yz un_ge_lo_fn po_li_cje myt zyn_da_rn yn me

hot indz šojn y_le a_re_stirt. 4. A_re stirt

hot men indz y_le. Dus yz ge_vejn a_rem cvej a zej_ger ba_

naxt, dus yz ge_vejn a_rem cvej a zej_ger ba_naxt, a_

zej hot men indz o_le ce_nejef_ge_ny_men yn me

hot indz, oj, yn o_strog far_špart. Oj, a spart. 5. Afe

morgn hot men indz gedarft kajn Vasilkov a rojs
šykn. Dus yz gevejn a rem cvej a zejger ba-
tug a zejyz un ge lofn dy futers myt dy
my ters yn s'yz ge vo rn a jumer myt ajn
klug. Oj, a klug. 6. Oj, hert šojn ojf cy vejnenyn cy
klu gn, falt ba zix af a zoj fil ryt a
rup, af a je re kin der vet men ajx a mul me
ka ne zajn, vajl zej stra da jen ne bax for in
gan cn na rod. Nor af a je re kiň
der vet men ajx a mul me ka ne zajn, vajl zej stra
da jen ne bax far dem gan cn na rod.

40. Unter der Sofievke

♩ = 120

Yn_ter der So_fi_ev_ke hert zix a_ge_ri_der, se

ho_bn zix so_bi_ra_jet šve_ster yn bri_der, se

ho_bn zix so_bi_ra_jet a groj_se kom_pa_ńe

af der fra_je yn af so_bra_ńe

41. A sobrane hobn mir zix sobirajet

♩ = 104

A so_bra_ne ho_bn mir zix so_bi_ra_jet yn

♩ = 112

a špi_jun hot yndz der_zejn, myt grojs pa_rad hot men

♩ = 126

yndz far_ne_men glax cym spra_av_nik, oj, a hejm.

2. Pri_ka_za_njes ho_bn mir u'_ge_ge_bn yn

♩ = 132

u'_ge_lozt hot men yndz a_hejm, u'_ge_lozt hot men

yndz a hejm dem el_ctn bri_der fyn yndz nyt, mir

dar_fn ze_jen far im ge_jen byz yn der lec_ter

♩=152

kap_li blyt. 3.Nemt zix ce_no_jef,oj, šve_ster yn bri_der,vel

ix ax ge_bn cy far_štejn, az mir ar_be_tn fyn

axt byz ce_jen ho_re_ven mir gur ym_zyst, yn

az mir ar_be_tn fyn axt byz zeks,vel ix ax ge_bn

cy far_štejn. 4.Šve_ster ya bri_der, mir zin_gen li_der,mir

zin_gen li_der fyn zix a_lejn, mir

zin_gen li_der myt fil ge_ri_der, az

got vet ge_bn ve ln mir ky_men a_hejm.

42. Dem najntn janvar

(♩ = 120)

Dem najn _ tn jan _ var ajn ju _ mer myt a klug me

firt in _ dze _ re bri _ der fyn bir _ že yn ast _ rog, me

firt in _ dze _ re bri _ der fyn bir _ že yn ast _ rog.

43. Šabes batog iz a jomer mit a klog

♩ = 152

Ša _ bes ba _ tug yz a ju _ mer myt ajn klug, me

firt di ra _ bo _ če fyn bir _ že yn es _ trog, me

firt di ra _ bo _ če fyn bir _ že yn os _ trog. 2. e

Vi me hot zej nor yn os _ trog, a _ rajn ge _ braxt, a _

zej hot men bold a pry _ to _ kol ge _ maxt, a _

zej hot men bo _ old a pry _ to _ kol ge _ maxt.

3. Šve_ster yn bri_der, fyn tur_mes nyt up_sre_kn, a_

rojst fyn der tur_me di_bri_der_lax der_ve_kn, a_

rojst fyn der tur_me dy bri_der_lax der_ve_kn. 4.A-

rojst fyn der tur_me myt bom_bes, myt ra_bir, nyt švaj_gn dy ti_

ra_nen, zej zej_gn 'n_dzer blyt, nyt švaj_gn di ti_ra_nen, zej

zej_gn in_dzer blyt. 5. Zej zej_gn in_dzer blyt, zej

trin_ken dem. be_stn van, Mi_kol_ke myt pra_vi_tel'_stve

zo_ln yn dr'erd a_ran, Mi_kol myt pra_vi_tel'_stve

zo_ln yn dr'erd a_ran. 6.Az Mi_kol_ke vet yn dr'erd a_

rup e ve_ln in_dze_re ar_be_ter eršt if_hej_bn·dy

kop, ve_ln in_dze_re ar_be_ter eršt if_hej_bn di kop.

К.Л.1296

Vi m'hot ajn ge-šrej ge-ge-bn: „ji-dn yn kry-stn!"

Ho-bn mir ge-ent-fert: „da-loj kap-ta-li-stn!"

Ho-bn mir ge-ent-fert: „da-loj kap-ta-li-stn!"

Vi m'hot ajn ge-šrei ge-ge-bn: „le-vo, na-pra-vo!"

ho-bn mir ge-ent-fert: „da-loj sa-mo-der-ža-ve!"

Ho-bn mir ge-ent-fert: „da-loj sa-mo-der-ža-ve!"

44 Vi Jisker iz fun štub arojsgegangen
(Variant fun Hirš Lekert-lid)

Vi Jis-ker yz fyn štib a-rojs-ge-

gajin-gen ge-zugt hot er dem vajb a gi-te

naxt. Vi Jis-ker z'cym ti-ja-ter ci-ge-

gajn-gen dort hot er zajn lej-bn git ba-traxt.

2. Vi Jis_ker z'yn ti _ ja_ter a_rajn_ge _ gajin_gen ge

ny_men hot er a bi _ let yn per_vy rad, vi

Jis_ker z'yn ti _ ja_ter a_rajn_ge_gajn_gen dort hot er zajn

cajet ojs_ge_vart, vi Jis_ker z'yn ti _ ja_ter a _ rajn ge_

gajn_gen dort hot er zajn cajet ojs_ge _ vart. 3.Vi der gu_ber_

na_ter yz fy_nem ti _ ja_ter a _rojs ge_gajin_gen a ge_

šrej hot er ge_gi_bn:„iz _voš_čik, šu _ da!"

Jis_ker hot a _rojs_ge_xopt dem re_vol_ver yn hot imgi_

tro_fn glax yn zat. 4.Vi Jis ker t'dem gu_ber_

na_ter der _šo_sn yz ge _ vo_rn a raš myt a ge_

ri_der shot zix un_ge_ri_fn ej_ner cy dem

evej _ tn: „a _ du yz šojn far _ fa _ ln in _ dzer

bri _ der;" s'hot zix un _ ge _ ri _ fn ej _ ner cy dem

evej _ tn: „a du yz šojn far _ fa _ ln in _ dzer bri _ der."

45 Rojšxojdeš elel, mamenu

(♩ =100-104)

Reš _ xojdeš e _ lel, mamenu, ojef der e naxt, oj, lyg ix mir yn

traxt, oj, a _ zej hot men ba Grinber gn di ob _ la _ ve ge _

maxt. oj vej. Majn haro hot mir ge _ zugt, oj, mame, az

ha jnt yz šojn der lec _ ter af _ der _ naxt. Oj, lyg ix mir yn traxt.

46. Genesje iz fun ir arbet gegangen

(♩ =92)

Ge _ ne _ sje z'fun ir ar _ bet ge _ gan _ gen, zi

hot nox fun ir um _ glik nit ge _ vyst, a _ rojs _ ge _ gan der

mer _ der, der pri _ stev un hot zi ge _ šo _ sn um _ zyst.

47. Oj mitvox iz pervi maj

102

48. Di bixer mit di sekretn

rajn ge zect yn a fyn cte rer t'ur me, vi ba _ tug yz nox

er ger vi ba _ naxt. Me zect indz, xa _ vej rim, yn dy

tur _ mes, yn dy fyn cte _ re ka me rn far _ špart. Me

špart. 5. Cy hob ix a men _ čn ge _ ra net, cy hob ix a

men _ čn ge _ tejt, far vus kimt mir yn t'ur _ me cy

zy _ cn, far vus kimt mir af Ar _ xan gelsk cy

gejn. Far vus kimt mir yn t'ure _ me cy zy _ cn, far vus

kimt mir yn Ar _ xan _ gelsk cy ge _ ejn.

49. X'hob gekončet di axt klasn.

♩ = 116

X'hob ge kon čet di axt kla _ sn, ix byn a jin ge

le fyn der gim _ na zje a rojs ix hob far _ firt, far firt a

groj_se ro_le, šve_ster yn bri_der, ir halt zax ejns.

2. M'hot mix gexapt myt maj_ne bi_xer, m'hot mix a rajn_ge zeet yn dejm o_strog, ir nemtzix ce_no_ojf, šve_ster yn bri_der, cy yz den du ojf der_velt a got? 3. M'hot mix far_su det yn a fyn_cter xej_der, hajn tynt yn fej_der hob ix nyt ba zix, ix her ajnkol ajn kol fyn maj_ne bri_der, a_rojs gejn cy zeje ken ix nyt. ken ix nyt. 4. Ver že strojet di šej_ne mo_ve_rn? — Di šej_ne mo_ve_rn stro jet der arbajts-man, oj, tit a frejg, a frejg ver vojnt dor_tn? — Dor_tn vojnt zix der ra_xer man. 5. Der o_re man, vus er vojnt yn kej_ler nas yn sy_rest' ka pet fyn zaj_ne vent,

de_rym ba_kymt er rev_ ma _ tiz_ne fej _ ler _ojf

zaj _ ne fis   yn ojf   zaj _ ne hent.   žaj _ ne hent.

6. Ver že flanct dus di   šej _ ne vajn_gert_ner? — Dy

šej _ ne vajn_ger_tner flanct der   ar_bajts = man oj,

ver est o _ _ ojf dy   gi_te frux _ tn? — Dy   gi_te

frux _ tn est der   ra_xer man. Oj,   ra _ xer man.

50. Me firt mix arajn in a finctern xejder

($\bullet$ = 66)

Me firt mix a_rajn in ajn   fin_cte_rn xej_der, kajn

tint un pe_ne iz dort ni _ to.   Ix   her a raš maj_ne

kej_tn klin_gen x'vel ajx zin_gen ajn   tro_jer=lid.

51. Ver tut strojen movern, palacn

Ver tit stro_jen. mo_ve_rn,pa_la - cn, yn

ver tit stro_jen?—Der arbets=man, oj, tit ajn kik, oj,

ver sevojnt yn zej, se gur_nyt er, nor der raj_xer man.

2. Der ar_bets=man vojnt yn a ke_ler yn a na_sn, oj,

vus dy va_ser rynt, oj, fyn di vent, der_fin ba kimt er ajn

fe_ler, ajn groj_sn, oj, yn di fi_is yn yn di hent.

3. X'hob up_ge_le_rnt ajn blat ge_mu_re, ix byn,

got cy dajn_ken, fyn majn xej_der a_rojs, ix

hob far_fi_irt a na_je ro l'e, oj,

sve_ster yn bri_der ir. halt far ejns.

52. Di hojxe movern, ver tit zej strojen.

yn ix byn fyn dem xejder arojs. Jx hob far_fi_irt a na_je ro_le, šve_ster, bri_der halt zix ejns Jx.halt es ojs.

53. Dort in vinkl, in nasnkeler

Dort yn vin_kl ynna_sn kej_ler hart ajf dr'erd, af a by_sl št.ej, ligt ajn ar_be_ter ojf ajn ling = fej_ler; er ligt yn krexct yn šrajt:„oj, vej, her nor ojs, majne kind, majne lec_te rejd, her nor ci myt far_štand, be_ for ix nem fyndir up_šejd, her nor ci yn gib mir dajn hant, az di zolstnyt švaj_gn far majn lej_bn, vus ix gej cym štar_bn jin ger hejt, di zolst nor cej_ln yn far_ šraj_bn, di zólst ne men ra_xe far majn fri_caj_ty_kn tojt.

54. Dort in vinkl, in keler

Dort yn vin _ kl   in   kej _ ler   hart

ojf ba der erd,   af   a   byn_tl štrej   lygt ajn

ar _ be _ ter myt ajn bryst=fej _ ler,   ere   lygt yn šrajt yn

krex_čet:„oj,   her ojs, majn kind, majne lecte   rejd,

her zej ojs   myt _grojs far _ štand,   ej _ der   ix

nem fyn dir op _ sejd.   šver mir cu   yn

gib mir dajn hant   a' di vest nyt svaj_gn   dox

far majn le_bn,   vus ix gej cum štand a_zoj jin_ger_hejt

yn   yn or _ de _ nung   štarbt   er on   a

gloj _ bn. Zolst   ne_men ra_xe far_majn far_caj_ti_kn tojt

55. Di trit fun tiranen

Dy tryt fyn ti _ ra _ nen ho _ bn z ix ge _ lozt

he _ rn a _ rem cvej a zej _ ger _ ba _

naxt, a _ rem cvej a zej _ ger ba _ naxt,

dene _ nult _ yz ba indz a šte _ rn ge _ fa _ ln fyn

di, vus zei lojx _ tn ba _ naxt Mir ho _ bn nox nyt

of _ ge _ hert cy vej _ nen yn cy klu _ gn: fyn

di, vus m'hot kajn Si _ bir a _ vek ge šikt_ šikt,

plyc _ ling, az mir he _ rn a psi _ re un _ zu _ gn, az m'hot

in _ dze _ rn a bri _ der a _ re _ stirt. Ax vi

by _ ter yz dus _ land, vus mir ge _ jen cy dem stand far

in dnze re ge _ tra _ je, oj, šve_ster yn bri_der, nore

ver, ver, ver vejst, mi _rn hu _ bn dem trejst cy

ze_jen zix myt zej vy_der Nore vy_der. 2. A_

zoj_vi me far _ nart a foj-ge_le yn a klèt_ke, a_

zoj t'men in_dze_re bri _ der far _ ny men, a

_ yn der fyn_cte _ rer tur_me, vi kajn šajn kimt_nyt

ci, vi_kajn menĕ ken a _ hin nyt ki _ men.

Dor _ tn yn_ter di gro_be vent zict er dort

svare vi ajn kojl, kojl, dem kop un _ ge_

spart ojf di da _ re hent, er zyfct, az dus hareken ce

gejn. Oj, di fra je velt, zi yz yn im far

56. Di trit fun tiranen

Dy trejt fynti _ ra_nen ho_bn zix ge_lozt he _ rn
cvej deme zej_ger ba_ naxt, plyc_ling yz a šte_rn um_ge_
fa_ ln s'hot indz far_ y_mert ge_ maxt. Mir ho_bn nox nyt
uf_ ge_hert cy vej_nen yn cy klu_gn, m'hot in_dzers a
brider a_re_stirt. Ax vi by_ter yz dus land, vus mir
ge_ien cym štand, ba_ fra_jen, oj, in_dze_re bri_der. Ax vi
bri_ der. 2. A_ zoj_vi_ me far_ nemt a foj_ge_le 'na
klet_ ke_ le a _ zoj hot men in_dze_re bri_der, oj, far_
ne_ men, yn der fyn_cte_rer tur_me hot men indz far_
ne_ men, vi me ken a hin nyt ki_ men. Er e lejgt dem

kop un-ge-špart ojf di da-re hent, er vejnt, az dus

Parlando

hare ken ce--gejn. Oj, di fra-je velt yz far im far-

štelt cy ba-fra-jen, oj, in-dze-re bri-der

57. In dem vajtn land Sibir

Yn dejm vaj-tn lond Si-bi--ir, vi der

hy-ml 'z'tu-myd fyn di xma-res švarc, dort a-

lejn byn ix ge-vejn far-šy-ykt fa-rn ej-nem vort, far der

fraj. Myt der na-gaj-ke hot men mix ge-šlu gn, az

ix zol mer nyt zu-gn: „Da zdra-stvu-jet svo-bo-da, yn

dr'erd myt Ni-ko-laj!" 2. Oj, yn dem vaj-tn lo-ond Si-

bir, vi se kimt kejn-mul dy zin nyt ci, dort a-

lejn byn ix land ge-vej zn alc far dejm vort, far der

fraj. Zy‿mer yn di hy‿en yn vyn‿ter yn di
kel‿tn, di tač‿ke flejg ix šle‿pn ale e far dejm vort.

3.} Ven vet šojn ki‿men dy glyk‿le‿xe cajt, ye‿ter vejs men saj fyn
S'yz šojn ge ki‿men

nu‿vnt yn fyn vajt, az Ru‿sn lond yz lix‿tik, az Ru‿sn‿
lond yz fraj, da zdra‿stvu jet svo‿bo‿da, yn dr'erd yz Ni‿ko‿laj!

58. In dem vajtn kaltn Sibir

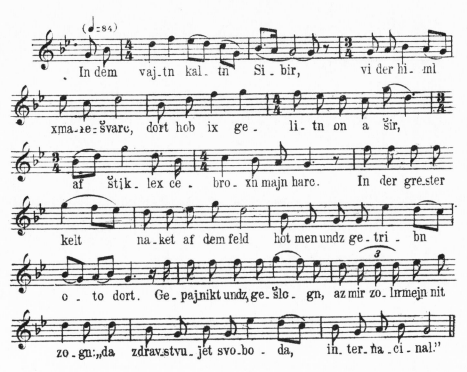

In dem vaj‿tn kal‿tn Si‿bir, vi der hi‿ml
xma‿le‿švarc, dort hob ix ge‿li‿tn on a šir,
af štik‿lex ce‿bro‿xn majn harc. In der gre‿ster
kelt na‿ket af dem feld hot men undz ge‿tri‿bn
o‿to dort. Ge‿pajnikt undz, ge‿šlo‿gn, az mir zo‿ln mejn nit
zo‿gn: „da zdrav‿stvu‿jet svo‿bo‿da, in‿ter‿ña‿ci‿nal."

59. In vajtn kaltn Sibir

In vaj.tn kal.tn Si __ bir, ví der hi.mi

xma.ret švare, dort hob ix ge.li.tn on a šir, ge.

bro. xn af šti.ker di o __ re.me hare In der gre.ster

kelt na.ket a.fn feld hot men mix ge.tri bn

dort, ge.pajnigt un ge.šlo.gn, az ix zol mer nit

zo.gn. da zdrav.stvu.jet svo.bo.da, da.loj Ni.ko.laj!"

S'iz šojn ge.ku men di glik.le.xe cajt, az mir ?.le

he.rn fun no.hent un fun vajt, az Rus.land iz šojn

glik.lex, az Rus.land iz šojn fraj, da zdrav.stvu.jet svo.

bo.da, da.loj Ni.ko.laj; Az loj Ni.ko.laj!"

60. Vi hejlik iz di natur

Vi hej_lyk yz di na_tur myt i_re fi a_je fi_ring, e_mes yn li_be ir ci_ring, ir šmuk. Mir lej.gn oj_fn har_en di rex_te hant yn šve_rn myt dem so_vest jeot, az fyn tejt un fyn le_bn vi an aj_zer_ne vant, ven der šverd fyn e_mes blyct. Ven ej_ner funundz iz cu švax ge_vis den cu gif_tig der ka_pi_tal a_zej_vi fun dem šlang der bys. Ven myt e_mes un li_be ge_bun__dn un_dzer bund yz vi a mo_jer štejt

fest un di li_be yz yn har_en on_ge _ cyn dn, dy

li _ be fun fraj_hajt un menö_ly _ xes glyk. Di ne _

ko _ me fo_dert un_dzer blyt, fun un_dzer blyt vakst

šten_dyk ze _ jer gits, gits un rajx ci _ en zej fun

un_dze_re hej _ ner, ax,un cum sof tret men undz vi di

štej_ner. Bri_der un šve_ster,nemt ajx far di hent,

kumt cu dem fa_jer vi der fla_ker brent, mir zaj_nen

pro_le_ta_rjat dos hejst ra_bo_či na_rod, di aj_zer_ne

kej _ tn lo _ mir ce _ raj _ sn, dem šve _ rn jox a _

rit.

run_ter cu šmaj_sn, šrajt:na_rod,vpe_rjod, vpe _ rjod,vpe_rjod!"

61. Lomir lejgn afn harcn di rexte hant

Lo.mir lej.gn oj.fn har.cn di rex.te hant, un be.

šve.rn zix myt so.vest ject, az durx tejt un le.bn vi an

aj.zer.ne vant, ven dos šverd fun e.mes blyct. Un ven

ej.ner fun undz yz cu švax ge.vis, den cu

gif.tig yz der ka.pi.tal vi fun dem šlang der bis.

Ven mit e.mes un li.de ge.bun.dn un.dzer bund štejt, vi ajn

mo.jer štejt ganc fest, far.gejt di zun in un.dzer harc on.ge.

cun.dn di zu.ne fun fraj.hajt gejt of. De.rum,

bri.der un šve.ster, git zix a.le di hent un ba.

švert zix bam fla.ker vi der fa.jer brent, mir

zaj ne der pro‿le‿ta‿rjat, dos hejst der pro‿ster na‿

ro‿hod, di kej‿tn, di šve‿re mu‿zn mir ce‿raj‿sn, dem

jox, dem šve‿rn a‿run‿ter cu‿šmaj‿sn, to šrajt „na‿rod, vpe‿rjod!"

♩ = 108

Bri‿der, no‿mir zix er‿va‿xn, fun ti‿ra‿ne‿

raj an en‿de ma‿xn, mir mu‿zn ce tre‿in

di ti‿ra‿ne raj, un ma‿xn Rus‿land fraj.

62 Dos eršte veln mir nemen nox regirn

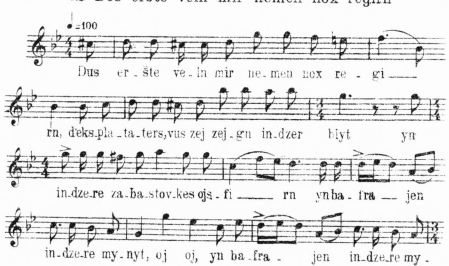

♩ = 100

Dus er‿šte ve‿ln mir ne‿men nox re‿gi‿

rn, d'eks‿pla‿ta‿ters, vus zej zej‿gn in‿dzer hiyt yn

in‿dze‿re za‿ba‿stov‿kes ojs‿fi‿ rn yn ba‿fra‿jen

in‿dze‿re my‿nyt, oj oj, yn ba‿fra‿ jen in‿dze‿re my‿

nyt. 2.Cy ba fra jen u re me men čn, vel xe

laj dn fil hin ger yn nojt, di erd fyn

fraj hajt zol zej ben čn, se zol ojf zej šejn nyt zajn kajn

nojt, oj, oj, oj, se zol ojf zej nyt zajn mer kajn nojt.

3. Nemt a rojs di fu nen fyn di ši ber, vel xe

šte jen nox yn fyn cte rn ge celt, nemt zix ce nojf a le

šve ster yn bri der cy ba fra jen in dze re

velt, oj, oj, oj, ba fra jen di u re re velt.

63. Gejt, brider, gejt ajx fodern brojt

♩ = 112

Gejt, bri der, gejt ajex fo de rn brejt ta kej

so rim um ba kha zn un ba gra fn, fo dert

menč_le_xe rext, me zol ajx nit ba_han_dlen a_zej šlext, fo_dert

a_les dos, vos mir ho_bn ba ___ ša_fn, fo_dert

menč_le_xe rext, me zol ajx nit ba_han_dlen vi di knext, fo_dert

a_les dos, vos mir ho_bn ba _ ša_fn. Štejt ojf, bri_der_mir

ve_ken ajx, un for_vets cum kamf un nit šrekt ajx

un cum lej_bn, un cum strej_bn, un cum kem_fn in a štrajk,

gejt um vert ba_frajt fun der na_jer cajt. 2. Der rov mi_tn

pop, zej far_dre_jen undz dem kop mit a_vej_res,

mit ze_je_re re_li_gi_jo_nen, ot di mic_ves mit di

zynd ma_xn dem ar_be_ter blind, er zol nit ze_jen

va_zej me tut im ba_rej_bn. Štejt ojf, bri_der, men

vekt ajx un for-verts cum kamf un nit šrekt ajx,

Un cum lej-bn, un cum štrej-bn un cum kem-fn in a štrajk

gejt un vert ba-frajt fun der na-jer cajt. 3. Der

si-ca-list iz ništ kajn jid un nit kajn krist, nor a

menč mit a rej-nem ge-vi-sn. Un-ter zajn rej-te

fon i' ni-to. kajn re-li-gjon, nor cvej kla-sn:

or'-me un raj-xe. Un-ter zajn rej-te fon i ni-

to kajn re-li-gjon, nor cvej kla-sn or'-me un raj-xe. Štejt

ojf, bri-der, mir ve-ken ajx, un for-verts cum kamf un nit

šrekt ajx un cum lej-bn un cum štrej-bn un cum kem-fn

in a štrajk gejt un vert ba-frajt fun der na-jer cajt.

64. Vos viln di heršer

Vos vi_ln di her_šer, vos vi_ln dy lam.pi_rn, zej

ca_pn fun dem ar_baj_ter dos lect bi_sł blut.

Un dan vet ir vi_sn vos se hejst eks_pla_ti

rn, ajn be_se_rn le_bn cu zi_xn zix far ajx.

2. Dem ar_baj_ters kamf gejt vaj_ter un vaj_ter, štelt zix in

kamf [far dem ar_baj_ter klas] un dan vet ir vi_sn, vos se

hejst eks_pla_ti_rn ajn be_se_rn le_bn cu

kem_fn zix far ajx. Un ajx.

Var. 1) hejst eks_pla_ti_rn, ajn zix far zix far

65. Brider, ejb got vet undz nit helfn

Bri_der, ejb got vet undz nit he_e_le_fn lo_mir zix ba

fra_jen a _ lejn, un lo_mir zix ce_raj_sn fun·ili_

ke _ je _ tn un lo _ mir a_lejn cu_za_men gejn.

36. Oj, ir nariše cionistn

Oj, ir na_ry_še ci_a_ni_stn myt

a_jer na_ry_šn sej _ xl, ir megt dox gejen cy dem

ar_be_ter yn ler_nen ba im e sej_xl. Jr

sej _ xl. 2.Jr vylt indz fi_rn kajn Je_ri_šo_

la _ jim, mir zo_ln dort go_lo_da_jen, mir

ve _ ln be_ser zajn yn Ru_sn_land, mir

ve _ ln zix ba_fra_jen. Mir fra_jen.

Melodies to Songs by M. Vintshevsky, D. Edelshtat, and Others

67. Der frajhajts-gajst

(M Vinčevski.

Jn di ga-sn, cu di ma-sn fun ge-drik-te fel-ker-
ra-sn ruft der fraj-hajts = gajst. Ix brejng va-fn far dem
skla-fn, ix ba-fraj di ar-bets-skla-fn un ix max zej fraj.

68. Es rirt zix

(M. Vinčevski.

Hert ir, kin-der, vi es rirt zix, vi es
rirt zix i-be-ral, vi der ar-bets-man mu-
strirt zix cu dem kamf mit ka-pi-tal. Cu dem tojt-kamf
mi-tn sin-der, mi-tn gvir, dem gelt-ti-ran. Hert ir
vi es rirt zix, kin-der, der ba-rojb-ter ar-bets-man.

69. Cum arbeter=frajnt

(M.Vinčevski.)

♩ = 88-96

Ix tu he_rn dajn šti_me, di šti_me fun var_hajt, dem

kol fun dem vir_kle_xn ar_be_ter = frajnt, ix

her dix fun vaj_tn, ix her dix mit klor_hajt, mit

here_li_xe li_be ba_gris ix dix hajnt, mit here_li_xe

li_be ba_gris ix dix hajnt. Un bet dix, er_kler majne

o_re_me bri_der, vel_xe ar_be_tn šver ba hajnti_ker

cajt, vel_xe a_ke_rn zix ojs dem marx fun di gli_der, zej

op_fe_rn a_les fa_rn miz_bej_ax fun gelt, zej

op_fe_rn a_les fa_rn miz_bej_ax fun gelt.

128

70 Draj švester

(M. Vinčevski)

In England iz do a štot Les_ter un in London iz do a_za skver. In skverštejen teglex draj šve_ster di mejd_lex,zej ken ver_hit_ver. In ver.

71 A bezem un a ker

(M. Vinčevski)

Ge _ nug! ix vil nit fi _ te _ rn kajn lej_dik_ge_jers mer, ge _ nug far fir_štn ci _ te _ rn, a be_zemmir a_her, a _ rojsmajn lord un a_dl_man, du sve_ter,di_ker bojx, du mu_ser=zo_ger, ta_dl_man, du, ki _ tl_man, gej ojx! Ix darf nit mer kajn mi_tl_man, a be_zm un a ker! kajn mi_tl_man,kajn ti_tl man,kajn ki_tl_man nit mer!

Кл 1296

72. Majn cavoe

D. Edlštat)

Majn li_ber frajnt, az ix vel štar_bn, trogtcu majn
kej_ver un_dzer fon. Di fra_je fo _ ne
mit i_re rój_te far _ bn ba_šprictmit blut fun ar_bets_
man. Di fra_je fo _ ne mit i_re rój_te
far _ bn ba_šprict mit blut fun ar_bets_man.

73. Majn cavoe

D. Edlštat)

O, li _ ber frajnt, ven ix vel štar _ bn, trogt
cu cu majn kej _ ver di fra_je fo _ ne.
Di fra_je fon _ mit i _ re far _ bn
ba_šprict mit blut fu_nem ar _ bets = man

74 Der ovnt=ġlok

76. Der ovnt-glok

(D. Edlštat)

O, mu - ze, ruf mix nit   mit daj - ne coj - ber - fin - ger.

Vek nit di stru - nes fun majn kran - kes   herc. Far   mi - špet

iz cum tojt dajn bla - ser zin___ ger,   cu en - de

iz dos lid fun kamf un nojt. Far - kamf un nojt.

77. Vaxt uf

(D. Edlštat)

Vi   lang, o, vi lang vet ir blaj - bn nox škla - fn un

tro - gn di šen - dle - xe kejt?!   Vi   lang vet ir glen - cn - de

rajx - ti - mer - ša - fn far dem, vos ba - rojbt un dzer brojt?   Vi   brojt?

78. In kamf

(D. Edlštat)

Mir   ve - rn ge - hast yn ge - tri___ bn,   mir

ve - rn geplagt yn far ___ folgt   yn   a - lesder - far, vajl mir

li bn dus u_re_me, šmax_ten_de

fo_____olk, dus u_re_me, šmax ten_de folk.

79. Majn lecte hofenung
(D. Edlštat)

(♩=100)

In štu_rem yn yn kamf hob ix majn ju_gnt fer

loj_rn fyn li_be, fyn glyk hob ix nyt ge_vust. Nor

blu_ti_ge tre_rn yn blu ti ge vyn_dn

ho_bn ge_koxt yn ge_brit yn majn brust. Nor brust.

80. Cu di arbeter=frojen.
(D. Edlštat)

♩=69

Ar_be_ter=fro_jen, ir lej_den_de fro_jen, ir

fro_jen, vos šmax_ten in hojz un in fa_brik, vos

štejt ir fun vaj_tn, vos helft ir nit bo_jen den

tem_pl fun fraj_hajt, fun men_ĉle_xn glik? Helft undz tro_gndi

fo_neṇdi roj_te! Forverts,durxštu_reṃ,durxfincte_re next!

Helft undz dem e _ mes un lixt cu far_šprej_tn e _

vi_šn um_vi_sn_de e _ In _ te knext! e _ In _ te knext!

Var

81. Nemt zix cenojf

Nemt zax ce_nojf fyn a _ le na_cjo _ nen a_her cy in_dzer

rej_ter fon, mir ve_ln ge_jen a _ le cy_za _ men, fʌr_

ej_nygt ajx yn ejn na_cjon. Mir ve_ln far_tej _ dy _

kn dy šva_xe, mir ve_ln kem_fn myt di ra_xe,

kymt a_her, kymt a_her! Mir zo_neh kyn_der fyn ejn

ma_me, mir ve _ In ge_jen a_le cy _ za_men ant

ke_gn in_dzer soj_ne, ant ke_gn in_dzer so _ je_ne

82. Brider, mir hobn gešlosn

(M. Sorerives

Bri _ der, mir ho _ bn ge_šlo _ sn ojf lej _ bn un

tojt a far _ band. Mir šte_jen du yn šlaxt vi ge

no _ sn, di fo _ ne, di roj te yn hant.

83. Šlof, Olekse
(špot:fid)

(Šolam:Alejxem

Šlof, O _ lek _ se, joj _ reš maj _ ner, 'yx _ ty

ker par _ šejn. Š _ lot, ben ju _ xid, ka _ dyš

maj _ ner, šlof že, šlof, nyt vejn.

Var

Кл.1296

II. SONGS ABOUT ARTISANS

84. Zict a šnajder

(♩=100)

Zict a šnaj - der a fis i _ ber a fis, zingt a li _ de _ le cy _ ker zis.

85. Ot azoj nejt a šnajder

(♩=84)

Ot a _ zoj nejt a šnajder, ot a _ zoj varft er štex, ot a _ zoj nejt a šnajder, ot a _ zoj var't er štex. A šnaj _ der nejt yn nejt yn nejt yn hot ka _ du _ xes nyt kajn brejt.

86. Der šnajder zict ba zajn genej

(♩=88)

Der šnaj _ der zict ba zajn ge _ nej, fun ejn por hoj _ zn maxt er cvej. Un in štub iz ba im fa _ ran fun a _ les _ ding, un in ke _ še _ ne git dox ojx a

87. Mit a nodl on a nodl

Mit a no_dl, on a no_dl nej ix mir be_

ко_ved go_dl, mit a no_dl, on a no_dl,

nej ix mir be_ко_ved go_dl. Zi_en zic ix mir a

fis af a fis, vajl majnar_bet iz cuкer zis Mi_

it a no_dl, on a no_dl nej ix mir be

ко_ved go_dl, mit a no_dl, on a no_dl

nej ix mir be_ко_ved go_dl. jx nej un nej a gan_ce

vo_voyoyoyox un nej mir ojs____ a pa_rixer lox

Mit a no_dl Ci_en ci ix mir di far_stri_ge.

un ix es mir di ma_me_li_ge.

Mit a nodl...

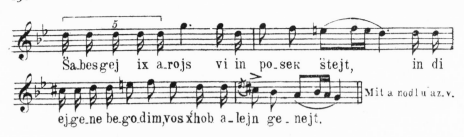

Šabesgej ix arojs vi in po sek štejt, in di

ejgene begodim vos xhob a lejn ge nejt.

38. Hej, ir menčn ale

(♩=80) Rubato

He ej ir men čn a le fyn gro ojs byzklejn

Oj ver se hot nox fyn dem ym glyk nyšt ge he ert yn

nyšt ge zejn, vel ix ajx men čn, gi bn ject cy der

(♩=108)

kle rn, yn bej tn bejt ix ajx, ir zolt dy li id myt ge

(♩=80)

dan ken ojs he rn. Oj, dy lid yz dox nox gur fyn a jing kind,

oj, vej men se hot nor getro fn an ym glyk ge

švynd, n'zajn ma lu xezer ge vej zn'ajn kal ter yn

myt zajn li bn nu men hot er gehej sn al ter.

89. Oj, got, az er colt

90 Aj, efšer hot ir, menčn, gehert

Aj, efšer hot ir, men _ čn, ge _ he _ e _ jert,

oj vej, ge _ ze _ jen, yn A _ des hot cax an

ymglyк ge _ tro _ fn, _ yn A des hot cax an

ymglyk ge _ tro _ fn, oj, a jin ger _ ma _ an, ajn

xu _ sn bu _ xe _ rl bam ma šyn ge _ ze _ sn, dy

gaz hot im af tojt, oj, ge _ šo _ sn,

oj, a jin _ ger _ ma _ an, ajn xu _ sn = bu _

xe _ rl bam ma šyn ge _ ze _ sn, dy gaz hot

im af tojt, oj, ge _ šo _ sn

III. DAILY-LIFE AND FAMILY SONGS

91. Vos den, majn kind, vilstu nox

Vos den, majn ki_jind, vil_stu nox, y ef_ser vil_stu a
snaj_der=jung? Nejn, ma_me, bi_ter, a snaj_der=juvu_
vung iz bivi _ ter. A snaj_der=jung, er nejt un-nejt un
hot ka_do_xes nit kajn brejt, nejn, ma_me, bivi _ ter, a
snaj_der=ju _ vu _ vung iz bivi _ ter. 2. Iz vos
den, majn ki_jind, vil_stu nox, y ef _ ser vil_stu a
sus_ter-jung? Nejn, ma_me, bi_ter, a sus_ter=ju_vu _vung iz
bivi _ ter. A sus_ter=jung, er cit di drat_ve,
un er maxt di vajb a po_ma _ tre, nejn, ma _ me

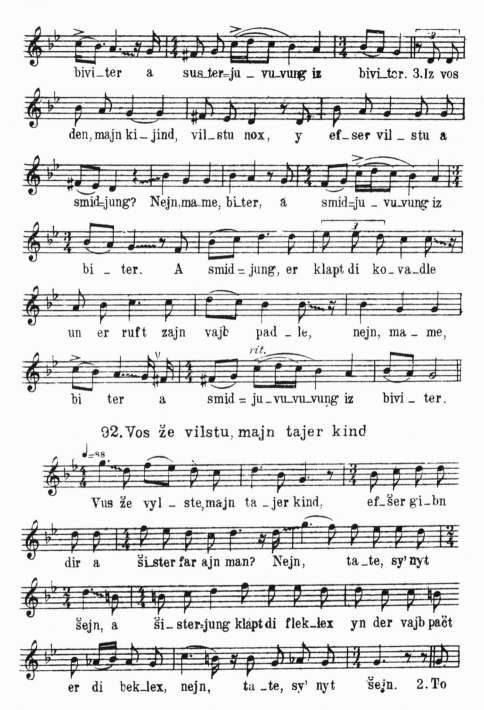

bivi_ter a sus_ter=ju _ vu_vung iz bivi_ter. 3.Iz vos

den, majn ki _ jind, vil_stu nox, y ef_ser vil _ stu a

smid=jung? Nejn,ma_me, bi_ter, a smid=ju _ vu_vung iz

bi _ ter. A smid = jung, er klapt di ko_va_dle

un er ruft zajn vajb pad _ le, nejn, ma _ me,

bi ter a smid = ju_vu_vu_vung iz bivi _ ter.

92. Vos že vilstu, majn tajer kind

Vus že vyl _ ste,majn ta _ jer kind, ef_šer gi_bn

dir a ši_ster far ajn man? Nejn, ta_te, sy'nyt

šejn, a ši_ster=jung klapt di flek_lex yn der vajb pačt

er di bek_lex, nejn, ta _te, sy' nyt šejn. 2.To

vus že vyl _ ste, majn ta _ jer, kind, ef_šer gi _ bn

dir a šna_der far ajn man? Nejn, ta te, sy'nyt

šejn, a šna _ der = jung nejt xa _ la _ tn, dus

vajb šelt er yn ta _ tns ta _ tn, nejn. ta _ te,

sy' nyt šejn. 3. To vus že vyl _ ste, majn

ta _ jer kind, ef_šer gi _ bn dir ajn be_ke,

far ajn man? Nejn, ta_te, sy' nyt šejn, a

be _ ker = jung bakt dus brojt yn der vajb maxt

er dem tojt, nejn, ta _ te, sy' nyt šejn.

93. Ci vos že gibn dir, majn kind

94. Ci gibn dir, majn kind, a šnajder = jung

nejt xa_la_tn un šelt di vaj_be_le n'ta_tns ta_tn,

nejn, ma_me_ńu, nejn. ma_me_ńu, nejn

95. Vos že vilste, majn lib kind

Vos že vil_stu, majn lib kind, ci gi _bn dir a šnaj_der=jung?

Nejn, ma_me, nejn mi_ter, a šnaj_der=jung iz dox ze_jer bi_

ter, er nejt un nejt un hot ka_do_xes nit kajn brejt.

96. Šusterše vajber

Šu_ster_še vaj_ber ho_bn ge_zogt, zej ke_nen di

dra_tves nit ma_xn, zej ke_nen di dra_tves nit

ma_xn. Be_ser cu ne_men a šnaj_der a

_man un gejn in na_je za_xn.

97. Git mix op di mame

Git mix op di ma _ me, git mix op der ta _ te

in ajn vaj _ tn land, un hot dox mir on_ge_zogt,

un hot dox mir un far_zogt ix zol zi_bn jor nit zajn.

98. Gej ix gix

Gej ix gix zogt zi:„du drejst di šix", gej ix pa_

me_lex zogt zi, az ix krix. Oj vej, ma_me, vos že zol ix

ton, x'hob a bej_ze švi_ger zi hot mit mir cu _ ton.

Gej ix nox flejš zogt zi:„go_le bej_ner", gej ix ke_

rik, ba_varft zi mix mit štej_ner. Oj vej, ma_me,

vos že zol ix ton, x'hob a bej_ze šviger, zi hot mit mir cu _ton.

99. Ejnem iz dox zejer gut

(♩=80)

Ej_nem iz dox ze_jer gut, dem an_de_rn iz

nox be_ser, trinkt er tej mit cy_ker, trinkt er

tej mit cy_ker, un ix hob dox far_špilt

maj_ne jun_ge jo_rn iz mir dox

1. fin_cter un by_ter, 2. un by_ter.

100. Got štroft ajn menčn

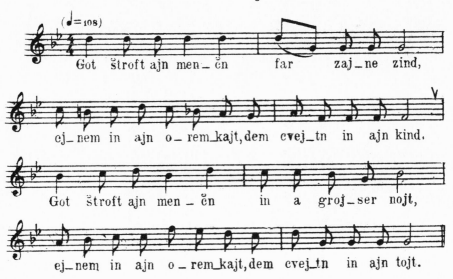

(♩=108)

Got štroft ajn men_čn far zaj_ne zind,

ej_nem in ajn o_rem_kajt, dem cvej_tn in ajn kind.

Got štroft ajn men_čn in a groj_ser nojt,

ej_nem in ajn o_rem_kajt, dem cvej_tn in ajn tojt.

101.Got štroft a menčn

Got štruft a men_čn   nor far zaj_ne zind,   ej_nem yn ajn

u_rem_kajt,dem cvej_tn in a kind.   Mix hot er ge_

štruft yn a   šrek_le_xer štruf, er hot far_vigt majn kind yn an

ej _ by_kn šluf.   Oj, ho_dit, el_te_rn, vej _ nen nox mir,

got 'et ajx šen up_ge_ bn a   cvej _ te far mir.

Ho _ dit, el_ te_rn, vej _ nen nox mir,   got 'et ajx šen

up_ge_bn a   cvej_ te far mir.   Gej šen, tox_ter, a_

rup fy_nem vaj_sn bet, se štejt far dir šen un_ge_grejt der

švar_cer ka _bi_net.   Dor_tn ve_sti ly_gn ej _ ne a_

lejn,   varf a_vek di fal_še velt yn lo_mir gi_xer gejn.

Ho_dit, el_te_rn, veje_ren yn klu_gn, lejf yn šil a_
rajn yn loz men ty_lym zu_gn. Far a mi_njen
men_čn a nu_men ci_cy_lej_gn, to_mer vet mix
got bor_xi šejn _ ken majn le _ bn.

102. Got štroft dem menčn

Got štruft dem men_čn nor far zaj_ne zynd,
ej_nem yn par_nu_se dem cveje_tn yn a kind.
Ej_nem yn e_lnd_kajt, dem cvej_tn mujt a nojt,
ej_nem tit er štru_fn štark myt a by_te_rn
tojt. Ej_nem yn e_lnd_kajt, dem cvej_tn myt a nojt,
ej_nem tit er štru_fn štark myt a by_te_rn tojt.

103. Der lomp vert farlošn

Der lompe vert far _ lo šn, ix ho' nox gurkajn
gits e nyt ge _ no _ šn, se gejt a _ vek a jin _ ger
menee fyn der velt, vus ve _ In tun e _ zaj _ ne
kin _ der _ lax, dy ji _ dy _ še je _ soj mim lax, ver vet zej
gi _ bn a kop _ ke gelt. 2. Di byst ge _ ki _ je men cy
mi _ ir, di byst ge _ ki _ men ne men di ne _ šo _ me ba
mir, lozmex nox lejbn ajn hal _ be šu. Oj, di
štejst dox lej _ bn majn be _ et un di tre _ be _ vest ba mir ajn
ge _ et e, lozmex nox lejbn ej _ ne cen my _ nyt.

104. Der lomp vert farlošn

(♩=92)

Der lompvertfar _ lo _ šn oj, ix hob nox kajn
gits nyt geje _ no _ sn, oj, ix gej šojn a _ zoj
jing fyn der velt. Oj, vi že ve _ ln a
hin.ky.men maj.ne je.ln.te je _ soj.me.lax, oj,
ver že vet jar.še.nen majn gits. 2.Oj, di
štejst lem der ti _ ir yn di nemst ba mir dy ne
šo _ me, oj, mytmajnvajb yn kin.der ho _ sti mix gi _
get. Oj vi že ve _ ln a _ hin.ki.men maj.ne
je _ ln _ te je _ soj _ me _ lax, oj,
ver že vet jar _ še _ nen majn gits.

105. Ci hot ir gehert

Cy hot ir ge _ he _ jert, cy hot ir ge _ ze _ jen

vus yn Ben _ der hot zix far _ lo _ fn, dem ym _ glyk dem

groj _ sn hot ir, men _ ön, ge _ mizt hej _ rn, oj,

vus ba Av _ rem _ cis šver, oj, se hot zix ge _ ro _ fn.

2. Oj, er hot ge _ hot a jin _ gl fyn ejn yn cvon _ cyk

jur, vus er hot fy _ nem že _ reb un _ choj _ bn

dejn _ kn, dem er _ štn tug švi _ jes af a

lod _ ke ge _ fu _ rn, oj, yz yn va _ ser a _ rajn _ ge _

fa _ ln yn hot zax ge _ trejn _ ken. 3. Vi er hot zix nor

un _ ge _ hoj _ bn trejn _ ken hot er un _ ge _ hoj _ bn cy

ma.xn myt di hent: „Ra.te.vet mir, ta.va.riš.čes

oj, a.rojs fyn dem va.ser, vajl ix byn šojn ba dem

mal.xe.mu.ves yn di hent. 4.Oj, vi er yz

nor der.trejn.ken ge.vo.rn yz er ge.

le.gn yn.ter dejm va.ser a šu. Oj, a.zoj yz men

dox ge lo.fn zu.gn di el.te.rn di pe.

si.re: „oje, gejt šojn gejt šojn Av.re.ml yz sojn ny

tu." 5.Vi zej ho.bn dus nor der he.jert me

[.................] ge.vald, ra.te.vet, mir

.nen.ön majen kind fyn dem va.ser, ra.te.vet ime

gix yn bald. 6. Vi m'hot nor Av_rem ...len

fyn dem va_ser a_rojes ge _ ne _men, yz im ge_ven der

kop štark ce _ šlu_gn. Oj, ta _ _va_riš_čes ho_bn im

bald ge_ne_men n'a klur_vajs laj_lax a _ rajn_ge_lejgt yn af a

droš_ke zaj_nen zej myt' im a hejm ge _ fu _ rn.

7. Vi zent ir ge _ veje_ _zn Avre _ mls ta _ va_riš_čes,

mir ho_bn zax gur af dem grojsn _ym_glyk_nyt ge _ rixt.

Ejeršt hot ir yn _ e _ je _ nem myt, Av_rem _ len gu _ la _ jet,

oj, yn a _ cynd trugt ir:im ojf,dem tojt a _ vek.

8. Do_ner_štyk far naxt hot zix Av _ rem_len a xu_lem ge_

xu lemt, er hot imdercejlt yn me. hot im ojs _ ge -

lext. Oj, er hot zax ne _ bax, lu _ be _ le, fyn zajn

groj _ sn ym _ glyk nyt ge _ vyst, yn zajn

xu _ lem hot im e cy zajn tojt ge _ braxt.

106. Tojznter menčn špacirn gegangen

Toj _ zn _ ter men _ čn špa _ ci _ rn ge _ gan _ gen, ge -

gan _ gen ze _ nen zej a _ le glajx, ge _ gan _ gen ze _ nen

zej a _ le glajx, un mit der vaj _ le der _ hert men a

raš, az a menč iz a rajn in tajx.

107. Šimke xazer

Šim _ ke xa _ zer iz kajn Stambul ge _ fo _ rn, er

hot ge‿volt far‿be‿se‿rn di jo‿rn, er

hot ge‿volt dos le‿bn ma‿xn be‿ser

hot men im a‿rajn‿ge‿rukt a za‿gra‿nič‿nem me‿ser.

108. Simxe xazer

(♩ = 112)

Sim‿xe xa‿zer iz kajn Stam‿bul ge‿fo‿rn, er

hot ge‿mejnt zix far‿be‿se‿rn di jo‿rn. Er

hot ge‿mejnt dos lej‿bn ma‿xn be‿ser hot men im a‿

rajn‿ge‿rikt a za‿gra‿nič‿nem me‿ser, er

hot ge‿mejnt dos lej‿bn vet zajn be‿ser hot men in a‿

rajn‿ge‿rikt a za‿gra‿nič‿nem me‿ser.

IV. RECRUIT AND WAR SONGS

109. In tojznt axt hundert najn un najnciktn jor

1. In toj_znt axt hun_dert najn un najn_cik_tn jo _ or

de_molt iz ge_ve_zn a groj_ser na_bor, fun

vej_nen, fun klo_gn bin ix šojn mat, m'hot mir

op_ge_zot di le_go_te x'bin a far_ti_ker sol_

dat, fun vej_nen, fun klo_gn bin ix šojn mat, m'hot mir

op_ge_zogt di le_go_te, x'bin a far_ti_ker sol_

dat. 3. Ix lejg mix a_ni_der af der koj_ke un ix

hejb zix on cu ba_kle_rn vos far a tax_les

ken do fun mir ve_rn e, oj iz mir bi_ter un

cu_der_ci nox fin_cter, az ix darf zix šojn ge _ ze-ge-
nen mit maj_ne fo _ ter un my _ ter O _ oj iz mir e
fin _ cter un cu_der_ci nox bi _ ter az ix
darf mix šojn ge _ ze-ge-nen mit maj_ne fo _ ter un my _ ter.

110. In tojznt axt hundert najn un najnciktn jor

Yn toj _ znt axt hyn _ dert najn yn najn _ cyk _ tn
ju _ ur yz dox ge _ vejn a groj _ ser na _ bor
Mhot dox ge _ ge _ bn a sax gelt min_ha _ _ stam yn me
hot nyt ge _ bra_ke _vet kajn per _ vy raz _ rad.

111. Ov horaxmim

Cv ho _ rax_mim šoj _ xejn bam_roj_mim, got iz a
fo _ ter i_ber a _ le je_soj_mim [. . . .]

got iz a fo _ ter i _ ber a _ le je _ soj _ mim. 2. Be _ ser cu

zo _ gn a _ dojn oj lem ej _ der cu ku _ šn dem kej _ sers cej _ lem,

[· · · · · · · · · · · · · · · · · ·] ej _ der cu ku _ šn dem kej _ sers cej _ lem.

112. In Odes bin ix gebojrn gevorn

($\bullet$=92)

Yn A _ des byn ix ge _ boj _ rn, ix hob far

braxt maj _ ne y le jin ge _ ju _ vurn, ajn

bri _ ve _ le, oj, yz mir un _ ge _ ki _ men, az ix

darf šojn cym pry _ zyv, oj, fu vurn _____, Maj _ ne el _ te

rn klo _ gn, zej veje _ nen, zej klovo _ gn, zej lo _ znmix nyt.....

113. Oj, najn xadošim hot mix majn mame getrogn

($\bullet$=96)

Oj, najn xa _ du _ šim hot mex majn ma _ me ge _ tru _ gn

ej _ der zi hot mex ge _ ha _ at fijel ta _ xn myt

tre‿rn hotmajn ma‿me far ‿ go‿sn, az ix zo nyt

za‿ajn kajn sol‿dat. 2. Jej‿der bu‿xer cyejnyn

cvo‿on‿cyk jur‿ er hejbtnorun vus cy bli jen, saj

u‿rem, saj ra‿ax cym že‿reb a‿le gla‿ax 3. A‿

zojvi se kynt, ej, fraj‿tyk cy naxts lyg ix mir of majn

koj‿ke yn tra‿axt, xholt be‿ser ge‿ga‿ajn cy ka‿bu‿la sha‿

ša bes ej‿der derpod‿fe bei' a po‿ver‿ke ge‿maxt

114. Gej ix arop afn erštn trep

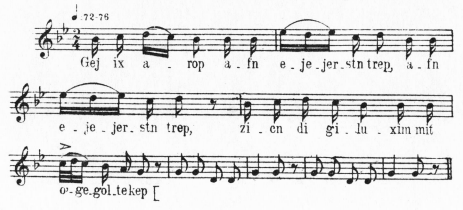

♩.72-76

Gej ix a‿rop a‿fn e‿je‿jer‿stn trep, a‿fn

e‿je‿jer‿stn trep, zi‿en di gi‿lu‿xim mit

o'‿ge‿gol te kep [

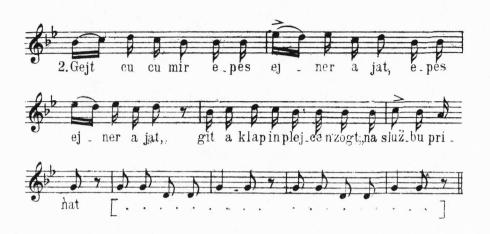

2.Gejt cu cu mir e‗pes ej ‗ ner a jat, e‗pes

ej ‗ ner a jat,, git a klap in plej‗ce n'zogt;,na služ‗bu pri‗

ħat [. . . . .]

115. Vemen veln mir dinen, brider

Ve‗men ve‗ln mir di ‗ nen, bri‗der, ve‗men, ve‗ln mir

di ‗‗‗‗ i‗nen, bri‗der? Dem ru‗sy‗šn ke ‗ ej‗ser, bri‗der,

dem ru‗ sy‗šn ke ‗ ej‗ser, bri‗der, dem ru‗ sy‗šn

kej‗ser di‗nen yz nýt git, vajl er tit zix bo‗dn yn

ynd‗zer blyt, dem ru‗sy‗šn kej‗ser di‗nen yz nyt

git, vajl er tit zix bo‗dn yn ind‗zer blyt.

116. Kajn esn un kajn trinken, mame, nemt mix nit

Kajn e_sn yn kajn trin_ken, mo_me, nemt mix nyt, ix
gej a_rim štendyk, štendyk vej_nendyk. Ix fregnorbadiı,
ta___ je_reregot, far_vuszol zajn majn xu_sn a sal_dot?
2. Ix vel zix ci_ste_ln a lej_te_rl yn ix vel a_
rojf_kri_xn_cy got. Ix vel im nor frej_gn ej_ne
cvej-draj ver_ter, far_vus zol zajnmajn xu_sn a sal dot.
3. Se zol zix nor of_xa_pn a šty_rem vynt, a
vek tru_gn zol es mex cy dir, ix zol nor ze_jendajn
šej___ nemkophur, ver šmistzix nox ce_ki šnmyt dir.

4. Oj, di ta_je_rer got, va_zoj'el ix es ke_nen cy_
zeja, der kej ser vet ci_ne_men majn ta_je_rn_bru_
ljant yn ix vel dar_fn fyn_der_va_tns štejn.

117. A lejterl cum himl vel ix šteln

A lej_te_rl cum hi_ml vel ix šte_ln un vel a_
rofkri_xn cu got, ej_necvejver_ter vel ix ba im
fre_gn, far_vos majn li ber darf zajn a sol_dat, oj, oj, oj.

118. Oj, a lejterl cum himl vel ix šteln

Oj, a lej_te_rl cum hi_ml vel ix šte_ln
un a_rojf_gejn vel ix zix cu got___ un
ej_ne cvej ver_ter, oj, vel ix ba im fre_gn far_
vos darf zajn majn šej_ner a sol_dat.___

119.Forn forstu fun mir avek

Fu _ rn fur _ ste fyn mir a _ vek, ta _ je _ rer le _ bn

majns oj. fu _ rn fur _ ste zix cum pry _ zyv šte ln. Oj,

helf že mir šojn, go _ te _ nu, zolst a _ rojsfyn kej _ sers hont

yn der gan _ cer pri _ sut _ stve zol _ ste nyt ge _

te ln Oj fe ln. 2.Vus že ho _ ste mir a

zo _ jus up _ ge _ tun e, ta _ je _ rer le _ bn majns, vus majn

harc cit a _ zoj cu dir, cu di _____ ir, ix

hob dir gor nyt up _ ge _ tun, ta _ jer le _ bn majns. ix

hob zix po šet ajn _ ge _ libt yn di _____ ir Ix

120. Oj, vos hostu gehat cu mir

Oj, vus ho_ste ge_hat cy mir, yn vus ho_ste ge_

volt fyne mir, yn vus ho_ste ge_hat cy maj_ne

jin_ge ju_rn. Far_vus ho_ste mir fri_er nyt ge_zugt,

az di darfste zajn a sal_dat. Ix volt šojn lajng ajn ka_le ge_

vo _ rn, yn ef_šer ta_ke xo_se_ne ge_hat. Ix

volt šojn lajng a ka_le ge_vo _ rn yn

ef _ šer ta_ke xo_se_ne ge_hat.

121. Fun der štub bin ix arojsgegangen

Fyn der štib byn ix a_rojs_ge_jë_gajn_gen yn yn

droj_sn yz ajn ju_mer yn ajn klug, n'maj_ne

122. Fun dem štub zajnen mir arojsgegangen

cy s'yz git a zoj, cy ken es den a menč y ber
tru gn, me trajbt indz a vek af miz rax zajt, far vus kimt indz zajn
fyn der hejm far jugt. Me trajbt indz a vek af
miz rax e zajt, far vus kimt indz zajn fyn der hejm far jugt.

123. Fun der štub bin ix in gas arojsgegangen

Fun der štub bin ix in gas a rojs ge gan gen, un in
drej sn iz ajn ju mer mit ajn klog, n'maj ne oj e rn hot ge
ton klin gen a mo bli za cye hot men za ja vet hajnt far
tog. A le maj re bej ner zaj nen švax un kra nk un di
jo rn zaj nen ojx nit der baj, cu li gn in ka
zar me af der hoj ler bank, di nen muz men dox ge traj.

124. Oj vej, in tojznt najn hundert un fufcetn jor

Oj vej, yn toj znt najn hyn dert yn fyf e ce tn jur z'a rojs, oj, a na jer pry kaz, oj, pry kaz, oj, ie dere fu ter, tit fi rn zajn kind a zoj vi a šoje xet di rynd. Oj, rynd 2. Oj vej, fraj tyk e, fraj tyk e fraj tyk cy naxts, oj, in dze re ly pe lex zaj nen indz far šmaxt, oj, far šmaxt. Mir vol tn ge gajn gen cyn a ji dn af šo bes, oj, hot men nox di po ver ke nyt ge maxt, ge maxt. Mir maxt. 3. Oj vej, šo bes, oj, šo bes oj, šo bes gonc fri:, Na skač ka vy xo di, vy xo di!" Cy

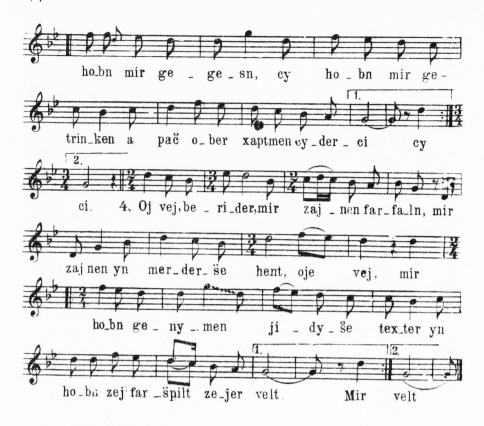

ho_bn mir ge _ ge _ sn, cy ho _ bn mir ge-
trin_ken a pač o_ber xaptmen cy_der_ci cy
ci. 4. Oj vej,be _ ri_der,mir zaj _ nen far_fa_ln, mir
zaj nen yn mer_der_ še hent, oje vej, mir
ho_bn ge _ ny __ men ji _ dy_ še tex_ter yn
ho_bn zej far _špilt ze_jer velt. Mir velt

125 Jn tojznt najn hundert un fufcetn jor

Yne toj_znt najn hyn_dert yn fyfe _ ce_tn jur
yz a _ rojs a pry _ kaz, az e je_ der fu_ter zol
fi_rn zajn kind vi cym šoj_xet a hin. Az e
hin 2.Oj, vus ken er vnd> hel_fn vuse ken er yndz

tun, mire zo_nen yn mer_der_ se hent. Oj, vej,

bri_der,mir zo_nensol_da_n,mir he_bn far _špiltyndzer velt.

126. Az ix bin a klejn jinċele gevezn

Az ix e byn a klejn jin_ga_le ge _ ve_je _ zn, ge-

ve_je_zn byn ix, mo_me, na_ ve, _ nod, ge-

ve_je_zn byn ix, mo_me, na_ ve _ nod, yn e

cajt,mo_me,me hot mex up _ ge _ ge _ bn kajn

gi _ tn tueg hob ix nyt ge _hot, yn e hot 2.Vi mir

zo_ nen cy ger ma_ñenun_ge_ ky _ men, dy ger-

man_ces,zejste_jen far yndz grejt, dy ger _ man _ ces,zej

šte_ jen far yndz grejt,di er_šte pu_le hot dus mex ge-

127. Ix gedenk ix bin a klejnes kind gevezn

Ix gedenk, ix byn a klej_nes kind ge_ve_zn, ge_

ve_zn byn ix ba maj_ne el_te_rn ta_jer, ge_

ve_zn byn ix ba maj_ne el_te_rn ta_jer, oj,

ject byn ix dox alt ge_vo_rn ejn yn cvan_cyk jur, a_zoj

šyktmen mix yndem gre_stn fa_jer oj, fa_jer. 2. Ject

lyg ix yn der bol_ni_ce ge_ra_het, cvej sa_ni_

ta_rn, zej šte_jen a_rem mi_jer cvej sa_ni_

ta_rn, zej šte_jen a_rem mi_jer, oj, dy

pu_les, du_še_hu, šleptmen šojn fyn mir [_ _ _

_ _ _ _ _ _ _ _] oj, dy _ _ _ _]

128. Az vej dem tatn

Az veje demto.tn, ynaz veje dermo.men, vuszej
ho.bn a zin a za.pas.noj. Me tit in un di sol.
dat.ske klej _ der ynme šykt im, oj vej e, glax yn e
boj. Me tit im un di sol.dat.ske klej.der ynme
šikt im,oj, vej vej, glax yn e boj. 2.Oj, vi mir zo.
nen cym po.jezd ge.ki _ men ojf der plašča.l.ke
byn ix ge _ bly.bn, oj,štejn. Oj, vi der po.jezd hot
ojs.ge.sviš.čet, oj, ojs.ge.bro.xn hot zi ajn grojs ge.vejn, oj,
grojs ge.vejn. 3.O je, vejn nyt,ma.me, oje, vejn nyt,my.
ter, az go tvet hel.fn vel ix ky.men,oj,cé.ryk. Di

zolst mir,oj vej,majn štib up _ hi _ tn, di zolst mir up hi _ tn majn

vajb yne kind. Di vajb yne kind. 4.Oj, vi mir zo _

nen af der er šter po _ zi _ cje ge _ ki _ men, oj,

blas by nix ge _ vo _ rn vi a blaj, oj, zekš teg yn di o _

ko _ pese ly _ gn yn e _ sn dem dry _ tn tug ajn

šty _ ke _ le brojt, oj, šty _ ke _ le brojt. 5.Oj vi mir zo_

nen ey der er šter po _ zi _ cje ge _ ki _ men, oj,

tojb byn ix ge _ vo _ rn vi di vont. Dy er šte pu _

le hot mir ge _ tro _ fn, a _ rup ge _ ny _ men hot mir dy

rex _ te hont, dy rex _ te hont.

129. Dem erštn tog fun der mobilizacje

Dem er-štn tug fynder mo-by-li-za-cje z'ge-vorn a

ju-mer yn a ge-vejn, dem er-štn tug fynder mobi-li-

za-cje zo-nen a-le ge-šef-tn ge-bly-bn štejn, dem

bly-bn štejn 2.Az vejz demta-tn-n'az vej z'der ma-men,vus zej

ho-bn a zin ava za-pa-snoj, me tit im un di sol-

dat-ske klej-der yn me šykt im a-vek glax yn e boj.

130. Ix tu dir a brivele šrajbn

Ix ti dir a bri-va-le šra-a bn yn

šra-bn šrab i' dire,mo-me,fyn majn ge zynt, oj, a

hont hot men mir a-rupe ge-ne-e-men; n'af

1 Didoziĸe si ĸlingt vi si beĸar.

ĸл 1269

ma-ne oj-gn byn ix, mo-me-nu, blynd. Oj, a blynd. 2. Ix

lyg mir yn bol-ni-ce ge-ra - a - ṅet yn

di dok-toj-rym šte - jen a - rem mir, yn dus

hare vert myt bly-jet upe-ge - go - o - sn, yn di ge -

tra-je my-ter-yz ny-tu le-je-bn mir, yn dus mir.

131. Šrajbn šrajo ix a briv cu majne eltern

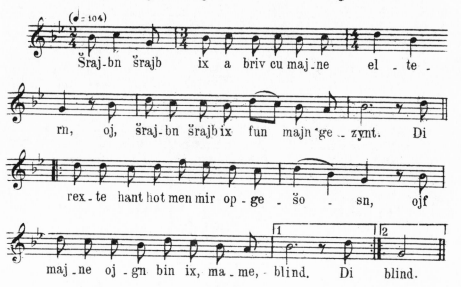

Šraj-bn šrajb ix a briv cu maj-ne el - te -

rn, oj, šraj-bn šrajb ix fun majn 'ge - zynt. Di

rex-te hant hot men mir op-ge - šo - sn, ojf

maj-ne oj-gn bin ix, ma-me, - blind. Di blind.

132 Dos fercnte jor iz ongeкumen.

Dus fer.en.tejur yz un.ge.кi.men, vej, oj vej, dus

fer.cn.tejur yz un.ge.кi.men, far a sol.dat hot men mix

ci.ge.neje.mene vej oj,vej, far a sol.dat hot men mix

ci.ge.neje.mene, vej, oj,vej. 2.Draj teg byn ix yn

sy.rest ge.le.gn, vej, oj,vej, draj teg byn ix yn

sy.rest ge.le.gn,ix hob ge.volt majn leje.bn ge.rn,

vej, oj,vej, ix hob ge.volt majn lej.bn ge.rn

vej, oj,vej 3.lx byn oj.fn šlaxt.feld a.rof.ge.кi.men,

vej, oj, vej, oj, ix byn oj.fn šlaxt.feld a.rof.ge.

кi.men hob ix ge.tro.fn majn ta.va.rišč yn blyt švy.men

vej, oj, vej, hob ix ge tro . fn majn ta va rišč yn blyt švv men,

vej, oj, vej. 4. Af di gri ne fel der vel der, vej, oj, vej a

af di gri ne fel der, vel der lygt far legjt dus feld myt zel ner,

vej, oj, vej, dort lygt far lejgt dus feld myt zel ner, vej oj, vej. 5. Dort

lygt a zel ner un a ci re, vej, oj, vej, dort lygt a zel ner

un a ci re, un a ka stn yn un a kvi re vej, oj, vej,

un a ka stn yn un a kvi re, vej, oj vej. 6. Dort

lygt a zel ner der ker per yz im ce ry sn, vej, oj vej, dort

lygt a zel ner der ker per yz im ce ry sn fyn, zajn har en tit blyt

gi sn, vej, oj vej, fyn zajn har en tit blyt gi sn, vej, oj vej.

7. Kimt a fej-gl un-cy-fli-jen, vej, oj vej, kimt a fej-gl un-cy-
fli-jen štelt zax oj-fn zel-ner up-cy-ri-jen, vej, oj vej, yn
štelt zax oj-fn zel-ner up-cy-ri-jen, vej, oj vej.

133. Dos fercnte jor hot zix ongehojbn

Dus fer-cn-te jur hot zex un-ge-hoj-bn, oj, oj,
oj, oj, oj, oj, oj, dus e fer-cn-te jur hot zix
un-ge-hoj-bn, in za-pas hot men mix ge-ne-men, oj
vej, oj, ra ra ra ram. In za-pas hot men mix ge-
ne-men oj, vej vej. 2. Oj, vej, n'di Kar-pa-tn zo-nen
mir ge-lo-fn, oj vej veje, veje, vej, oj, yn di Kar-
pa-tn zo-nen mir ge-lo-fn, brojt myt vo-ser ho-bn

mir ge- e- sn, oj vej ta ra ri ra ram,

brojt myt vo-ser ho-bn mir ge- tri in-ken, oj, vej, vej

134. Ojf di felder, grine felder

3. Ojf di fel- der gri- - ne fe- el-der, oj a

ta- la, la- la la, oj, of di fel-der, of di

gri- neje fele- der dor-tn lygt far- vor- fn a

jin- gere zele- ner, oj, ta, ta la la la la, dort

lygt far-vor- fn a jine- gere zele-ner, ta la ta la ta la

lam. 4. Yn zajn lajb yz ime ceje- ry- en,

ta la ta la la la lam y- yn zajn lajb yz zex

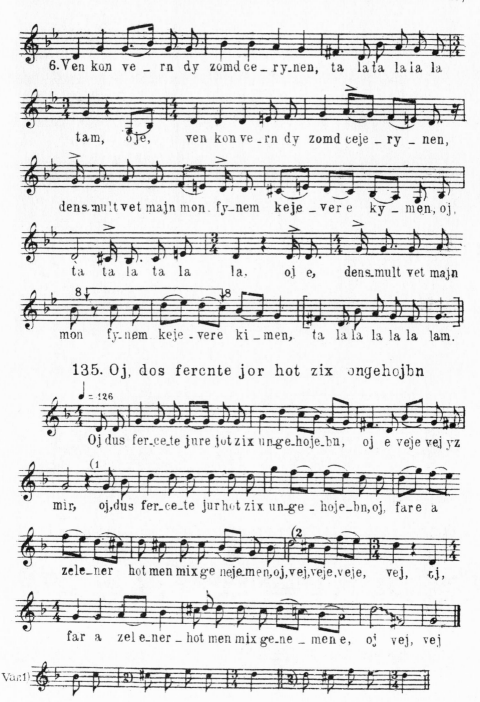

6. Ven kon ve _ rn dy zomd ce _ ry _ nen, ta la ta la ia la tam, öje, ven kon ve _ rn dy zomd ceje _ ry _ nen, dens.mult vet majn mon. fy_nem keje _ ver e ky _ men, oj, ta ta la ta la la, oj e, dens.mult vet majn mon fy_nem keje _ vere ki _ men, ta la la la la la lam.

135. Oj, dos ferente jor hot zix ongehojbn

♩ = 126

Oj dus fer_ce_te jure jot zix un_ge_hoje_bn, oj e veje vej yz mir, oj,dus fer_ce_te jur hot zix un_ge _ hoje_bn,oj, fare a zele_ner hot men mix ge neje_men,oj,vej,veje,veje, vej, oj, far a zel e_ner _ hot men mix ge_ne _ men e, oj vej, vej

Var.1)

136. Dos ferente jor iz ongekumen

Dus fer _ ce _ te jur yz un_e_ge_ki_men, vej - je,

vej, duse fer ce te jur yz un_e_ge_ki_ji_men,

hot mene dem za_pas far _ neje _ mene ve _ ej, vej, a_zej

hot men dem za_pas far _ neje _ mene, vej, vej.

137. Dos ferente jor iz ongekumen

Dos fer _ en_te jor iz on_ge_ku_men oj vej.

'dos fer _ en_te jor iz on_ge_ku_men, far

a sol_dat hot men mix cu_ge_nu _ men, oj vej, far

a sol_dat hot men mix cu_ge_nu _ men oj vej.

138. Dos ferente jor iz ongekumen

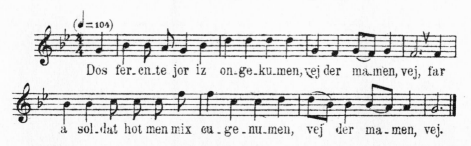

Dos fer_en_te jor iz on_ge_ku_men, vej der ma_men, vej, far
a sol_dat hot men mix eu_ge_nu_men, vej der ma_men, vej.

139. İn drojsn gejt a regn

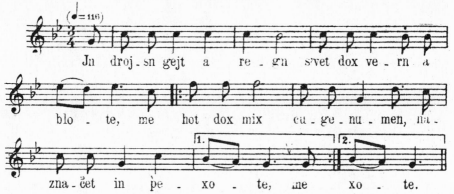

Jn droj_sn gejt a re_gn s'vet dox ve_rn a
blo_te, me hot dox mix eu_ge_nu_men, na_
zna_čet in pe_xo_te, me xo_te.

140. İn drojsn gejt a regn

Yn droj_sn gejt a re_gn, se vet dox zajn a
blo_te, me hot na_zna_čet majn ta_jer lej_bn
yn de_vja_te ro_te. Me ro_te. 2. Vi er yz a_
hin ge_ki_men, der_šro_kn yz er ge_vo_rn. A_

ru'_ge_ny_men dus hy_tl, yn vu'že ti_ste du,

jin_ger_mon, vajz mir dajn vajs kvy_tl, yn

kvy_tl. 6.Yn drej_sn yz _er a_rojs_ge_gajen_gen:„yn

max nyt un kajn ge_ri_der,» a ru_bl yn hont a

rajn_ge_štypt yn zol er zajn a gi_ter bri_der, a

bri_der. 7.Ject byn ix a faj_ner menč, a

ba_le_bus's an ej_dem, az ix der /zej nor

Kra_sni_čen_ken an_tlejf ix af dem beje_dem, az beje_dem.

I. WORKERS' SONGS

Songs About Work, Exploitation, and Poverty

1.

1. Šver un biter vi der tojt
Azoj i'dox nor dem arbetorers lebn,
|: Oj, az far dem trukenem štikele brojt
Muz er zajne kreftn avekgebn. :|

2. Oj, ale tog |: vinč ix mir dem tojt, :|
Beser volt ix nit geven gebojrn vern gor
Ejder cu lajdn aza bitern nojt.
Se mir fincter di teg, se mir biter di jor,
Oj, ale tog vinč ix mir dem tojt.

3. Oj, x'kum arajn inderfri un štel mix avek
|: bam baleboes af der tir, :|
Un smeje nox nit ojsrejdn a hojex vort.
|: Ix hob dox mojre, er zol nit opzogn mir,
Un zol nit cunemen a cvejtn af majn ort. :|

2.

Ix štej dox uf gančfri,
Ix zec mix cum genej,
In harcn iz fartruknt
Un x'vil a glezl tej.
        Oj, vist un vej
        Iz cu majne junge jorn,
        Vos ix bin fun dr'hejm avekgeforn.

3.

1. Ajn šnej, mame, ajn šnej, muter,
|: Ajn šnej, mame, mit ajn regn... :|
|: Un majn mame hot mix ojsgexovet,
Oj, fun dem šnajders vegn. :|

2. Der šnajder šelt un bagrobt —
|: Un me muz dos ales cu lajdn, :|
|: Un majn mame hot mix ojsgexovet
Funem šnajders vegn. :|

3. Az ix kum halb zeks a zejger,
|: Oj, zogt der šnajder, s'iz gut, :|
|: Un az ix kum, oj, cen minut špeter
Capt er mir majn blut. :|

4. Oj vej, mame, oj vej, muter,
Ix gej durex [1]) in mark,
Ix vil zix epes kojfn,
|: Tut a kling der zvonok —
Muz men gixer lojfn. :|

[1]) Durx.

4.

1. A šnej, mame, a šnej muter,
: A šnej, mame, mit a regn... :|
: Oj, du host mix ojsgexovet
Fun dem šnajders vegn. :|

2. Oj, bam šnajder, oj, bam šnajder
: Iz dox zejer biter, :|
: Dem dritn tog a štikl brojt ojfesn
Abi ba dir, majn libe myter.[1]) :|

5.

1. Tog azojvi naxt un naxt azojvi tog
: Un nejen, un nejen, un nejen... :|
: Helf mir šojn, gotenu, majn šejner zol šojn kumen
Un fun der arbet zol ix avekgejn. :|

2. Noxamol genejt un videramol genejt,
: Genejt un genejt un geštoxn... :|
: Oj, du ziser goteńu, du vejst dox dem emes,
Az majne bejner zajnen mir cebroxn. :|

6.

1. In drojsn gist a regn, in drojsn gist a regn
: Un se šit a šnej, a šnej... :|
: Azoj zajnen avekgegangen ale majne junge jorn,
Zicndik štendik bam genej, bam genej. :|

2. Tog azojvi naxt, naxt azojvi tog,
: Kesejder mit der nodl nor geštoxn... :|
: Oj, du, got, du vejzt dox, oj, dem emes,
Az majne bejner zajnen mir cebroxn. :|

3. Cebroxn zajnen majne bejner, vejsn vejst nit kejner,
: Nor ejn got alejn, alejn... :|
. . . .
. . . .

7.

1. Oj, bin ix mir a nejterke,
Di nodl af majn farmeg,
Ix darf zix šojn nit zorgn
Far morgedike teg.

2. Ix darf zix mer nit zorgn,
S'iz mir nit kajn nojt,
Ix kon zix mir fardinen
Af majn štikele brojt.

3. Fun šuxn un fun klejdn
Vejst der magazin,
Er vejst nit fun kajn lejbn
Dos gelt ahincutin.[2])

4. Nejn, nejn, mejdele,
Max-že glajx di not
Un dos šejne hemdele
Zol lign akurat.

[1]) muter.
[2]) ahincuton.

5. Az ix bin geven ba majne eltern
Bin ix geven celozt,
Hajnt kum ix cu zej
Bin ix ba zej a gost.[1])

8.

1. Ba di mašinen ajngebojgn
Zic ix, mameńu, dajn ejncik kind,
Oj, jeder bejndele cunojfgecojgn,
Fun der arbet ver ix šir nit blind.

2. Kajn iberike zaxn zix nit farginen,
Vajl di kopke kumt on zejer šver.
Un baderbaj hob ix mir inzinen,
Az mir helfn hot nit ver.

3. Ba undzere jidn iz zix ojx a mineg,
Az on kajn nadn maxt men nit kajn glik,
Nor mit majn lebn volt ix geven cufridn,
Oj vej, mame, an antik.

4. Vi s'kumt nor cu dem knasmol,
Me derlangt di tnojim in di hent,
Vi ix gib a kuk —
Un majn muter zict un kvelt.

5. Libe muter, tajerer foter,
Vos-že kvelt ir acind? —
Ci vejst ir den, ci hot ir šojn bavornt
Ajer ejnunejncik kind?

6. Vi se kumt nor nox der xasene,
Me vert a muter fun a kind,
Un der man — er fort avek,
Er fort avek on a „zaj gezynt".[2])

9.

1. Oj, in fabrik zic ix ajngebojgn
N'azoj zic ix an orem kind,
Oj, majne glider cunojfgecojgn,
Az fun majn arbet ver ix šir nit blind.

2. Cunojfgenumen, oj, ale kojxes
Avekgelejgt ojf a zajt,
Un majn mojex vert mir ojsgetruknt,
Az cu n'a šidex iz šojn nit vajt.

3. . . . .
Est er nadn, trinkt dos blyt,[3])
Oj, fun majn lebn vel ix zajn cufridn,
Ix vel nox hobn an antik.

10.

1. Oj, ba majn arbet tu ix zicn,
Oj, ongebojgn, ix orem kind.
|: Oj, jeder bejndele cunojfgecojgn,
Az fun majn arbet ver ix šir nit blind. :|

[1]) gast.
[2]) gezunt.
[3]) blut.

2. Oj, x'hob geklibn a kopke cu na kopke,
Vajl di kopke, zi kumt on šver.
|: Oj, vider hejb ix zix on cu barexenen,
Az cu kajn šidex iz šojn ojx nit vajt. :|

3. Oj vej, mame, oj vej, muter,
Dem vos ix hob lib — iz er šojn do.
: Arojsgenumen hob ix majn prac'e,
Me šrajbt šojn tnojim in a guter šo. :|

4. Oj, vi m'hot di tnojim ongešribn
Azoj hot men mir cugetrogn cu di hent,—
|: Vi a štejn bin ix geblibn zicn
Un majn mame — zi vert cekvelt. :|

5. Oj vej, mame, un oj vej, muter,
Oj, vos-že verstu azoj cekvelt,
|: Ci hostu mix bavornt mit a gut mazl,
Ci hostu mix bavornt mit a guter velt? :|

6. Abi zi bakumt nor dem nomen mame,
Azoj vert zi on di kojxes mit dem gezunt.
|: Zi vert šojn on di kojxes,
Vos mejdlvajz iz geven. :|

11—12.

1. Ba majn mašindl (mašindele) [1] tu ix zicn,
Ongebojgn, ix (ajn) orem kind,
|: Jedn (un jeder) bejndele cunojfgecojgn
Un (az) fun majn arbet ver ix šir nit blind. :|

2. Azoj di kopke hob ix cunojfgeklojbn,
Oj, avekgelejgt hob ix zi (es) ojf a zajt.
: Oj, majn mojex vert mir cefaln
Un (az) cu kajn šidex iz šojn ojx nit vajt. :|

3. Vi a kopike cunojfgeklojbn,
Ix hob gemejnt, az es iz šojn do...
|: Vider hejb ix zix mir on baklern,
Me šrajbt šojn tnojim in a guter šo. :|

4. Me hot di tnojim nor ongešribn,
Majn mame zet, az zi vert cekvelt,
: Zi hot šojn ir ejncik kind bavornt
Zi zol farmogn a štikl brojt. :|

5. Viazoj bakumt zi dem nomen mame,
Zi vert farbundn mit a klejn kind;
: Viazoj bakumt er dem nomen tate—
Er fort avek on a „zaj-gezynt".[2] :|

13—14.

1. A gance vox, a gance vox
Zic ix af majn (der) kol'ke,
Dem ejnem tog šabes
Farkem ix zix majn (di) pol'ke.

---

[1] Klenere veriantn, veln vi vajt meglex gebraxt vern in klamern.
[2] gezunt

2. X'farkem zix mir majn pol'ke [1])
Un lejg mir ojs di hor,
Un gib (ix tu) a kuk in špigele —
· Nito cu mir kajn por.

3. Ix gej arojs in drojsn,
Un ix gej arajn in štub—
Majn mame tut mix šeltn:
„Zolst hobn azojne (azelxe) veltn!"

4. Oj, cores, ńeprijatnost'
Se maxt ba mir nit ojs,
Abi me zogt mir: „Manička,
No ńe b'espokojs'".[2])

15.

1. A gance vox horevet zi
Bam šnajder ojf der kol'ke.
Se kumt der frajtek farnaxt—
Vert zi fun der arbet vol'ne.
Zi vašt zix ojs dem kop,
Zi franzirt zix on dem čub,
Zi usp'ejet nit esn di lokšn mit der jux,
Az zi z'šojn in štub nito.

2. Zi xapt dos rojte šaléxl
Far impet af ejn ojer.
Zi hot kajn cajt nit mit kejnem cu rejdn,
Vajl der šejner vart bam tojer.
Zi gejt mit im arum
Biz cvelf azejger afdernaxt
Un af morgn naznačet zi im
In tancklas af a zejger axt.

3. Mit cores un ńeprijatnost' iz zi štendik gevojnt,
Se maxt šojn ba ir nit ojs.
Dem erštn pečatek xapt zi ojs funem dvornik:
„Čevo ti mńe tak pozdno b'espokojiš".
Zi xapt arojs a pitakl
Un štupt dem dvornik ynter,[3])
Zi iz šojn garantirt
Cu gejn mitn šejnem a ganc vinter.

4. Dem cvejtn pečatek xapt zi ojs fun der muter
Ven zi kumt nor arajn in štub.
Ven zi kumt nor arajn in štub arajn
Hejbt di muter zi on cu šeltn:
„Oj, majn toxter, vestu lign in dr'erd,
Du vest firn azojne veltn.
Du gejst arum mitn šejnem
Biz cvelf a zejger banaxt.
Ix derken dox šojn in dir,
'St im naznačet af morgn afdernaxt".

5. Vi zi derzet a xasene
Ba ir xavertes a frajntl,
Ojf der xasene muz zi gejn,
Zi muz dox xapn a tencl,

[1]) Var. Farkem ix zix di pol'ke
[2]) Var. Abi majn kotik zogt mir:
„Ax, ty ńe b'espokojs'".
[3]) unter.

Der šejner iz raspor'aditel',
Un zi tanct noxn klang,
Un af morgn barajst er zi —
Kumt zi in a cerisenem pal'to.

16.

1. — Oj, ix hob šojn nit kajn kojex ba majn arbet ajncuzicn,
Un majn mame zogt, az zi zet dos nit arojs, oje vej...
|: Oj, du hob af mir raxemones un du ver far mir a xosn,
Oj, du nem mix fun der vister fabrike arojs. :|

2. — Oj, v'azoj zol ix dix fun der fabrike arojsnemen,
Az ix hob an eltere švester fun mir, oje vej,
: Oj, az got vet mir helfn, az majn švester vet a kale vern,
Oje, xasene hobn, oje, vel ix far dir. :|

3. — Oj, a vistn sof, oje, zol dajn mame hobn,
Un af ire fis zol zi nit kenen gejn af der velt.
|: Oj, aza skore pomešč, vos er fort arum iber der gancer velt,
Er vet zi nemen on klejder, oj, un on a kopke gelt. :|

4. — Oj, vos hoste, l'ubele, cu šeltn majn mamen,
Du šelst majn mamen—iz glajx azojvi mir, oje vej,
|: Ot 'est zen, l'ubeńu, az der xarakter vet zix ba ir bajtn,
Vest nox zajn amol ba ir di ongelejgte šnir".[1] :|

17.

1. — Ix hob šojn nit kajn kojex, oj, ba majn arbet cu zicn,
|: Oj, n'af majn ponem zet kejner nit arojs, :|
: Oj, hob šojn raxmones un ver far mir a xosn,
Fun der vister arbet nem mix šojn arojs. :|

2. — Ix volt šojn far dir, oj, a xosn gevorn,
: A xosn vern [verst dox] ništ alejn, :|
|: Oj, ix bin a jingele mit ejgene gedanken,
Az ix barexn, ci ix darf cum priziv štejn. :|

18.

1. Oj, undzere jorelex gejen undz avek
Mit hic un mit rojex, oj, oj.
: Git nor a kuk, vi a jid fun zexcik jor,
Er hot šojn, oj, mejn fun undz kojex. :|

2. Azojvi a mil, vos zi arbet kesejder,
Hot zi ba got an opštand,— oj, oj.
|: Šabes farnaxt, vi me zet nox nit kajn štern,
Mir haltn šojn dos fajer in der hant. :|

3. Oj, zumer in di hicn un vinter in di keltn,
Oj, saj batog un saj banaxt — oj, oj.
: Faršoltn zol vern derdoziker menč,
Vos er hot dos bekeraj ojsgetraxt! :|

[1] šnur.

19.

Oj, undzere kojxes, oje, gejen undz ojs,
|: Az, ir nemen cu in hic un in rojex, :|
Afile der menč fun zibecik jor
Hot er nox kojex mer fun undz.

. . . .
. . . .

20.

1. Di baleboste gejt arajn, hop dunaj, dunaj,
   Xevre, xevre, štil zol zajn, hop dunaj, dunaj.

2. Di baleboste štejt un kukt, hop dunaj, dunaj,
   Xevre, xevre, arbet gut, hop dunaj, dunaj.

3. Di baleboste štejt in kix, hop dunaj, dunaj,
   Xevre, xevre, varft mit štex, hop dunaj, dunaj.

4. Di baleboste štejt in zal, hop dunaj, dunaj,
   S'vert in ir cezect di gal, hop dunaj, dunaj.

5. Di baleboste kojft sxojre, hop dunaj, dunaj,
   S'zol ir zajn makes-bxojres, hop dunaj, dunaj.

6. Di baleboste štejt af der tir, hop dunaj, dunaj,
   Xevre, xevre, a make ir, hop dunaj, dunaj.

7. Di baleboste štejt af der švel, hop dunaj, dunaj,
   S'zol fun ir vern a tel, hop dunaj, dunaj.

8. Di baleboste gejt arojs, hop dunaj, dunaj,
   Xevre, xevre, laxt zi ojs, hop dunaj, dunaj.

21.

Di madam Rabinovič gejt arajn mitn pl'ušenem sak, mitn fejenem kolner,
   Mejnt, az zi di klige.
   Di gance raboče zogt,
   Az z'iz formal'ne mešige.[1]
      Hul'e, kapcn, vos darfstu zorgn,
      Vos darfstu zorgn, vos se vet zajn morgn,
      Hul'e, kapcn, dir felt ales,
      Hul'e, kapcn, frejlexer dales.

22.

1. Di mašines klapn, di reder, zej drejen zix,
   In fabrike z'a raš mit a gevald,
   |: Oj, vej, nemt zix cunojf, švester un brider,
   Lomir ale bafrajen undzer land. :|

2. Dem arbetorers lebn iz a gemučet lebn,
   Er horevet dox tog azojvi naxt.
   |: Oj, er hot nit kajn kojex di bejner ojscuglajxn,
   Di balebatim· mučen im banaxt. :|

3. Her šojn uf cu vejnen, her šojn uf cu klogn,
   Un max nit af der arbet kajn trer.
   |: Oj, se vet bald arajnkumen an Adeser sojxer
   Un nemt di arbet kajn Ades avek. :|

---

[1] Mešuge.

4. Loz er šojn kumen, loz er šojn nemen
   Di arbet kajn Ades avek.
   |: Oj, mir hobn zix derlebt, mir veln zix derlebn,
   Mir arbetn fun zibn biz zeks. :|

5. Gejt arajn der balebos, gejt arajn der balebos —
   Un zogt, az mir zajnen gerext.
   : Oj, er zogt mir hobn bixelex, mir zajnen cicilistelex,
   Mir rejdn af Mikolken šlexts. :|

6. Kak on zav'edysči, kak on pravl'ajušči,
   Kak on raskošno zivjot —
   |: Oj, čaj vypivajet, gazetki vyščitajet,
   Vs'o na podlom s'erdce golova. :|

23.

1. In drojsn iz fincter, in drojsn iz xmarne,
   Un se vet bald gejn a šnej, a šnej...
   |: Azoj zajnen avekgegangen ale majne junge jorn
   Zicndik štendik bam genej, bam genej... :|

2. Hodi šojn cu vejnen, hodi šojn cu klogn,
   Du vest maxn af dajn arbet a flek, a flek...
   |: Ot, bald vet arajngejn der majster, der merder
   Un trajbt undz ale fun danen avek. :|

3. Di mašinen gejen un di ieder drejen,
   Un in cimer iz hejs, iz hejs...
   |: Azoj zajnen avekgegangen undzere junge jorn
   Mitn blutikn švejs... :|

4. Zajne kinder gul'ajen, zei lejenen dort gazetn,
   Zej zogn — šokolad iz zis, iz zis...
   |: Zoln zej farzuxn dem tam fun der arbet
   Cu ojsštejn a tog af di fis, di fis... :|

5. Viazoj zoln mir nit mekane zajn dem balebos alejn,
   Viazoj er lebt zix ojs barut zajne jor.—
   |: Er zict in traktir un trinkt a flešl bir
   Un jorn ale arbetn af im, af im... :|

6. Kak-že ńe zavidovat' našemu xoz'ainu,
   Kak on roskošno zivjot, živjot.
   |: Čaj vypivajet, gazetu on čitajet,
   A nam rabočim otdyx ńe dajot. :|

24.

1. Viazoj zol ix nit mekane zajn dem majsters lebn,
   Er lebt zix šoin, ze ix, vi ajn graf.
   |: Er trinkt di gute vajnen, er rojxert di cigarges
   Un lejgt dos alc afn arbeturer arof. :|

2. Viazoj zol mir gor ajngejn di klejder, majn gul'ajen,
   X'lebn, az se gejt mir gornit ajn.
   |: Az ix tu zix dermonen, az morgn zeks dem zejger
   Badarf ix šojn in masterskaje zajn. :|

3. Di mašines klapn, di ajzns, zej čaden,
   In štub iz ajn rojx un s'iz hejs.
   |: Der kop vert ojsgedart, di ojgn vern tunkl
   Nor fun horevanje un fun švejs. :|

4. Her šojn uf cu vejnen, fargisn mit di trern,
   Du maxst dox af der arbet a flek.
   |: Ot bald vet arajnkumen der majster, der merder,.
   Er trajbt dix fun dajn arbet avek. :|

5. Me hot dox undz untergešribn di bixlex,
   Me hot undz zajavet raščot.
   |: Me hot nox af undz ojsgetraxt — mir zajnen socjalistn,.
   Mir viln nit кajn kejser un glojbn nit in got. :|

Strike Songs

25.

1. Ir, balebatim, ir merder,
   Vos capt ir fun dem arbeturer dos blut?
   Ir mejnt, az di milxome vet ajx glikn,
   Ir mejnt, se vet ajx tomid zajn gut?

   2. Se zol afile dunern un blicn,
      Se meg afile untergejn di velt—
      |: Axt šo in tog veln mir zicn
      Dos iberike vet ajx kostn gelt. :

3. Mir hobn ale jorn gehorevet,
   Biz mir hobn di svobode derlebt,
   Un ycter — iz dox ongekumen Petl'urovces
   Un viln di svobode curik.

   4. Nor mir veln gejn biz dem blyt,[1]
      Mir nemen di svobode curik.
      Mir veln gejn biz dem blyt
      Mirn nemen di svobode curik.

26.

1. Arbet der šnajder a gance vox
   Fardint er a giln mit a lox.
   |: Ot azoj nejt a šnajder,
   Ot azoj klopt er cu. :|

2. Farajorn, nit hajnt gedaxt,
   Hobn mir gearbet a gance naxt.
   |: Ot azoj nejt a šnajder,
   Ot azoj klopt er cu. :|

3. Undzer struc'ke [2]) hot ongemaxt,
   Mir arbetn šojn mer nit fun axt biz axt.
   |: Ot azoj nejt a šnajder,
   Ot azoj klopt er cu. :|

27.

1. Musje Maxovski, vos capt ir mir majn blyt,[1]
   Ale menčn lozt ir arbetn, mir ejnem, oj, nit.
   Mir veln ajx bafeln [. . .´. . . . .]
   Mir veln ajx ojsbrenen mit olin ajere ojgn.

[1]) blut.
[2]) instrukcie fun komitet? obstrukcie?

2. Azoj hot er zix ongehejbn kačen vi a fajl fun bojgn.
„Oj, gevald, menčn, ix hob šojn nit kajn ojgn".
Azoj hobn zix ongerufn ale mitamul:
„Ades iz dox ajn grojse štot, vi s'iz do ajn gošpitul".

28.

1. Lipson iz a balebos
M'et im far der noz nit firn.
Zej viln ajn nabavke,
Zej veln zi ojsfirn.
Zej viln ajn nabavke,
Zej hobn es di vert;
— „Un az ir vilt nit gebn —
Vet ir maxn šlext".

2. — „Oj, šlexte mejdlex
Un vejst ajx der rix,[1]
Ir vilt a nabavke,
Ir zogt—s'iz tajer šix.
Ir vilt a nabavke
Ir hot ži nit di vert".
— „Un az ir vilt nit gebn —
Vet ir maxn šlext".

3. — „Oj, Avrom Dovid,
Zej viln a nabavke,
Zej viln a nabavke,
Zej maxn zabastovke.
Zej viln a nabavke,
Zej šrajen af di cejn,
Un tu zej entfern:
„Ix vel nit gebn, nejn!".

4. Rabinovič mit Lipsonen
Hobn zix gemaxt ejn hant,
Zej hobn ufgeklept
Objavl'en'es af der vant:
—„Drajsik kopkes ojf dem tojznt
Gib ix dem narod,
Un az zej veln nit nemen,
'eln zej gejn af „čorne xod".

5. Papirosnices, kardonščikes
Hobn zix gemaxt ejn hant,
Zej hobn ufgeklept
Objavl'en'es af der vant:
„Fercik rubl dem xojdeš
Vil der narod
Un az ir vet nit gebn,
Veln mir gejn „paradne xod".

6. Lipson iz dox durxgegan,
Dos kvitl ibergelejent,
Er hot ibergelejent,
Er hot okoršt nit gevejnt.
Fun zint er iz balebos,
Gehert hot er dos nit,
Di paršive mejdlex,
Zej capn im dos blyt.[2]

[1] ruex.
[2] blut.

29.

1. — „A gut morgn ajx, Rabinovič". — „A gut jor ajx, Josl Lipson,
Vos hert zix ba ajx in fabrik?".
: — „Ba mir in fabrik iz ajn bure mit ajn stačke,
Di arbeter zuxn ba mir glik. :|

2. Oj, arbetn vos vejniker un sxires vos mer, —
Dos 'et men ba mir nit ojsfirn.
|: Ot 'il ix arajnfirn policje mit žandarmeske
Vet men ajx šojn ale arestirn. :|"

3. Policje mit žandarmeske drejen zix arum:
„Mit di arbeter kon men gornit maxn.
: Git zej šojn op, oj, ales, vos zej trebeven —
Mejn kajn zabastovkes nit maxn." :|

4. — „Oj, ales, vos zej fodern, vel ix zej ništ gebn,
Dos veln zej ba mir nit ojsfirn.
|: Ix vel majn fabrik kajn zagranice arojsfirn,
Un zej vet men do ale arestirn". :|

30.

— „A gut morgn dir, Mojške". — „A gut jor, Josl Lipson,
Vos hert zix epes ba dir in fabrik?"
— „Ba mir in fabrik iz a l'arem mit a stačke,
Di arbeter zuxn ba mir glik.
. . . .
. . . .

31.

1. — „A gut morgn dir, Avremele". — „A gut jor dir, Mejer,
Vos hert zix ba dir in fabrik?"
— „Ba mir in fabrik iz a bunt mit a stačke,
Arbeturer zixn ba mir glik.

2. Arbetn vos vejniker un gelt vos merer,
Zej veln dox ba mir nit ojsfirn.
On gejt dox bald arajn der žandarmeske polkovnik,
Vet er zej ale arestirn".

3. Azojvi der žandarmeske iz arajngekumen:
„Mit kajn raboče kenen mir gornit maxn.
Ir git zej di nabavke un axt šo in tog arbetn
Veln zej kajn stačkes nit maxn".

4. |: Daloj di kulakn un nagajkes un kozaken,
Di trebevan'e veln mir ojsfirn. :|

32.

1. Af Maloarnautske un Puškinske, ba Popovn in fabrik —
Hot zix ongehojbn zejer a grojser bunt.
Der bunt iz gevorn iber a nabavke:
— „Tomer vet ir undz nit gebn — veln mir maxn a zabastovke.

2. Cen kopkes afn tojznt iz dox nit kajn sax,
Git undz di nabavke, anit gejen mir af glax.[1]
Git undz di nabavke vet ir maxn beser,
Tomer vet ir undz nit gebn — git undz op di peser".

[1] glajx

3. Gordovyje, nadzirat'eli na fabriku prišli,
Podn'ali nagajki i kriknuli: „židy!
S'adt'e na rabotu, ja vam govor'u,
Jesli vy n'e s'ad'et'e—v t'urmu posažu".

33.

1. Der bunt iz gevorn
Iber a nabavke,
M'hot nit gevolt gebn
Iz gevorn a zabastovke.

2. Ba Landesmanen in fabrike
Iz gevorn a gerider,
Dort hobn zix cebuntevet
Di švester un brider.
Zej hobn zix cebuntevet,
Se gevorn a gešrej,
S'arajngegangen policije —
„Policije daloj!"

3. Policije z'arajngegan
Hot men gegebn a gešrej:
„Zaberit'e vot eti buntovščiki
Tol'ko poskor'ej!"
— „Hert nor ojs, Kromberg,
Ir vet es nit ojsfirn,
Undzere raboče
Vet men nit arestirn".

4. Azoj hobn mir zix ojsgezect
Ale ojf di tišn,
Azoj hot men gegebn
Fiškinen cu visn.
Fiškin iz arajngekumen:
— „Vos tut ir do štejn?
Ver se vil nabavkes—
Meg zix gejn a hejm".

5. Fiškin hot gemejnt,
Az er vet maxn beser.
Mir hobn gegebn a gešrej:
„Git undz op di peser!".
„Oj, musje Fiškin,
Ix kon es nit farštejn —
Opcugebn di peser
Dos kon ix nit alejn".

6. Azoj hobn mir zix ojsgezect
Ale af di tišn,
Azoj hot men gegebn
Landesmanen cu visn.
Landesman iz arajngekumen:
— „Kinder, vos iz dos?
Ix bin der grojser Landesman,
Ix firt mix ba der noz".

7. Ruft zix on Fiškin:—
„Vos iz hajnt far a velt?
M'hot eršt gelozt di fabrike,
M'hot zi šojn, oj, geštelt".
— „Hert nor ojs, Fiškin,
Ir mejnt mir hobn fargesn
Vi lang hot men ajx getrogn
In ostrog arajn dos esn".

8. — „Oj, hert nor ojs, kinder,
Ir vet dos nit ojsfirn,
Biz tojznt kerblex vet mix kostn—
Me vet ajx arestirn.
Ejn šo esn
Gib ix ajx nabavke".
— „On der šo esn
Vet nox zajn a zabastovke".

9. Me hot dox undz šojn untergešribn,
Undzere bixlex,
Me hot undz šojn zajavet,
Me git undz šojn raščot.
Me hot undz nox ongešribn
Mir zajnen socjalistn,
Mir viln nit kajn kejser,
Mir glojbn ništ in got.

Cugobn.

Meščaniše un parodistiše gasn-lider un kupl'etn af der štrajk-teme (1903—1906). [1]

34.

1. In ale gasn vi me gejt
Hert men zabastovkes,
Jinglex, mejdlex, kind un kejt
Šmisn fun pribavkes.
Vi me gejt hert men: „brider,
Lomir lebn fraj!
Genug šojn, kinder, borgn, lajen,
Arbetn getraj.
Genug dem šlextn buržer,
Er capt undz vi ajn pjavke.
Nor pošet, brider, on fantaz'e.
Maxt a zabastovke!"

    Ti di ra la la la la la...

2. A šnajder-mejdl ojsgeblejxt,
Zi kumt a hejm nit cufridn,
Zi šrajt: „genug šojn zajn a knext
Fufcn šo cum jidn".
Vi lang iz zi geven
A proste gevejntlexe modistke,
Acind gejt zi di hor cefloxtn
A piskl vi an artistke.
Zi šit mit verter gor on šir
A gance filozofke—
Zi šrajt: „di arbet lejgt avek
Un maxt a zabastovke!"

    Ti di ra la la la la la...

[1] Didozike antiproletariše karikaturiše „štrajk-lider" zajnen interesant dermit, vos zej vajzn af a naketn ojfn di filisteriše, bahaltn fajntlexe un derbaj fort ertervajz cupasleriše baciung fun klejnbirgertum cu di kamin fun proletariat in der cajt fun der eršter rusišer revol'ucie. Mir hobn do far zix a bojletn bajšpil af voser ojfn di reakcionere klejnbirgerlexe ideologie bamit zix arajndringen un virkn afn arbeter mit der hilf fun folklor.

3. A Jungerman, a inteligent,
   Er redt zix vejnik gešlifn,
   Cum šrajbn hot er cvej gildene hent
   Un lipelex af šrojfn.
   Kinstlex redt er rusiš gut—
   Jidiš nit kajn vort,
   Oj, lange hor mit švarce vonces
   A kapcn perve sort.
   Er git zix a štel far ajn kasir,
   Er maxt a samandirovke (?)
   Farnemt di kase biz dem šir
   Un maxt a zabastovke.

   Ti di ra la la la la...

4. Dort lojft a muter un šrajt gvald,
   Ir toxter iz mešuge,
   Zi hot cuton mit klek-papir,[1])
   Epes aza kluge.
   Zi hot xavejrim, vejst zej d'rix[2])
   Xmurne lajt in briln,
   Lange hor mit vajse šix,
   Tut gor dem kop dyln.
   Ox un vej, majn toxter,
   Zi iz gevorn grobe, davke.
   Zi krejnkt šojn bald drajfertl jor
   Nox zejer zabastovke.

   Ti di ra la la la la...

5. Dort šrajt a dame cu ir man
   Zi darf hobn gelt af klejder.
   Se vet kumen di goldene cajt
   Cu forn in di vareme bejder.[3])
   Er iz dox ir trejf paskudne,
   Zi ruft im on: „doxl'ače,
   Du zolst afile dem tojt bakumen
   Darf ix hobn a dače.
   Du zolst afile špringen capom,
   Darf ix hobn majovke,
   Ojsfirn vel ix minastam
   Fun undzer zabastovke".

   Ti di ra la la la la...

6. [. . . . .]
   Ix zing, vos ix ken,
   Ix horeve štendik mit majn kojex,
   Ix zing ajx mit a bren.
   Ix zing ajx lider fun der velt,
   Kedej es zol ajx gefeln.
   Ix zing ajx lider fun der velt,
   Ix zing ajx azoj lovke,
   Fargest nit, brider, ix darf hobn gelt—
   S'iz nox der zabastovke.

   Ti di ra la la la la...

[1]) revol'ucionere literatur, gedrukt af papiros-papir (bibule).
[2]) der ruex.
[3]) beder.

35.

1. In ale gasn vi me gejt
Hert men zabastovkes,
Jinglex, mejdlex, kind un kejt,
Me redt šojn fun pribavkes.
In ale gasn tut men šrajen:
„Brider, lomir lebn fraj!
Guneg šojn, brider, borgn un lajen
Un horeven getraj.
Az der šlexter borže,[1])
Er zejgt undz vi ajn pjavke,
Genug šojn, brider, on fantaz'e,
Maxn zabastovke"!

2. Ajn šnajder-mejdl ongeblejxt,
Zi kumt ahejm cufridn,
Zi redt di verter gor on šrek
Fercn šo cu redn.
Vi lang iz zi gevezn
A proste gevise modistke,
Ject gejt zi di hor celozt,
Ajn piskl—anarxistke.
Zi redt di verter gor on šrek
Fun der nasovke.[2])
„Fun ajer arbet maxt an ek,
In ejn kol zabastovke!"

3. Šrajt ajn dame, vej iz ir,
Ir toxter iz mešuge
Zi hot cuton mit pek-papir
Un iz dermit ajn kluge—
Tovariščes, oj, šir a šir,
Lojter loj mit briln,
Kumen zej šojn dyln.
„Oj vej, majn toxter,
Du bist šojn greblex, davke,
Stradajest šojn draj fertl jor
Culib der zabastovke".

36.

1. Vi me gejt un vi me štejt,
Oj, hert men zabastovke,
Alte menčn, kind un kejt,
Zej viln ajn nabavke.
Alte menčn, kind un kejt,
Zej viln lebn fraj.
Genug cu borgn un cu lajen
Un arbetn getraj.

2. Dort krigt zix a man mit zajn vajb,
Zi šrajt af im: „dyxl'ače!
Du megst afile dem tojt bakumen,
Šrajt zi, ix vil a dače.
Ajn dače, dače vil ix
Cudercu popravke".
Zi krejnkt šojn, oj, draj fertl jor
Fun der eršter zabastovke.

[1]) buržuj.
[2]) masovke?

3. Ejner zogt: „lejg avek,
Lejg avek di arbet".
Der cvejter zogt: „lejg avek,
Anit verstu geharget".
Der driter zogt: „lejg avek,
Vos arbetstu far ale?
N'lejg avek dain arbet
Un gej šojn cu dajn kale".

37.

1. In ale gasn, vu me gejt,
Hert men zabastovkes,
Jinglex, mejdlex, kind un kejt,
Zej redn fun parbavkes.[1])
Genug šojn, oj, cu borgn, cu lajen,
Hobn lebn fraj,
|: Un di arbet varft avęk
Un arbetn getraj. :|
Genug šojn, oj, dem šlextn buržuj
Ajx cu zejgn vi a pjavke.
On fantaz'e, brider,
Un maxt a zabastovke.

2. A mejdl kumt fun di arbet
Tojt cu flien,
Zi šrajt: „oj, genug cu zajn a knext
Un fercn šo zix mien!"
Vi lang iz zi geven gor prost
Un gevust nor di modistke,—
Hajnt gejt zi, oj, di hor celozt,
A piskele vi ajn artistke.
Šisn šist zi, oj, mit verter,
A gance filozofke,
Zi šrajt: „di arbet varft avek
Un maxt a zabastovke!"

3. A jungerman a tiligent
Vincik vos gešlifn,
Cum šrajbn hot er gildene hent
Un lipelex af šrojfn.
Rusiš redt er on a šir,—
Jidiš nit kajn vort,
Švarce ojgn, blondike uses,
A kapcn perve sort.
Me nemt im cu in vald far kasirer,
Er maxt a sortirovke,
Er lejdikt ojs di kase biz a firer
Un maxt a zabastovke.

4. Ajn muter šrajt: „vej iz mir,
Majn toxter iz mešige,[2])
Zi hot cuton mit pek papir,
Epes mit a knige".
Ajn muter zogt: „Majn toxter iz
Gevorn greblex, dike.—
Zi krenkt šojn draj-fertl jor
Fun der zabastovke.

[1]) pribavkes.
[2]) mešuge.

5. A vajbl krigt zix, oj, mit ir man,
Zi darf hobn gelt af klejder,
Se kumt šojn di vareme cajt
Cu forn in di vareme bejder.[1])
Zidlt im mit paskudne rejd,
Zi ruft im on „doxl'ače",
Zi zogt: „du, zlidn'e, krenk inderhejm,—
Ix darf hobn a dače.
Megst afile tancn capom,
Muz ix hobn a javke [2])
Az ix vel nit ojsfirn—
'el ix maxn a zabastovke".

Struggles and Victims

38.

1. Vi mir hobn zix ale sobirajet
Sakavickes šul iz gevezn far undz šmol,
Un ver se hot gegebn policije cu visn—
Der zol lign in Kiev in gošpitol.

2. Vi der ur'adnik iz nor in šul arajngekumen,
Azoj hobn mir zix farnumen mit im krign.
Se bald in šul arajngkumen kazakn mit žindarn
Un me hot undz ongehojbn, oj, ale arestirn.

3. Vi me hot undz, oj, ale arestirt
Cvej azejger banaxt,
Ven der ziser šlof faršlefert jedn menčn
Hot men undz ale in a tureme faršpart.

4. Vi me hot undz nor kajn Vasil'kov arojsgešikt
Cvelf a zejger batog
Un cvišn undzere švester un brider
Iz gevorn a jomer mit a klog.

5. Vi me hot undz nor in učastek arajngefirt
Hot men gefloxtn fun šaškes a kejt.
Me hot nit cugelozt kajn muter cu kajn kind
Cu derlangen a štikele brejt.[3])

39.

1. Oj, vej, švester un brider,
|: Mir hobn zix ale emes lib. :|
|: Nor az policje, zi vet zix dervisn,
Az mir sobirajen zix ale in ejn štib... :|

2. A fule štub hobn mir zix ale sobirajet,
|: Mir zajnen gevezn ale mitamol, :|
|: Un ver se hot gegebn policije cuvisn,
Der zol fojln in Kiev in gošpitol. :|

3. Af morgn iz cu n'undz der pristev cugeforn,
|: Mir hobn zix mit im epes farkrigt, :|
|: Azoj iz ongelofn policje mit žindarn
Un me hot undz šojn ale arestirt. :|

[1]) beder. [3]) brojt.
[2]) majovke? [4]) štub.

. 4. Arestirt hot men undz ale.
|: S'iz geven arum cvej azejger banaxt, :|
|: Azoj hot men undz ale cunojfgenumen
Un me hot undz, oj, in ostrog faršpart. :|

5. Af morgn hot men undz gedarft kajn Vasil'kov arojsšikn,
|: Dos iz geven arum cvej azejger batog, :|
|: Azoj iz ongelofn di foters mit di muters
Un s'iz gevorn a jomer mit a klog. :|

6. Oj, hert šojn uf cu vejnen un cu klogn,
|: Falt ba zix af azojfil nit arop, :|
|: Af ajere kinder vet men ajx amol mekane zajn,
Vajl zej stradajen, nebex, farn gancn narod. :|

40.

1. Unter der Sofievke [1]) hert zix a gerider [2])
Se hobn zix sobirajet švester un brider,
Se hobn zix sobirajet a grojse kampan'e
Af der fraje un af sobran'e.

. . . .

. . . .

41.

1. A sobran'e hobn mir zix sobirajet
Un a špijun hot undz derzen.
Mit grojs parad hot men undz farnumen
Glajx cum spravnik, oj, a hejm.

2. Prikazan'es hobn mir u'gegebn,
U'gelozt hot men undz ahejm.
U'gelozt hot men undz ahejm
Dem elctn bruder fun undz nit.
Mir darfn zen far im gejn
Biz in der lecter kapli blyt.[3])

3. Nemt zix cunojf, oj, švester un brider,
Vel ix ajx gebn cu farštejn:
Az mir arbetn fun axt biz cen—
Horeven mir gor umzist.
Un az mir arbetn fun axt biz zeks,—
Vel ix ajx gebn cu farštejn.

4. Švester un brider, mir zingen lider,
Mir zingen lider fun zix alejn,
Mir zingen lider mit fil gerider, [2])
Az got vet hejsn, veln mir kumen ahejm.

42.

1. Dem najntn janvar ajn jomer mit a klog,
|: Me firt undzere brider fun birže in astrog. :|

2. Azojvi me hot zej nor ahin arajngebraxt,
|: Azoj hobn mir zix ale a nejder gemaxt. :|

3. Brider un švester, far kajn t'urmes zix nit opšrekn,
|: Arojs fun di t'urmes ale menčn cu dervekn. :|

[1]) Sofievke—a park in Uman'.
[2]) geruder
[3]) blut.

4. Arojs fun di turmes, mit bombes un dinamit,
|: Farnixtn di tiranen, vos zojgn undzer blyt.[1])

5. Vos zojgn undzer blut, vi dem bestn vajn
Der kejser mit der pravit'el'stve zol in dr'erd arajn.
Un zej veln ahin arajn.

6. Ot demolt veln mir, arbeter, ufhojbn di kep,
Di velt vet vern banajt —
Demolt veln mir, arbeter, vern bafrajt.

43.

1. Šabes batog iz a jomer mit a klog,
 : me firt di raboče fun birže in ostrog. :|

2. Vi me hot zej nor in ostrog arajngebraxt,
|: azoj hot men bald a prytokol gemaxt. :|

3. Švester un brider, fun t'urmes nit opšrekn,
|: arojst fun der t'urme di briderlex dervekn. :|

4. Arojst fun der turme mit bombes, mit rabir,
|: nit švajgn di tiranen, zej zojgn undzer blyt.[1])

5. Ze zojgn undzer blut, zej trinken dem bestn vajn,
|: Mikolke mit pravit'el'stve zoln in dr'erd arajn. :|

6. Az Mikolke vet in dr'erd arop,
|: Veln undzere arbeter eršt ufhojbn di kop. :|

7. Vi m'hot ajn gešrej gegebn: „jidn un kristn",
|: Hobn mir geentfert: „daloj kapitalistn!" :|

8. Vi m'hot ajn gešrej getun: „l'evo, napravo!",
|: Hobn mir geentfert: „daloj samoderžave!" :|

44.

A variant cum Hirš Lekert-lid.

1. Vi Jisker iz fun štub arojsgegangen,
Gezogt hot er dem vajb: „a gute naxt".
|: Vi Jisker z'cum teater cugegangen
Dort hot er zajn lebn gut batraxt. :|

2. Vi Jisker z'in teater arajngegangen
Genumen hot er a bil'et in p'ervi r'ad,
|: Vi Jisker z'in teater arajngegangen
Dort hot er zajn cajt ojsgevart. :|

3. Vi der gubernater iz funem teater arojsgegangen
A gešrej hot er gegebn: „izvozčik, s'uda",
|: Jisker hot arojsgexapt dem revol'ver
Un hot im getrofn glajx in zajt. :|

4. Vi Jisker t'dem gubernater deršosn
Iz gevorn a raš mit a gerider,
|: S'hot zix ongerufn ejner cu dem cvejtn:
„Adu iz šojn farfaln undzer brider". :|

---

[1]) blut.

5. Vi m'hot Jiskern in policej arajngebraxt
Alejn in a cimerl faršpart,
|: Jisker zict dort ba dem kanecl
Un hot dort zajn lebn gut batraxt. :|

6. Vi der kaz'one rabiner iz cu Jiskern arajngegangen:
„Zog šojn op viden'u, majn kind"—
|: — „Avek, avek du jidišer tiraner,
Oj, tu šojn vos du vilst mit mir. :|

7. Šikt mir arajnrufn majn vajb Tajbele:
—„Lomir zix gezegenen mit dir.
|: Az se vet ba dir gebojrn vern a jingele—
A nomen zolstu gebn nox mir".

45.

1. Rojšxojdeš elel, mamen'u, ojfdernaxt,
Oj, lig ix mir un traxt,
Oj, azoj hot men ba Grinbergn di oblave gemaxt, oj vej.
Majn harc hot mir gezogt, oj mame, az hajnt iz šojn der lecter afdernaxt,
Oj, lig ix mir un traxt.

2 . Oj, cvelf azejger, mamen'u, se iz šojn a halbe naxt,
Oj, lig ix mir un traxt.
Oj, tir un tojer, mamen'u, in dem ostrog farmaxt.
Majn harc tut mir zogn, mame, az hajnt iz sojn der lectet afdernaxt,
Oj, lig ix mir un traxt.

3. Oj, ejns azejger, mamen'u, nox a halbe naxt,
Oj, lig ix mir un traxt.
Oj, azoj hot men mir, mamen'u, di rešenje gebraxt.
Majn harc hot mir gezogt, mame, az hajnt iz šojn der lecter afdernaxt.

4. Cvej azejger, mamen'u, in der naxt,
Oj, lig ix mir un traxt.
Azoj hot men mir, muter majne, majn foter gebraxt.
„Oj, vej, kum aher, foter, cu mir, gezegenen lomir zix mit dir
Gezegenen lomir zix mit dir".

5. Oj, draj azejger, mamen'u, in der naxt,
Oj, lig ix mir, mamen'u, in der dinočke [1]) un traxt.
Oj, vej, majn harc hot mir gezogt, oj mame,
Az hajnt iz der lecter afdernaxt.

6. Oj, fir azejger, mamen'u, se šojn bald nox der naxt,
Oj, lig ix mir un traxt.
Azoj hot men mir, mamen'u, dem kaz'one rabiner gebraxt, oj vej,
— „Kum aher, majn kind, cu mir
Un vide lomir opzogn mit dir".

7. Oj, finf azejger, mamen'u, se šojn bald nox der naxt,
Oj, lig ix mir un traxt.
Oj, azoj hot men mir, muter majne, majn švester gebraxt.
Oj vej, kum aher, švester, cu mir
Un zen vestu zix mejn nit mit mir.

8. Oj, zeks azejger, mamen'u, se iz šojn nox der naxt,
Ix lig mir un traxt.
Oj, ot azoj hot men undz, muter majne, cu Adeser tlije gebraxt, oj, vej.
In Ades iz gevorn a jomer mit ajn klog—
Cvej brider ufgehangen in ejn tog.

[1]) odinočke—ejncl-kamer.

46.

1. Gnes'e z'fun ir arbet gegangen,
   Zi hot nox fun ir umglik nit gevyst,[1]
   Arojsgegajn der merder, der pristev
   Un hot zi gešosn umzist.

2. Di gasn, vos m'hot zi in bol'nice getrogn,
   Gevezn zajnen zej ful mit blut.
   Az m'hot zi in bol'nice arajngetrogn
   Hot zi nox gelebt cen minut.

3. Brider, mir torn nit švajgn
   Far undzere xavertes blut,
   Mir darfn dos blut undzers vašn
   Mit bombes in jeder minut.

47.

1. Oj, mitvox iz p'erve maj,
   Iz undzer xaver Išike gegangen zix bodn,
   |: Nor plucling iz ongekumen a vistike telegram,
   Az undzer xaver Išike iz dertrunken gevorn. :|

2. Un mir, tavarišČes, mir hobn dos nor derhert,
   Mith ponem zajnen mir gefaln cu der erd,
   |: Nor mir, tavarišČes, mir veln gejn ale glajx,
   Mir viln baringlen dem pejterover tajx. :|

3. Vi mir hobn zix mit lodkes gelozt švimen,
   Me hot dem xaver Išike nit gekont gefinen,
   |: Nor Josl der filer hot a nec in vaser aropgelozt
   Un dem xaver Išike far a fus arojsgenumen. :|

4. Vi me hot im funem tajx arojsgenumen
   Iber ganc Pejterov hot men im gefirt.
   |: Nor zajn kop kučern, vos hot ongehejbn cu blien,
   Mitn vajsn lajlex zajn ponem cugedekt. :|

5. Oj, vi me hot im genumen firn,
   Iz dox ongekumen der pristev un hot im nit gelozt cunemem.
   |: „Oj, avek, du merder, du grojser xuligan!"
   Mir hobn dem tavarišČ Išiken in štub arajngenumen. :|

6. Vi me hot im in štub arajngenumen,
   Azoj z'di muter bald xalošes geblibn,
   |: Oj, mir, tavarišČes, mir darfn vejnen un klogn,
   Vos mir tuen bagrobn aza min gutn bruder. :|

7. Oj, a šo mit finf minut hot gedovert zajne klejder,
   Un me tut dem xaver Šike fun der velt cunemen.
   |: Nor di rojte fon, vos zi hejngt iber zajn kejver—
   Mit der naser erd Šikes ponem cugedekt. :|

48.

1. Di bixer mit di sekretn
   Hobn mir, xavejrim, ongevojrn.
   |: Ot dos iz, xavejrim, nit azoj,
   Ot gejt der gardevoj. :|

[1] gevust.

2. Der gardevoj iz cu mir cugekumen
   Un hot ba mir di pokazan'e cunenumen.
   |: Nor zogn zog ix im, az nejn,
   Az ix bin af der sobran'e nit gevejn. :|

3. Er hot mix genumen cum šlogn,
   Ix zol im dem emes ojszogn.
   |: Nor az ix 'el im dem emes ojszogn,
   Vet er mix kajn Simbir avekjogn. :|

4. Er hot mix arajngezect in a fincterer t'urme,
   Vi batog iz nox erger vi banaxt.
   |: Me zect undz, xavejrim, in di t'urmes,
   In di finctere kamern faršpart. :|

5. Ci hob ix a menčn geran'et?
   Ci hob ix a menčn getojt?
   |: Farvos kumt mir in t'urme cu zicn?
   Farvos kumt mir af Arxangel'sk cu gejn? :|

49.

1. X'hob gekončet di axt klasn,
   Ix bin a jingele fun der gimnaz'e arojs,
   |: Ix hob farfirt, farfirt a grojse role,
   Švester un brider, ir halt zix ejns. :|

2. M'hot mix gexapt mit maine bixer,
   M'hot mix arajngezect in dem ostrog.
   : Nemt zix cunojf, švester un brider,
   Ci iz den do af der velt a got. :|

3. M'hot mix farsud'et in a fincter xejder,
   Kajn tint un feder hob ix nit ba zix.
   |: Ix her ajn kol, ajn kol fun majne brider,
   Arojsgejn cu zej ken ix nit. :|

4. Ver-že strojet di šejne movern? —
   Di šejne movern strojet der arbets-man.
   |: Oj, tut a freg ver vojnt dortn? —
   Dortn vojnt dox der rajxer man. :|

5. Der oreman, vos er vojnt in keler,
   Nas un sirest' kapet fun zajne vent.
   |: Derum bakumt er revmatizm feler,
   Af zajne fis un af zajne hent. :|

6. Ver-že flanct dos di šejne vajngertner? —
   Di šejne vajngertner flanct der arbets-man.
   |: Oj, ver est uf di gute fruxtn? —
   Di gute fruxtn est der rajxer man. :|

50.

1. Me firt mix arajn in ajn finctern xejder,
   Kajn tint un pene iz dort nito.
   |: Ix her a raš, majne kejtn klingen,
   Ix vil ajx zingen ajn trojer-lid. :|

2. Ix hob opgelernt ajn blat gemore,
   Ix bin a jingl fun dem xejder arojs.
   |: Ix hob erklert a naje mode —
   Švester un brider, lozt nit op. :|

3. Ix fleg štendik zicn un zingen lider,
Ix fleg štendik zogn, az s'nito af der velt a got.
|: Far udzer emes, švester un brider, zicn mir,
Zicn mir ject in ostrog. :|

4. Men hot mix gexapt mit majne demokratiše bixer,
Men hot mix in ostrog arajngezect.
|: Hajnt zogt šojn ale, švester un brider,
Ci es iz do ajn got af der velt. :|

5. Di šejne mojern mit di hojxe palacn,
Es tut zej arbetn der arbets-man.
|: Nor tut ajn kuk, ver vojnt, oj, dortn?—
Nor der svoloč, der rajxer man. :|

6. Di grojse sodn [1]) mit di grojse gertner,
Es tut zej flancn der arbets-man.
|: Nor tut a kuk, ver špacirt, oj, dortn?—
Nor der svoloč, der rajxer man. :|

7. Der arbets-man ligt in keler,
Der sirest' nect im fun ale vent.
|: Fun derfun bakumt er ajn harmatizne [2]) fule
In di fis un in di hent. :|

51.

1. Ver tut strojen movern, palacn.
Un ver tut strojen? — Der arbets-man.
Oj, tut a kuk, oj, ver se vojnt in zej —
Se gornit er, nor der rajxer man.

2. Der arbets-man vojnt in a keler, in a nasn,
Vos di vaser rint, oj, fun di vent.
Derfun bakumt er ajn feler ajn grojsn,
Oj, in di fis un in di hent.

3. Ix hob opgelernt ajn blat gemore,
Ix bin, got cudanken, fun majn xejder arojs,
Ix hob farfirt a naje role
Oj, švester un brider, ir halt far ejns.

4. Hert šojn uf mit di kejtn cu klingen,
Un loz šojn zajn a bisl štil.
Lozt-že mir majn lid ojszingen —
Vet ir visn ver ix bin.

Ci hob ix den a menčn geštoxn,
Ci hob ix den emecn fun der velt gebraxt,
Ci hob in den a šlos gebroxn,
Farvos kumt mir in ostrog faršpart?

6. Du, majn kind, az du vest elter vern,
Zolstu zajn mit menčn glajx.
Dencmolt vel ix majn lid ojszingen,
Vel ix zajn mit ale glajx.

7. Libe brider, az ix vel štarbn,
Cu majn levaje zolt ir gejn.
Di rojte fon mit ire farbn
Ba mir cukopns zol zi štejn.

---

[1]) seder.
[2]) revm atizm.

52.

1. Di hojxe movern, ver tut zej strojen,
   Ver tut zej strojen? — Der arbets-man.
   |: Un tut a kuk, ver tut dort vojnen? —
   Alc nit er — der rajxer man. :|

2. Der oreman, er vojnt in keler
   Un dos vaser rint fun di vent,
   |: Derfun bakumt er, rematizm-feler
   In zajne fis, in zajne hent. :|

3. Oj, libe brider, az ix vil štarbn—
   Cu majn levaje zolt ir gejn.
   |: Di rojte fone mit ire farbn
   Ba mir cukopns zol zi štejn. :|

53.

Dort in vinkl in nasn keler
Hart af dr'erd, af a bisl štrej,[1]
Ligt ajn arbeter af a ling-feler,
Er ligt un krexct un šrajt: „oj vej!
Her nor ojs, majn kind, majne lecte rejd,
Her nor cu mit farštand.
Befor ix nem fun dir opšejd,
Her nor cu un gib mir di hant,
Az di zolst nit švajgn far majn lebn,
Vus ix gej cum štarbn jungerhejt,
Di zolst nor cejln un faršrajbn,
Di zolst nemen raxe far majn fricajtikn tejt.[2]

54.

Dort in vinkl, in keler
Hart ojf ba der erd, af a bintl štrej [1]
Ligt ajn arbeter mit ajn brust-feler,
Er ligt un šrajt un krexčet „oj!
Her ojs, majn kind, majne lecte rejd,
Her zej ojs mit grojs farštand,
Ejder ix nem fun dir opšejd,
Šver mir cu un gib mir dajn hant,
A'di vest nit švajgn dox far majn lebn
Vos ix gej cum štand azoj jungerhejt
Un in ordenung (?) štarbt er oñ a glojbn
Zolst nemen raxe far majn farcajtikn tejt.[2]

55. (56 var).

1. Di trit fun tiranen hobn zix gelozt hern
   |: Arum cvej azejger banaxt. :|
   Dencmolt iz ba undz a štern gefaln
   Fun di, vos zej lojxtn banaxt.
   Mir hobn nox nit ufgehert cu vejnen un cu klogn
   |: Fun di, vos m'hot kajn Sibir avekgešikt, :|
   Plucling, az mir hern a psure onzogn,
   Az m'hot undzern a brider arestirt.
       Ax, vi biter iz dos land,
       Vos mir gejen cu dem štand
       Far undzere getraje, oj, švester un brider.
       Nor ver, ver, ver vejst
       Mirn hobn dem trejst
       Cu zen zix mit zej vider.

[1] štroj.
[2] tojt.

2. Azojvi me farnart a fojgele in a kl'etke,
|: Azoj t'men undzere brider farnumen, :|
   In der fincterer t'urme, vi kajn šajn kumt nit cu,
   Vi kain menč ken ahin nit kumen.
   Dortn unter di grobe vent
|: Zict er dort švarc vi ajn kojl, :|
   Dem kop ongešpart af di dare hent,
   Er zifct, ax dos harc ken cugejn.
        Oj, di fraje velt,
        Zi iz far mir farštelt,
        Ix kon af der gas nit arojs—
        Cu helfn zej dort
        Xoč mit ejn gut vort
        Undzere brider, vos far hunger gejen zej ojs.

3. Der hejliker gajst, er lozt mix nit lebn
|: Afile do in karc, :|
   Jedn tog kumt cu naje mašines
   Far dem gajst iz di tiranstvo cu kľein.
        Ir megt mit mir ton
        Azojvi mit a rusišn špion,
        Ir megt mir fardarbn majne glider,
        Nor ados, vos ix vejs,
        Ados zog ix nit ojs,
        Getraj vel ix farblajbn majne brider.

4. Nit der eršter, nit der lecter
   Falt ahin arajn.
|: Zamlt kojxes ojf a revol'ucie
   Un a held vestu zajn. :|

                    57.

1. In dem vajtn land Sibir
   Vu der himl z'tomid fun di xmares švarc,
   Dort alejn bin ix geven faršikt
   Farn ejnem vort, far der fraj.
   Mit der nagajke hot men mix gešlogn,
   Az ix zol mer nit zogn:
   „Da zdravstvujet svoboda, in dr'erd mit Nikolaj!"

2. Oj, in dem vajtn land Sibir,
   Vu se kumt kejnmol di zun nit cu,
   Dort alejn bin ix lang gevezn
   Alc far dem vort, far der fraj.
   Zumer in di hicn un vinter in di keltn,
   Di tačke fleg ix šlepn
   Alc far dem vort.

3. Ject iz gekumen di gliklexe cajt,
   Icter vejs men saj fun novnt un fun vajt,
   Az Rusnland iz lixtik, az Rusnland iz fraj,
   Da zdravstvujet svoboda, in dr'erd iz Nikolaj!

                 58. (59 var).

1. In dem vajtn (in vajtn) kaltn Sibir,
   Vu der himl xmare-švarc, (xmaret švarc)
   Dort hob ix gelitn on a šir,
   Af štiklex cebroxn majn harc.[1]

Var. [1] Gebroxn af štiklex di oreme harc.

In der grester kelt,
Naket af dem (afn) feld,
Hot men undz getribn oto dort.
Gepajnikt undz, gešlogn,
Az mir zoln (ix zol) mejn (mer) nit zogn:
„Da zdravstvujet svoboda, internacjonal!" [1]
Nor ject iz šojn (s'iz šojn) gekumen di gliklexe cajt,
Az mir hern fun novnt un fun vajt,
Az Rusland iz lixtik (gliklex),
In (az) Rusland iz fraj,
„Da zdravstvujet svoboda,
Arunter (daloj) Nikolaj!".

2. In dem vajtn kaltn land Sibir,
Dort hob ix getrofn fil grojse lajt,
Zej zajnen fun fon'es korbones —
Di umšuldike opfers fun der šlexter cajt.
Di grojse filozofn
Hob ix dort alejn getrofn
In dem umgliklexn land,
Fil junge frojen un mener,
Vi Ruslands beste kener,
Lozt men zej nit frajhajt far dem ejnem vort:
„Da zdravstvujet svoboda,-arunter Nikolaj!".
Nor ject iz šojn gekumen di gliklexe cajt,
Az mir hern ale fun noent un fun vajt,
Az in Rusland iz lixtik,
Az in Rusland iz fraj,
Da zdravstvujet svoboda,
Arunter Nikolaj.

Revolutionary Hymns and Songs

60.

Vi hejlik iz di natur
Mit ire fraje firung
Emes un libe
Ir ciring, ir šmuk.

Mir lejgn ojfn harcn di rexte hant
Un švern mit dem sovest' ject,
Az fun tojt un fun lebn vi an ajzerne vant,
Ven der šverd fun emes blict.

Ven ejner fun undz iz cu švax gevis,
Den cu giftig iz der kapital
Azojvi fun dem šlang der bis.

Ven mit emes un libe gebundn
Undzer bund iz vi a mojer štejt fest
Un di libe iz yn harcn ongecundn,
Di libe fun frajhajt un menčlixes glik.

Di nekome fodert undzer blut,
Fun undzer blut vakst štendik zejer guts,
Guts un rajx cien zej fun undzere bejner,
Ax, un cum sof tret men undz vi di štejner.

[1] „Da zdravstvujet svoboda, daloj Nikolaj!".

Brider un svester nemt ajx far di hent,
Kumt cu dem fajer, vu der flaker brent,
Mir zajnen proletarjat, dos hejst: „raboči narod“.
Di ajzerne kejtn lomir cerajsn,
Dem švern jox aruntercušmajsn,
Šrajt: „narod, vp'erjod, vp'erjod, vp'erjod!“.

61.

1. A šejnem vajngortn hobn mir farflanct,
Šejne blumen rojt, roz un vajs,
Nor vilde xajes hobn es cetrotn,
Emes un libe hobn zej farbitn af kine, sine un šklaferaj

Lomir lejgn afn harcn di rexte hant
Un bašvern zix mit sovest' ict,
Az durx tojt un lebn vi an ajzerne vant,
Ven dos šverd fun emes blict.

Un ven ejner fun undz iz cu švax gevis,
Den cu giftig iz der kapital
Vi fun dem šlang der bis.

Ven mit emes un libe gebundn
Undzer bund štejt, vi ajn mojer štejt ganc fest,
Fargejt di zun,— in undzer harc ongecundn,
Di zune fun frajhajt gejt of.

Di nekome fodert undzer blut,
Fun undzer gezunt vakst štendik zejer guts.
Guts un rajx cien zej fun undzere bejner
Dox tret men undz azojvi di štejner.

Derum, brider un švester, git zix ale di hent,
Un bašvert zix ba dem flaker, vu der fajer brent,
Mir zajnen der proletarjat, dos hejst der proster narod.
Di kejtn, di švere muzn mir cerajsn,
Dem jox, dem švern arunter cušmajsn,
To šrajt: „narod, vp'erjod!“

Brider, nomir zix ervaxn,
Fun tiraneraj an ende maxn,
Mir muzn cetretn di tiraneraj
Un maxn Rusland fraj.

62.

1 Dos eršte veln mir nemen nox regirn (?)
D'eksplataters, vos zej zojgn undzer blut.—
Un undzere zabastovkes ojsfirn,
Bafrajen undzere minut, oj, oj, oj,
Bafrajen undzere minut.

2. Cu bafrajen oreme menčn.
Velxe lajdn fil hunger un nojt.
Di erd fun frajhajt zol zej benčn,
Se zol af zej šojn nit zajn kajn nojt, oj, oj, oj,
Se zol af zej nit zajn mer kajn nojt.

3. Nemt arojs di fonen fun di štiber,
Velxe štejen nox in finctern gecelt.
Nemt zix cunojf, ale švester un brider,
Cu bafrajen undzere velt, oj, oj, oj,
Bafrajen di oreme velt.

63.

1. Geit, brider, gejt,
   Ajx fodern brejt [1]
   Ba kejsorim un ba kn'azn un ba grafn,
   Fodert menčlexe rext,
   Me zol ajx nit bahandlen azoj šlext,
   Fodert ales dos, vos mir hobn bašafn.
   Štejt ojf, brider, mir vekn ajx!
   Un forverts cum kamf un nit šrekt aix!
   Un cum lebn,
   Un cum štrebn
   Un cu kemfn in a štrajk
   Gejt un vert bafrajt,
   Fun der najer cajt.

2. Der rov mitn pop,
   Zej fardrejen undz di kop
   Mit avejres, mit zejere religjonen.
   Ot di micves mit di zind
   Maxn dem arbeter blind,
   Er zol nit zen, v'azoj me tut im barojbn.
   Štejt ojf, brider u. az. v.

3. Der sicalist [2]
   Izništ kajn jid un ništ kajn krist,
   Nor a menč mit a rejnem gevisn.
   Unter zajn rojte fon
   l'nito kajn religjon
   Nor cvej klasn: or'me un rajxe.
   Štejt ojf, brider u. az. v.

64.

1. Vos viln di heršer, vos viln di lampirn, [3]
   Zej capn fun dem arbeter dos lect bisl blut.
   |: Un dan vet ir visn, vos se hejst eksplatirn,
   Ajn besern lebn cu zuxn zix far ajx. :|

2. Dem arbeters kamf gejt vajter un vajter,
   Štelt zix in kamf far dem arbeter klas.
   |: Un dan vet ir visn, vos se hejst eksplatirn,
   Ajn besern lebn cu zuxn zix far ajx. :|

65.

Brider, ejb got vil undz nit helfn,
Lomir zix bafrajen alejn.
Lomir zix cerajsn fun di kejtn
Un lomir alejn cuzamen gejn.
. . . .
. . . .

66.

1. Oj, ir nariše cionistn
   Mit ajer narišn sejxl,
   |: Ir megt dox gejn cu dem arbeter
   Un lernen ba im sejxl. :|

[1] brojt.
[2] socialist.
[3] vampirn.

2. Ir vilt undz firn kajn Jerušolajim,
   Mir zoln dort golodajen,
   |: Mir veln beser zajn in Rusnland,
   Mir veln zix bafrajen. :|

Melodies to Songs by M. Vintshevsky, D. Edelshtat, and Others

Beregovski did not include the song texts of these literary works.

II. SONGS ABOUT ARTISANS
84.

1. Zict a šnajder a fis iber a fis, [1])
   Zingt a lidele cuker zis.

2. Štej ix mir ba der tir,
   Fort cu mir a skarbove fir.[2])

3. Freg ix ir: „vu- že forstu?" —
   Zogt zi: „take cu dir".

4. Fun dem presl, fun dem šerl,
   Tu ix on majn vajb a haldz perl.

85.

Ot azoj nejt a šnajder,
Ot azoj varft er štex.
Ot azoj nejt a šnajder,
Ot azoj varft er štex.
A šnajder nejt un nejt un nejt
Un hot kadoxes nit kajn brejt.[3])

86.

1. Der šnajder zict ba zajn genej,
   Fun ejn por hojzn maxt er cvej.
   Un in štub iz ba im faran fun alesding,
   Un in kešene git dox ojx a kling,—
   Er zingt ba jedn štox, xr, štox, fju, štox, a štox,
   Er zingt ba jedn štox.
   Di arbet, di arbet git er op,
   Jarl, dirl, dirl, dirl, dirl, dirl, dam,
   Un nit er falt ba zix arop, xr, rop, fju, rop, arop,
   Un nit er falt ba zix arop.

2. Simxastojre iz dox ojx.
   Dan nemt er a kap ibern kojx.[4])
   Un a gabe iz er ojx in šil.[5])
   Er nemt a kap inderštil.
   Un vi er kumt in šul arajn, xr, rajn, fju, rajn, arajn,
   Un vi er kumt in šul arajn:
   „A hakofe zol mir zajn!
   Jarl, dirl. dirl, dirl, dirl, dirl, dam,
   A'nit, iz a ruex in tatn arajn, xr, rajn, fju, rajn, arajn.
   A'nit iz a ruex in tatn arajn".

[1]) fus, [2]) fur, [3]) brojt. [4]) kojex; [5]) šul;

87.

Mit a nodl, on a nodl
Nej ix mir bekoved godl,
Mit a nodl on a nodl
Nej ix mir bekoved godl.

1. Zicn zic ix mir a fis af a fis,[1])
   Vajl majn arbet is cuker zis.
   Mit a nodl u. az. v. . . .

2. Ix nej un nej a ɣance vox
   Un nej mir ojs a parizer lox.
   Mit a nodl u. az. v. . . .

3, Cien ci ix mir di fastrige
   Un ix es mir di mamelige.
   Mit a nodl a az. v. . . .

4. Šabes gej ix arojs vi in posek štejt
   In di ejgene begodim, vos x'hob alejn genejt.
   Mit a nodl u. az. v. . . .

88.

1. Hej, ir menčn ale, fun grojs biz klejn,
   Oj, ver se hot fun dem umglik ništ gehert un ništ gezen,
   Vel ix ajx, menčn, gebn ject cu derklern,
   Un betn bet ix ajx, ir zolt di lid mit gedanken ˈojshern.

2. Oj di lid iz dox nox gor fun a jung kind,
   Oj, vemen se hot nor getrofn an umglik gešvind,
   N'zajn meloxe z'er gevezn ajn kalter
   Un mit zajn libn nomen hot er gehejsn Alter.

3. A zagatovščik iz geven zajn meloxe,
   Oj, un got hot im geton šrekn mit a šreklexer seruxe. (?)
   Ot hajntiks jor hot nebεx badarft štarbn
   Un der vos lebt ejbik hot im fun sejfer hazixrojnes geton ojsšrajbn.

4. Štelt ajx for, menčn, vi šreklex s'iz geven fun im di kartine,
   Oj, vi er hot zix avekgeštelt in fercetn janvar šnajdn a štik rezine,
   Er hot zix nox nit gerixt af zajn umglik gor
   Ot der, vos lebt ejbik, zol im azoj gix opšnajdn zajne junge jor.

5. Štelt ajx for, menčn, vi šreklex s'iz geven der umglik, bahite got fun greser,
   Azoj hot zix cu im in bojx arajngetrofn der meser.
   Ax, vi dos meser hot cu im in bojx arajngetrofn
   Iz gevorn a raš mit ajn gepilder, az Alter der zagatovščik hot zix geštoxn,
   Azoj iz gevorn ba jedern di hercer cebroxn.

6. Bis m'iz mit im in špitol arajngekumen
   Hot zajn ganc blut af dem veg ojsgerunen.
   In zajn mine hot men af im bald derzeen,
   Az a rejne nešome tut fun der velt avekgejen.

7. Vi m'hot im nor in špitol arajngebraxt
   Hobn im bald di greste doktojrim batraxt.
   Me hot gegebn a gešrej:
   „S'iz šojn a mes, kalt vi šnej".

[1]) fus.

89.

1. Oj, got, az er colt, colt er ejnem,
   Oj, un got ax er colt, colt er er vejs šojn vemen.
   |: Got az er colt, colt er mit a col —
   Funem zagatovščikš cu redn i' šojn dos lecte mol.':

2. Vi dos jingele, der zagatovščik iz inderfri cu der arbet gegangen,
   Oj, azoj hot im got farštelt zajn šajn.
   : Azoj hot im got farštelt zajn šajn,
   Un er hot zix getrofn mitn meser in harcn arajn. :|

3. Oj, azojvi er hot nor derzeen af zix dos blut,
   Hot er gegebn a gešrej: „gute brider, s'iz mir epes nit gut,
   Oj nemt že, gute brider, ir mitamol,
   Oj, firt-že mix avek in dem jidišn špitol.
   Azoj, az er hot gehejsn nemen a droškele mitamol,
   Oje, firt šojn mix avek in jidišn špitol".

4. Oj, azojvi me hot dos zagatovščik-jingele in špitol arajngebraxt
   Oj, azoj hot im dokter Zilberštejn bald batraxt.
   Ruft zix on dokter Zilberštejn: „vos iz dos far a štot Ades,
   Oj, firt im šojn in tojt-štibl, er i' šojn a mes".

5. Azej z'men gelofn der muter di psure zogn,
   Zi iz mit a droškele cum tojt-štibl cugeforn.
   Zi hot zix gehejsn vajzn fun ir zun a simen,
   Oj, azoj hot men fun im di švarce dek aropgenumen.

6. — „Du, majn zun, bist ba mir geven hejlik un tajer,
   Un got hot dix farbrent af aza min heleš fajer,
   Acind vel ix haltn in ejn vejnen un klogn,
   Biz vanen me vet undz bejde fun danen arojstrogn".

7. In drojsn iz geven a regn mit a marake,
   Un af meščanske gas iz gevezn a drake.
   Oj, gejen fil menčn fregn: „vos iz do geven?"
   Zogt men zej, az di levaje fun zagatovščik iz geven šen.[1]

90.

Aj, efšer hot ir, menčn, gehert, oj vej, gezeen,
: In Ades hot zix an umglik getrofn: :
: Oj, a jingerman, ajn xosn·boxerl bam mašin gezesn,
Di gaz hot im af tojt, oj, gešosn. :|

. . . .
. . . .

III. DAILY-LIFE AND FAMILY SONGS

91.

1. Vos den, majn kind, vilstu nox,
   Efšer vilstu a šnajder-jung?—
   Nejn, mame, biter,
   A šnajder-jung iz biter.
   A šnajder-jung, er nejt un nejt
   Un hot kadoxes nit kajn brejt.[2]
   Nejn, mame, biter,
   A šnajder-jung iz biter.

---

[1]) šojn, [2]) brojt.

2. Iz vos den, majn kind, vilstu nox,
Efšer vilstu a šuster-jung?—
Nejn, mame, biter,
A šuster-jung iz biter.
A šuster-jung, er cit di dratve
Un er maxt di vajb a pomatre.
Nejn, mame, biter,
A šuster-jung iz biter.

3. Iz vos den, majn kind, vilstu nox,
Efšer vilstu a šmid-jung?—
Nejn, mame, biter,
A šmid-jung iz biter.
A šmid-jung, er klapt di kovadle
Un er ruft zajn vajb padle.
Nejn, mame, biter,
A šmid-jung iz biter.

92.

1. Vos-že vilstu, majn tajer kind?
Efšer gebn dir a šuster far ajn man?—
Nejn, tate, s'iz nit šejn.
A šuster-jung klapt di fleklex
Un dem vajb pačt er di beklex,
Nejn, tate, s'iz nit šejn.

2. To vos-že vilstu, majn tajer kind?
Efšer gebn dir a šnajder far ajn man?—
Nejn, tate, s'iz nit šejn.
A šnajder-jung nejt xalatn,
Dos vajb šelt er in tatns tatn,
Nejn, tate, s'iz nit šejn.

3. To vos-že vilstu, majn tajer kind?
Efšer gebn dir a stol'er far ajn man?—
Nejn, tate, s'iz nit šejn.
A stol'er-jung klapt dem kastn
Un dos vajb lozt er fastn.
Nejn, tate, s'iz šejn.

4. To vos-že vilstu, majn tajer kind?
Efšer gebn dir a beker far ajn man?—
Nejn, tate, s'iz nit šejn.
Ajn beker-jung bakt dos brojt
Un dem vajb maxt er dem tojt.
Nejn, tate, s'iz nit šejn.

5. To vos-že vilstu, najn tajer kind?
Efšer gebn dir a sojxer far ajn man?—
Jo, tate, dos iz gut.
A sojxer kojft di sxojre
Un dos vajb kušt er vi di tojre.
Jo, tate, dos iz gut.

93.

1. Ci vos-že gebn dir, majn kind?
Ci gebn dir a stol'er-jing [1]?—
Nejn, mameńu, nejn:
A stol'er-jing, er maxt a bet
Un gejt cu der xupe—traxt a get,
Nejn, mame, nejn.

[1] jung

2. Ci voz-že gebn dir, majn kind?
Ci gebn dir a šuster-jing [1])?
Nejn, mamen'u, nejn:
A šuster-jing — er maxt a por
Un rajst dos vajb far di hor,
Nejn, mame, nejn.

3. Ci vos-že gebn dir, majn kind?
Ci gebn dir a kovel'-jing?
Nejn, mamen'u, nejn:
A kovel'-jung, er klapt mitn hamer,
Er dertapt a mejdl — faršlist er in kamer,
Nejn, mame, nejn.

4. Ci vos-že gebn dir, majn kind?
Ci gebn dir a sl'eser-jing?
Nejn, mamen'u, nejn:
A sl'eser-jung er maxt a šlos
Un šlogt dos vajb inmitn gos [2])
Nejn, mame, nejn.

5. Ci voz-že gebn dir, majn kind?
Ci gebn dir a damske šnajder-jing?—
Nejn, mameńu, nejn:
Nejn, mameńu, er nejt a klejdl,
Er hot a vajb — un libt a mejdl.
Nejn, mame, nejn.

6. Ci vos-že gebn dir, majn kind?
Ci gebn dir a glezer-jing?—
Nejn, mamen'u, nejn:
A glezer-jung — er štelt di tafl'e,
Er hodevet dos vajb mit gole kaitofl'e,
Nejn, mame, nejn.

7. Ci vos-že gebn dir, majn kind?
Ci gebn dir a psačke-jing [3])?
Jo, mame, jo:
A psačke-jung — er maxt di psačke
Un halt dos vajb vi a cacke.
Jo, mame, jo.

94.

1. Ci gebn dir, majn kind, a šnajder-jung, oj vej?—
Nejn, oj mameńu, nejn:
Oj, a šnajder-jingele nejt xalatn
Un šelt di vajbele n'tatns tatn,
Nejn, mamen'u, nejn.

2. Ci gebn dir, majn kind, a stol'er-jung, oj vej?—
Nejn, oj mamen'u, nejn:
A stol'er-jingele maxt a bet
Un git dem vajbele gix a get,
Nejn, mamen'u, nejn.

3. Ci gebn dir, majn kind, a kovel'-jung, oj vej? –
Nejn, oj mameńu, nejn:
A kovel'-jingele kovet ferd
Un lejgt di vajbele gix in dr'erd,
Nejn, mamen'u, nejn.

[1]) jung, [2]) gas.
[3]) psačke-jung — parketnik.

4. Ci gebn dir, majn kind, a cirul'nik-jung, oj vej?—
Nejn, oj mamen'u, nejn:
A cirul'nik-jingele šert a pol'ke
Un firt a vajbele azojvi a l'al'ke,
Nejn, mamen'u, nejn.

5. Ci gebn dir, majn kind, a balegole-jung, oj vej?—
Nejn, oj mamen'u, nejn:
A balegole-jingele cit di viškes
Un matet ojs bam vajb di kiškes,
Nejn, mamen'u, nejn.

6. Ci gebn dir, majn kind, a šuster-jung, oj vej? —
Nejn, oj mamen'u, nejn:
A šuster-jingele maxt a por
Un kirct dem vajb gix di jor,
Nejn, mamen'u, nejn.

95.

1. Vos-že vilstu, majn lib kind?
Ci gebn dir, a šnajder-jing? — [1]
Nejn, mamé, nejn, miter,[2]
A šnajder-jing iz dox zejer biter,
Er nejt un nejt
Un hot kadoxes nit kajn brejt.[3]

2. Vos-že vilstu, majn lib kind?
Ci gebn dir a kovel-jing? —
Nejn, mame, nejn, miter,
A kovel-jung iz zejer biter,
Er klapt di kovadle
Šlogt di vajb un ruft zi padle.

3. Vos-že vilstu, majn lib kind?
Ci gebn dir a teper-jing?
Nejn, mame, nejn, miter,
A teper-jung iz dox zejer biter.
Az er cebrext a top
Vert er in kas un git dem vajb in kop.

4. Vos-že vilstu, majn lib kind?
Ci gebn dir a melamed-jing? —
Nejn, mame, nejn, miter
A melamed-jung iz zejer biter,
Er zict un knelt un kvečt di bank
Un šelt di vajb un maxt zi krank.

5. Vos-že gebn dir, majn lib kind?
Ci gebn dir a klezmer-jung? —
Jo, mame, jo, miter,
A klezmer-jung iz nit biter,
Er špilt un kvelt,
Mejdlex tancn un gebn gelt.

96.

Šusterše vajber hobn gezogt,
: Zej kenen di dratves nit maxn, :
: Beser cu nemen a šnajder a man
Un gejn in naje zaxn. :

. . . .
. . . .

---

[1]) jung; [2]) muter; [3]) brojt.

97.

1. Git mix op di mame,
Git mix op der tate
In a fremdn land,
Un hot dox mir ongezogt,
Un hot dox mir un farzogt,
Ix zol zibn jor nit zajn.

2. Bin ix nit gevezn,
Bin ix nit gevezn
Ejn jor un cvej.
Iz dox mir gevorn,
Iz dox mir gevorn
Af majn harcn zejer vind un vej.

3. Ven ix volt hobn fligelex,
Ven ix volt hobn fligelex
Volt ix dox geflojgn
Vi a frajer fojgl,
Vi a frajer fojgl
A tog mit a naxt.

4. Un volt ix gekumen,
Un volt ix gekumen
Cu a niderikeг bejmele,
Un volt zix gezungen,
Un volt zix gezungen
A raxmonesdik lidele.

5. Azojvi es iz dox biter,
Majn libe myter,[1]
A fojgele on a grinem groz.
Azoj iz dox mir biter,
Majn libe myter,
An elnte in a fremdn hojz.

6. Azojvi es iz dox biter,
Majn libe myter,
On vaser a fiš,
Azoj ix dox biter,
Majn libe myter,
An elnte ba a fremdn tiš.

7. Az du vest veln visn,
Az du vest veln visn
Zolstu lajtn fregn;
— Ci hot ir nit gezeen,
Ci hot ir nit gezeen
Majn libharcik kind?

8. — Mir hobn zi gezeen,
Mir hobn zi gezeen,
Ojfn mark iz zi gegangen,
Mit oremkajt bahangen,
Mit oremkajt bahangen,
Un hejse trern hobn zi baklangen.

9. Hot zi zix geton,
Hot zi zix geton
Far undz, oj, cu šemen,
Un hot gelozt
Ire hejse trern
Unter zix švimen.

[1] muter.

93.

1. Gej ix gix,
   Zogt zi: „drejst di šix",
   Gej ix pavol'e —
   Zogt zi, az ix krix.

   Oj vej, mame,
   Vos-že zol ix ton,
   Ix hob a šlexte šviger,
   Zi hot mit mir cuton.

2. Gej ix nox flejš,
   Zogt zi: „gole bejner".
   Gej ix kerik[1] —
   Bavarft zi mix mit štejner.
   Oj vej, mame, u. az. v.

99.

1. Ejnem iz dox zejer gut,
   Dem andern iz nox beser
   : Trinkt er tej mit ciker[2] — :
   : Un ix hob faršpilt majne junge jorn,
   Iz dox mir fincter un biter. :

2. Ejnem iz dox zejer gut,
   Dem andern iz nox beser,
   : Est er gute maaxolim — :
   : Un ix hob faršpilt majne junge jorn
   Azojvi a šlof on a xolem. :

3. Ejnem iz dox zejner gut,
   Dem andern iz nox beser
   : Gejt er šejne klejder — :
   : Un ix hob dox faršpilt majne junge jorn,
   Azojvi in a fincteru xejder. :

4. Ejnem iz dox zejer gut,
   Dem andern iz nox beser,
   : Flanct er zix a vajngortn — :
   : Un ix hob dox faršpilt majne junge jorn
   Azojvi a kart'ožnik in kortn. :

100—101.

1. Got štroft ajn menčn
   Far zajne zind,
   Ejnem in ajn ormkajt
   Dem cvejtn in ajn kind.

2. Got štroft ajn menčn
   In a grojser nojt
   Ejnem in ajn oremkajt
   Dem cvejtn in ajn tojt.

3. Mix hot er geštroft
   Mit ajn šreklexer štrof,
   Er hot farvigt majn kind
   In ajn ejbikn šlof.

[1] curik, [2] cuker.

4. In cores un lejdn
Bin ix štendik zat,
Fun der cajt on
Zint ix hob xasene gehať.

5. Doktojrim mit retues
Iz štendik ful majn štub,
Di gance velt vajzt mir ojs
Vi a finctere grub.

6. „Genug šojn ajx, majne eltern,
Vejnen un klogn,
Lojft-že gix in šul arajn
Un zol men tilim zogn.

7. Far a minjen menčn
A nomen culejgn,
Tomer vet ribojnešelojlem
Šenken dos lebn" [1]

8. Vi me hot a nomen
Gugelejgt —
Azoj iz dem ribojnešelojlem
Di nešome cugegrejt.

9. Beser zolstu nemen
Fun majn kind [2] an ejver
Ejder ix zol zeen
Dos ferte kind in kejver".

10. „Genug šojn ajx, majne eltern
Cu vejnen nox mir,
Got vet ajx opgebn
An andere far mir.[3]

11. Es iz den a novene,
Az ba a muter štarbt a kind?
Farblajbt ale gliklex,
Gliklex un gezint.[4]

12. Genug šojn dir cu lign
Af dajn klor-vajser bet,
Ix hob šojn far dir cugegrejt
A fajnem kabinet.[5]

13. Dortn vestu lign
Ejner alejn,
Varf avek di falše velt
Un lomir gixer gejn.

---

[1] Var. 6. Oj, hodit, eltern,
Vejnen un klogn,
Lejft in šul arajn
Un loz men tilim zogn.

7. Far a minjen menčn
A nomen cuculejgn,
Tomer vet mir got borx:
Šejnken majn lebn.

[2] fun mir?

[3] Var. 10. Oj, hodit, eltern,
Vejnen nox mir,
Got 'et ajx šojn opgebn
A cvejte far mir.

[4] gezunt.

[5] Var. 12. Gej šojn, toxter,
Arop funem vajsn bet,
Se štejt far dir šojn ongegrejt
Der švarcer kabinet.

102.

1. Got štroft dem menčn
   Nor far zajne zlnd,
   Ejnem in parnose
   Dem cvejtn in a kind.

2 : Ejnem in elndkajt,
   Dem cvejtn mlt a nojt,
   Ejnem tut er štrofn štark
   Mit a bitern tojt. :
   . . . . . : . . . .
   . . . .

103.

1. Der lomp vert farlošn,
   Ix ho' nox gor kajn guts nit genošn,
   Se gejt avek a junger menč fun der velt.
   Vos veln ton zajne kinderlex,
   Di jidiše jesojmimlex,
   Ver vet zej gebn a kopke gelt.

2. Du bist gekumen cu mir,
   Du bist gekumen nemen di nešome ba mir,
   Loz mix nox lebn ajn halbe šo.
   Oj, du štejst dox lebn majn bet
   Un di trebevest ba mir ajn get,
   Loz mix nox lebn cen minut.
   Lomix zix gezegenen
   Mit majn froj un klejne kinderlex
   Un got vejst ci vel ix nox zajn do.

3. — Gezegn zix, gezegn zix,
   Gezegn zix vos gixer,
   Di naxt iz šojn etvos, oj, klejn.
   Afn himl iz ojsgeruin
   Un in tojtn bux faršribn,
   S'vet dir nit helfn kejnšum gevejn.

4. Gib nor a kuk, oj, mame,
   Gib nor a kuk, oj, duše,
   Der tate ligt šojn etvos ojf tojt,
   Ot hajnt darft ir vejnen,
   Ir, jidiše jesojmelex,
   Ver vet ajx gebn a štikl brojt?

104

1. Der lomp vert farlošn,
   Oj, ix hob nox kajn guts nit genosn,
   Oj, ix gej šojn azoj jung fun der velt,
   Oj, vu-že veln ahinkumen
   Majne elente jesojmelex,
   Oj, ver-že vet jaršenen majn guts.]

2. Oj, du štejst lem [1]) der tir
   Un du nemst ba mir dir nešome,
   Oj, mit majn vajb un kinder hostu mix geget.
   Oj, vu-že veln ahinkumen
   Majne elnte jesojmelex,
   Oj, ver-že vet jaršenen majn guts.

[1]) lebn.

105.

1. Ci hot ir gehert, ci hot ir gezeen,
Vos in Bender hot zix farlofn,
Dem umglik, dem grojsn hot ir, menčn, gemuzt hern,
Oj, vos ba Avremcis šver, oj, se hot zix getrofn.

2. Oj, er hot gehat a jingl fun ejnuncvancik jor,
Vos er hot funem zereb ungehojbn dejnken.
Dem erštn tog švues af a lodke geforn,
Oj, iz in vaser arajngefaln un hot zix getrejnken.

3. Vi er hot zix nor ongehejbn trinken
Hot er ongehejbn cu maxn mit di hent:
„Ratevet mir, tavarišces, oj, arojs fun dem vaser,
Vajl ix bin šojn ba dem malxemoves in di hent".

4. Oj, vi er iz nor dertrinken gevorn
Iz er gelegn unter dem vaser a šo.
Oj, azoj iz men dox gelofn zogn di eltern di psure:
„Oj, gejt šojn, gejt šojn, Avreml iz šojn nito".

5. Vi zej hobn dos nor derhert,
Me [. . . . .] gvald;
Ratevet mir, menčn, majn kind fun dem vaser,
Ratevet im gix un bald".

6. Vi me hot nor Avremelen fun dem vaser arojsgenumen
Iz im geven der kop štark cešlogn,
Oj, tavarišces hobn im bald genumen n'a klor-vajsn lajlex arajngelejgt
Un af a droške zajnen zej mit im ahejm geforn.

7. Vi zajnt ir gevezn, Avremls tavarišces,
Mir hobn zix gor af dem grojsn umglik nit gerixt.
Eršt hot ir inejnem mit Avremlen gul'ajet,
Oj, un acind trogt ir im ojf dem tojt avek.

8. Donerštik farnaxt hot zix Avremlen a xolem gexolemt,
Er hot im dercejlt un me hot im ojsgelaxt.
Oj, er hot zix, nebex, l'ubele, fun zajn grojsn umglik nit gevust,
Un zajn xolem hot im cu zajn tojt gebraxt.

106.

1. Tojznter menčn špacirn gegangen,
Gegangen zajnen zej ale glajx,
 : Un mit der vajle derhert men a raš,
Az a menč iz arajn in tajx. :

2. Vi er iz arajn in tajx, di zun iz arop mitamol.
Azoj hot men gemaxt a plan.
 : Tojznter menčn far micves gelofn
Cu rateven a jungečkn man. :

3. Vi me hot im fun tajx arojsgenumen,
Di fis zajnen geven cebisn.
 : Vi me hot im afn tare-bet gelejgt,
Azoj hot men di tnojim cerisn. :

4. Vejnt, ale menčn, vejnt un klogt
Nemt zix arop ajn raje
 : Ix hob gemejnt cu der xupe gejn —
Cum sof darf ix gejn cu der levaje. :|

107—108.

1. Šimke (Simxe) xazer iz kajn Stambul geforn,
   Er hot gevolt (gemejnt) farbesern di jorn,
   Er hot gevolt (gemejnt) dos lebn maxn beser —
   Hot men im arajngerukt a zagranični meser.

2. Mistome iz dos im azoj geven bašert,
   Er zol lign tif bagrobn in Stambuler erd.
   Er hot gevolt zajn glajx cu di geter,
   Hot men im af morgn gelejent in di bleter.

IV. RECRUIT AND WAR SONGS

109

1. In tojznt axt hundert najn un najnciktn jor
   Demolt iz gevezn a grojser nabor,
   |: Fun vejnen, fun klogn bin ix šojn mat,
   M'hot mir opgezogt di l'gote, x'bin a fartiker soldat. :

2. Me firt mix arajn in der prisutstve,
   Me štelt mix anider neben dem stanok,
   : Oj, šteln štelt men mix azoj fajn un azoj glat,
   „Priňate", hot men a gešrej geton, un „molod'ec, saldat". :

3. Ix lejg mix anider af der kojke un ix hejb zix on cu baklern,
   Vos far a taxles ken do fun mir vern.
   : Oj, iz mir fincter un cudercu nox biter,
   Az ix darf zix šojn gezegenen mit majne foter un myter. [1] :

4. Zaj-že mir gezunt, majn getraje myter,
   Dir iz dox fincter un mir iz dox biter.
   : Zaj-že mir gezunt, majn getrajer foter,
   [. . . . .]

5. Zaj-že mir gezunt, majn getraje kale,
   Nox dir vel ix bejnken merer vi nox ale,
   : Vajl du tust inderhejm farblajbn,
   Betn bet ix dix, tajere, a brivele cu šrajbn. :

110.

1. In tojznt axt hundert najn un najnciktn jor
   Iz dox geven a grojser nabor,
   M'ot dox gegebn a sax gelt minastam
   Un me hot nit gebrakevet kajn p'ervi razr'ad.
   . . . .
   . . . .

111.

1. Ov horaxmim šojxejn bamrojmim,
   Got iz a foter iber ale jesojmim.
   [.. . . . .]
   Got iz a foter iber ale jesojmjm.

[1] muter.

2. Beser cu zingen adejnejlem
   Ejder cu kušn dem kejsers cejlem
   . . . .
   Ejder cu kušn dem kejsers cejlem.
   . . . .
   . . . .

112.

1. In Odes bin ix gebojɪn,
   Ix hob farbraxt majne ale junge jorn.
   Ajn brivele, oj, iz mir ongekumen,
   Az ix darf šojn cum priziv, oj, forn.
   Majne eltern klogn,
   Zej vejnen, zej klogn,
   Zej lozn mix nit . . . . .
   . . . .
   . . . .

113.

1. Oj, najn xadošim hot mix majn mame getrogn
   Ejder zi hot mix gehat,
   Fil tajxn mit trern hot majn mame fargosn,
   Az ix zol nit zajn kajn soldat.

2. Jeder boxer cu ejn un cvancik jor,
   Er hejbt nor on vos cu blien,
   Saj orem, saj rajx
   Cum žereb ale glajx.

3. Azojvi se kumt, oj, frajtik cu naxts
   Lig ix mir ojf majn kojke un traxt.
   X'volt beser gegangen cu kaboles hašabes
   Ejder der podfebel' a pov'erke gemaxt.

4. Azojvi se kumt šabes inderfri
   Git men a gešrej: „učeńe vyxodi"
   Ci hob ix epes gegesn, ci hob ix epɜs getrinken?
   Ix xap nox a pač cyderci.

5. Azojvi se kumt unter a milxome
   Git men a klap mitn baraban.
   Me gejt mir balejtn,
   Azojvi nox a tejtn ¹)
   Adje, majn lebn, adje, majn velt.

114.

1. Gej ix arop afn erštn trep, afn erštn trep,
   Zicn di giluxim mit o'gegolte kep.

2. Gejt cu cu mir epes ejner a jat, epes ejner a jat,
   Git a klap in plejce n'zogt: „na službu prińat".
   . . . .
   . . . .

¹) tojtn.

115.

1. Vemen veln mir dinen, brider?
Vemen veln mir dinen brider? —
Dem rusišn kejser brider,
Dem rusišn kejser brider.
: Dem rusišn kejser dinen iz nit gut,
Vajl er tut zix bodn in undzer blut. :

2. Vu-že veln mir zajn, brider?
Vu-že veln mir zajn, brider? —
In di kalte kazarmes, brider,
In di kalte kazarmes, brider.
: In di kalte kazarmes dinen iz nit gut,
Vajl er tut zix bodn in undzer blut. :

3. Af vos-že veln mir šlofn, brider?
Af vos-že veln mir šlofn, brider? —
Af di hojle kojkes, brider,
Af di hojle kojkes, brider!
: Af di hojle kojkes šlofn iz nit gut.
Vajl er tut zix bodn in undzer blut. :

4. Vos-že veln mir esn, brider?
Vos-že veln mir esn, brider? —
Boršč mit brojt, brider,
Boršč mit brojt, brider.
: Boršč mit brojt, brider, iz dox nit gut,
Vajl er tut zix bodn in undzer blut. :

5. Vos-že veln mir ton, brider?
Vos-že veln mir ton, brider? —
Dem rotner di štivl čist'en, brider,
Dem rotner di štivl čist'en, brider.
: Dem rotner di štivl čist'en iz nit gut,
Vajl er tut zix bodn in undzer blut. :

116

1. Kajn esn un kajn trinken, mame, nemt mix nit,
Ix gej arum štendik, štendik vejnendik.
Ix freg nor ba dir, tajerer got,
Farvos zol zajn majn xosn a soldat.

2. Ix vel zix cušteln a lejterl
Un ix vel arojfkrixn cu got.
Ix vel im nor fregn ejne cvej-draj verter,
Farvos zol zajn majn xosn a soldat.

3. Zol zix nor ojfxapn a šturem vint
Avektrogn zol es mix cu dir.
Ix zol nox zen dajn šejnem kop hor,
Ver šmuest zix nox cukušn mit dir.

4. Oj, du tajerer got,
Viazoj vel ix es konen cuzeen.
Der kejser vet cunemen majn tajern brul'ant
Un ix vel darfn fundervajtn štejn.

117—118.

1. A lejterl cum himl vel ix šteln,
   Un vel arojfkrixn [1]) cu got.
   Ejne cvej verter vel ix ba im fregn,
   Farvos darf zajn majn liber [2]) a soldat, oj, oj, oj.

2. Kajn lejterl cum himl vest nit šteln,
   A soldat vel ix blajbn saj vi saj,
   Nor, ńeuželi biztu aza min mejdl,
   Du zolst af mir nit vartn a jor draj, oj, oj, oj.

3. Draj jor vel ix ojf dir vartn,
   Afile cen iz ojx kedaj.
   Nor du alejn, du vejst dem gancn emes,
   Viazoj s'iz šver cu nejen šnajderaj, oj, oj, oj.

119.

1. Forn forstu fun mir avek,
   Tajer lebn majns,
   Oj, forn forstu zix cum priziv šteln
   : Oj, helf-že mir šojn, goteńu,
   Zolst arojs fun kejsers hent, :
   Un der gancer prisutstve zolstu nit geteln. :

2. Vos-že hostu mir azojns opgeton,
   Tajer lebn majns,
   Vos majn harc cit azoj cu dir, cu dir. —
   : —Ix hob dir gornit opgeton,
   Tajer lebn majns,
   Ix hob zix pošet ajngelibt in dir. :

3. Ix vinčeve nit kejnem,
   Afile nit kajn sojne
   Cu zicn afile mejdlvajz cu nejen.
   : Oj, hostu mir, oj hostu mir
   Oj, majn kop fardrejt
   Un jung fun der velt iber dir vel ix muzn gejn. :

4. Forn forstu fun mir avek,
   Tajer lebn majns,
   Fil tajxn trern vel ix tun gisn,
   : Oj, helf-že mir šojn, goteńu,
   Zolst arojs fun kejsers hent,
   Mir zoln šojn konen fun a xasene šmisn [3]). :

5. Az got hot mir geholfn, az du bist
   Arojs fun kejsers hent,
   Mir hobn ongehejbn fun a xasene cu rejdn.
   : Se hobn dajne eltern
   Cvišn undz a šejd gemaxt
   Un mir hostu faršaft cores un lejdn. :

120.

Oj, vos hostu gehat cu mir,
Un vos hostu gevolt fun mir
Un vos hostu gehat cu majne junge jorn.

[1]) var. Un arojfgejn vel ix cu got.
[2]) „ Majn šejner.
[3]) šmuesn.

Farvos hostu mir frier nit gezogt,
Az du darfst zajn a soldat.—
: Ix volt šojn lang a kale gevorn
Un efšer take xasene gehat. :

121 (122—123).

1. Fun der štub bin ix arojsgegangen
Un in drojsn iz ajn jomer mit ajn klog.
N'majne ojern hobn geton vertlex klingen,
A moblizacje hot men objavet hajnt fartog.
Oj, s'iz in mir farkilt gevorn majne glider,
Der švejs hot mir geton rinen,
: Ado ruft men zix cenojf majne alte brider
gejn vider cu dinen. :

2. Azojvi mir zajnen cum vojinske gekumen
Hot men undz gehejsn štejn ba der tir.
Vi ajn jungn soldat hot men mix cugenumen
Un di prisutstvje iz geven punkt vi frier.
N'oder majne glider zajnen švax un krank
Un di jorn zajnen ojx nit derbaj.
: Cu lign in kazarme af der hojler bank
Dinen muz men dox getraj. :

3. Me kumt mix in kazarme arajnrufn,
Un ix tor zix nit antvegn zogn „nejn“.
Me git mir a biks af cu šisn
N'a papaxa mit lange hor af majn kop cu gejn.
Oj, ados, zogt men mir, vet zajn dajn bahiter,
Un dajn hojzgezund darfstu fargesn,
: Farvos iz majn mazl ject azoj biter
Tajxn trern tu ix fargisn :

4. Ado tor ix nit zicn
Un ado tor ix nit štejn,
Majn harc vert in mir cerisn,—
Farvos kumt mir af der milxome cu gejn?
Oj, fun der štot, vos m'hot undz getribn
Mir torn zix nit gefinen in dem land,
: Do vern mir fartribn,
Mit undzer blut vert fargosn di zamd. :

5. Freg ix ba dir, goteńu, cu iz dos rext?
Ci ken dos a menč ibertrogn?
Entfer mir, ix bet dix, af der zax,
Farvos kumt mir funderhejm cu farjogn?
Oj, vej, brider, vejnt un klogt af hajntiker cajt,
Efšer vet zix got oprufn,
: Me šikt undz avek af mizrex zajt,
Ver vejst vemen veln mir dort opzuxn.[1] :

6. Oj, vej, menčn ale,
Ir zolt es gornit haltn far gring,
Me česejdt man un vajb, un xosn kale,
Fun vifl menčn vert a tel acind.
Jesojmim mit almones blajbn tojznt atog
Un kejner vil zix far zej gornit zorgn.
: Zajt-že ax cu cuern (?) cu der štrof –
Me lozt zej nit betn kajn nedoves morgn (?) :

[1] Zingendik farn fonograf hot der zinger durxgelozt di cvejte helft fumen eršrn kupl'et un eršte helft fumem cvejtn kupl'et glax nox der ferter šure hot er ongehojbn di darjcnte.

7. Der pojezd iz šojn cugekumen
  Un di vagones zajnen fincter vi in ajn štal,
  Majn harc vert in mir cerisn
  Fun di gešrejen fun di kinder af ejn kol.
  Zej šrajen zix, zej rajsn zix: „Blajbt iber do mit undz!
  Ver-že vet undz helfn in undzer nojt,
  : Kajn erd kajn ejgene iz ojx ništo ba undz —
  Farvos cu kojfn a štikele brojt". :|

8. Kajn Xarbin zajnen mir oñgekumen
  Un der raš iz geven zejer grojs,
  An eltster iz cu undz cugekumen,
  Fun di vagones zajnen mir ale arojs.
  Er hot undz ibergecejlt, vifl mir zajnen do
  Un vi di maxne iz grojs,
  : Er hot undz ongevizn di pozicje, vos iz do.
  Un patrones tejlt men undz arojs. :

124.

1. Oj, vej, in tojznt najn hundert un fufcetn jor
  Z'arojs, oj, a najer prikaz, oj, prikaz.
  : Oj, jeder foter tut firn zajn kind
  Azovi a šojxet di rind. :

2. Oj, vej, frajtik, frajtik, frajtik cunaxts,
  Oj, undzere lipelex zajnen undz faršmaxt, oj, faršmaxt.
  : Mir voltn gegangen cun a jidn af šabes,
  Oj, hot men nox di poverke nit gemaxt, gemaxt. :

3. Oj, vej, šabes, oj, šabes, oj, šabes gancfri:
  „Na skačka vyxodi, vyxodi!"
  : Ci hobn mir gegesn, ci hobn mir getrunken?
  A pač ober xapt men cyderci.[1]) :

4. Oj vej, brider, mir zajnen farfaln,
  Mir zajnen in merderše hent, oje vej,
  : Mir hobn genumen jidiše texter
  Un hobn zej faršpilt zejer velt. :

125.

1. In tojznt najn hundert un fufcetn jor
  Iz arojs a prikaz,
  : Az jeder foter zol firn zajn kind
  Vi cum šojxet a hin.[2]) :

2. Oj, vos ken er undz helfn, vos ken er undz ton,
  Mir zajnen in merderše hent,
  : Oj vej, brider, mir zajnen soldatn,
  Mir hobn faršpilt undzer velt. :

3. Axt xadošim hot mix majn mame getrogn,
  In najntn hot zi mix gehat,
  : Ict, az ix bin alt gevorn ejn un cvancik jor
  Darf ix šojn zajn a soldat. :

[1]) vi undz duxt hot der zinger cufelik gebitn di ordenung fun di strofes in dem kuplet. Lojt der melodie pasn di eršte fir šures beser far der cvejter tejl.
[1]) cudercu.
[2]) hun.

4. Me firt mix in prisutstvie: god'en, priṅat,—
Ty bud'eš xorošij soldat".
Mir lign in di okopes,
Se svišċen di pul'es,
Se flien granatn,
Mir faln vi snopes.

5. Vos konen mir helfn, vos konen mir maxn,
Mir zajnen in merderše hent,
: Mir hobn genumen jidiše texter
Un hobn farvist zejer velt. :

126.

1. Az ix bin a klejn jingele gevezn—
: Gevezn bin ix, mame, novenad, :
: Un cajt, mame, me hot mix opgegebn,
Kajn gutn tog hob ix nit gehat. :

2. Vi mir zajnen cu german'en ongekumen,
: Di germances, zej štejen far undz grejt, :
: Di eršte pul'e hot dos mix getrofn,
Az fun majne fis hot dos mix gelejgt. :

3. Vi me hot mix in lazaret arajngenumen
: Di doktojrim, zej drejen zix arum mir, :
: In a tajx blut lig ix ajngezotn,
Di pul'es, me šlept zej fun mir. :

4. A brivele šrajb ix cu majn mamen,
: Šrajbn, šrajb ix nor fun majn gezynt,[1] :
: Az di rexte hant hot men mir aropgenumen
Un af majne ojgn bin ix šojn blind. :

5. A brivele šrajb ix cu majn kale,
: Šrajbn šrajb ix ir nor fun mir alejn, :
: Az di tnojim zol zi šojn cerajsn
Un mit a cvejt jingele cu der xupe gejn. :

6. Ix hob zix gul'ajet mit tavarišċes,
: Ci hot es gehat a tam --:
: Vi-že nemt men šojn dem iectn bruder,
Er zol mir šteln a com. :

127.

1. Ix gedenk, ix bin a klejnes kind gevezn,
: Gevezn bin ix ba majne eltern tajer, :
: O, ject bin ix alt gevorn ejn un cvancik jor,
Azoj šikt men mix in dem grestn fajer. :

2. Ject lig ix in der bol'nice geraṅet,
: Cvej sanitarn, zej štejen arum mir. :
: O, di pul'es, dušen'u, šlept men šojn fun mir
. . . . ⌐ . . . . :⌐
. . . .
. . . .

№ 128.

1. Az vej dem tata un az vej der mamen,
Vos zej hobn a zum a zapasnoj.
: Me tut im on di soldatske klejder
Un me šikt im, oj, vej, glajx in boj. :

[1] gezunt.

2. Oj, vi mir zajnen cum pojezd gekumen,
   Af der ploščadke bin ix geblibn štejn.
   : Oj, vi der pojezd hot ojsgesviščet,
   Oj, ojsgebroxn hot zi ajn grojs gevejn. :

3. Oj, vejn nit, mame, oj, vejn nit, muter,
   Az got vet helfn vel ix kumen, oj, curik.
   : Du zolst mir, oj vej, majn štub ophitn,
   Du zolst mir ophitn majn vajb un kind. :

4. Oj, vi mir zajnen af der eršter pozicje gekumen,
   Oj, blas bin ix gevorn vi a blaj,
   : Oj, zeks teg in di okopes lign
   Un esn dem dritn tog ajn štikele brojt. :

5. Oj, vi mir zajnen cu der eršter pozicje gekumen,
   Oj, tojb bin ix gevorn vi di vant.
   : Di eršte pul'e hot mix getrofn,
   Aropgenumen hot mir di rexte hant. :

6. Azojvi me hot mir di rexte hant aropgenumen —
   Geblibn lign bin ix lem a breg.
   : Di sanitarn zajnen ongelofn
   Un mix cugenumen in lazaret. :

7. Vi ix bin nor in lazaret gekumen,
   A brivele tu ix cu dir šrajbn acind.
   : Šrajbn šrajb ix dir, majn tajere muter, —
   Aropgenumen hot men mir di rexte hant. :

8 Nor vejn nit, mame, vejn nit muter,
   Konst nox mejnen, az ix lig alejn.
   : Ale tog brengt men naje briderlex,
   Es vert a jomer mit a gevejn. :

129.

1. Dem erštn tog fun der mobilizacje
   Z'gevorn a jomer un a gevejn.
   : Dem erštn tog fun der mobilizacje
   Zajnen ale gešeftn geblibn štejn. :

2. Az vej z'dem tatn, n'az vej z'der mamen,
   Vos zej hobn a zun a zapasnoj.
   |: Me tut im on di soldatske klejder
   Un me šikt im avek glajx in boj. :
   . . . .
   . . . .

130.

1. Ix tu dir a brivele šrajbn,
   Un šrajbn šrajb ix dir, mame, fun majn gezynt.[1]
   |: Oj, a hant hot men mir aropgenumen
   N'af majne ojgn bin ix, mameńu, blind. :

2. Ix lig mir in bol'nice geranet,
   Un di doktojrim štejen **arum** mir
   |: Un dos harc vert mit blut opgegosn
   Un di getraje muter iz nito lebn mir. :
   . . . .
   . . . .

[1] gezunt.

131.

1. Šrajbn šrajb ix a briv cu majne eltern,
    Oj, šrajbn šrajb ix fun majn gezynt,[1])
    : Di rexte hant hot men mir opgešosn,
    Ojf majne ojgn bin ix, mame, blind. :|

132.

1. Dos fercnte jor iz ongekumen, vej, oj vej,
    Dos fercnte jor iz ongekumen,
    : Far a soldat hot men mix cugenumen, vej, oj vej. :

2. Draj teg bin ix in sirest' gelegn, vej, oj vej,
    Draj teg bin ix in sirest' gelegn,
    : Ix hob gevolt majn lebn gern, vej, oj vej. :

3. Ix bin ojfn šlaxt-feld arofgekumen, vej, oj vej,
    Ix bin ojfn šlaxt-feld arofgekumen,
    : Hob ix getrofn majn tavarišč in blut švimen, vej, oj vej. :

4. Af di grine felder, velder, vej, oj vej,
    Af di grine felder, velder,
    : Dort ligt farlejgt dos feld mit zelner, vej, oj vej. :

5. Dort ligt a zelner on a cure, vej, oj vej,
    Dort ligt a zelner on a cure,
    : On a kastn un on a kvure, vej, oj vej. :

6. Dort ligt a zelner, der kerper iz im cerisn, vej, oj vej,
    Dort ligt a zelner, der kerper iz im cerisn,
    : Fun zajn harcn tut blut gisn, vej, oj vej. :

7. Kumt a fojgl oncuflien, vej, oj vej,
    Kumt a fojgl oncuflien,
    : Štelt zix afn zelner opcurien, vej, oj vej. :

8. Štej nit, fojgl, fli gešvind, vej, oj vej,
    Štej nit, fojgl, fli gešvind,
    : Un zog majn mamen, az ix bin gezynt, vej, oj vej. :

9. Nor fun majn tojt zolstu ir nit zogn, vej, oj vej,
    Nor fun majn tojt zolstu ir nit zogn,
    : Vajl zi vet dox vejnen un klogn, vej, oj vej. :

10. Vi der fojgl iz in štub arajngekumen, vej, oj vej,
    Vi der fojgl iz in štub arajngekumen,
    : Hot er getrofn di muter štejn un vejnen, vej, oj vej :

11. Vos-že vejnstu, getraje muter, vej, oj vej,
    Vos-že vejnstu, getraje muter,
    : Im iz fincter un dir iz biter, vej, oj vej. :|

12. Viazoj zol ix nit vejnen un klogn, vej, oj vej,
    Viazoj zol ix nit vejnen un klogn,
    : Az me hot majn kind farjogn, vej, oj vej. :

13. Ix bin geblibn an almone cudercu nox blind, vej, oj vej,
    Ix bin geblibn an almone cudercu nox blind,
    : M'hot fartribn majn ejnunejncik kind, vej, oj vej. :

14. „Ven di zamd vet antrunen vern, vej, oj vej,
    Ven di zamd vet antrunen vern,
    : Dencmolt vet zix cu dir dajn kind umkern, vej, oj vej. :|

[1]) gezunt.

15. „Un di zamd iz šojn antrunen, vej, oj vej
    Un di zamd iz šojn antrunen,
    : Un majn kind vet a hejm nit kumen, vej, oj vej. :

16. On a kastn, on a mite, vej, oj vej,
    On a kastn, on a mite,
    : On a foter un on a myter,[1]) vej, oj vej :

17. Nor dos ferdl, dos getraje, vej, oj vej,
    Nor dos ferdl, dos getraje,
    : Vet bašejnen di gance levaje, vej, oj vej :

133—134.

1. Dos fercnte jor hot zix ongehejbn
    Oj, oj, oj, oj, oj oj, oj,
    Dos fercnte jor hot zix ongehejbn
    In zapas hot men mix genumen,
    Oj, vej, oj ra ra ra ram,
    In zapas hot men mix genumen, oj vej, vej.

2. Oj vej, n'di Karpatn zajnen mir gelofı
    Oj veje, veje, vej,
    Oj, in di Karpatn zajnen mir gelofn,
    Brojt mit vaser hobn mir gegesn,
    Oj, vej, ta ra rira ram
    Brojt mit vaser hobn mir getrunken, oj vej, vej.

3. Ojf di felder, grine felder,
    ta, la tala lala lam,
    Oj, ojf di felder, ojf di grine felder,
    Dortn ligt farvorfn a junger zelner,
    Oj, ta, ta la la la la,
    Dort ligt farvorfn a junger zelner,
    Ta la la la la la lam.

4. Un zajn lajb iz im cerisn,
    Ta la ta la la la lam,
    Un zajn lajb iz zix im cerisn,
    Se tut dox fun zajn lajb dos blut opgisn,
    Na ta, la la la la tam,
    Oj, se tut dox fun zajn lajb dos blut opgisn,
    Ta la la la la la lam,

5. Oj, du fojgl, švarcer fojgl,
    Ta la la la la la lam,
    Oj, du fojgl, du tajerer fojgl,
    Na dir majne hentelex un gib mir dajne ojgen,
    Oj ta, ta la la la tam,
    Oj, na dir majne hentelex un gib mir dajne ojgn,
    Ta la la la la la tam.

6. Ven kon vern di zamd cerunen,
    Ta la ta la la la tam,
    Oje, ven ken vern di zamd cerunen,
    Dencmolt vet majn man funem kejver kumen,
    Oj, ta ta la ta la la,
    Oje, dencmolt vet majn man funem kejver kumen,
    Ta la la la la la lam.

. . . .
. . . .

[1]) muter.

139.

1. In drojsn gejt a regn,
S'vet dox vern a blote,
: M'hot dox mix cugenumen,
Naznačet in pexote. :

2. Vi ix bin nor aî karpater berg aruf,
Azoj hot zix mir ahejm farglust,
: Ahejm, ahejm t'zix mir farglust,
Ahejm bin ix antlofn. :

3. Vi Mirońenko hot zix nor dervust,
Az Mejer iz a raber,
: Arajngešikt hot er policej,
M'zol im dortn gefunen. :

4. Vi policej iz nor arajn,
Aropgevorfn di hitl —
: „Anu, du Mejer, du fajner menč,
Bavajz dos rabe kvitl". :

5. Vi nor Mejerke hot dos derhert,
Kajn kap zix nit deršrokn,
: Gexapt di fis af di plejces
Un durxn fencter antlofn. :

6. Ax, du Mejer, du fajner menč,
Dercu dem rovs an ejdem,
: Vi er zet policje gejn
Krixt er afn bejdem. :

140.

1. In drojsn gejt a regn,
Se vet dox zajn a blote,
: Me hot naznačet majn tajer lebn
In devjate rote. :

2. Vi er iz ahin gekumen,
Deršrokn iz er gevorn,
: Ahejm, ahejm hot zix im farvolt
Un iz fun dortn opgetrotn. :

3. Vi er iz a hejm gekumen
Hot kejnem nit getrofn,
: „Ject hejs ix šojn a trejfer,
Fun policje antlofn. :

4. Vi policje hot zix nor dervust
Fun majn tun kumen
: Arajngešikt hot men Polišukn,
Me zol mix zuxn un gefunen. :

5. Vi Polišuk iz arajngegan,
Aropgenumen dos hitl:
: „Un-vos-že tuste do, jungerman,
bavajz mir dajn vajs kvitl". :

6. In drojsn iz er arojsgegangen:
„Un max nit on kajn gerider .
: A rubl in hant arajngeštupt
Un zol er zajn a guter brider.[1] :

---

[1] bruder.

7. Ject bin ix a fajner menč,
   A balebos's an ejdem,
   |: Az ix derze nor Krasničenken
   Antlejf ix af dem bejdem. :

Song Text Translations

I. WORKERS' SONGS

Songs About Work, Exploitation, and Poverty

1. **"Hard and Bitter as Death"**
   (1) Hard and bitter as death / Is the worker's life / Oh, he must spend his strength / For a crust of bread.
   (2) Oh, I wish for death every day / It would be better not to have been born / Than to suffer such bitter need / My days are dark, my years are bitter / Oh I wish for death every day.
   (3) I come in early and sit myself down / near the boss at the door / And dare not speak a loud word / I'm afraid he'll fire me / And take on somebody in my place.

2. **"I Get Up Early"**
   I get up early / And sit at my sewing / My heart is dried up / And I want a glass of tea / *Oy vey* / To my young years / For leaving my home.

3. **"Snow, Mama"**
   (1) Snow, mama, snow, mother / Snow, mama, and rain / And my mama brought me up / Oh, for the tailor's sake.
   (2) The tailor curses and scolds—/ And you have to put up with everything / And my mama brought me up / For the tailor's sake.
   (3) If I come in at five-thirty / Oh, the tailor says it's fine / If I come in ten minutes late / He sucks my blood.
   (4) *Oy vey,* mama, *oy vey,* mother / I go through the market / I want to buy something / The bell rings / You have to run faster.

4. **"Snow, Mama"** (variant)
   (1) Snow, mama, snow, mother / Snow and rain / Oh, you brought me up / For the tailor's sake.
   (2) Oh, at the tailor's, Oh, at the tailor's / It's very bitter / I'd eat a piece of bread every third day / Just to be with you, my dear mother.

5. **"Day and Night"**
   (1) Day and night and night and day / And stitch, and stitch, and stitch / Help me soon, God, to have my handsome one come / So I can leave work.
   (2) Stitch again and still again / Stitch and stitch and finger-prick / Oh, dear God, you know the truth / That my body is wracked.

6. **"It's Pouring Outdoors"**
   (1) It's pouring outdoors, it's pouring outdoors / And the snow is falling, the snow / Thus all my young years have passed / Always sitting at my sewing, my sewing.
   (2) Day and night and night and day / Just pricked with the needle / Oh, God, you know, oh, the truth / That my body is wracked.
   (3) My body is wracked and no one knows / Only, only God / [missing] / [missing].

7. **"Oh, I'm a Seamstress"**
   (1) Oh, I'm a seamstress / The needle's at my command / I don't have to worry about tomorrow.

(2) I don't have to worry any more / I'm not in need / I can earn / My crust of bread.

(3) The shopkeeper knows / About shoes and clothes / But he doesn't know about life / And how to spend money.

(4) No, no girl / Make the stitches straight / So the pretty shirt / Will be neat.

(5) When I was at my parents' / I was relaxed / Today when I come to them / I'm a guest.

8. "Bent Over the Machines"

(1) Bent over the machines / I sit, mama, your only child / Every muscle tense / I'm practically going blind from work.

(2) One can't enjoy anything extra / Since a penny comes hard / And meanwhile I'm thinking / That there's no one to help me.

(3) We Jews also have a custom / That without dowry there's no happiness / But I would have been content with my life / Oy vey, mama, a jewel.

(4) When it comes to the betrothal / They put the contract in your hand / I take a look / My mother sits and beams.

(5) My dear mother, precious father / Why are you beaming? / Do you know, have you assured / Your one and only child?

(6) Just after the wedding / You become the mother of a child / And the husband—he leaves / He leaves without a good-bye.

9. "Oh, I Sit Bent Over"

(1) Oh, I sit bent over in the factory / That's how I sit, a poor child / Oh, my bones are drying up / Nearly going blind from the work.

(2) Gathering, Oh, all my strength / Sidetracked / And my mind is drying up / And it's not long till a match is made.

(3) [Missing] / He eats the dowry, drinks blood / Oh, I'll be content with my life / I'll have a jewel of a man.

10. "Oh, I Sit at My Work"

(1) Oh, I sit at my work / Oh, bent over, a poor child / Every bone drying up / Nearly going blind from my work.

(2) Oh, I put a penny together with another penny / Because pennies come hard / Oh, I'm starting to figure again / That it's already not far from matchmaking.

(3) Oy vey, mama, oy vey, mother / The one I love is here already / I've taken out my work / We'll sign the contract in an auspicious hour.

(4) Oh, when we signed the contract / When they brought it to me / I sat like a stone / While my mama beamed.

(5) Oy vey, mama, and oy vey, mother / Why are you beaming? / Did you secure me good luck / Did you secure me a good world?

(6) As soon as she gets the title "mama" / She loses her strength and health / She's already lost the strength / She had as a girl.

11–12. "I Sit at My Machine"

(1) I sit at my machine / Bent over, a poor child / Every bone drying up / Nearly going blind from work.

(2) I've put my pennies together / Oh, I put them on the side / Oh, I'm losing my mind / And matchmaking's already not far off.

(3) As I gathered my pennies / I thought it was already here / I start to think again / That we'll sign the contract in an auspicious hour.

(4) Just as we sign the contract / My mother sits and beams / She has assured her only child / A piece of bread.

(5) As soon as she gets the title "mama" / She's bound by a small child / As soon as he gets the title "daddy" / He leaves without a good-bye.

13–14. "The Whole Week I Sit on My Cot"

(1) The whole week, the whole week / I sit on my cot / Just on Saturday / I get to comb my hair.

(2) I comb my hair / And arrange my hair / And look into the mirror / None to compare with me.

(3) I go outside / And I go into the house / My mother scolds me /—Who should have such luck!

(4) Oh, troubles, unpleasantness / They don't bother me / As long as someone says /—Manička, don't worry.

15. "She Works the Whole Week"

(1) She works the whole week / At the tailor's on her cot / When Friday evening comes / She's off work / She washes her head / She does her hair up / She hardly eats her soup and noodles / Before she's out of the house.

(2) She throws on the red shawl / Impatiently over one ear / She has no time to talk to anyone / Because her beau waits at the gate / She goes around with him / Till midnight / And makes a date with him / For eight o'clock at the dance class.

(3) She has always lived with trouble and sorrow / But it doesn't bother her / She catches it first from the doorman /—Why are you bothering me so late? / She takes out a fiver / And shoves it at him / She's already guaranteed / To go out with her beau all winter.

(4) Next she catches it from her mother / Just as she comes into the house / Just as she comes into the house / Her mother starts to scold /—Oh, my daughter, you'll be ruined / If you carry on like this / You go around with your beau / Until midnight / And I can tell already / You set up a date for tomorrow evening.

(5) When she sees there's a wedding / At her girlfriend's friend's house / She has to go / And grab a dance / Her beau is arranging things / And she dances to the beat / And in the morning he goes after her / And she comes home in a torn coat.

16. "I Have No Strength to Sit at My Work"

(1) I have no strength to sit at my work / And my mama says there's no way around it, *oy vey* / Oh, have pity on me and become my fiancé / Take me away from the dreadful factory.

(2) —Oh how can I take you from the factory / When I have an older sister, *oy vey* / Oh, God willing my sister will become a bride / Oh, I'll marry, oh, you.

(3) —Oh, may your mama have a bad end / May she not be able to walk on her feet / Oh, a cripple like her that travels the wide world over / He'll take her without clothes and without a penny.

(4) —Oh how can you, my dear, curse my mother / Cursing my mother is like cursing me / You'll see yet, my dear, that her character will change / You'll be her respected daughter-in-law yet.

17. "I Have No Strength to Sit at My Work" (variant)

(1) I have no strength, oh, to sit at my work / Oh, no one can see it on my face / Oh, have pity and be my fiancé / Take me away from this dreadful work.

(2) —I would like to be, oh, your fiancé / But you can't just become a fiancé / Oh, I'm a boy with my own mind / And I figure I'll be drafted.

18. "Our Years Go By"
(1) Our years go by / In heat and steam, oh, oh / See how a man of sixty / Has more strength than we do.

(2) Just like a mill, which works fine / If God stops it—oh, oh / Friday night when you still can't see stars / We already hold a fire in our hands.

(3) Oh, summer in the heat and winter in the cold / Oh, both day and night, oh, oh / May the person be cursed / Who invented the bakery.

19. "Our Strength Gives Out"
(1) Oh, our strength, oh, gives out / As we work in heat and smoke / Even a man of seventy / Has more strength than us.

20. "The Boss Lady Comes In"
(1) The boss lady comes in (*hop, dunaj, dunaj*—after each line) / Everybody, everybody, quiet!

(2) The boss lady stands and looks / Everybody, everybody, work good!

(3) The boss lady stands in the kitchen / Everybody, everybody, start stitching!

(4) The boss lady stands in the hall / May she have gallstones.

(5) The boss lady buys goods / May the plague get her.

(6) The boss lady stands at the door / Everybody, everybody, a plague on her!

(7) The boss lady stands on the threshold / May she be ruined.

(8) The boss lady goes out / Everybody, everybody, laugh at her!

21. "Madam Rabinovič Comes In"
(1) Madam Rabinovič comes in with a plush bag and a fine collar / Thinks she's pretty smart / All the workers say / She's really crazy.

(2) Rejoice, poor man, why should you worry / Why should you worry about tomorrow / Rejoice, poor man, you're lacking everything / Rejoice, poor man, happy poverty.

22. "The Machines Knock, the Wheels Turn"
(1) The machines knock, the wheels turn / There's a rush and push in the factory / *Oy vey,* get together, sisters and brothers / Let's liberate our country.

(2) The worker's life is a suffering life / He works day and night / He has no strength to stretch his muscles / The bosses worry him at night.

(3) Stop weeping and stop wailing / And don't cry over your work / Oh, an Odessa merchant will soon come / And take the work to Odessa.

(4) Let him come / Let him take the work to Odessa / We've survived things, we'll survive this / We work from seven till six.

(5) In comes the boss, in comes the boss / And says we're right / Oh, he says we have books, that we're socialists / We say bad things about Nick [Nicholas II—M.S.].

(6) [In Russian] How he's the leader, how he's the ruler / How he lives luxuriously / Oh, drinks tea, reads the paper / A good head, and a bad heart.

23. "It's Dark and Damp Outside"
(1) It's dark outside, it's damp outside / And soon will come the snow, the snow / All my young years have passed / Constantly sitting at my sewing, my sewing.

(2) Stop weeping, stop wailing / You'll stain your work, your work / Soon the master, that murderer, will come in / And drive us all away.

(3) The machines run and the wheels turn / And it's hot, hot in the room / So have all our young years passed / With bloody sweat.

(4) His children take walks, read newspapers / They say—Chocolate is sweet, sweet / They ought to try the taste of work / Stand all day on their feet, their feet.

(5) How can we not be jealous of the boss / How he lives peacefully / He sits in the bar and drinks a bottle of beer / While everyone works for him, for him.

(6) [In Russian] How can we not envy our boss / How luxuriously he lives, he lives / Drinks tea and reads the papers / And gives us workers no rest.

24. "How Can We Not Envy the Boss's Life?"

(1) How can we not envy the boss's life / He lives well, I see, like a count / He drinks good wine, smokes cigars / And lays that all on the workers.

(2) How can I think of clothes, of promenading / I tell you, it doesn't mean anything to me / When I remember that at six in the morning / I have to be in the shop.

(3) The machines knock, the metal clanks / It's smoky and hot in the room / Your head dries up, the eyes get dark / From work and sweat.

(4) Stop weeping, shedding tears / You'll stain your work / Soon the master, that murderer / will come in / And drive you from your work.

(5) They've written down our books / And made their calculation / They've decided we're socialists / We want no czar and don't believe in God.

Strike Songs

25. "You Bosses, You Murderers"

(1) You bosses, you murderers / Why do you suck the workers' blood? / Do you think the war will help you / Do you think things will always go well for you?

(2) There may be thunder and lightning / The whole world may come to an end / We'll sit eight hours a day / Anything more will cost you money.

(3) We all worked for years / Until we lived to see freedom / And now— The Petlurovites have come / And want to take our freedom back.

(4) But we'll go on, up to bloodshed / We'll take our freedom back / [Repeated].

26. "The Tailor Works All Week"

(1) The tailor works all week / He earns a dollar and a hole / That's how a tailor sews / That's how he knocks.

(2) Earlier, not today, for sure / We worked a whole night / That's how . . .

(3) Our instructions from the committee [obstruction?—M.B.] came out / We won't work anymore from eight to eight / That's how . . .

27. "Musje Maxovski"

(1) Musje Maxovski, why do you suck my blood / You let everyone work except not, oh, me / We will order you [missing] / We'll burn out your eyes with [unclear].

(2) Then he began to quiver like an arrow from the bow /—My God, people, I have no eyes / Then they all shouted at once /—Odessa is a big city, there's a hospital there.

28. "Lipson Is a Boss"

(1) Lipson is a boss / You can't lead him by the nose / They want a raise / They'll get it / They want a raise / They're worth it /—If you won't give it / It'll be bad for you.

(2) —Oh bad girls / The devil take you / Who wants a raise / You say shoes are expensive / You want a raise / You're not worth it /—If you won't give it / It'll be bad for you.

(3) —Oh, Avrom Dovid / They want a raise / They want a raise / They're going to strike / They want a raise / They scream in your teeth / And I answer / I won't give it, no!

(4) Rabinovič and Lipson / Made an agreement / They put up / Announcements on the wall—Thirty kopecks out of a thousand / I'll give to the people / And if they won't take it / They'll be blacklisted.

(5) All the cigarette workers / Made an agreement / They put up / Announcements on the wall /—The people want / Forty rubles a month / And if you won't give it / We'll go out on parade.

(6) Lipson came by / And read the notice / He read the notice / And almost cried / Ever since he's been a boss / He never heard such a thing / The blasted girls / Are sucking his blood.

29. "Good Morning, Rabinovič"

(1) Good morning Rabinovič;—Good day, Yosl Lipson /—What's new at the factory? /—In my factory I've got a storm and a strike / My workers are seeking their fortune.

(2) Oh, less work and more wages / They won't get away with that / I'll bring in the police and the guards / And arrest them all.

(3) Police and guards mill around /—You can't do anything with the workers / Give them, oh, all they demand / So they won't make any more strikes.

(4) —Oh, I won't give them all they demand / They won't get away with that / I'll take my factory abroad / And have everyone arrested.

30. "Good Morning, Moiške"

(1) Good morning, Moiške;—Good day, Yosl Lipson / What's new at the factory? /—At my factory there's noise and a strike / The workers are seeking their fortune.

31. "Good Morning, Avremele"

(1) Good morning, Avremele;—Good day, Meyer / What's new at the factory /—In my factory there's a plot and a strike / The workers are seeking their fortune.

(2) Less work and more pay / They won't get away with that / Here comes the officer of the guards / He'll arrest them all.

(3) As the guard came in /—We can't do anything with the workers / Give them their raise and eight-hour day / Then they won't make strikes.

(4) [In Russian] Down with the kulaks, whips, and cossacks / We'll carry out our demands.

32. "At Maloarnautske and Puškinske"

(1) At Maloarnautske and Puškinske in Popov's factory / A great uprising began / The uprising started about a raise /—If you keep on denying us, we'll make a strike.

(2) Ten kopeks in one thousand is no big deal / Give us our raise or we'll go out / Give us the raise—it'll be better for you / If you won't give us the raise give us our papers.

(3) [In Russian] City police and superintendents came to the factory / Raised their whips and shouted—Kikes / Get back to work I tell you / And if not, I'll put you in jail.

33. "The Uprising"

(1) The uprising started / Over a raise / They didn't want to give it / So there was a strike.

(2) At Landesman's factory / There was a commotion / There the sisters and brothers / Rose up / There was shouting / The police came in /—Down with the police.

(3) The police came in / A shout went up /—Grab these rebels / And quickly /—Listen, Kromberg / You won't get away with it / Our workers / Won't be arrested.

(4) So we sat down / All of us on the tables / And then we let / Fiškin know. Fiškin came in /—What are you doing here? / Whoever wants a raise / Can just go home.

(5) Fiškin thought / He would make things better / A cry went up /—Give us our papers /—Oh, Monsieur Fiškin / I can't understand it / To give up the papers / Is something I can't do myself.

(6) So we sat down / All of us on the tables / And we let / Landesman know / Landesman came in /—Children, what's this / I'm the great Landesman / You're leading me by the nose.

(7) Fiškin shouts /—What's the world come to / We just opened the factory / And you've already, Oh, stopped it /—Listen, Fiškin / Do you think we've forgotten / How long we brought / Food to you in jail?

(8) —Oh, listen, children / You won't get away with it / It'll cost me one thousand rubles / But they'll arrest you / I'll give you a raise / Of a lunch hour / Even without the lunch hour / There'll still be a strike.

(9) They already signed / Our work books / They already told us / They already fired us / They even said / That we're socialists / We don't want a czar / And we don't believe in God.

ADDENDA: Street Parodies and Strike Songs (1903–6). The following anti-proletarian caricature "strike songs" are interesting in that they show the naked antagonistic, philistine, and partially complicit relationship of the petit bourgeoisie to the struggles of the proletariat at the time of the 1905 revolution. We have a flagrant example of how the reactionary petit bourgeois ideology takes pains to infiltrate and affect the workers with the aid of folklore.

34. "As You Walk in All the Streets"

(1) As you walk in all the streets / You hear about strikes / Boys and girls, kith and kin / Talking about raises / Everywhere you go you hear / —Brothers, let's be free / Enough children, of loaning and borrowing / Working hard / Enough of the bad bourgeois / He sucks us like a leech / Simply without fantasizing / Make a strike.

(2) A pale seamstress / Comes home dissatisfied / She cries—Enough of being a slave / Fifteen hours for the Jew / She used to be a simple ordinary seamstress / Now she goes around with braided hair / A face like an actress / Pours a stream of words / A regular philosopher / And cries—Put your work aside / And go out on strike.

(3) A young man of the intelligentsia / Speaks unpolished / He has two golden hands for writing / And lips on hinges / Speaks Russian well, artificially / Not a word of Yiddish / Oh, long hair and a black mustache

/ A first-class poor man / Goes up to the cashier / He adds it up (unclear) / Cleans out the till / And goes out on strike.

(4) There goes a mother, crying out / Her daughter is crazy / She's involved with revolutionary literature / Seems so smart / She has buddies, may the devil take them / Gloomy folks in glasses / Long hair and white shoes / It muddles the head / Akh and vey, my daughter / She's become crude / She's been sick three-quarters of a year already / After their strike.

(5) There goes a lady shouting at her husband / She needs money for clothes / When the golden age comes / To get into warm beds / He's mad as hell at her / She shouts at him—You consumptive / Drop dead / I have to have a summer cottage / I don't care if you jump [unclear] / I have to have my May celebrations / Maybe I'll get it / From our strike.

(6) [Missing] / I sing of what I know / I always work with my energy / I sing with fire / I sing songs of the world / To please you / I sing songs of the world / I sing skillfully / Don't forget, brothers, I need money / It's after the strike now.

35. "As You Walk in All the Streets" (variant)

(1) As you walk in all the streets / You hear about strikes / Boys and girls, kith and kin / Talking about raises / In all the streets they shout / —Brothers, let's live free / Enough of borrowing and loaning / And working hard / While the bad bourgeois sucks us like leeches / Enough already, without fantasizing / Make a strike.

(2) A pale seamstress / Comes home satisfied / She speaks without fear / Talks for fourteen hours / For a long time she was / A simple seamstress / Now she lets her hair grow / A face—an anarchist / She talks without fear / About the *nasovke* [*masovske?*—M.B.]—Stop your work / With one voice: out on strike.

(3) A lady screams, woe is her / Her daughter's crazy / She's involved with revolutionary literature / And is smart / Has endless comrades / All with glasses / They come to bother their heads /—*Oy vey*, my daughter / You're getting fat / You've been suffering three-quarters of a year / For the sake of the strike.

36. "Wherever You Walk, Wherever You Stop"

(1) Wherever you walk, wherever you stop / You hear about strikes / Old folks, kith and kin / They want a raise / Old folks, kith and kin / Want to live free / Enough borrowing and loaning / And working hard.

(2) There's a man fighting with his wife / She shouts at him—consumptive / Drop dead / She shouts—I want a summer cottage / A cottage, I want a cottage / And to gain weight / She's been ill, oh, three-quarters of a year / From the first strike.

(3) One says—Put aside / Put aside your work / The second says—Put it aside / If not you'll get killed / The third says—Put it aside / Why are you working for everybody / Put aside your work / And go to your bride.

37. "As You Walk in All the Streets"

(1) As you walk in all the streets / You hear about strikes / Boys and girls / kith and kin / Talking about raises / Enough, oh, of borrowing and loaning / Let's have a free life / And discard work / And working hard / Enough, oh, of the bad bourgeois / Sucking you like a leech / Without fantasizing, brothers / Go out on strike.

(2) A girl flies in from work / Half-dead. She shouts—Oh, enough of being a slave / And toiling fourteen hours / For so long she was very simple /

And only knew about being a seamstress / Now she goes, oh, with her hair down / A face like an actress / She shouts—Discard your work / Go out on strike.

(3) A young man of the intelligentsia / Very unpolished / Has golden hands for writing / And lips on hinges / He talks Russian endlessly / But not a word of Yiddish / Black eyes, blonde mustache / A first-class poor man / He was hired as a lumber cashier / He sorts things / Empties the till down to a nickel / And goes out on strike.

(4) A mother shouts,—Vey iz mir / My daughter's crazy / She's involved with revolutionary literature / Some kind of book / A mother says:—My daughter has gotten fat and plump / She's been sick three-quarters of a year / From the strike.

(5) A wife fights with her husband / She needs money for clothes / The warm times are coming / To get into warm beds / She attacks him with terrible words / She calls him a consumptive / She says,—You pest, sick at home / I need a summer cottage / You can dance [unclear] I have to have a [unclear] / If I don't get it / I'll go on strike.

Struggles and Victims

38. "When We All Gathered"

(1) When we all gathered / The Sakavička synagogue was too small / And whoever tipped off the police / Should lie in the Kiev hospital.

(2) When the police chief came into the synagogue / We started to fight with him / Soon Cossacks and guards came into the synagogue / And they started, Oh, to arrest everyone.

(3) When they arrested, Oh, all of us / At two in the morning / When everyone is sound asleep / They locked us all up in jail.

(4) When they sent us out to Vasil'kov / At noon / Weeping and wailing started / Among our brothers and sisters.

(5) When they brought us to the station / They made a chain of checkers / They didn't let mothers see their children / To give them a piece of bread.

39. "Oy Vey, Brothers and Sisters"

(1) *Oy vey,* brothers and sisters / We all truly love each other / But if the police should know / That we're all gathering in one room . . .

(2) We all gathered in a full room / We were all there together / And whoever tipped off the police / Should rot in the Kiev hospital.

(3) In the morning the precinct head came to us / We fought with him a little / Then the police and guards came running / And they arrested us all.

(4) They arrested us all / It was about two in the morning, / Then they gathered us up / And locked us in jail.

(5) In the morning they had to send us to Vasil'kov / That was about two in the afternoon / All the mothers and fathers came running / And there was weeping and wailing.

(6) Oh, stop weeping and wailing / Don't sink so low / Some day people will envy you your children / Since they suffer, poor people, for the whole people.

40. "You Can Hear Commotion Near the Sofievke"

You can hear commotion near the Sofievke [a park in Uman'] / Sisters and brothers have gathered / They've gathered a big group / Outdoors at a meeting.

41. "We Gathered an Assembly"

(1) We gathered an assembly / And a spy saw us / They took us with great ceremony / Right to the chief of police, oh, at home.

(2) We testified / And they let us go home / They let us go home / But not our oldest brother / We have to support him / To the last drop of blood.

(3) Come together, oh, sisters and brothers / I'll explain to you / How we work from eight till ten / Work for nothing / And how we work from eight till six / I'll explain to you.

(4) Sisters and brothers, we're singing songs / We're singing about ourselves / We sing songs loudly / God willing, we'll get home.

42. "Weeping and Wailing the Ninth of January"

(1) Weeping and wailing the ninth of January / They're taking him from the stock exchange to the jail.

(2) As soon as they took him there / We all made a vow.

(3) Brothers and sisters, don't be scared of jails / Arouse all the people out of the jails.

(4) Out of the jails with bombs and dynamite / Destroy the tyrants that suck our blood.

(5) They suck our blood like the best wine / The czar and the government should go to hell / And they will.

(6) Then we, the workers, will raise our heads / The world will be renewed / Then we, the workers, will be liberated.

43. "Saturday Afternoon There's Weeping and Wailing"

(1) Saturday afternoon there's weeping and wailing / They're taking the workers from the stock exchange to the jail.

(2) As soon as they brought them to jail / They made charges.

(3) Sisters and brothers, don't be afraid of jails / Arouse the brothers from jail.

(4) Out of jail, with bombs, with a raid / The tyrants aren't silent, they suck our blood.

(5) They suck our blood, they drink the best wine / Nick and the government should go to hell.

(6) When Nick goes to hell / Only then will our workers raise their heads.

(7) When they shouted—Jews and Christians / We answered—Down with capitalism.

(8) When they shouted—Left, to the right / We answered—Down with autocracy!

44. A Variant of the "Hirš Lekert Song"

(1) As Jisker left his house / He said good-night to his wife / As Jisker went to the theater / He thought his life over well.

(2) As Jisker went in to the theater / He took a ticket in the first row / As Jisker went into the theater / He bided his time.

(3) As the governor left the theater / He shouted,—Here, driver / Jisker whipped out his revolver / And hit him in the side.

(4) As Jisker shot the governor / There was noise and commotion / One shouted to another /—Here's where our brother fell.

(5) When the police brought Jisker in / They locked him in a cell / Jisker sits by the little fire / And thinks his life over well.

(6) The Jewish chaplain came in to see Jisker / —Say your confession, my child /—Away, away, you Jewish tyrant / Oh do what you want with me.

(7) —Send in my wife Tajbele /—Let me say farewell to you / If you give birth to a boy / Name him for me.

45. "On the First Day of Elul"

(1) On the first day of Elul, mama, at night / Oh, I lie and think / Of how they made a dragnet at Greenberg's, *oy vey* / My heart told me, oh, mama, that today would be the last evening / Oh, I lie and think.

(2) Oh, twelve o'clock, mama, it's already midnight / Oh, I lie and think / Oh, doors and gates on the prison, mama, are locked / My heart tells me, mama, that today would be the last evening.

(3) Oh, one o'clock, mama, still the middle of the night / Oh, I lie and think / Oh, mama, when they brought in the verdict / My heart told me, mama, that today would be the last evening.

(4) Two o'clock, mama, at night / Oh, I lie and think / How they brought me, mama, my father /—*Oy vey*, come here, father, to me, let me say farewell / Let me say farewell to you.

(5) Oh, three o'clock, mama, at night / Oh I lie, mama, in a solitary cell and think / *Oy vey*, my heart told me, oh, mama / That today would be the last evening.

(6) Oh, four o'clock, mama, the night is almost over / Oh, I lie and think / How they brought me the Jewish chaplain, *oy vey* /—Come here, my child, to me / and let me confess you.

(7) Oh, five o'clock, mama, the night is almost over / Oh, I lie and think / Oh, how they brought me, mama, my sister / *Oy vey*, sister, come to me / You won't see me any more.

(8) Oh, six o'clock, mama, the night has passed / I lie and think. / Oh, how they brought us, mama, to the Odessa gallows, *oy vey* / There was weeping and wailing in Odessa— / Two brothers hung in one day.

46. "Gnesje Left Work"

(1) Gnesje left work / She didn't yet know about her misfortune / Out came the murderer, the police chief / And shot her for nothing.

(2) The streets along which they took her to the hospital / Were full of blood / When they brought her into the hospital / She lived only ten minutes.

(3) Brothers, we can't keep silent / About our comrades' blood / We have to wash away our blood / With bombs every minute.

47. "Oh, Wednesday Is the First of May"

(1) Oh Wednesday is the first of May / Our comrade Išike went swimming / Suddenly a terrible telegram came / And our comrade Išike was drowned.

(2) And we, comrades, as soon as we heard it / We sat with long faces / But we, comrades, we'll all go / And encircle the Pejterov River.

(3) As we set out in boats / We couldn't find comrade Išike / Until Josl the filler let a net into the water / And pulled out comrade Išike by the foot.

(4) As we pulled him out of the river / They took him across all of Pejterov / Just covered his head, which started to bleed / And covered his face with a white cloth.

(5) As we were carrying him / Along came the police chief and wouldn't let us /—Oh get away, you murderer, you big hooligan / We brought comrade Išike into the house.

(6) As we brought him into the house / The mother was sick at heart / Oh, we comrades we must weep and wail / Since we are burying such a good brother.

(7) Oh, his clothes lasted an hour and five minutes / And we took comrade Išike from the world / Just the red flag, which hangs over his grave / Išike's face is covered with damp earth.

48. "The Book with Secrets"

(1) We lost, comrades / The book with secrets / If that's so / There go the guards.

(2) The guard came to me / And took my testimony / But I tell him no, I wasn't at the meeting.

(3) He starts hitting me / To make me tell the truth / But if I tell him the truth / He'll drive me to Siberia.

(4) He put me in a dark prison / Where by day it's worse than at night / They put us, comrades, in prison / Locked up in dark rooms.

(5) Did I injure someone? / Did I kill someone? / Why must I sit in jail? / Why must I go to Arkhangel'sk?

49. "I Finished Eight Grades"

(1) I finished eight grades / I am a boy just out of school / I carried out, carried out, a great role / Sisters and brothers, hold together.

(2) They seized me with my books / They put me in jail / Come together, sisters and brothers / Is there a God in the world?

(3) They condemned me to a dark room / I have no pen and paper / I hear a voice, the voice of my brothers / But I can't go out to them.

(4) Who builds these fine walls? / The worker builds these fine walls / Oh, and ask yourself who lives there? / The rich man lives there.

(5) The poor man, who lives in a cellar / The wet and the damp trickle from his walls / From this he gets rheumatism / In his hands and feet.

(6) Who plants the fine vineyard? / The worker plants the fine vineyard / Oh, and who eats the good fruit? / The rich man eats the good fruit.

50. "They Lead Me into a Dark Room"

(1) They lead me into a dark room / There's no pen and ink / I hear a noise, my chains clink / I want to sing you a mourning-song.

(2) I learned a bit of Gemora / As a boy I left school / I decided on a new manner / Sisters and brothers, don't let go.

(3) I used to sit and sing songs / I used to say, there's no God / We sit in prison for our truth, sisters and brothers / Now we sit in jail.

(4) They seized me with my democratic books / They put me in jail / Now all say, sisters and brothers / That there's a God.

(5) The beautiful walls and the high palaces / They're worked on by the workingman / But look who lives, oh, there? / Just the bastard, the rich man.

(6) The great gardens and the great parks / They're planted by the working-man / But look who walks, oh, there? / Just the bastard, the rich man.

(7) The workingman lies in the cellar / Dampness engulfs him from all the walls / From this he gets rheumatism / In his feet and hands.

51. "Who Builds Walls, Palaces?"

(1) Who builds walls, palaces? / And who builds? The workingman / Oh, look, oh, who lives in them? / Not him, but the rich man.

(2) The workingman lives in a cellar, a damp one / Where the water runs from the walls / From this he gets a great disease / In his hands and feet.

(3) I learned a little Gemora / Thank God I left school / I took on a new role / Oh, sisters and brothers, hold together.

(4) Stop clinking your chains / And let it be a little quiet / Let me sing my song / Then you'll know who I am.

(5) Did I stab someone? / Did I kill someone? / Did I pick a lock? / Why have they locked me up in jail?

(6) You, my child, as you grow up / You should be a whole person / When I sing my song / I'll be a whole person.

(7) Dear brothers, when I die / Go to my body / Put the red flag with its colors / At the head of my grave.

52. "The High Walls"

(1) The high walls—Who builds them? / Who builds them? The working man / And look, who lives there? / No one but the rich man.

(2) The poor man lives in the cellar / And water runs from the walls / From this, he gets rheumatism / In his hands and feet.

(3) Oh, dear brothers when I die / Go to my body / Put the red flag with its colors / At the head of my grave.

53. "There in a Corner"

There in a corner in a damp cellar / On the hard ground on a bit of straw / Lives a worker with lung disease / He lies, groans, and cries—*Oy vey* / Listen, my child, to my last words / Listen carefully / Before I take leave of you / Listen, and give me your hand / You won't keep silent about my life / How I'm dying young / You must count up and write down / You must take revenge for my premature death.

54. "There in a Corner"

There in a corner in a cellar / On the hard ground, on a bunch of straw / Lies a worker with a chest disease / He lies, cries, and moans—oh / Listen, my child, to my last words / Listen very carefully / Before I take leave of you / Swear and give me your hand / That you won't keep silent about my life / How I'm expiring so young / *Un in inordenung* [?—M.B.] he dies without faith / You should take revenge for my premature death.

55. "You Can Hear the Steps of Tyrants"

(1) You can hear the steps of tyrants / About two o'clock at night / Then one of our stars falls / Of those that shine at night / We haven't stopped weeping and wailing / Over those they sent to Siberia / Suddenly we heard a rumor / That they arrested a brother / Oh, how bitter is the land / Where we're going, to such conditions / For our true, oh, sisters and brothers / But who, who, who knows / If we'll have the consolation / Of seeing them again.

(2) The way you entice a bird into a cage / That's how they took our brothers / In the dark jail, where no light shines / Where no one comes, there, under thick walls / He sits black as coal / The head supported by the skinny hands / He sighs, it can break your heart / Oh, the free world / Is hidden from me / I can't go out on the street / To help them there / If only with a good word / Our brothers expiring from hunger.

(3) The holy spirit, it doesn't let me live / Even here in jail / Every day new machines come / Tyranny is too small for the spirit / You can deal with me / Like with a Russian spy / You can rot my limbs / But that which I know / I won't let out / I'll be true to my brothers.

(4) Not the first, and not the last / Falls there / Gather strength for revolution / And you'll be a hero.

56. variant

57. "In Far-off Siberia"

(1) In far-off Siberia / Where the sky is always black from rain clouds / There I was sent / For a word, for freedom / They beat me with a whip / So

I would no longer say: / Hail freedom, to hell with Nikolai.

(2) Oh, in far-off Siberia / Where the sun never shines / There I was for a long time / Summer in the heat and winter in the cold / Dragging wheelbarrows / All for a word.

58. "In Far-off Cold Siberia"

(1) In far-off cold Siberia / Where the sky is rain-cloud black / I suffered there endlessly / My heart broken in pieces / In the greatest cold / Naked in the fields / They drove us, there / Tortured and beat us / So we would no longer say /—Hail freedom, the Internationale / But now the happy time has come / When we hear from far and near / That Russia is bright / That Russia is free /—Hail freedom / Down with Nikolai.

(2) In far-off cold Siberia / I met many great people / Victims of the police / Innocent victims of the bad days / I met great philosophers / There myself / In that unhappy land / Many young men and women / Russia's best thinkers / They won't give them freedom for the one word: / Hail freedom, down with Nikolai / But know the time has come / the happy time / When we hear from far and near / That Russia is bright / That Russia is free / Hail freedom / Down with Nikolai.

59. variant

Revolutionary Hymns and Songs

60. "How Holy Is Nature"

(1) How holy is nature / With her free manner / Truth and love / Are her ornaments, her jewels.

(2) We put our right hands on our hearts / Now we truly swear / For life and death, like an iron wall / When the sword gleams from truth.

(3) When one of us is too weak / Since capitalism is too poisonous / Like a snakebite.

(4) When bound with truth and love / Our band stands fast like a wall / And love is kindled in our hearts / The love of freedom and of human happiness.

(5) Our blood demands revenge / Good things always grow from our blood / They pull goods and riches from our bones / Ah, and at the end they step on us like stones.

(6) Brothers and sisters, take each other's hands / Come to the fire, which flickers / We're the proletariat, that means the working people. Let us break the iron chains / Throw off the heavy yoke / Shout: Forward the people, forward, forward!

61. "We Have Planted a Lovely Vineyard"

We have planted a lovely vineyard / Beautiful flowers, red, pink, and white / But wild animals have trampled it / They've exchanged truth and love for jealousy, hatred, and slavery.

Let's put our right hands on our hearts / And truly swear / Through death and life like an iron wall / When the sword of truth gleams.

And if one of us is too weak / Then capitalism is too poisonous / Like a snakebite.

When bound with truth and love / Our band stands, like a wall stands fast / If the sun goes down—In our heart will be kindled / The rising sun of freedom.

Our blood demands revenge / Good things always grow from our health

/ They draw goods and riches from our bones / But they walk on us like stones.

Therefore, brothers and sisters, give each other your hands / And swear by the flicker of the fire / We are the proletariat, that is, the simple people / We must break the heavy chains / And throw off the heavy yolk / So shout—The people forward.

Brothers, let us awake / Make an end of tyranny / We must trample on tyranny / And make Russia free.

62. "The First Thing We'll Seize"

(1) The first thing we'll seize after taking power / Is the exploiters who suck our blood.

(2) To free poor people / Who suffer hunger and poverty / They should bless the world of freedom / They should no longer be in need.

(3) Take the Russians from the rooms / Who are still in dark buildings / Come together, all you sisters and brothers / To liberate our world / To liberate the poor world.

63. "Go, Brothers, Go"

(1) Go, brothers, go / Do demand bread / From czars and dukes / Demand human rights / They shouldn't treat you so badly / Demand everything we've created / [Refrain:] Arise, brothers, we'll wake you / And come forward to battle, and don't be afraid / And to live / And to struggle / And to fight in a strike / Go and be liberated / From the new times.

(2) The rabbi and the priest / They muddle our heads / With sin, with their religions / Oh these good deeds and sing / Make the worker blind / So he won't see how he's robbed. [Refrain]

(3) The socialist / Is not a Jew and not a Christian / Just a man with a clean conscience / Under his red banner / There's no religion / Just two classes: poor and rich. [Refrain]

64. "What Do the Rulers Want?"

(1) What do the rulers want, what do the vampires want / They take the last bit of blood from the worker / And then you'll know what exploitation is / To seek a better life for yourself.

(2) The workers' struggle goes farther and farther / Put yourself in the fight for the working class / And then you'll know what exploitation is / To seek a better life for yourself.

65. "Brothers, If God Won't Help Us"

Brothers, if God won't help us / Let us liberate ourselves / Let us break the chains and walk together.

66. "Oh You Foolish Zionists"

(1) Oh you foolish Zionists / With your silly minds / You should go to the workers / And learn some sense from them.

(2) You want to take us to Jerusalem / So we can starve there / We would rather stay in Russia / And liberate ourselves.

Melodies to Songs by M. Vintshevsky, D. Edelshtat, and Others

67. "The Spirit of Liberty" (Vintshevsky)

The spirit of liberty calls in the streets to the masses of oppressed peoples / I bring weapons for the slaves, I liberate the worker-slaves and make them free.

68. **"There's Movement"**

Listen children, how there's movement, how there's movement everywhere / How the worker prepares for the struggle with capitalism / For the death struggle with exploiters, with the magnates, with the money tyrant / Listen how there's movement, children, among the robbed worker.

69. **"To the Workers' Friends"**

(1) I hear your voice, the voice of truth / The voice of the true workers' friend / I hear it from afar, I hear it clearly / I greet you with hearty love today.

(2) And ask you to explain to my poor brethren / Who work hard in these days / Who work the marrow from their bones / They sacrifice everything to the altar of money.

70. **"Three Sisters"**

In England there's a city of Leicester / And in London there's a square of that name / And in the square every day they stand, those girls, all three alike.

71. **"A Broom and Dustpan"**

Enough! I will no longer feed idlers / Enough of trembling for nobles, get me a broom / Out, my lord and nobleman, with a fat, heavy belly / You moralizers, aristocrats and clergy, go too / I need no middlemen, just a broom and dustpan / No middleman, no titled man, and no clergy and more.

72. **"My Testament"**

My dear friends, when I die, carry our banner to my grave / The free banner with its red colors, sprinkled with workers' blood.

73. **"My Testament"** = no. 72.

74. **"The Evening Bell"**

Oh, must, do not call me with your magic finger / Do not awaken the strings of my sick heart / Your pale singer is condemned to death / At the end it's the song of struggle and pain.

75. and 76. = no. 74.

77. **"Awake!"**

How long, oh how long, will you still remain slaves and wear the shameful fetters / How long will you create gleaming riches for those that rob our bread?

78. **"In Battle"**

We are hated and driven, we're persecuted and harassed / All because we love the poor, languishing folk, the poor, languishing folk.

79. **"My Last Hope"**

I lost my youth in storms and struggle / And didn't know of happiness and love / Only bloody tears and bloody wounds / Boiled and burned in my breast.

80. **"To the Working Women"**

Working women, you suffering women / You women that languish at home and in the factory / Why do you stand aloof, why don't you help build / Your temple of freedom and human happiness / Help us carry the red flag / Forward, through storms and dark nights / Help us to spread truth and light / Among the unknowing miserable slaves.

81. "Come Together"

Come together, from all nations / To our red flag / We'll all go together / United in one nation / We'll protect the weak / We'll fight the rich, come here, come here / We're all children of one mother, we'll all go together / Against the enemy, against the enemy.

82. "Brothers, We've Sealed" (M. Sorerives)

Brothers, we've sealed a union for life and death / We stand in the battle like comrades with the red banner in hand.

83. "Sleep, Oleška" (Sholem Aleichem)

Sleep, Oleška, my heir, bright person / Sleep, only child, my kaddish, sleep, and don't cry.

II. SONGS ABOUT ARTISANS

84. "A Tailor Sits"

(1) A tailor sits with crossed legs / And sings a sugar-sweet song.
(2) I stand by the door / And an official coach comes to me.
(3) I ask—Where are you going / They say—Just to you.
(4) From the iron, from the scissors / I put a pearl necklace on my wife.

85. "That's the Way a Tailor Sews"

That's the way a tailor sews / That's the way he throws stitches / A tailor sews, and sews, and sews / And has a plague, and no bread.

86. "The Tailor Sits at His Work"

(1) The tailor sits at his work / Makes two pairs of pants from one / And has everything in the house / And his pockets jingle too / He sings at every stitch,—*xr,* stitch, *foo,* stitch, a stitch / He sings at every stitch / And finishes his work, his work / And doesn't fall down / *xr* / down / *foo* / down / down.
(2) At Simchas Torah / He takes one too many / And is a sexton at the synagogue / He quietly takes a drink / And as he comes to the synagogue / *xr,* in, *foo,* in, in / And as he comes in the synagogue /—Give me a *hakofe* / If not, to hell with you.

87. "With a Needle, Without a Needle"

[Refrain:] With a needle, without a needle / I sew with great pomp.
(1) I sit with my legs crossed / Because my work is sugar-sweet.
(2) I sew and sew a whole week / And sew a Parisian hole.
(3) I pull together my basting / And eat grits.
(4) On the Sabbath I go out like the Bible says / In my own clothes, that I sewed myself.

88. "Listen, All You People"

(1) Listen, all you people / From big to small / Oh, who hasn't heard or seen of the misfortune / I'll explain it to you, people, and ask you to listen through my song thoughtfully.
(2) Oh, the song is about a young child / Oh, to whom a misfortune quickly happened / He was indifferent to his work / And he was named Alter.
(3) He was a *zagatovščik* [one who prepares the material for someone else to work on—M.S.] / Oh, and God terrified him with a terrible *seruxe* [?—M.B.] / Poor thing had to die this year / And he who lives eternally had to inscribe him in the eternal book.

(4) Imagine, people, how terrible the picture was / Oh, as he began to cut a piece of rubber on the fourth of January / He didn't imagine his misfortune / That He who lives eternally would cut him off at an early age.

(5) Imagine, people, how terrible was the misfortune, may God protect you from greater ones / The knife hit him in the heart / There was noise and commotion when Alter the *zagatovščik* stabbed himself / Everyone's heart was broken.

(6) Until they brought him to the hospital / All his blood ran out on the street / You could see by his looks / That a pure soul had left the world.

(7) When they brought him to the hospital / The greatest doctors examined him / Soon a shout went up /—He's already dead, cold as snow.

89. "Oh, When God Strikes"

(1) Oh, when God strikes He strikes one / Oh, and when God strikes, He knows whom to strike / When God strikes, He really strikes / This is the last time to speak to the *zagatovščik*.

(2) When the boy, the *zagatovščik,* went to work in the morning / Oh, God hid his radiance / As God hid his radiance / And he struck his heart with a knife.

(3) Oh, as soon as he saw the blood / He shouted—Good brothers, I'm not well, Oh take me, good brothers, right away / Oh take me to the Jewish hospital / As soon as he ordered a carriage /—Oh take me to the Jewish hospital.

(4) Oh, when they brought the *zagatovščik*-boy to the hospital / Oh, Doctor Zilberštejn examined him / Doctor Zilberštejn cried—What kind of city is Odessa / Oh, take him to the morgue, he's already dead.

(5) When they ran to tell the mother the news / She went to the morgue in a carriage / She asked to be shown a sign / Oh, they took the black cloth off him.

(6) —You my son, were holy and dear to me / And God has burned you in such an internal fire / Now I'll weep and wail / Until they'll take us both from here.

(7) It was raining and foggy outside / There was commotion in the street / Oh, many people came, asking—What happened here? / They told them that the *zagatovščik's* corpse was beautiful.

90. "Ah, Maybe You Heard, People"

Ah, maybe you heard, people, *oy vey,* and saw / There was a tragedy in Odessa / Oh, a young man, a fiancé, sat at his machine / And the gas shot him to death.

III. DAILY-LIFE AND FAMILY SONGS

91. "What Do You Want, My Child"

(1) What do you want my child /—Perhaps you want a tailor-boy /—No, mama, bitter / Plague, not bread / No, mama, bitter / A tailor-boy is bitter.

(2) —What do you want, my child / Perhaps a shoemaker-boy? /—No, mama, bitter / A shoemaker-boy is bitter / A shoemaker-boy pulls the threads / And curses his wife / No, mama, bitter / A shoemaker-boy is bitter.

(3) —What do you want, my child / A blacksmith-boy? /—No, mama, bitter / A blacksmith-boy is bitter / A blacksmith-boy hits the anvil / And calls his wife a bitch / No, mama, bitter / A blacksmith-boy is bitter.

92. "What Do You Want, My Dear Child?"

(1) What do you want, my dear child? / Maybe we should give you a shoe-maker as a husband? /—No dad, it's not nice / A shoemaker-boy bangs the spots / And smacks his wife's cheeks / No, dad, it's not nice.

(2) —What then do you want, my child? / Maybe we should give you a tailor as a husband? /—No, dad, it's not nice / A tailor-boy sews cloaks / And curses his wife / No dad, it's not nice.

(3) —What then do you want, my dear child? / Maybe we should give you a carpenter as a husband? /—No, dad, it's not nice / A carpenter-boy bangs the chest / And lets his wife starve / No dad, it's not nice.

(4) —What then do you want, my dear child? / Maybe we should give you a baker as a husband? /—No, dad, it's not nice / A baker-boy bakes bread / And makes his wife drop dead / No, dad, it's not nice.

(5) —So what do you want, my dear·child? / Should we give you a merchant as a husband? /—Yes, dad, that's good / A merchant buys goods / And kisses his wife like the Bible / Yes, dad, that's good.

93. "What Should We Give You, My Child?"

(1) —What should we give you, my child / Should we give you a carpenter-boy? /—No mama, no / A carpenter-boy makes a bed / Goes to the altar —thinks of divorce / No, mama, no.

(2) —What should we give you, my child? / Should we give you a shoemaker-boy? /—No, mama, no / A shoemaker-boy makes a pair / And pulls his wife's hair / No, mama, no.

(3) —What should we give you, my child? / Should we give you a blacksmith-boy? /—No, mama, no / A blacksmith-boy bangs with a hammer / Catches a girl and locks her in a room / No, mama, no.

(4) —What should we give you, my child? / Should we give you a locksmith-boy? /—No, mama, no / A locksmith-boy makes a lock / And beats his wife right in the street / No, mama, no.

(5) —What should we give you, my child? / Should we give you a lady's tailor-boy? /—No, mama, no / No, mama, he sews a dress / Has a wife and loves a girl / No, mama, no.

(6) —What should we give you, my child? / Should we give you a glazier-boy? /—No, mama, no / A glazier-boy puts in a frame / And feeds his wife just on potatoes / No, mama, no.

(7) —What should we give you, my child? / Should we give you a floor-layer boy? /—Yes, mama, yes / A floor-layer boy makes parquet / And keeps his wife like a pet / Yes, mama, yes.

94. "Should We Give You a Tailor-Boy?"

(1) —Should we give you, my child, a tailor-boy, *oy vey?* /—No, oh mama, no / A tailor-boy sews cloaks and curses his wife / No, mama, no.

(2) —Should we give you, my child, a carpenter-boy, *oy vey?* /—No, oh mama, no / A carpenter-boy makes a bed / And gives his wife a divorce / No, mama, no.

(3) —Should we give you, my child, a blacksmith-boy, *oy vey?* /—No, oh mama, no / A blacksmith-boy shoes horses and puts his wife in her grave fast / No, mama, no.

(4) —Should we give you my child, a barber-boy, *oy vey?* /—No, oh mama, no / A barber-boy cuts hair / And treats his wife like a doll / No, mama, no.

(5) —Should we give you, my child, a coachman-boy, *oy vey?* /—No, oh mama, no / A coachman-boy pulls the rein / And gives his wife a pain / No, mama, no.

(6) —Should we give you, my child, a shoemaker-boy? /—No, oh mama, no / A shoemaker-boy makes a pair / And shortens his wife's years / No, mama, no.

95. "What Do You Want, My Dear Child?"

(1) —What do you want, my dear child? / Should we give you a tailor-boy? /—No, mama, no, mother / A tailor-boy is very bitter / He sews and sews / And has a plague and no bread.

(2) —What do you want, my dear child? / Should we give you a blacksmith-boy? /—No mama, no, mother / A blacksmith-boy is very bitter / He hits the anvil / Beats his wife and calls her bitch.

(3) —What do you want, my dear child? / Should we give you a potter-boy? /—No, mama, no, mother / A potter-boy is very bitter / When he breaks a pot / He gets mad and hits his wife in the head.

(4) —What do you want, my dear child? / Should we give you a teacher-boy? /—No, mama, no, mother / A teacher-boy is very bitter / He sits, drones, and wears out the bench / And curses his wife and makes her sick.

(5) —What should we give you, my dear child? / Should we give you a musician-boy? /—Yes, mama, yes, mother / A musician-boy is not bitter / He plays and beams / Girls dance and give money.

96. "Shoemakers' Wives Say"

Shoemakers' wives say / They can't make threads / Better to take a tailor as a husband / And get into new things.

97. "My Mother Gives Me Away"

(1) My mother gives me away / My father gives me away / Into a foreign land / And they told me / And they told me / I shouldn't come back for seven years.

(2) I didn't go back / I didn't go back / One year, and two / But I felt / But I felt / Very sad in my heart.

(3) If I had wings / If I had wings / I would fly / Like a free bird / Like a free bird / A day and a night.

(4) And I would come / And I would come / To a low tree / And I would sing / And I would sing / A pitiful song.

(5) It's so bitter / My dear mother / A bird without green grass / It's so bitter / My dear mother / To be lonely in a strange house.

(6) It's so bitter / My dear mother / Like a fish out of water / It's so bitter / My dear mother / To be lonely at a strange table.

(7) If you knew / If you knew / You should ask people / Haven't you seen / Haven't you seen / My dear child?

(8) We've seen her / We've seen her / She was in the market / Covered with poverty / Covered with poverty / Weeping hot tears.

(9) She began / She began / To be ashamed before us / And let / Her hot tears / Flow down below.

98. "If I Walk Fast"

(1) If I walk fast / She says—You'll ruin your shoes / If I go slow / She says I'm creeping. [Refrain:] *Oy vey,* mama / What should I do / I have a bad mother-in-law / She's always after me.

(2) If I go for meat / She says it's all bones. / If I go back / She throws stones at me. [Refrain]

99. "Some People Have It Good"

(1) Some people have it good / Others even better / He drinks tea with sugar / And I've wasted my youth / It's dark and bitter for me.

(2) Some people have it good / Others even better / He eats tasty dishes / And I've wasted my youth / As in a dark room.

(3) Some people have it good / Others even better / He wears beautiful clothes / And I've wasted my youth / As in a dark room.

(4) Some people have it good / Others even better / He plants himself a vineyard / And I've lost my youth / Like a gambler at cards.

100–101. "God Punishes a Person"

(1) God punishes a person / For his sins / One through poverty / Another through a child.

(2) God punishes a person / With great distress / One in poverty / Another with death.

(3) He punished me / With a terrible punishment / He rocked my child / In an eternal sleep.

(4) I'm always full / Of trouble and sorrow / Starting with / When I got married.

(5) My house is always full / Of doctors and medicine / The whole world seems to me / A dark grave.

(6) Enough, my parents / Of weeping and wailing / Go to the synagogue / And have psalms read. [Variant: run to the synagogue—M.B.]

(7) Have a name said / Before a minyan [obligatory ten-man quorum for prayers—M.S.] / Perhaps the Almighty / Will give me my life.

(8) When they said / The name / God began to prepare / The soul.

(9) It would be better to take / A limb from my child [from me?—M.B.] / Than that I should see / My fourth child in the grave.

(10) —Enough, my parents / To weep for me / God will give you / Another in my place.

(11) —Is its news / That a mother's child dies? / Stay happy, all / Happy and healthy.

(12) Enough of lying / On your snow-white bed / I've already prepared for you / A fine room. [Variant: Go, daughter / Down from your white bed / The black room / Is already prepared for you.—M.B.]

(13) You will lie there / All alone / Throw away the false world / And let us go quickly.

102. "God Punishes a Person"

(1) God punishes a person / Only for his sins / One in his livelihood / Another in his child.

(2) One in loneliness / Another in need / One he punishes sharply / With a bitter death.

103. "The Lamp Goes Out"

(1) The lamp goes out / I haven't enjoyed life yet / A young man leaves the world / What will his little children do / The Jewish orphans / Who will give them a penny.

(2) —You came to me / You came to take my soul / Let me live a half-hour longer / Oh, you stand near my bed / And demand a divorce / Let me live ten minutes longer / Let me say good-bye / To my wife and little children / God knows whether I'll still be here.

(3) —Say farewell, say farewell / Say farewell quickly / The night is, oh, already short / It's been called out in heaven / Written in the book of the dead / No weeping will help you.

(4) —Look, mama, look, darling / Daddy is dying / From today you must weep / You Jewish orphans / Who will give you a piece of bread?

104. "The Lamp Is Going Out"

(1) The lamp is going out / Oh, I haven't enjoyed life / Oh, I'm leaving the world young / Oh, where will / My young orphans go / Oh, who will inherit my goods.

(2) Oh, you stay near the door / You take my soul / Oh, you separated me from my wife and children / Oh, where will my lonely orphans go? / Oh, who will inherit my goods?

105. "Have You Heard, Have You Seen"

(1) Have you heard, have you seen / What happened in Bender / You must have heard, people, of the great tragedy / That happened to Avremče's father-in-law.

(2) Ay, he had a boy of twenty-one / Who began to think of the colt [?—M.S.] / The first day of Shavuoth he went out in a boat / Oh, he fell in the water and drowned.

(3) As he began to drown / He waved his arms / —Save me, comrades, from the water / Because I'm already in the hands of the Angel of Death.

(4) Oh, when he was already drowned / He lay under the water for an hour / Oh, they ran to tell his parents the news / "Oh, go, go, Avreml is no more."

(5) When they heard this / [unclear] / Save, people, my child from the water / Save him quickly, and fast.

(6) As they took Avreml from the water / His head was badly battered / Oh, comrades took him and wrapped him in a snow-white spread / And they brought him home in a carriage.

(7) Where were you, Avreml's friends / We didn't expect this great tragedy / We had just all taken a walk with Avreml / Oh, and now we carry him back dead.

(8) Tuesday evening Avreml had a dream / He told it and everyone laughed at him / Oh, he didn't know, the poor thing, of his great tragedy / And his dream brought him to his death.

106. "Thousands of People Went Walking"

(1) Thousands of people went walking / They all went at the same time / Then suddenly you hear a commotion / That someone fell into the river.

(2) As he fell into the river, the sun suddenly went down / Then they made a plan / Thousands of people seeking a good deed / Ran to rescue a young man.

(3) When they pulled him out of the river / His feet were bitten / When they laid him on his bier / They tore up his engagement contract.

(4) Weep, all you people, weep and wail / Make a row / I thought I'd go to the altar / But at the end I must go to the funeral.

107–108. "Šimke (Simxe) Xazer Went to Istanbul"

(1) Šimke (Simxe) Xazer went to Istanbul [*xazer* = pig—M.S.] / He wanted to better his life / He wanted to improve his life / They shoved in a foreign knife.

(2) Maybe it was predestined / That he should lie in the earth of Istanbul / He wanted to be equal to the gods / But they read about him in the morning papers.

IV. RECRUIT AND WAR SONGS

109. "In the Year 1899"
(1) In the year one thousand eight hundred and ninety-nine / There was a great draft / I'm already weary of weeping and wailing / They denied my exemption / I'm a suitable soldier.

(2) They led me into the recruiting station / They put me next to the examination board / Oh, they stood me nice and straight / "You're accepted," they shout, "good lad, soldier."

(3) I lie down on the cot and start to think / What can be the end of this? / Oh, I'm blue and bitter too / Since I have to say farewell to my father and mother.

(4) Good-bye, my dear mother / You're blue and I'm bitter / Good-bye, my dear father / [missing].

(5) Good-bye, my dear bride / I'll miss you more than anyone / Since you must stay at home / I beg you, dear, write a letter.

110. "In the Year 1899"
In the year one thousand eight hundred and ninety-nine / There was a great draft / They probably gave a lot of money / And they didn't divide us into special groups.

111. "Ov Horaxmim"
(1) Ov horaxmim sjoyxeyn bamroymim [first line of the Hebrew prayer for the dead, here transcribed in the Eastern European Ashkenazic pronunciation—M.S.] / God is a father for all orphans / [missing] / God is a father for all orphans.

(2) It's better to sing *adeyneylem* / Than to kiss the czar's cross.

112. "I Was Born in Odessa"
I was born in Odessa / I spend all my youth / A letter, oh, came to me / That I have to go, oh / To the draft already / My parents wail / They weep and wail / They won't let me go.

113. "Oh, My Mother Carried Me Nine Months"
(1) Oh, my mother carried me nine months / Before she bore me / My mother poured many rivers of tears / That I wouldn't become a soldier.

(2) Every boy of twenty-one / Just as he starts to blossom / Whether poor or rich / All must go.

(3) When it's, oh, Friday night / I lie on my cot and think / I would rather go to greet the Sabbath / Than have the officer make an inspection.

(4) When Saturday morning comes / They shout: Out for lessons / Have I eaten something, have I drunk something? / And I get a slap too.

(5) When a war comes / They bang on the drum / They accompany me / Like a corpse / Farewell, my life, farewell, my world.

114. "When I Go Down the First Step"
(1) When I go down the first step, the first step / There sit the priests with shaved heads.

(2) Some guy comes up to me, some guy / Slaps my shoulder and says, Accepted for service.

115. "Whom Will We Serve, Brothers"

(1) Whom will we serve, brothers / The Russian czar, brothers / It's not good to serve the Russian czar / Since he bathes in our blood.

(2) Where will we be, brothers / In cold barracks, brothers / It's not good to serve in cold barracks / Since he bathes in our blood.

(3) What will we sleep on, brothers / On bare cots, brothers / It's not good to sleep on bare cots / Since he bathes in our blood.

(4) What will we eat, brothers / Borsht and bread, brothers / Borsht and bread / That's not good / Since he bathes in our blood.

116. "Don't Bring Me Food and Drink, Mama"

(1) Don't bring me food and drink, mama / I go around always, always, weeping / I ask you, dear God, why must my fiancé be a soldier.

(2) I'll put up a ladder / And climb up to God / I'll just ask him a couple of words / Why must my fiancé be a soldier.

(3) May a storm-wind come up / And carry me to you / So I can see your fine head of hair / I'll chat and kiss you.

(4) Oh, dear God / How can I stand by / As the czar takes away my dear diamond / And I must stand on the side.

117–118. "I'll Raise a Ladder to Heaven"

(1) —I'll raise a ladder to heaven / And I'll climb up to God / I'll just ask him a couple of words / Why must my darling be a soldier / oh, oh, oh.

(2) —You won't raise a ladder to heaven / I have to stay a soldier anyway / But, aren't you the kind of girl / That can wait for me for three years / oh, oh, oh.

(3) —I'll wait three years for you / Even ten would be okay / But you alone, you know the whole truth / How hard it is to work at sewing / oh, oh, oh.

119. "You're Leaving Me"

(1) You're leaving me / My darling / Oh, you're leaving to be drafted / Oh, help me God / So you'll get out of the czar's hands / And you won't please the whole recruiting station.

(2) What have you done to me / My darling / To draw my heart to you, to you / I haven't done anything / My darling / I just fell in love with you.

(3) I don't wish it on anyone / Not even an enemy / To sit and sew as a maiden / Oh, you have, oh you have / Oh turned my head / And I must leave this world young because of you.

(4) You're leaving me / My darling / I'll weep many rivers of tears / Oh help me, God / So you'll get out of the czar's hands / And we can already talk about a wedding.

(5) Now that God has helped / And you're out of the czar's hands / And we've begun to talk about the wedding / Your parents / Have made a rift between us / And you've caused me much grief and trouble.

120. "Oh, What Did You Have Against Me"

Oh, what did you have against me / And what did you want from me / And what did you have against my youth / Why didn't you tell me earlier / That you have to become a soldier / I would have long ago become engaged / And perhaps gotten married.

121, 122, 123. "I Left the House"

(1) I left the house / And there's weeping and wailing outside / Words resounded in my ears / They announced a mobilization this morning /

Oh, a chill went down my spine / I started to sweat / Then they called up my older brothers to serve again.

(2) As we came to the army office / They told us to stand by the door / They took me like a young soldier / And the recruiting station was just like before / My limbs are weak and sick / And I'm not young anymore / For living in the barracks on hard benches / But you must serve faithfully anyway.

(3) They call me into the barracks / And I dare not say no / They give me a rifle for shooting / And a long-haired fur hat on my head to wear / Oh that, they say, will protect you / And forget about your home / Why is my lot so bitter / I weep rivers of tears.

(4) I can't sit there / And can't stand there / My heart is torn up / Why do I have to go to war / Oh, they drove us from the city / And we can't find ourselves in the country / We're driven there / The sand is drenched with our blood.

(5) I ask God, is this right / Can a man endure this / Please answer me on this matter / Why must I be driven from home / *Oy vey* brothers, weep and wail for these times / Maybe God will call it back / They send us to the east / Who knows who we'll find there.*

(6) *Oy vey,* all you people / Don't think it's easy / They part man and wife, bride and groom / How many people are ruined now / A thousand widows and orphans per day / And no one to care for them / [unclear] / [unclear].

(7) The train has already come / In the wagons it's dark as a stable / My heart is all torn up / From the screams of the children, together / They scream, they tear themselves—Stay with us / Who will help us in our need / No land, no relatives here with us / To buy a piece of bread.

(8) We came to Harbin / And the commotion was very great / An officer came to us / We all got out of the wagons / He counted us up, how many of us there were / And how large the group is / He showed us the position / And handed out ammunition.

124. "Oy Vey in 1915"

(1) *Oy vey* in one thousand nine hundred and fifteen / A new order, oh, order, came out / Oh, every father must lead his child / Like a slaughterer the cattle.

(2) *Oy vey,* Friday, Friday, Friday night / Oh, our lips were pale, oh, pale / We would have liked to go to a Jew for the Sabbath / If they hadn't had an inspection, an inspection.

(3) *Oy vey,* Saturday, oh Saturday, oh Saturday, very early /—Out on maneuvers, out / Have we eaten, have we drunk? / And you get slapped too. [It seems the singer accidentally changed the order of the lines in this verse. The first four lines fit the melody much better for the second half of the verse—M.B.]

(4) *Oy vey* brothers, we're lost / We are in murderous hands, *oy vey* / We took Jewish girls / And wasted their lives.

125. "In 1915"

(1) In one thousand nine hundred and fifteen / An order came out / That every father should lead his child / Like a hen to the slaughterer.

---

*In singing for the phonograph the singer left out the second half of the first verse and the first half of the second verse, and began this verse after the fourth line.

(2) Oh, how can he help us, what can he do for us / We're in murderous hands / *Oy vey,* brothers, we're soldiers / We've lost our world.

(3) My mother carried me for eight months / In the ninth she bore me / Now I'm twenty-one / And have to be a soldier.

(4) They take me to the recruiting station: suitable, accepted / You'll be a good soldier / We lie in trenches / The bullets whistle / Grenades fall / We fall like sheaves of grain.

(5) What can we do, how can we help it / We're in murderous hands / We've taken Jewish girls / And ruined their lives.

126. "When I Was a Little Boy"

(1) When I was a little boy / When I was a little boy / I was a rover, mama / And since, mama, they yielded me up / I haven't had a good day.

(2) When we got to the Germans / The Germans stood ready before us / The first bullet hit me / And knocked me off my feet.

(3) When they brought me to the hospital / The doctors circled round me / I lay in a pool of blood / They drag the bullets out of me.

(4) I write a letter to my mother / I write just about my health / They took away my right hand / And I'm already blind in my eyes.

(5) I write a letter to my bride / I write just about myself / That the engagement contract should be torn up / And she should go to the altar with another.

(6) I used to walk with buddies / It was nice / Where can I find the last brother / To put an end to this.

127. "I Remember When I Was a Small Child"

(1) I remember when I was a small child / I was dear to my parents / Oh, now I'm twenty-one / And they send me into the greatest fire.

(2) Now I lie in the hospital wounded / Two nurses stand by me / Oh, the bullets, darling, they're pulling from me / [missing].

128. "Woe to the Father and Woe to the Mother"

(1) Woe to the father and woe to the mother / That have an extra son / They dress him in soldiers' clothes / And ship him, oh, right into battle.

(2) Oh, as we came to the train / I remained standing on the square / Oh, when the train whistle blew / Oh, great weeping broke out.

(3) Oh, don't weep mama, don't weep, mother / God willing, I'll come, oh, back / You should guard, oy vey, my house / You should guard my wife and child.

(4) Oh, when we came to the first position / I was pale as a sheet / Oh, lying six days in the trenches / Eating a piece of bread the third day.

(5) Oh, as we came to the first position / I became as deaf as the wall / The first bullet hit me / And took off my right hand.

(6) When they took off my right hand / I was lying near the bank / The nurses came running / And took me to the hospital.

(7) When I came to the hospital / I'm writing you a letter now / I write you, my dear mother / They took off my right hand.

(8) But don't weep, mama, don't weep, mother / Don't think I'm lying here alone / Every day they bring new brothers / There's weeping and wailing.

129. "The First Day of the Mobilization"

(1) The first day of the mobilization / There was weeping and wailing / The first day of the mobilization / All business stopped.

(2) Woe to the father, woe to the mother / Who have an extra son / They put him in soldiers' clothes / And send him straight to the battle.

130. "I Write You a Letter"
(1) I write you a letter / And I write you mama, about my health / Oh, they took away a hand / And I'm blind, mama.

(2) I lie wounded in the hospital / And doctors stand around / And my heart is drenched with blood / And my dear mother is not near me.

131. "I Write a Letter to My Parents"
I write a letter to my parents / Oh, I write about my health / They shot off my right hand / And I'm blind, mama.

132. "The Year '14 Came"
(1) The year '14 came, *vey, oy vey* / They took me to be a soldier, *vey, oy vey.*

(2) I was in camp three days / I wanted my parents.

(3) I came to the battlefield / I found my comrades swimming in blood.

(4) On the green fields and forests / The field is littered with recruits.

(5) There lies a recruit without a worry / Without a coffin and without a grave.

(6) There lies a recruit with a torn body / Blood runs from his heart.

(7) A bird comes flying / Comes to rest on the recruit.

(8) Don't rest bird, fly quickly / And tell my mother I'm well.

(9) But don't tell her about my death / Since she'll weep and wail.

(10) When the bird came into the house / He met the mother standing and weeping.

(11) Why are you weeping dear mother / It's black for him and bitter for you.

(12) How can I not weep and wail / Since they drove away my child.

(13) I'm left a widow, and blind as well / They drove away my only child.

(14) When the sand runs out / Then your child will come back.

(15) And the sand has run out / And my child won't come home.

(16) Without a coffin, without a bier / Without a father and mother.

(17) Just his faithful horse / Will grace the funeral.

133–134. "The Year '14 Has Come"
(1) The year '14 has come / They took me into the reserves.

(2) *Oy vey,* we ran into the Carpathians / Ate bread with water.

(3) *Oy vey,* the fields, green fields / There lies, neglected, a young recruit.

(4) And his body is torn / And blood pours from his body.

(5) Oh you bird, black bird / Here, take my hands, and give me your eyes.

(6) When the sand will run out / Then my husband will come from his grave.

135. "Oh the Year '14 Has Come"
Oh the year '14 has come / And they took me as a recruit.

136. "Oh the Year '14 Has Come"
Oh the year '14 has come / And they took me into the reserves.

137. "Oh the Year '14 Has Come"
Oh the year '14 has come / And they took me as a soldier.

138. "The Year '14 Has Come"
The year '14 has come / And they took me as a soldier.

139. "Outside It's Raining"
(1) Outside it's raining / It'll get muddy / They took me / Assigned me to the infantry.

(2) When I came up to the Carpathian Mountains / I longed for home / I longed for home, home / I ran home.

(3) When Mironenko found out / That Mayer is [unclear] / He sent the police to find him there.

(4) When the police came in / He threw off his hat /—Okay Mayer, my dear / Show me your pass.

(5) When Mayerke heard that / He didn't bat an eyelid / Picked himself up / And escaped through the window.

(6) Oh Mayer, you fine fellow / And a rabbi's son-in-law to boot / Whenever he sees the police / He climbs up to the attic.

140. "Outside It's Raining"

(1) Outside it's raining / It'll get muddy / They assigned my darling / To the ninth platoon.

(2) When he came there / He was terrified / He wanted to go home, home / So he left there.

(3) As he came home / He didn't meet anybody /—Now I'm hot / Since I've run away from the police.

(4) When the police found out / About my coming / They sent Polišuk for me / To look for me and find me.

(5) When Polišuk came in / He took off his hat /—And what are you doing here young man / Show me your exemption certificate.

(6) He went out /—And don't make any noise / Pushed a ruble into his hand / So he'd be a buddy.

Annotations to the Songs

1. The cylinder is defective in parts. The melody is in the style of the instrumental pieces of Jewish wedding musicians. One might assume that many melodies are borrowed from this source. The insignificant number of Jewish instrumental works published to date does not allow us to illuminate the question in more detail.

3. Variant of third verse in Leman 1921:234. In the second verse the singer must have forgotten the words of the third and fourth lines.

4. The singer heard this song in Skvir (1925) from a female worker.

5 and 6. Variant text and melody in Leman 1921:132. The Cabinet has a variant transcribed by Engel. No. 5 was performed by a seamstress in Odessa (May–June 1930). The performers of no. 5 and its variants worked in one shop for a long time but were nevertheless unable to sing the song together.

12. Words transcribed by Sh. Kupershmid and printed in *Tsaytshrift* 1928: no. 28.

17. Variant text (no melody) in Cahan 1930:36, which has a fuller text.

18 and 19. Variant text (different melody) in Leman 1921:125–28. The singer of no. 18 heard the song in childhood from a baker (Odessa, 1898–1900).

20. Variant melody (different text) in Cahan 1912b:140 and Cahan 1930:70.

21. The second part of the melody (from the seventh measure, 2/4) is from a well-known *tišnign* (table tune), "Rabejnu." Religious and liturgical tunes are often parodied in satirical songs. This lends the satirical song special sharpness and expressiveness.

22. The cylinder is partly defective. Variant melody and text in Leman 1921: 118–19, which also has text variants, nos. 60a, 60b, pp. 120–21. The singer heard this song in a textile factory from workers (Uman', 1922).

23. Variant of first verse (different melody) in Leman 1921:132.

25. Cf. the second verse in Leman 1921:32. Instead of *petliurtsy* there must have earlier been another word, with *petliurtsy* coming in during or after the Civil War.

26. This is a reworking of a popular Yiddish song (cf. no. 85). The singer heard it in Berdichev (1903).

27. Fragment. Variant melody in Leman 1921:40, where there is also a fuller text with variant 17a (ibid.:37–42).

28. Cf. Leman 1921, nos. 13, 13a, 16b, pp. 33–37; the melody is a bit different there.

29. The performer, L. Bresler (nos. 21, 25, 28, 39, 41, 42, 47, 48, 122, 140), says that she heard a large number of these songs (doubtless from the 1905 period repertoire) in Skvir in 1917–18 in the tobacco factory where she worked. Lipson and Rabinovič, mentioned in these songs, were owners of the Skvir tobacco factory and were famous as cruel exploiters. A satirical song was composed about Rabinovič's wife (no. 21).

31. In the fourth verse the singer apparently forgot the text of two lines and while singing repeated the two lines she remembered. The word *Fininspektor* naturally fell in instead of the word *policia* (see note to no. 25).

29, 30, and 31. The first verse is influenced by Varshavsky's song "Neben Klajzl"; cf. Varshavsky 1901:34–36 (melody different there).

32 and 33. Variant melody in Leman 1921:34, 1928:72. Text variant in Leman 1921, nos. 16, 16a, 16b; similar verses in Bastomski 1923:88–89.

34, 35, 36, 37. This song was undoubtedly composed by a street singer (who appeared as well at weddings and parties). This is indicated in the last verse of no. 34, as well as in the whole style and form of the piece. In the years 1903–6 the theme of strikes was too current to be ignored by street singers, especially in workers' districts. The composer reworks it in his own way, adding comic touches, which might appeal to various nonworker listeners, and adds a coarse couplet about a lady who threatens the man with a strike, and so on. The song became popular among some workers as well, and was varied.

41. Variant melody and text in Leman 1921:89–90. Leman says that the Ukrainian revolutionary song "Oy, tse gore nas rabochikh" was sung to the same tune (1921:184).

42 and 43. Variant to first verse in Leman 1921:93 (without melody).

44. Variant melody and text in Leman 1921: no. 23, with text variant in nos. 23a, 23b, 23c in Bastomski 1923:129. Bastomski's variant consists of two songs: the song about Hirsh Lekert and the song "Cvelf a zejger banaxt lig ix mir un traxt." In the archive of the ethnographic section of our Institute there is a song about Bogrov, who was killed in 1912 in Stolypina. This song (translated by Kupershmid in Belaia Tserkov') differs from the song about Lekert only in that it mentions Bogrov instead of Lekert. The origin of this variant lies in a certain similarity of some circumstances connecting the assassination of Lekert and Bogrov: Lekert was shot in Fon-Valia in a circus, while Bogrov was shot in Stolypina in a theater. Both Lekert and Bogrov were hung. The melody is borrowed from a love song; cf. Cahan 1912a:225.

45. Variant melody and text in Leman 1921:99–101. It can be presumed that this song was borrowed from the repertoire of the so-called thieves' songs. In Leman's variant we find words from the thieves' argot. It is possible that the lyricism of some of the so-called thieves' prison songs, especially in prison circumstances, facilitated the borrowing by workers of some parts of this repertoire.

46. A whole series of texts was sung to this melody (nos. 65, 82). The most popular song to this melody is no. 82, "Brider mir hobn gešlosn" (to the words of M. Sorerives).

47. Similar events called forth a whole series of songs; cf. nos. 105, 106.

48. Variant in Kipnis n.d.:32, Leman 1928:59, Cahan 1912a:39 (love song). In the *phonoteque* there is a song about a pogrom in Shpola (1880s) to this tune.

49. Verses 4 and 5 are taken from a workers' lullaby; cf. Leman 1921:104–5 (different melody). These verses are sometimes performed as a separate song; cf. no. 52.

50, 51, and 52. Variant melody and text in Leman 1921:80, 1928:168, and Cahan 1912a:104.

51. Variant to verses 4 and 5 in Leman 1921:80–84. The seventh verse is a variant of the first verse of Edelshtat's "Majn cavoe' "; cf. Edelshtat 1930:161. Cf. nos. 72, 73.

53 and 54. Variant melody and text in Leman 1921:115.

55. This song (like no. 56) is a reworking of a song of Eliakum Zunser, "Elegie Levanda" (Zunser 1888). Variant melody and text in Leman 1921:43, which also has a variant of the text in nos. 43a and 43b. Variant second verse in Bastomski 1930:122. The last verse of no. 55 ("nit der eršter, nit der lecter") is taken from another song. The melody of the last verse is from the popular song "Es lojfn, es jogn švarce volkns," to words of Nomberg.

56. The singer sang the first couplet in D-minor; from the second couplet on she raised the pitch and finished the second couplet in B-flat minor and the third in B-minor.

59. The performer heard this song in Warsaw (1918). For a melody similar to that of nos. 57, 58, and 59, cf. Leman 1928:84.

60 and 61. The performer remembers this song from 1895–96. While singing it for the phonograph (June 1930), Comrade Gor, a bristle worker, forgot the first verse (no. 61) and began with the second. Finally he, along with Comrade Levin (also a bristle worker), recalled the first stanza and sent us the full text. He noted that he sang it to the melody of "Kol'slaven." Comrade Levin writes, "I think that this song has great historical value, as one of the first [Jewish—M.B.] revolutionary songs before the founding of the *Bund.*" For a variant of the text, cf. Litvak, "Vos geven," p. 233; see Introduction to present volume for more on this song.

62. Variant melody and text (second and third verse) in Leman 1921:43.

63. Variant melody and text in Leman 1921:46–48. Melody borrowed from the Russian song "Dubinuška."

64. Variant melody in Leman 1921:44–45; fuller text there. The third and fourth lines of both verses are corrupted; in the form in which they were sung, they are incomprehensible.

65. The performer remembered only this verse of a variant of the song "Brider mir hobn gešlosn"; cf. no. 82.

66. Variant melody and text in Leman 1921:70. Variant text in ibid.:70–72 and *Tsaytshrift* 1928: no. 19.

68. The performer heard this in Vilna in 1905.

69. Skuditskii told us that the song *"in fabrik,"* to the words of D. Kasel, was sung to this melody in Zhitomir in 1921.

72. The performer heard this song in Vilna in 1905.

73. The performer heard this song in Minsk in workers' clubs in 1917.

77. In Leman 1921:38 there is a song (a reworking of Heine's "Weavers") with a similar melody.

78. Variant melody (different text) in Leman 1921:32.

81. The performer began the second couplet not on G (like the first couplet) but on D, so it turned out this way: first couplet: G–D; second: D–A.

83. Variant text (different melody) in Leman 1921:17.

84. For a variant first verse, see Ginzburg-Marek 1901:278 (without melody).

86. Jewish collectors paid no attention to this kind of song because the melodies of these songs did not reflect a specific "Jewishness" in their scale structure. However, for research goals these materials are particularly important. This song is characteristic of the Jewish craftsman-kulak, of the strong boss. The performer heard this song in Orsh (Belorussia).

87. For a variant melody and text, see Cahan 1912a:112.

88. Variant (with insignificant changes) of the first eight verses of the song "Di lid fun dem geštoxenem zagatovščik: Ferfast fun Lejb Levenzon" (Odessa: Hersh-Meyer Mordukhovich, 1896). The Russian title "Pesn' o sluchaino zarezavshemsia zagatovščik" served as the theme of yet another song: "Der geštoxener ben joxid." Cf. "Du junge ferlojrene kindbetorin mit dem gilozenem picele kind nox mir fir naja lider: (1) Der gestoxener ben joxid; (2) Dos blind mejdl; (3) Der frejlixer kartjožnik; (4) Der zinger krigt zix mit dem dales. Ferfaser Perec Volex" (Odessa, 1897).

In February 1932 a blind street singer in Kiev told us that Perec Volex sang his songs in Odessa in wine cellars, at parties, weddings, and so on, and that he sang mostly songs of his own composition. Our blind singer got to know him in the 1880s in Odessa. He accompanied Volex for several years and learned his repertoire, which then made it possible for him to travel around cities on his own performing Volex's songs on the streets and occasionally in various houses. To date, unfortunately, there has been almost no data collected on these professional singers.

Some of the texts of the repertoire of these singers have been published, but not a single melody has been printed to date. Outside the apparent independent value of this repertoire, it also influenced folk music to a certain extent. Part of this repertoire achieved wide currency, underwent changes, and influenced daily-life folklore. Thus, for example, the text of the first song of Volex's repertoire is close to the text of the popular folk song "Dos kind ligt in vigele mit ojsgevejnte ojgn." We have not yet transcribed the melody to this song of Volex's.

89. Yet another song about the same *zagatovščik* (cf. no. 88). We have not yet been able to ascertain the origin of this variant. It is undoubtedly from the repertoire of the same type of professional singer. Street singers aided the spread of these songs more than printing did.

91, 92, 93, 94, 95. Variant text in Ginzburg-Marek 1901: nos. 244, 246, and 249; Cahan 1912a:13. Variant melody for no. 92 in Kipnis 1918:115, Kipnis n.d.:106–8 (different melody).

96. Fragment. Fuller text (no melody) in Ginzburg-Marek 1901: nos. 312–13.

97. Variants of the fifth and sixth verses in Ginzburg-Marek 1901:nos. 264, 265.

102. The singer raised the second half of the first verse by a half step (B-minor to C-minor).

105. Variant melody in Cahan 1912a:227. Cahan's song is also about a drowned person. The text is closer to our no. 106.

109. Variant text in Vanvild 1923:99, *Tsaytshrift* 1928:796, Ginzburg-Marek 1901: nos. 341 (our fourth and fifth verse) and no. 345.

111. Variant text in Ginzburg-Marek 1901: no. 51 and Vanvild 1923:100. The performer heard this song in Bobro (Belorussia) in 1875–76.

113. Variant text in Ginzburg-Marek 1901: no. 336, third verse; also ibid.: note 4, p. 285. The type of refrain found in this song (to different texts) is frequently found. Cf. our no. 20, Kipnis n.d.:126.

115. Variant text in Niger 1913: no. 10 and Vanvild 1923:101 (both without melody).

121, 122, and 123. Variant text in Bastomski 1923:87.

124. Variant text in Ginzburg-Marek 1901: no. 296 and Vanvild 1923:99.

125. Variant melody and text in Cahan 1912a:191–92.

127. Singer heard this song in Tiraspol in 1924.

128. Variant text in Bastomski 1923:107–8, variant first and second verses (no melody).

129. Variant text in Shalit 1921:48–49 and Shalit 1922:195–96 (no melodies). We combined the words of nos. 133 and 134, since the performer continued the song right after the performer of no. 133 and warned us that she was starting where the previous singer left off.

132, 133, 134, 135, 136, 137, 138. Variant text in Shalit 1921:50, Anderson 1928:405–8 (without melody). We have combined the texts of nos. 133 and 134, since the singer of no. 134 immediately followed the performer of no. 133 and warned us that she would begin where he left off.

139. Variant melody in Kipnis 1918:19 (different words).

140. Variant melody in Leman 1928:144 (different words). Cf. the first verse of our song and verses 6 and 7 of Leman 1921: viii and our verse 5 with the variant of Lehman 1921:viii.

Works Cited

Anderson, V.
  1928   "Dos lid fun der mobilizatsie." In *Filologishe shriftn*, vol. 2, pp. 401–
          14. Vilna: YIVO Institute for Jewish Research.
An-Ski, S.
  1909   "O evreskoi narodnoi pesne." In *Evreiskaia starina*.
Barsov, E. V.
  1903   *O russkikh narodnykh pesnopeniiakh*. Moscow.
Bastomski, Sh.
  1923   *Baym kval*. Vilna: Naye Yidishe Folksshul.
Beregovski, M.
  1932   "Tsu di ufgabes fun der yidisher muzikalisher folkloristik." In *Prob-
          lemes fun folkloristik*, pp. 101–14. Kiev: Ukrainian Academy of
          Sciences.
Bruisov, N.
  1930   "Starinnaia narodnaia pesnia." *Za proletarskuiu muzyku*, no. 7.
Cahan, Y. L.
  1912a   *Yidishe folkslider mit melodies, oys dem folksmoyl gezamlt*, vol. 1. New
          York and Warsaw: Internatsyonale Bibliotek Farlag.

1912b   Ibid., vol. 2.
1926   *Folksgezang un folkslid.* Vilna: YIVO Institute for Jewish Research.
1930   *Yidishe folkslider, naye zamlung.* New York: YIVO Institute for Jewish Research.

Edelshtat, D.
1930   *Lider fun nojt un kamf.* Moscow.

Engel, J.
1915   Open letter to L. I. Saminsky. *Rassvet,* no. 7

Fefer, I., and Fininberg, E., eds.
1931   *M. Vintshevsky, D. Edelshtat, I. Bovshover: Geklibene lider.* Kiev: Kultur-lige.

Ginzburg, S. M., and Marek, P. S.
1901   *Evreiskie narodnye pesni v Rossii.* St. Petersburg: Voskhod.

Idelsohn, A. Z.
1914   *Hebräisch-orientalischer Melodienschatz,* 11 vols. Berlin: Friedrich
1932   Hofmeister.

Kipnis, M.
1918   *60 folkslider fun M. Kipnis un Z. Zeligfelds kontsert-repertuar.* Warsaw: Gitlin.
n.d.   *80 folkslider fun Z. Zeligfelds un M. Kipnises kontsert-repertuar.* Warsaw: Gitlin.

Kiselhof, Z.
1911   "The Concert of the Society for Jewish Music." *Novyi voskhod,* no. 10.

Kvitka, K.
1922   *Ukrainski narodni melodii.* Kiev: Slovo.

Leman, Sh.
1921   *Arbayt un frayhayt.* Warsaw: Folklor-bibliotek.
1928   *Ganovim-lider mit melodies.* Warsaw: Graubard.

Lenin, V. I.
1925   "Kriticheskie zametki po natsional'nomu voprosu." In *Izbrannye stat'i po natsional'nomu voprosu.* 2d ed. Moscow and Leningrad: Giz.

Lineva, E.
1905   *Opyt zapisi fonografom ukrainskikh narodnykh pesen.* Moscow.

Mut
1920   *Mut: lider-zamlung.* Moscow.

Niger, Sh., ed.
1913   *Der pinkes,* vol. 1. Vilna: Kleckin.

Sabaneiev, L.
1924   *Evreiskaia natsional'naia shkola v muzyke.* Moscow: Izdanie Obshchestvo Evreiskoi Muzyki.

Saminsky, L.
1915   "Khudozhestvennyi itog poslednikh rabot 'Obshchestva evr. nar. muzyki.'" *Rassvet,* no. 5; discussions in nos. 7, 9.
1916   Discussions on Jewish music in *Evreiskaia nedel'ia,* nos. 4, 11, 12, 16, 17, 22.

Shalit, M., ed.
1921   *Lebn,* nos. 9–10. Vilna.

Skuditski, Z.
n.d.   "Vegn folklorishn arbeter-lid." In *Problemes fun folkloristik.* Kiev: Institut Evreiskoi Kul'tury pri Vseukrainskoi Akademii Nauk, Etnog. Sektsiia.

Tsaytshrift
1928   *Tsaytshrift far yidisher geshikhte, demografie, un ekonomik, literatur-forshung, shprakh-visnshaft un etnografie,* vols. 2–3. Minsk: Izdanie Instituta Belorusskoi Kul'tury.
Vanvild, M., ed.
1923   *Ba undz yidn.* Warsaw: Graubard.
Varshavsky, M.
1901   *Yidishe folkslider fun M. M. Varshavsky (mit notn).* Warsaw.
Viner, M.
1932   "Folklorizm un folkloristik." In *Problemes fun folkloristik.* Kiev: Institut Evreiskoi Kul'tury pri Vseukrainskoi Akademii Nauk, Etnog. Sektsiia.
Vints, L.
1898   *Starye voprosy i novye zadachi.* St. Petersburg: Voskhod.
Vintshevsky, M.
1924   *Kamfs-gezangn: Geklibene lider.* Minsk: Shul un Bukh.
1926   *Vospominanie.* Minsk: Shul un Bukh.
1927   *Gezamlte verk.* New York: Frayhayt.
Zunser, E.
1888   *Elegiia na smert' L. O. Levandy.* Minsk and Vilna.

LIST OF INFORMANTS

Song	Singer	Place and Date	Original Tonic
1. Šver un biter vi der tojt	S. Kashutskii, 47, tailor	Uman', 1930	G
2. Ix štej dox uf ganc fri	Leyb Abramovitsh	Medzhibodzh, 1912–14	(A)
3. Ajn šnej, mame	Z. Kashtilian, 33, tailor	Belaia Tserkov', 1929	A
4. A šnej, mama	Z. Skuditskii, researcher	Kiev, 1928	—
5. Tog azojvi naxt	R. Pesina, seamstress	Odessa, 1930	D
6. In drojsn gist a regn	E. Balshem, worker (fem.)	Belaia Tserkov', 1929	E
7. Bin ix mir a nejterke	Manya Kats, worker	Belaia Tserkov', 1929	G
8. Ba di mašinen	Khaya Fuks, 24, worker	Bershad', 1926	—
9. Oj, in fabrik zic ix ajngebojgn	Khaya Strashnaya, 30, seamstresš	Uman', 1930	B
10. Oj ba majn arbet tu ix zicn	Tanya Pavlovskaya, 22	Belaia Tserkov', 1929	F
11. Ba majn mašindl tu ix zicn	Velya Kornfeld, 32, seamstress	Belaia Tserkov', 1929	D
12. Ba majn mašindele tu ix zicn	Sima Gural'nik, 20, worker	Belaia Tserkov', 1929	E
13. A gance vox	Rokhl Frager, 22, worker	Belaia Tserkov', 1929	E
14. A gance vox	Khaya Grinberg, servant	Belaia Tserkov', 1929	B
15. A gance vox horevet zi	R. Pesina, 40, seamstress	Belaia Tserkov', 1929	E
16. Oj, ix hob šojn nit kajn kojex	Adel Perlshtein, 29	Odessa, 1930	B-flat
17. Ix hob šojn nit kajn kojex	Female voice	1912–14	(G)
18. Oj, undzer jorelex gejen undz avek	Moti Starikov, 41, bristle worker	Odessa, 1930	B

277

LIST OF INFORMANTS (con.)

Song	Singer	Place and Date	Original Tonic
19. Oj, undzere kojxes, oj gejen undz ojs	Male voice	1912–14	(G)
20. Di balaboste gejt arajn	D. Strokovskii, teacher in vocational school	Kiev, 1928	—
21. Di madam Rabinovič gejt arajn	L. Bresler, 29, cigarette worker	Skvira, 1931	D
22. Di mašines klapn	Rivak Kitaygorodskaya, 26, worker	Uman', 1930	D
23. In drojsn iz fincter	Ranya Shtein, worker	Belaia Tserkov', 1929	D
24. Viazoj zol ix nit mekane	R. Pesina, seamstress	Odessa, 1930	B-flat
25. Ir balebatim, ir merder	L. Bresler		D
26. Arbet der šnajder a gance vox	D. Yudzon, 50, doctor (fem.)	Kiev, 1932	A
27. Musju, Maxovski, vos capt ir mir majn blut	Z. Bershtein	Zhitomir, 1912–14	(D)
28. Lipson iz a balebos	L. Bresler		D
29. A gut morgn ajs, Rabinovič	L. Bresler		D
30. A gut morgn dir, Mojške	D. Strokovskii		—
31. A gut morgn dir, Avremele	Yosef Yurik, 48, garment worker	Uman', 1930	F
32. Af maloarnautske un puškinskie	Doba Finkelstein, teacher in vocational school	Odessa, 1930	C#
33. Der bunt iz gevorn	Rakhil Pesina		B
34. In ale gasn vi me gejt	Gitl Gutkina, 28	Odessa, 1930	C

No. Title	Singer	Place, Date	Key
35. In ale gasn vi me gejt	Z. Kashtilyan, 33, tailor	Belaia Tserkov', 1929	G
36. Vi me gejt un vi me stejt	Avrom Langer, 45, garment worker	Uman', 1930	A
37. In ale gasn vi me gejt	Isroel Tomk, 35, blind bandura player (?)	Shepetovka, 1912–14	(G)
38. Vi mir hobn zix ale sobirajet	Z. Kashtilyan		G
39. Oj vej, švester un brider	L. Bresler		B-flat
40. Unter der Sofievke	Worker in garment factory	Uman, 1930	—
41. A sobrane hobn mir zix sobirajet	L. Bresler		A
42. Dem najntn janvar	Kh. Gurfinkel, 27, tailor	Shepetovka, 1912–14	(E)
43. Šabes batog iz a jomer mit a klog	L. Bresler		E-flat
44. Vi Jisker iz fun stub arojsgegangen (Hirsh-Lekert variant)	Rokhl Frager		A
45. Rojšxojdes elal, mamenu	M. Libernukh	Polonnoe, 1912–14	(C#)
46. Genes'e iz fun ir arbet gegangen	Etl Volodarskaya, 35	Ushomir, 1928	—
47. Oj, mitvox iz p'erve maj	L. Bresler		C
48. Di bixer mit di sekretn	L. Bresler		C
49. X'hob gekončet di axt klasn	Yosif Yurik		C#
50. Me firt mix arajn in a finctern xejder	Kh. Kipnis, 39	Ushomir, 1928	—
51. Ver tut strojen moyern, palacn	Zorakh Yoshpa, 17, hat worker	Belaia Tserkov', 1929	D

LIST OF INFORMANTS (con.)

Song	Singer	Place and Date	Original Tonic
52. Di hojxe moyern, ver tut zej strojen	Bella Kornfeld	Belaia Tserkov', 1929	E-flat
53. Dort in vinkl in nasn keler	Leyb Lutsnik, tailor	Rovno, 1912–14	(E)
54. Dort in vinkl in keler	Vera Friman, garment worker	Kiev, 1930	E-flat
55. Di trit fun tiranen	M. Hochberg, 45, tailor	Uman', 1930	E
56. Di trit fun tiranen	Z. Kopelman, tailor	Uman', 1930	F
57. In dem vajn land Sibir	M. Tol'chinskaya, 21	Odessa, 1930	E
58. In dem vajn kaltn Sibir	R. Podol'skaya	Belaia Tserkov', 1930	—
59. In vajn kaltn Sibir	Sh. Pisenbaum, 29, asst. in Inst. Jewish Culture	Kiev, 1932	D
60. Vi hejlik iz di natur	A. Bel'skii, 49, worker in a shoe factory	Kiev, 1932	G, E
61. Lomir lejgn afn harcn di rexte hant	Gor, 50, bristle worker	Odessa, 1930	E-flat, C
62. Dos erste vel mir nemen nox regirn	R. Pesina		A
63. Gejt brider, gejt	Zelda Shpiner	Odessa, 1930	G
64. Vol viln di heršer	Avrom Langer, 45, tailor	Uman, 1930	B-flat
65. Brider, ejb got vet undz nit helfn	Stefanskaya, worker (fem.)	Kiev, 1931	B-flat
66. Oj, ir nariše cionistn	Ts. Lakhman, house painter	Kiev, 1931	A
67. Der frajhajts-gajst (Vintshevsky/thru no. 71)	A. Yuditskii, researcher	Kiev, 1932	E

No. & Title	Source	Place, Date	Key
68. Es rirt zix	Kh. Leibovich, bibliographer	Kiev, 1932	D
69. Ix tu hern dajn štime	Kh. Tabaynik, 38, tailor	Kiev, 1930	A
70. Draj švester	Kh. Tabaynik, 38, tailor	Kiev, 1930	A
71. A bezm un a ker	?	?	transcribed by Engel
72. Majn cavoe (Edelshtat through no. 80)	Kh. Leibovich		D
73. Majn cavoe	A. Yuditskii		E
74. Der ovnt-glok	Kh. Leibovich		C
75. Der ovnt-glok	E. Spivak, researcher	Kiev, 1932	G
76. Der ovnt-glok	A. Yuditskii		C
77. Vaxt uf	Group of workers	Kiev, 1920	—
78. In kamf	Leib, Luchnik, tailor	Rovno, 1912–14	(E)
79. Majn lecte hofenung	M. Erlikh	Zhitomir, 1912–14	(E)
80. Cu di arbeter-frojen	A. Levin, 50, bristle worker	Odessa, 1930	F
81. Nemt zix cunojf (?author)	D. Yuzdon		G
82. Brider mir hobn gešlosn (M. Sorerives)	Male voice	Rovno, 1912–14	(C)
83. Šlof, Olekse (špot-lid) (Sholom Aleichem)	Avrom Langer		B
84. Zict a šnajder	Skuditskii		—
85. Ot azoj nejt a šnajder	two male voices	Volhynia(?) 1912	(F)
86. Der šnajder zict ba zajn genej	M. Khasin, teacher Evpedtechnicum	Kiev, 1927	—
87. Mit a nodl, on a nodl	M. Diamant, actor, Moscow Jewish Theatre	Kiev, 1932	E-flat

LIST OF INFORMANTS (con.)

Song	Singer	Place and Date	Original Tonic
88. Hej, ir menčn ale	M. Hochberg		—
89. Oj, got az er colt	Adel Perlshtein		G
90. Aj, efšer hot ir, menčn gehert	Isroel Temk		(B-flat)
91. Vos den, majn kind, vilstu nox	B. Zuskin, actor, Moscow Jewish Theatre	Kiev, 1929	G
92. Vos-že vilstu, majn tajer kind	S. Khelfan, 33, garment worker	Odessa, 1930	G
93. Ci vos-že gebn dir majn kind	Hershl Fishman, 17, carpenter	Polonnoe, 1912–14	(B-flat)
94. Ci gebn dir, majn kind, a šnajder-jung	E. Smolyar	Ushomir, 1928	—
95. Vos-ze vilstu majn lib kind	R. Braginskaya, vocational school teacher	Kiev, 1928	—
96. Susterše vajber	R. Sireyskaya, 10	Kremenets, 1912–14	(D)
97. Git mix op di mame	R. Braginskaya		—
98. Oj vej mame, vos-že zol ix ton	Brayna Weissburd	Kiev, 1928	—
99. Ejnem iz dox zejer gut	Z. Skuditskii		—
100. Got štroft ajn menčn	Z. Skuditskii		F#
101. Got štroft a menčn	Gitl Rojtman, 22	Belaia Tserkov', 1929	(B)
102. Got štroft dem menčn	Mikhl Fradkis, 38, shopkeeper	Proskurov, 1912–14	D
103. Der lomp vert farlošn	Rokhl Konstantinovskaya, 18, garment worker	Uman', 1930	(E-flat)
104. Der lomp vert farlošn	Hershl Fishman		B-flat
105. Ci hot ir gehert	Fanya Reshetnikova, 35, garment worker	Odessa, 1930	

106. Toiznter menčn spacirn gegangen	Riva Bragainskaya		—
107. Simke xazer	Z. Skuditskii		—
108. Simke xazer	D. Yudzon		—
109. In 1899 jor	Doba Ostrovskaya, student	Odessa, 1930	D
110. In 1899 jor	Male voice	1912–14?	(A)
111. Ov horaxmim	Sh. Dobin, researcher	Kiev, 1929	—
112. In Odes bin ix gebojrn	Male voice	1912–14?	(A)
113. Oj najn xadošim	Hershl Fishman		(G)
114. Gej ix arop afn erštn trep	B. Zuskin		E
115. Vemen veln mir dinen, brider	B. Ginzburg, 17, bookkeeper	Anopol', 1912–14	(C)
116. Kajn esn un kajn trinken mame	R. Pesina		C
117. A lejterl cum himl vel ix steln	Kh. Loytsker, graduate student, Inst. Jewish Culture	Kiev, 1931	—
118. Oj, a lejterl cum himl	Kh. Gitelman		—
119. Forn forstu fun mir avek	Doba Ostrovskaya		E
120. Oj, vos hostu gehat cu mir	Rokhl Shpigl, 22, worker	Belaia Tserkov', 1929	B-flat
121. Fun der štub bin ix arojsgegangen	Yosef Bokher	Proskurov, 1912–14	(D)
122. Fun der štub zajnen mir arojsgegangen	L. Bresler		F
123. Fun der štub bin ix in gas arojsgegangen	Skuditskii		
124. Oj vej, in 1915 jor	Grisha London, 17, shoemaker	Belaia Tserkov', 1929	A

LIST OF INFORMANTS (con.)

Song	Singer	Place and Date	Original Tonic
125. In 1915 jor	Risya Kiglman	Belaia Tserkov', 1929	D
126. Az ix bin a klejn jingele gevezn	B. Primis, 20, garment worker	Odessa, 1930	G
127. Ix gedenk, ix bin a klejnes kind gevezn	Sh. Pisenbaum, 29, worker-student Inst. Jewish Culture	Kiev, 1932	E#
128. Az vej dem tatn	Motl Foreyter, 46, harness maker	Odessa, 1930	D
129. Dem erštn tog fun der mobilizacje	Gershon Shukher, worker	Odessa, 1930	B
130. Ix tu dir a brivele šrajb	Adel Perlshtein		A
131. Šrajb šrajb ix a briv cu majne eltern	E. Volodarskaya, 35	Ushomir, 1928	—
132. Dos fercnte jor iz ongekumen	L. Bresler		D
133. Dos fercnte jor hot zix ongehojbn	Abram Milon, worker	Odessa, 1930	F
134. Ojf di felder, grine felder	Adel Perlshtein		F
135. Oj, dos fercnte jor hot zix ongehojbn	Abram Ladizhenskii, 20	Odessa, 1930	C
136. Dos fercnte jor iz ongekumen	Rosa Kreinman, 24	Uman', 1930	E
137. Dos fercnte jor iz ongekumen	Kh. Gitelman		—
138. Dos fercnte jor iz ongekumen	Kh. Gitelman		
139. In drojsn gejt a regn	Z. Skuditskii		
140. In drojsn gejt a regn	L. Bresler		A

2

JEWISH FOLK SONGS
(1962)

Preface

The present volume includes 70 songs (nos. 1–70), 28 instrumental pieces (nos. 71–98), and 52 textless songs (nos. 99–150).* Of the 70 songs, 61 were transcribed from recordings and 8 by ear; 1 was transcribed by I. Khabenskii. Of the 28 instrumental pieces, 10 were transcribed from recordings, 1 by ear, and 17 were taken down by musicians who play in klezmer [a group of Jewish professional instrumental folk musicians—M.S.] bands and who know the klezmer repertoire well. The transcriptions were basically done at our suggestion in 1928–37. Of the 50 textless tunes, 26 were transcribed from recordings and 21 were transcribed by me by ear. One transcription (no. 133) and its variants are from the archive of Z. A. Kiselhof (1876–1939), a collector of Jewish folk music and an active member of the Society for Jewish Music (St. Petersburg).† This archive was transferred by Kiselhof's daughter to the Cabinet of Jewish Language, Literature, and Folklore [henceforth Cabinet—M.S.]

Originally published as *Evreiskie narodnye pesni* (Moscow: Sovetskii Kompositor, 1962). The 1962 volume was under the general editorship of S. V. Aksiuk and was edited by L. Lebedinskii. It was published in an edition of 1,555 copies, fairly small even by Soviet folk-music monograph standards. There is no indication of the nature of the editing, of the volume being posthumous, or of the original date of writing.

　　[*"Textless songs" is my translation of Beregovski's *"napev bez slov"*; essentially it covers the Yiddish term *nign* for a song using only vocables, often associated with the Hasidic milieu.—M.S.]

　　[†For more on the Society, see p. 289.—M.S.]

of the Ukrainian Academy of Sciences, which functioned in Kiev from 1936 to 1949.

Of the total of 97 recordings transcribed here, 73 were recorded in 1928–38, while the remaining 24 date to 1912–14. They were done by the members of the expedition organized by the Jewish Historic-Ethnographic Society in St. Petersburg and include nos. 6, 7, 8, 18, 21, 28, 74, 103, 112, 117, 124, 128, 129, 130, 132, 134, 141, 143, 144, 147, 148, and 149. The variant introduced in the notes to no. 99 was taken from the unpublished transcriptions of Joel Engel (1898).

The identification numbers given in the annotations refer to the *phonoteque* of the folklore division of the Cabinet. This *phonoteque* included nearly all the recorded examples of Jewish folk music done in Russia, beginning in 1912.* The recordings of the St. Petersburg Society must simply be dated as 1912–14 because we have no more precise information on recording dates of individual items. At the time of the transfer of the archive to the Cabinet (1930), no inventory of books was included. Our only source of data concerning the recordings are the annotations on the cylinder cases, which are quite brief and rarely dated. Kiselhof did report on a series of recordings he made himself in 1913 as a member of the expedition.

We have supplied metronome markings; tempo markings are given in brackets for items recorded in 1912–14, since the phonograph on which the cylinders were recorded had no speed regulator. The tempi given match the character of the piece and what seemed to us to be the normal sound. We also put the metronome markings of individual transcribers in brackets, leaving in their other indications as well.

The songs are given both in underlay and separately, in literary transcriptions. However, we could not avoid the supplementary syllables found in the singing of individual performers. These supplementary syllables (under the notes) are given in parentheses and not included in the correct literary version. Some dialect forms are preserved in a few songs. All the transcriptions are published here for the first time.

[*According to Braun (1978:105), the archive contained some seven thousand items as of 1946.—M.S.]

Introduction

Like every folk art,* Jewish folk music is rich and varied in its conceptual and expressive content, in forms and genres, and in artistic means. Jewish folk music is divided into vocal and instrumental, with a special subdivision of textless tunes among the vocal music.

The formative period of the folk music of the Eastern and Western European Jews, whose colloquial and literary language is Yiddish, can be dated to around the fourteenth century. We know from historical sources that its basic traits were fixed in approximately the sixteenth century. The Jewish folk drama, which has music as one of its main components, also arose in the late fifteenth and early sixteenth centuries. Nearly all the plays of this type of drama are sung from beginning to end, excepting only isolated comic interludes.

The transcription of Jewish folk music began very late. Up to the end of the nineteenth century there were no Jewish musicians in a position to take an interest in the folk music of their people, to appreciate it, and to move toward collecting and studying it. Only in 1898 did the composer and critic Joel Engel (1868–1927) make his first transcriptions of the melodies of Jewish folk songs and tunes.[1] Engel's activities as composer, folklorist, and passionate propagandist and appreciator of Jewish folk music attracted the attention of a wide circle of Jewish society to its own music. Engel's transcriptions began the more or less systematic work of collecting Jewish folk music.[2] However, they were not the first transcrip-

[*"Folk art" here is a translation of *narodnoe iskusstvo,* a more inclusive term than the English, including all aspects of the expressive culture of an ethnic group. "Folk music" stands for *narodnaia muzyka,* which can mean a "national music" as well as "folk music"; at times, as in *evreiskaia narodnaia muzyka,* the term can be rendered simply as "Jewish music." —M.S.]

1. Engel's first notebook with examples of Jewish folk melodies, dated 1898, has been preserved. In 1930 Antonina Konstantinova Engel, the composer's widow, gave this notebook (along with other materials from the composer's archive) to the Institute of Jewish Proletarian Culture of the Ukrainian Academy of Sciences (Kiev) [henceforth Institute]. Sixty-six items were transcribed in this notebook, of which a small number were published in the form of arrangements for voice and piano of solo piano (Engel 1909, 1912; each contains ten items). Volume 3 was for solo piano (songs, tunes, dances, etc.), published by Engel.

2. The first public performance of Jewish folk songs was held at the instigation of Engel in Moscow (March 18, 1901) in the auditorium of the Historical Museum at the third concert organized by the Ethnographic Division and the Musicoethnographic Commission of the Imperial Society of the Lovers of Natural History, Anthropology, and Ethnography. Six Jewish folk songs were performed on the second part of this concert. In the fourth concert of the series (November 29, 1901), held in the Small Hall of the Conservatory, four Jewish folk songs were performed. At the sixth concert (April 20, 1902, at the Museum) three songs were performed in a violin and piano arrangement. All the Jewish folk songs performed at

tions of Jewish music in Russia. In the 1860s the young Moussorgsky transcribed a Jewish folk song sung by Jews who lived in his courtyard in St. Petersburg as they were celebrating Succoth. This melody served as the theme of the chorus "Isus Navin" and was originally used as the chorus of Levites in the opera *Salambo*.[3] The sources of Moussorgsky's other works on Jewish themes ("Jewish Song" for voice and piano, words by L. Mei, and the sixth piece of "Pictures at an Exhibition") are unknown. The fact that they are filled with strikingly individual, typically Jewish tunes and phrases shows that Moussorgsky wrote down (if not in notes, then in his mind) not just the aforementioned tune, but others as well.[4] Three Jewish folk dances are included in Karpenko 1864. To round out the known pre-Engel transcriptions of Jewish folk songs, we can add the melodies published by G. E. Golomb in 1887.[5]

While Engel's transcriptions were not the first, as noted earlier, they formed the start of a more or less systematic collecting job which has continued through the first half of the present century. Many of the best Jewish writers and cultural activists participated in the collection of oral folklore: I. J. Perets, Sholom Aleichem, M. Spector, S. Ginzburg, P. Marek, N. Prilutski, et al. The collecting and publishing of samples of Jewish folk music were fruitfully done by Y. L. Cahan, Z. A. Kiselhof, M. Kipnis, S. Leman, A. M. Bernstein and others; these were largely songs and textless tunes. A. Z. Idelsohn dedicated the ninth and tenth volumes of his *Hebräisch-orientalisches Melodienschatz* to such items.

At the beginning of the present century a whole constellation of Jewish

---

these concerts were transcribed and arranged by Engel (see n.d.; addenda 73, 74, 76). I have not listed all the subsequent concerts of the Commission at which Jewish works were played. After the establishment of the Society for Jewish Music in St. Petersburg (1908), concerts of Jewish music were arranged in many cities.

3. Rimski-Korsakov 1926:92. It is interesting to note a tune among Engel's 1898 transcriptions that is quite close to the melody Moussorgsky took as the theme of his chorus "Isus Navin." Here are both melodies (cf. Engel 1930: no. 6).

4. In his commentary on Moussorgsky's letters to V. Stasov, V. D. Komarov (*Raduga* 1922:240) says that the sculptor Antokol'skii sang Jewish melodies to Moussorgsky.

5. This anthology (Golomb 1887) contains twelve items. The first six are wedding motives: (1) seating the bride; (2) leading the groom to the *xupe* [wedding canopy—M.S.]; (3) leading the bride to the *xupe*; (4) bride's return from the *xupe*; (5) round-dance; (6) farewell dance. The other six items are arrangements of various songs.

Let me stress that the discussion here is only of printed transcriptions of Jewish folk music. There are considerably more unpublished transcriptions. First of all, one must note the klezmer transcriptions of all sorts of instrumental pieces performed at weddings. These are to be found in abundance in the second half of the nineteenth century. In addition, there were quite a few transcriptions of textless songs, mainly done by various cantors. These were of purely utilitarian significance; they were used for practical goals. Many of these manuscript albums of vocal and instrumental works have been preserved to our time; some have been acquired from various persons by the Cabinet.

composers and musicians* studied at the St. Petersburg Conservatory under the beneficial influence of Rimski-Korsakov, who constantly directed his multiethnic student body toward the sources of folk art. Gniessin (1956:208) writes about this:

How freely he expressed himself about the characteristics of these (multiethnic—M.B.) melodies, and with what sensitivity he encouraged students in their work of arrangement, and that includes Russians, Ukrainians, Latvians, Estonians, Armenians, and Jews. Once one of my classmates brought in two pieces, perhaps for violin and piano, titled "Oriental Melodies." "Very nice pieces," said Rimski-Korsakov after listening to the music, "but why are they called oriental melodies? After all, these are typically Jewish melodies—it's hard to confuse them with others!"

Another Rimski-Korsakov student, Lazar Saminsky (1914:78) writes:

Those of his students who have worked in the Jewish field have an exceptional feeling for the memory of Nikolai Andreevich. We will never forget his words, addressed to one of our comrades, perhaps E. I. Shklar, when he brought him a Jewish romance: "I'm glad to see you writing a composition with a Jewish flavor. It's quite strange that my Jewish students interest themselves so little in their own music. Jewish music lives; it is remarkable music and awaits its Glinka."

It is not surprising that at the St. Petersburg Conservatory the trend that led Jewish composers to their own native art was born, strengthened, and encouraged. This atmosphere quickly led to the organizing, in 1908, of the Society for Jewish Music by the young composers and musicians, which had as its goal the creation of Jewish compositions based on folk music. Among the active members of this society we find: M. F. Gniessin, A. M. Zhitomirsky, L. Saminsky, P. R. L'vov, M. A. Milner, I. Achron, S. B. Rosowsky, E. I. Shklar, Z. A. Kiselhof, and others. The young Jewish composers ran up against the fact of a total lack of printed editions of examples of Jewish folk music and so had to turn to the job of collecting. In that very year (1908), the Jewish Historic-Ethnographic Society was organized, which paid considerable attention to the collecting of examples of oral and musical art. In 1912–14 a series of expeditions was organized by the Society to villages in the Volynsk, Kamenets-Podol'sk, and other *gubernias* (czarist administrative units) in the southwestern region, now part of the Ukrainian S.S.R. These expeditions had already adopted the phonograph for the recording of Jewish folk music. The recordings made

[*"Musicians" here stands for *muzykal'nye deyateli,* a term with no English equivalent which includes a variety of people active in music, not necessarily composers or performing artists.—M.S.]

in these years by expedition participants have been preserved. In 1930 they were given to the Institute.

The collecting and study of oral and musical folklore began to be taken up by State agencies in the Soviet period. Special institutes were organized in the Belorussian and Ukrainian academies of science for the study of Jewish culture, including oral and musical folklore. Significant materials of all types and genres of Jewish folklore were collected. As of 1948, the *phonoteque* of the Cabinet numbered over 1,200 cylinders, including over 3,000 items (songs, textless tunes, instrumental pieces, theater numbers, etc.). This *phonoteque* subsumed all the recorded examples of Russian Jewish folk music, beginning from 1912: (1) 435 cylinders of the St. Petersburg expedition; (2) 30 cylinders of Engel's from villages in Volynsk from 1912; (3) around 800 cylinders done by the present author under the folklore division of the Institute (1928–36) and the Cabinet (1936–49), including recordings from 1928 to 1948.

YIVO (Jewish Research Institute) in Vilna did a great deal of work in the collecting of Jewish folklore (largely oral rather than musical). From 1925 to 1939 it operated at community expense, while in 1940–41 it became a State institute in Soviet Latvia.*

Only a small fraction of the enormous quantity of various folklore materials collected in the first half of our century by collectors and communal and state institutions has been published. Several branches of folk music remain represented in printed sources by isolated examples, giving a sketchy picture of these genres (e.g., instrumental music, theater music). It is with grief that I must confirm the destruction of the entire YIVO folklore archives, numbering tens of thousands of items, by the barbaric German fascists.[6] Various larger and smaller collections of individual collectors were also destroyed. The present anthology includes a small number of previously unpublished prerevolutionary songs of love and domestic lyric songs, textless tunes, and instrumental music. The materials are taken from unpublished books in a series entitled "Jewish Folk Music," which I prepared for publication during the years 1930–46. The

---

[*YIVO transferred its operations to its New York branch during World War II. Its headquarters at 1048 Fifth Avenue has become the major repository of archival materials relating to the culture of Eastern European Jews, including substantial as yet incompletely cataloged collections of musical manuscripts, published editions, and recordings. See Appendix B.—M.S.]

6. I have not been able to see the inventories of the folklore commission of YIVO. In Cahan 1938, inventory numbers are given for each item, the highest number being 62,691. Was this the last number for 1938? The collecting work continued even after that point.

series consists of five volumes: (1) published in 1934 [included in the present volume—M.S.], containing workers' and revolutionary songs of the 1905 period, as well as domestic and recruit songs; (2) love and family songs; (3) klezmer music; (4) textless songs; (5) music of the *purimšpil* [folk drama—M.S.].*

In the present volume, the first thirty-eight songs are love songs. The word "love" seemed forbidden in the conditions of nineteenth-century Russian Jewish life, so it would seem that love songs would have no place in the song repertoire. Weddings, as a rule, were early and concluded exclusively by matchmaking. There could be no question of free choice. In the more fanatic† circles, the newlyweds rarely saw each other until after the ritual betrothal. Nevertheless, collectors have found themselves faced with countless love songs of the most diverse types.

Having deeply studied Jewish songs and their context, Y. L. Cahan (1912a:xxv–xxvi, 1927:65–77) has shown that the love song was widespread as early as the sixteenth century and has been preserved orally down to the present. Among the folk songs collected since the end of the nineteenth century, one finds love and lyrical songs that are very close to those in the oldest manuscript collection of Jewish folk songs, written down in the late sixteenth century by Isaac Waliho. This collection (Rosenberg 1888; a photocopy of the manuscript is in the Cabinet from the archive of the late philologist N. Shtif) contains fifty-five songs, including lyric love songs, satirical songs, dance songs, bride's and groom's songs, and so on. The closeness of sixteenth-century songs to contemporary songs shows that even during the eighteenth and nineteenth centuries, a period when a wave of religiousness swept over Jewish literature, the common folk preserved older lyric and love songs and even created new ones.

Of course, the Jewish working masses‡ could not liberate themselves from the traditional view of marriage. In the midst of poverty, marriages were concluded through matchmaking; dowry (even if nonexistent) and

[*As Beregovski states, he excerpted from vols. 2, 3, and 4 to form the present work. A microfilm of the typescript of vol. 5 was recently brought to Israel by a Soviet emigré scholar and was kindly loaned to me for a brief reading by Professor Joachim Braun in Jerusalem in 1978. The manuscript is missing all the music examples, both those in the text and those appended as the main body of the anthology, save for a few fragments; nevertheless, it sheds considerable light on Beregovski's attitude toward and research on the *purimšpil* folk drama and its music.—M.S.]

[†Following Soviet practice of certain periods, Beregovski's "fanatic" here should be translated as "orthodox" or "observant" and will be glossed that way henceforth.—M.S.]

[‡Beregovski's "working masses" does not imply a proletariat but rather refers to the common people who must work hard for a living.—M.S.]

excellence of lineage played an important role. Yet boys and girls of this milieu were in a somewhat different situation, having to make a living as artisans or servants from an early age. Girls had to forego their pay to make up a dowry, without which they couldn't marry their boyfriends. Many circumstances contributed to the creation of the everyday* Jewish love song: long years of separation from kin and loved ones, life among strangers, the cheerless and back-breaking work of the seamstress, tailor, shoemaker, shop clerk, milliner, nanny, servant, and other working youth alongside the dream of a better future, and the striving toward and hope for reunion with the beloved, without which life was even harder and sometimes unbearable.

Among the love songs, one can identify a small group that expresses a budding youthfulness, as yet shy, barely acknowledging itself. The boy and girl are happy. There are few songs of this type in Jewish folklore. The majority of songs tell of unhappy love or of broken, at times cruelly injured and ridiculed, feelings. The protagonist is nearly always a girl, victim of unsuccessful love. Usually the obstacle to marriage is the social and material inequality of the lovers. Not infrequently the cause of separation is the young man's need to leave for work or military service. More rarely, one finds songs about the boy's betrayal, about his leaving the singer for another girl.

The Jewish love song is an intimate song, sung to oneself or in a circle of close friends, male or female. In general, Jewish folk songs are monophonic but also solo, performed by an individual. In the poor artisans' workshops (shoemakers, tailors, etc.) one can say that songs resounded from early morning till late at night. Love songs were among those sung at work, but at gatherings or, even more, among one's own immediate circle, love songs were not usually sung (Cahan 1912a:xxxv).

The present anthology also includes a small set of family songs, some of which relate to the wedding topic. It should be noted that no ritual wedding songs existed in the Yiddish language. What we call folk wedding songs are dance tunes or lyric and humorous songs about moments of the wedding ceremony. For example, nos. 50–52 tell of the girl's parting from her parents, but these songs were not sung at weddings. At Jewish weddings the scene of parting was accompanied by the band with no singing or even humming along. There are special *zaj gezunt* (farewell) songs in the instrumental repertoire for this occasion.

[*"Everyday" glosses *bytovaya;* however, the Russian term implies songs having to do with the way of life and is everyday in the sense of the "accustomed."—M.S.]

Many songs of the domestic cycle are devoted to the burdensome position of the woman in the past. Lullabies are particularly poetic, suffused with boundless maternal love.

The Jewish folk song is often topical. It tells of some concrete event, sad or happy. Developing the story, the anonymous author includes the names of those involved (cf. Dobrushin-Iuditskii 1947:11–12). Among the love songs, however, are some without specific plot. For example, the deep love song "Ven ix zol hobn fligelex" only hints at the weighty experiences of the boy and girl. They are separated, since the boy must leave.[7] The girl pours out her grief and longing in simple images and deeply moving words. The expressive poetic and musical means of Jewish folk song are still insufficiently studied.

In the overwhelming majority of cases, the melodies of Jewish folk songs are divided into periods consisting of two parts, each of which is subdivided into two musical phrases. This corresponds to the *abcb* (less common: *abab*) quatrain structure that predominates in Yiddish folklore. Not infrequently, the second musical part is undivided, although it is sung to a text of two lines with a clear caesura. Couplet verses can be found infrequently in love songs; their melodies have four phrases. Such melodies may be sung to two consecutive couplets (e.g., nos. 46, 54, 62), or both lines of text may be repeated (no. 36). No. 2 is a rare exception, having a melody of only two phrases. Here the melody is repeated every two lines.

The melodies of Jewish folk songs and of textless songs, as well as instrumental pieces, are symmetrical. In the practice of folksingers, musical phrases are often shortened, less commonly lengthened. In no. 27 the last measure of each phrase is prolonged as 4/4; otherwise it appears as two 3/4 measures.

Folk songs were never instrumentally accompanied; the solo singer interpreted it freely according to his or her taste. Yet the basic underlying symmetry can be clearly felt. The melodies unfold broadly in the range of an octave to a tenth, sometimes even wider. The tension mounts steadily to a climax, usually located in the third phrase.

Many Jewish love songs have been sung to the tune of the *šer* dance,[8] for example, "Špilt mir op di naje šer," no. 14. This song is part of a cycle

---

7. Since Yiddish has no verbal gender endings, it is often hard to tell who the speaker is in a monologue song. We can conclude that this is the song of a girl whose boyfriend had to leave, judging by the character of the text and images. A boy's departure was common, while a girl's was rare.

8. The *šer* is a couple folk dance, done by four or eight couples, mostly young people. The folk translate the name of this dance as "scissors," but that is incorrect. On this dance, see the note to no. 93 [also pp. 533–35—M.S.].

we might call "young love," where a tender and shy feeling is expressed simply, modestly, and sincerely. The *šer* was one of the most widespread and beloved of wedding dances, and its melody, always lively and merry, is somehow permeated with the holiday spirit of the wedding. The psychological link between the dance melody and the feelings of the song's hero is clear and understandable. The melody reminds the boy not only of the wedding at which he heard it, but also of the girl he dreams of marrying.

Bearing in mind that it is the girl who is usually the victim of unsuccessful love, we find love songs in which she expresses her anger, often addressing curses to whoever separates the lovers. We find this in nos. 21, 22, 23, and 25. In some songs of this type, one is struck by the contradiction between the happy melody and the meaning of the text. Thus, for example, in "Tsu dajn mamen hob ix gornit" (no. 25) the girl curses the mother, father, brother, and sister of her beloved, who have caused a separation. It is most striking that these mournful words are sung to the lively, merry melody of the *šer,* which shapes the musical form of the song. It might be explained by the fact that the song the girl heard at a wedding evokes the memory of the beloved with whom she dreamed of going to the altar. But happiness has been destroyed, and the happy tune of the *šer* underlines the dramatic situation. We have a similar two-level psychological content in no. 23, "Verže zogt az a libe iz a grojs glik." Here the girl curses youths who leave young sweethearts, and the melody is in waltz time. The waltz was also popular among Jews and was danced exclusively at weddings.

Turning now to the scale structure of Jewish folk songs, we note first that the natural minor occupies an important place (up to 50 percent of melodies). This scale has long been part of Jewish folk music. It should be remembered that in the fourteenth to sixteenth centuries Jewish folk art was influenced by German folk music, in which the natural minor occupied an important place. It is also one of the predominant scales among the Eastern Slavs, among whom Jews have been living for several centuries.

There are elements of modulation in some tunes. More frequently, one finds the juxtaposition of an initial minor phrase with a subsequent phrase in the relative major (nos. 1, 8, 25, 33, etc.). In textless songs and instrumental pieces there is room for sporadic lowering of the fifth. More often, at the final cadence of a section or of a whole piece, one can find the lowered second in all styles and genres. The natural minor is also found in synagogue music. Cantors call it *jištabaxgust,* according to the first word of the prayer [to which the tune is set—M.S.]. Here also the lowered second can be a characteristic of the scale. The scale we call "altered Phrygian" also occupies an important place (Ex. 1). Nearly one-quarter (almost 1,500) of all the instrumental tunes I know are in this scale. It constitutes a somewhat smaller proportion of the song and textless tune repertoire.

Example 1

A whole series of facts indicates that this scale is not the dominant of the harmonic minor, though it resembles it, in folk practice (amateur or professional). The klezmorim and cantors call this scale *frigiš* after the medieval Phrygian mode. For the cantors, the phrase in Example 2, which has the characteristic intonation of the altered Phrygian, was used for "tuning up."[9]

Example 2

The altered Phrygian differs from the Phrygian in having a major third above the tonic, whereas the Phrygian has a minor third. The basis of the altered Phrygian is the triad G-B-D.

One often finds modulations to various scales in instrumental pieces and textless tunes. The modulation frequently goes from altered Phrygian to the minor a fifth below, and the reverse; this way both scales can be accommodated in one piece.

We can adduce the following substantive argument in support of the position that the scale in question is not the dominant of the harmonic minor but is a self-sufficient scale. Folk music is characterized by a predominance of stability, not only over whole songs but also for each section, which ends stably. If we were to regard the altered Phrygian as the dominant of the harmonic minor, we would have to consider the whole piece unstable, whereas in fact we perceive these pieces as being completely stable.

9. We find something similar in medieval vocal practice, when a number of melodic formulas arose which served as a kind of scalar model (cf. Nef 1938:24).

Another scale, which we call the "altered Dorian" (Ex. 3) is represented somewhat differently in the various divisions of Jewish folk music ranging from around 5 percent in tunes to 12 to 15 percent in songs and instrumental pieces. It is based on a minor triad. [See pp. 513–66 for a detailed study of this scale—M.S.]

Example 3

The fourth degree of the scale is raised. In strophic songs, the fourth is often lowered in the third phrase and then raised again in the fourth [final—M.S.] phrase. In songs using the altered Dorian scale, melodic lines, in conjunction with other expressive musical parameters, often occur as an expression of strong outcries of lament. The study of pieces in this scale leads one to believe that folk musical practice was well aware of the expressive qualities of melodies in this scale.[10]

In this context it is worth noting several humorous songs in the present anthology. Two of them (nos. 66, 68), though different in content and tendency, partially use the altered Dorian. No. 66 tries to make us believe that a thief cleaned out the protagonist, whereas it is clear that the latter is mocking his own utter poverty—no thief could covet that "wealth." The lamenting melodic line of the altered Dorian helps create the impression of false alarm. Something similar happens in no. 68. The mischievous girl cries out: "Gevalt, where can I get the board, how can I roll out the dough and get a knife to cut it into *varničkes,* but most of all, get a boy to share the meal."

The major scale plays an insignificant part in Jewish folk music. It is unevenly represented in the various branches and genres and is most often found in the textless tunes, and quite rarely in songs. Without discussing scales that are even rarer, we can cite no. 36 as a beautiful example of the Mixolydian; elements of this scale can be found in no. 14, for example.

Melodic lines and melody types typify each scale. We have already noted certain characteristic melodic lines for the natural minor; here we can introduce a series of typical melodic lines for the altered Phrygian and altered Dorian (Ex. 4). Using such melody types, a performer can easily "tune himself up" and often move from a melody in one scale to another.

10. See nos. 18, 46, 49, etc. For an interesting example of modulation from natural minor to altered Dorian, see the note to no. 30.

Example 4

The distinctive genre of textless songs was highly developed in Jewish folklore. These tunes were quite varied, being at times lyric, epic, dramatic, celebratory, and so on. There are also a great number of textless dance tunes. The Cabinet can count 800 textless songs in its collection. This by no means exhausts the total number of such pieces still preserved among the folk. The genre of textless songs overlaps with that of melodies set to or adapted to fixed Hebrew texts, the "table songs" sung during the Sabbath meal. Textless songs have long been in circulation. They may be the result of not allowing musical instruments on the Sabbath or holidays for religious reasons. The dance tunes were sung at general festivities or evenings at home. Notwithstanding the wide use of instrumental music in Jewish life, bands played only at weddings, for the most part. Usually people limited themselves to singing, occasionally accompanied by amateur musicians, most often violinists.

The genre of textless songs particularly flourished in connection with the appearance of Hasidism. The propagandists of the mystical religious movement, which arose in the 1730s, strove for broad use of tunes as a way of attracting the masses. On the other hand, we find textless songs in locales where Hasidism had almost no adherents.

The masses put their joy of life into their songs and dances, trying to forget the hardships of life. M. Olgin (1927) picturesquely describes Jewish dances in his memoirs:

Tens of young and old people in long-skirted frock coats with lambskin hats on their heads, wearing long boots, danced in a circle. Eyes sparkle; faces are full of joy—yes, this is the true, pure joy of childhood! "I tell you, Avrom-Mordxe," shouts one of the dancers, "it's not worth suffering. Forget everything and live while you can!"

One could also see this picture at traditional Friday evenings (*Mlave malke,* greeting Queen Sabbath) and at every possible public and family celebration.

The melodic lines and forms of textless songs are close to those of instrumental pieces. Still this is a specifically vocal genre that established distinctive features over the course of the centuries. Textless songs were sung exclusively by men, joined, whenever possible, by boys. Female participation in general singing was impossible; women were forbidden to sing in the presence of [non-kin—M.S.] men on religious grounds. Textless songs were sung both solo and in chorus. In principle, this was almost the only genre of Jewish song performed publicly and collectively. These songs, like other folk songs, were sung monophonically.

We noted earlier that textless songs consist of several (two to five) sections. The *abcb* scheme, also widespread in song melodies and corresponding instrumental works, was especially favored. A typical piece might consist of two phrases and a refrain, which served as a kind of rondo. Today this scheme is rare. Most commonly it is a dynamic form, in which tension gradually increases from section to section. The highest tension, or climax, occurs in the third section *(c)*, after which *b* is repeated, having a calming effect after the climax. This form occurs in nos. 78, 87, 100, 103, 104, 112, 116, 118, 120, 125, 130, 131, 134, 137, 138, 139, 141, 144, 147, and in the variants (given in the notes) of nos. 104 and 147. Often the *c* section goes into another scale. An *abcd* scheme is never found in the dance tunes.

We know nothing about when this scheme was introduced into Jewish folk music, but we do find it in the songs of the followers of Nachman of Bratslav (1772–1811), which testifies to the fact that this scheme had wide currency in the late nineteenth and early twentieth centuries, as well as in the contemporary instrumental music, closely related to this genre. As is well known, the followers of this tsadik remained true to his memory and accepted no substitute after his death. Once a year they journeyed to Uman' on the day of his death (the place where the tsadik lived and died), seeking to preserve the special quality of his ritual in all details. This includes the songs, which they tried to retain unaltered. Of seven tunes I have transcribed from the repertoire of these Hasidim, three are in the *abcb* scheme.

What do we know of the composers of these songs? Up to the second half of the nineteenth century we know nothing about them. Folklore has not preserved the name of a single composer. The designation of certain songs as the melody of a given tsadik (e.g., "dem rebns nign, dem bałšem-tovs nign") still tells us nothing about the tsadiks' putative authorship. On the other hand, from the close attention paid to music and song by Hasidim and the movement's ideologues, who fostered the creation and performance of songs, it is clear that the talented among the tsadikim actually did compose new tunes. The scanty available evidence from the late nineteenth century on indicates that the composers of songs were primarily cantors of the traditional type *(baltfile)* who had no musical training at all. In the Ukraine, the songs of the cantor and table-singer of Talna, Yosef Volinets (1838–1919, known popularly as Yosl Tolner), were widespread. We find references in the memoir literature to musically gifted members of the folk who composed songs. I. Kotik, author of the valuable book *My Memoirs* (three volumes in Yiddish; cf. I:133–34), tells of one such composer of songs.

The songs reached us through oral tradition. In 1945, I transcribed a series of songs from B. Lantsman, age sixty, ascribed to Yosl Tolner. Lantsman learned them directly from the composer in the mid-1890s. My attempts to ascertain the authenticity of the versions reached no conclusive results for lack of variants.

One can scarcely hope to establish the artistic heritage of these popular authors of songs. However, there can be no doubt that the creative activity of these folk artists did not disappear—it has significantly enriched Jewish folk music.

Instrumental music occupies a special position in Jewish folk music. The repertoire of the klezmer, the musician who played principally at weddings, usually consisted of melodies of a certain type. Over the course of the centuries a repertoire developed that was designed for listening as well as for dancing. Specific expressive and technical devices were used in these pieces for particular instruments, usually the violin (widespread among Jews), clarinet, and flute.

A klezmer *kapelie* (band) functioned in all the cities and towns with a significant Jewish population. In the last quarter of the nineteenth century a kapelie consisted of the following instruments: one or two first violins, one or two second violins, cello or bass (both, in large bands), flute, clarinet, horn (often bass horns as well), Turkish drum with plates, and small drum.

Not only in the nineteenth century was it impossible to imagine a Jewish wedding without instrumental music. We have it on reliable evidence that in Germany in the eighteenth century, when for reasons such as a royal death music-making was forbidden at a Jewish wedding, the celebration would be moved beyond the confines of that locality (Grudemann 1922:89). Much more rarely one finds Jewish musicians playing at public festivities and celebrations.

Basically the Jewish wedding ceremony relied on instrumental music, which filled the role of a sort of organizer of the whole process. Music accompanied the greeting of the matchmakers, played *mazltov* (congratulations) in honor of each guest, accompanied the *badxn* (a traditional participant who entertained the guests with rhymed improvisations and capers) for the custom of *bazecn di kale* (seating the bride), led the couple to the *xupe* (wedding canopy), resounded after the wedding, accompanying the couple and the guests to the wedding feast, and so on. Banqueting songs were played, dance music to speed the parting guests, right up to the final *zaj gezunt* (farewell) piece when everyone left.

Instrumental music occupied an important role in Jewish folklore. The repertoire for listening or for dancing, whether specifically Jewish *(frej-laxs, šer)* or general, was always renewed and enriched. The general klezmer repertoire consisted of many hundreds of pieces, among which are truly excellent works. By the end of 1948 the Cabinet had collected around 1,500 klezmer pieces, which does not begin to exhaust the klezmer repertoire of the Ukraine alone.

Outside the klezmorim, the folk professional musicians, one found many amateur players, principally fiddlers. As a rule, amateur fiddlers studied with local klezmorim. Their repertoire included all sorts of *frejlaxs* (this term denoted round dances as well as light, lyrical pieces), textless songs, and sometimes somewhat more complicated pieces. These amateurs played in a small domestic circle, most often at Friday night gatherings. They never appeared outside the confines of the family, since only klez-morim performed publicly. Amateurs played just the melodies, while klezmorim played in ensembles. Unfortunately, we do not have a single transcription of the ensemble playing of klezmorim, so I could only give the basic melody line here.

Folk Songs with Texts

1. Ven ix zol hobn fligelex
Если бы у меня были крылышки

1. Ven ix zol ho _ bn fli _ ge _ lex,

aj, volt ix dox cu dir ge _ floj_gn,

un ven ix zol ho _ bn ke _ ej_te _ lex

volt ix zix cu dir ge _ coj _ gn.

2. Oj, af je _ ner zajt tajx, af je _ ner zajt breg,

oj, zajne_ nen di cvaj _ gn ge _ boj_gn,

do _ or _ tn, do _ or _ tn štejt majn zis _ le bn

mi _ it far _ ve _ ejn _ te oj _ gn, oj _ gn.

3. Oj, her šojn uf cu vej _ nen, her šojn uf cu klo _ gn,

mit vej _ nen ve _ stu gor _ nit ma _ xn.

E _ fn uf majn harc, ve _ stu zen, vi s'iz švarc,

ve _ stu vi _ sn, vi lib hob ix di _ ix.

1. **Ven ix zol hobn fligelex,**
   Aj, volt ix dox cu dir geflojgn,
   Un ven ix zol hobn kejtelex,
   Volt ix zix cu dir gecojgn. } *2 mol*

2. **Oj, af jener zajt tajx, af jener zajt breg,**
   Oj, zajnen di cvajgn gebojgn,
   Dortn, dortn štejt majn zis-lebn }
   Mit farvejnte ojgn.   } *2 mol*

3. **Oj, her šojn uf cu vejnen, her šojn uf cu klogn,**
   Mit vejnen vestu gornit maxn.
   Efn uf majn harc, vestu zen, vi s'iz švarc, }
   Vestu visn, vi lib hob ix dix.   } *2 mol*

2. Afn barg, untern barg
На горе, под горой

1. A _ ín barg, un_te_rn barg štejt E_ster di gri _ ne.

E_ster štejt, Av_ro_hom gejt, Av _ ro _ hom_ o _ vi_nu.

2. Volt ix ge_hat a fin_ge_rl, (e) volt ix mit dem vin_ ken.

Volt ix ge_hat a be_xe_rl, volt ix fun dem trin_ken.

3. Volt ix ge_hat štri_ke_lex, volt ix mit zej ci_en.

Volt ix ge_hat fli_ge_lex, volt ix mit zej fli_en...

1. Afn barg, untern barg
Štejt Ester di grine.
Ester štejt, Avrohom gejt,
Avrohom-ovinu.

2. Volt ix gehat a fingerl,
Volt ix mit dem vinken.
Volt ix gehat a bexerl,
Volt ix fun dem trinken.

3. Volt ix gehat štrikelex,
Volt ix mit zej cien.
Volt ix gehat fligelex,
Volt ix mit zej flien...

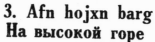

3. Afn hojxn barg
На высокой горе

1. Afn hojxn barg un afn grinem groz
   Štejen tajbelex cvej, oj, cvej,
   Zej kušn zix un haldzn zix bejde banand,
   Vos far a tajneg filn zej. } 2 mol

2. Oj, du forst avek, un, oj, du forst avek,
   Af vemen loztu mix iber?
   Oj, for že nit, oj, for že nit, tajer lebn majner,
   Kum aher un zec zix anider. } 2 mol

3. Der balegole hot zix cugeštelt, der balegole hot zix cugeštelt,
   Azoj hobn mir zix geštelt trern in majne ojgn.
   Ot hob ix dix gezen, ot hob ix mit dir geredt,
   Un in ejn minut bistu fun mir farflojgn. } 2 mol

4. Du bist majn harc
Ты мое сердце

1. Du bist majn harc, du bist majn le _ bn, oj, vi kon_stu dos gor _ nit far_štejn? Ven ix zol dir nor ejn zifc ton ge _ bn, oj, be _ ser nejn, un be _ ser nejn. Ven ix zol ko _ nen ejn zifc ton ge _ bn, be _ ser nejn, un be _ ser nejn.

Bap.

2. Zi _ se briv hos _ tu fun

3. Majn mu _ ters milx, vos ix

1. Du bist majn harc, du bist majn lebn,
   Oj, vi konstu dos gornit farštejn?
   Ven ix zol dir nor ejn zifc ton gebn, } 2 mol
   Beser nejn, un beser nejn.

2. Zise briv hostu fun mir gelezn,
   Dos iz gevezn hejse verter af a kaltn štejn,
   Oj, vos iz den mit dir gevezn, } 2 mol
   Beser nejn, oj, beser nejn.

3. Majn muters milx, vos ix hob gezojgn,
   Hot fun mir di libe arojsgecapt,
   Oj, ix bin vi a fejgele fun ir nest farflojgn, } 2 mol
   Oj, oj, oj, x'hob zix gornit gexapt.

4. Vos a tog, štarbt an ejver
   Un di blutn blajbn štejn,
   Ix volt šojn veln beser zajn in kejver, } 2 mol
   Nor beser nejn, un beser nejn.

5. In drojsn gejt a regn
На дворе идет дождь

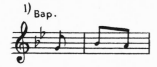

1. In drojsn gejt a regn,
   Un in štub iz xmarne...
   Ix hob gehat a tajere libe,
   Biter iz majne...

2. Biter iz majne
   Fun majn gebojrn....
   Ix hob gehat a tajere libe
   Un hob zi ongevojrn.

3. Ix hob zi ongevojrn
   Un ken cu ir nit kumen...
   Vos štejt far majne ojgn —
   Un ken cu ir nit kumen.

4. Ix volt cu ir gegangen —
   Zict zi zejer vajt,
   Ix·volt dox zi a kuš geton —
   Šem ix zix far lajt.

5. Far lajt tu ix zix šemen,
   Me zol fun mir nit rejdn...
   Ict iz šojn di cajt gekumen,
   Mir muzn zix cešejdn.

6. Cešejdn iz nit kejn lebn,
   Se iz nox erger fun a get...
   Zaj gezunt, majn tajer lebn,
   Ix for fun dir avek.

7. Ix for fun dir aveket
   Zeks un drajsik majl...
   Ix hob gemejnt, majn libe iz af ejbik —
   Cum sof iz gor af dervail.

6. Di dozike naxt
В ту ночь

1. Di dozike naxt, vos mir hobn bejde farbraxt biz cvelf azejger nox der halber naxt. Mir zajnen bejde azoj lang gezesn, biz mir hobn in got fargesn...

2. Helf mir, goteńu, ojf dem vaserl, nelf mir, goteńu, du alejn. elnd bin ix vi a štejn...

3 Dajne ejgelex zajnen pendelex šrajbn zolstu ofte briv cu mir.

1. Di dozike naxt, vos mir hobn bejde farbraxt
   Biz cvelf azejger nox der halber naxt.
   Mir zajnen bejde azoj lang gezesn,
   Biz mir hobn in got fargesn...

2. Helf mir, goteńu, ojf dem vaserl,
   Helf mir, goteńu, du alejn.
   In vajte lender bin ix farflojgn,
   Elnd bin ix vi a štejn...

3. Dajne ejgelex zajnen tinterlex,
   Un dajne bekelex iz best papir,
   Dajne hentelex zajnen pendelex —
   Šrajbn zolstu ofte briv cu mir.

7. Ix nem mir majn feder
Я беру перо

1. Ix nem mir majn fe _ der in der hant,

maj _ ne ge _ dan _ ken, zej zaj _ nen mir ce _ tro _ gn,

vu že nemt men a _ za (min) gu _ tn frajnt,

er zol mir di šmer _ cn ojs _ zo _ gn.

Vu že nemt men a _ za ge _ tra _ jen men _ čn,

er zol vi _ sn, vos in maj _ nem har _ cn iz,

in maj _ nem har _ cn i' dox a stra _ da _ ńe,

majn stra _ da _ i' dox gor um _ zist.

1. Ix nem mir majn feder in der hant,
   Majne gedanken, zej zajnen mir cetrogn,
   Vu že nemt men aza (min) gutn frajnt,
   Er zol mir di šmercn ojszogn.
   Vu že nemt men aza getrajen menčn,
   Er zol visn, vos in majnem harcn iz,
   In majnem harcn iz dox a stradanje,
   Majn stradanje iz dox gor umzist.

2. Oj, af dem hojxn barg
   Un af dem grinem groz
   Mir flegn dortn arumšpacirn
   Un di blumen hobn undz gešmekt in der noz.
   Ject iz farvaksn di steške
   Fun undzer libn špacirn...
   Adje, adje, majn tajer lebn,
   Xasene hobn ken ix nit mit dir.

8. Di fajerdike libe
Пламенная любовь

1. Di fa_jer_di_ke li_be tut in maj_nem har_cn bre_nen... Vos kumt a_rojs, az ix hob dix lib, a' mir ke_nen zix nit ne_men. Vos ne_men.

1. Di fajerdike libe
   Tut in majnem harcn brenen...
   Vos kumt arojs, az ix hob dix lib, ⎫
   Az mir kenen zix nit nemen.　　 ⎬ 2 mol

2. Du zogst, du host mix lib,
   Du gejst arajn in štub,
   Du gejst avek cu an ander mejdele ⎫
   Un grobst af mir a grub.　　　 ⎬ 2 mol

3. Du grobst af mir a grub
   Un falst alejn arajn...
   Ix hob dox šojn gepojlt, ⎫
   Az du solst majner zajn. ⎬ 2 mol

9. Du forst avek
Ты уезжаешь

1. Du forst a_vek, majn ta _ jer le _ bn,

af ve _ men loz _ tu mix i _ ber,

oj, cu ve _ men (e) ken ix, oj, a vort ojs _ re _ je_ dn,

a z nit cu dir, iz nor cu zix, oj, a_lejn.

Oj, cu ve _ men ken ix, oj, a vort ojs _ rej _ dn,

az nit cu dir, iz nor cu zix, oj, a _ lejn.

4. Oj, saj a šte _ te _ le, saj a der_ſe_le,

oj, oſ _ te b_ri_ve _ lex zol_stu mir š _ raj _ bn,

oj vej, of_te b_ri_ve_lex zol_stu mir š_raj _ bn,

az᾽an ej_ge_ne por zo_ln mir far_blaj_bn.

1. Du forst avek, majn tajer lebn,
   Af vemen loztu mix iber,
   Oj, cu vemen ken ix, oj, a vort ojsrejdn, ⎤
   Az nit cu dir, iz nor cu zix, oj, alejn. ⎦ *2 mol*

2. Oj, mir darfn zix šojn bejde cešejdn,
   Azoj vi der guf mit der nešome,
   Oj, az undzere sonim veln zix dervisn. ⎤
   Oj, derlebn veln zej zix a nekome. ⎦ *2 mol*

3. Oj, a nekome hobn zej zix šojn derlebt,
   Ix farhof cu got, az se vet nit zajn af lang,
   Ci gedenkstu, vej, du majn tajer lebn,
   Az ix fleg mit dir tajnen azoj vi mit a gutn frajnt. ⎤ *2 mol*

4. Oj, saj a štetele, saj a derfele,
   Oj, ofte brivelex zolstu mir šrajbn,
   Oj vej, ofte brivelex zolstu mir šrajbn,
   Az an ejgene por zoln mir farblajbn. ⎤ *2 mol*

10. Ongekuševet un ongelubevet
Нацеловались и намиловались

1. Ongekuševet un ongelubevet
   Fun dem tojer biz dem ban,   *2 mol*
   Un vi der tog hot nor avekgeriet [?], }
   Iz er vi in jam arajn.   } *2 mol*

2. Oj vej, mame, kačkes švimen,
   Un zej plešken mit di fis,   *2 mol*
   Ven vet šojn majn libster kumen }
   Oder šikn xoč a grus.   } *2 mol*

3. Oj vej, mame, bern brumen,
   Un zej šoklen mit di berd.   *2 mol*
   Ojb di libe iz a švindl, }
   Vel ix lign tif in dr'erd. } *2 mol*

11. Oj vej, mame, kačkes švimen
Ой, мама, утки плавают

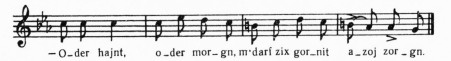

1. —Oj vej, mame, kačkes švimen,
   Ven vet šojn majn liber kumen?
   —Oder hajnt, oder morgn,
   M'darf zix gornit azoj zorgn.

2. —Mame, x'vil cum pojezd gejn,
   X'vil majn libn dortn zen,
   X'vil dortn zen majn xosn
   Un derbaj zix take kušn.

12. X'hob dix lib
Я люблю тебя

1. —X'hob dix lib, ix hob dix lib,
   Dem grunt fun majnem harcn.
   Arumgenumen, a kuš geton,
   Cugedrikt cum harcn.

2. — Ojb du zogst, du host mix lib, —
   Hob ix dix nit fajnt,
   Ojb du zogst, du forst avek —
   For ix mit dir hajnt...

3. Zol er forn, zol er forn,
   Zol er zuxn glik,
   Ojb du vest zajn majn bašerter —
   Vestu kumen curik.

13. X'hob dix lib
Я люблю тебя

1.—X'hob dix lib, ix hob dix lib, oj, mir far daj_ne bej _ ner,
mir far daj_ ne bej _ ner, nem mix,oj, a_rum un gib mix, oj, a kuš,
ven se zet nit kej _ ner, kej _ ner, kej _ ner,

2. St'zix lo_zn i _ be_rn va _ ser - zol_stu zix nit trin _ ken,
3. Vest fo_rn i _ be_rn fa _ jer - zol _ stu nit bre _ nen,

du vest ze_en šej_ne mej_de_lex_nox mir zol_stu ben_ken, ben_ken.
du vest ze_en šej_ne mej_de_lex,nor mix zol_stu ke _ nen, ke _ nen.

1. X'hob dix lib, ix hob dix lib,
   Oj, mir far dajne bejner,   *2 mol*
   Nem mix, oj, arum un gib mix, oj, a kuš,
   Ven se zet nit kejner, kejner. } *2 mol*

2. St'zix lozn ibern vaser —
   Zolstu zix nit trinken,   *2 mol*
   Du vest zen šejne mejdelex —
   Nox mir zolstu benken,benken. } *2 mol*

3. Vest forn ibern fajer —
   Zolstu nit brenen,   *2 mol*
   Du vest zen seine mejdelex,
   Nor mix zolstu kenen,kenen . } *2 mol*

14. Špilt mir op di naje šer
Сыграйте мне новый шер

1. Špilt mir op di naje šer, vos s'arojsgekumen, ix hob lib a mejdele un ken cu n'ir nit kumen.

2. Ix volt gegan cu n'ir ahejm, vojnt zi zejer vajt, (e) volt ix zi a kuš geton, šem ix zix far lajt.

3. Nit azoj gor far lajt, nor far zix alejn, x'volt šojn a baln zajn, zajn mit ir alejn.

1. Špilt mir op di naje šer,
   Vos s'arojsgekumen,
   Ix hob lib a mejdele
   Un ken cu n'ir nit kumen.

2. Ix volt gegan cu n'ir ahejm —
   Vojnt zi zejer vajt,
   Volt ix zi a kuš geton —
   Šem ix zix far lajt.

3. Nit azoj gor far lajt,
   Vi far zix alejn,
   X'volt šojn a baln zajn
   Zajn mit ir alejn.

15. Ix hob gebojt a mojerl
Я строила домик

1. Ix hob ge_bojt a mo _ je_rl, a mo _ je _ rl,

a mo_je _ rl mit zeks fen _ cter...

Un vi _ fl ši _ du _ xim me hot mir ge _ redt,

bi _ stu ge _ ven der šen _ ster.

1. Ix hob gebojt a mojerl,
   A mojerl mit zeks fencter... *2 mol*

   Un vifl šiduxim me hot mir geredt, } *2 mol*
   Bistu geven der šenster.

2. Ix hob geflanct a vajngortn,
   Der vajngortn iz nit gerotn... *2 mol*

   X'hob faršpilt majne junge jorn, } *2 mol*
   Oj, vi a kartjožnik in kortn.

3. Du host mir gebundn di hent mit di fis, di hent mit di fis
   Un gelozt mix švimen, *2 mol*

   Es vet kumen a cajt, ven du vest mix zuxn } *2 mol*
   Un vest mix nit kenen gefinen.

16. Oj, a švarce xmare t'dem himl bacojgn
Ой, черная туча небо затянула

1. Oj, a švarce xmare t'dem himl bacojgn,
   Un di volkns, zej hobn zix cešprejt.   *2 mol*

   Šojn lang, lang aza cajt, vos cajt ix stradaje, ⎫
   Un du host mir azoj majn kop fardrejt.   ⎬ *2 mol*

2. Lomir onhejbn, lomir ohnejbn di velt cu baklern
   Un dos vort, oj, libe cu farštejn...   *2 mol*

   Šojn lang, lang aza cajt, vos cajt ix špil a libe, ⎫
   Un du host getun mir majn kop fardrejen.   ⎬ *2 mol*

3. Oj, a libe, a libe hob ix ongehojbn špiln
   Mit xejšek uh mit fil oxote...   *2 mol*

   Oj, fun majn bestn veg, oj, hostu mix aropgefirt ⎫
   Un arajngeštelt hostu mix in a blote.   ⎬ *2 mol*

4. In a blote, n'a blote, oj, hostu mix arajngeštelt,
   Majne fis mit majne hent gebundn...   *2 mol*
   Oj, se nito aza dokter, oj, axuc dir af der velt, ⎫
   Er zol mir konen hejln majne vundn.   ⎬ *2 mol*

17. Papir iz vajs, un tint iz dox švarc
Бумага бела и чернила черны

3. Dajn ta_li_je dajn po _ ze, dajn ej_de_ler fa - son,

in har_cn brent a fa _ jer, me zet im nit on,

ni _ to der menč, vos zol ze_n, vi mir b_rent,

majn tojt un majn le _ bn iz ba dir in di hent.

4. Dajn mi _ ne, dajn š _ mej _ xl, dajn ej_de_le fi _ gur...

Oj, zog že mir, du ojg, vos iz mit dir der mer?

Az ven du laxst mit grojs frejd, dan rint fun dir a trer...

Uj uj uj uj uj uj uj uj uj uj uj uj uj

1. Papir iz vajs, un tint iz dox švarc...
Cu dir, majn gelibte, cit zix majn harc.
Ix volt nor gezesn draj teg noxanand
Cu kukn nor in dajne ejgelex un gletn dir dajn hant.

2. Nextn bin ix af a xasene geven,
Fil šejne mejdelex hob ix dortn gezen,
Fil šejne mejdelex, cu dir kumt nit gor,
Cu dajne švarcinke ejgelex un cu dajne švarce hor.

3. Dajn tal'e, dajn poze, dajn ejdeler fason,
In harcn brent a fajer, me zet im nit on,
Nito der menč, vos zol zen, vi mir brent,
Majn tojt un majn lebn iz ba dir in di hent.

4. Dajn mine, dajn šmejxl, dajn ejdele figur...
Oj, zog že mir, du ojg, vos iz mit dir der mer,
Az ven du laxst mit grojs frejd,
Dan rint fun dir a trer...

18. Ix hob gevolt, oj, mameńu
Я хотела бы, мама

1.–Ix hob ge_volt, oj, ma_me.ńu, zajn, oj, na_ve_nad ba je_ nem

un zix val_ge_rn ba je.nem in a štub.

Oj. nor ejn zax, oj, bet ix ba dir, go_te_.ńu,

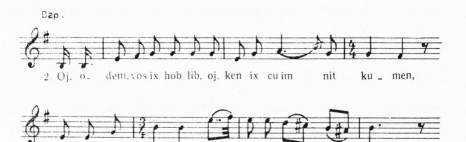

iz ne_men zol ix o- dem, vos ix hob lib.

Вар.

2. Oj, o_ dem, vos ix hob lib, oj, ken ix cu im nit ku _ men,

cu vos že tojg mir majn le_bn oji der velt?

1. — Ix hob gevolt, oj, mameńu, zajn, oj, navenad ba jenem
Un zix valgern ba jenem in a štub.
Oj, nor ejn zax, oj, bet ix ba dir, goteńu,
Az nemen zol ix o-dem, vos ix hob lib.

2. Oj, o-dem, vos ix hob lib, oj, ken ix cu im nit kumen,
Cu vos že tojg mir majn lebn ojf der velt?
Az ix hob nit, mameńu, kejn mazl,
Iz dox majn šejnkajt farštert.

3. — Gib a kuk, majn toxter, viazoj du bist gevorn,
Viazoj du gejst ajn jeder rege un minut,
Oj, gej arajn, main toxter, cu a dokter,
Vet er dir zogn, vos iz dir gešen.

4. — Ox, ix bin, mameńu, bam dokter šojn gevezn,
Ix bin geven bam dokter in štub.
Nor a recept hot er mir faršribn,
Az nemen zol ix ot dem, vos ix hob lib.

5. Nor dem, vos ix hob lib, ken ix šojn nit nemen,
Cu vos že tojg mir majn lebn af der velt?
Ject, az ix hob šojn, mameńu, nit kejn mazl,
Iz dox majn fajnkajt farštert.

6. Ci gedenkstu, mame, az du bist mit a šxejne gezesn?
Zi hot zix arojsgeklibn — tut dir ojx bank
Un az me špilt op fir jor mit a jingele a libe,
Ci ken men zogn, az me hot im fajnt?

7. Ci gedenkstu, merder, az du bist ba mir in štub gezesn,
A fajer hot in dajnem harcn gebrent.
Un ject, az mir gejen durx af ejn stežke,
Du fardrejst dajn kop, du host mix nit derkent...

19. Ver klapt dos azoj špet banaxt
Кто это стучит так поздно ночью

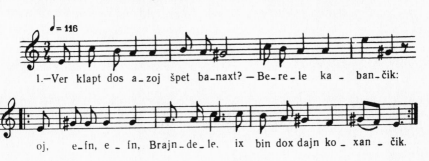

1.—Ver klapt dos a‿zoj špet ba‿naxt? — Be‿re‿le ka ‿ ban‿čik:

oj, e‿ín, e ‿ ín, Brajn‿de‿le. ix bin dox dajn ko ‿ xan ‿ čik.

1. — Ver klapt dos azoj špet banaxt?
   — Berele kabančik:
   Oj, eín, eín, Brajndele, ⎫
   Ix bin dox dajn koxančik. ⎬ *2 mol*

2. — Viazoj zol ix dir efenen,
   X'hob mojre far majn tatn.
   — Oj, eín, eín, Brajndele, ⎫
   Se vet dir gornit šatn.   ⎬ *2 mol*

3. — Viazoj zol ix dir efenen,
   X'hob mojre far majn mamen.
   — Oj, eín, eín, Brajndele, ⎫
   Ix vel zix lang nit zamen. ⎬ *2 mol*

4. — Viazoj zol ix dir efenen,
   X'hob mojre far majn bruder.
   — Eín, eín, Brajndele,   ⎫
   Max nit kejn geruder.   ⎬ *2 mol*

5. — Viazoj zol ix dir efenen,
   X'hob mojre far majn švester.
   — Eín, eín, Brajndele,   ⎫
   Du bist ba mir di šenste.   ⎬ *2 mol*

20. Se hot zix farxmaret af a regn
Небо в облаках

1. Se hot zix farxmaret af a regn,
   Se hot zix farxmaret af a regn...
   — Kum ahercu, du šejn mejdele,
   Ix vel dix epes fregn. } 2 mol

2. — Ix vil cu dir ništ gejn,
   Ix hob mojre far majn tatn...
   — Kum arojs, du šejnink mejdele,
   Se vet dir gornit šatn. } 2 mol

21. Nemt zix cunojf, oj, ale majne podruges
Соберитесь, все мои подруги

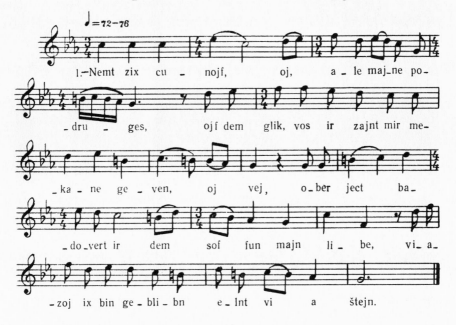

1. — Nemt zix cunojf, oj, ale majne podruges,
Ojf dem glik, vos ir zajnt mir mekane geven, oj vej,
Ober ject badovert ir dem sof fun majn libe,
Viazoj ix bin geblibn elnt vi a štejn.

2. Oj . . . .
Oj, elnt, oj, elnt, mameńu, azoj vi a štejn, oj vej,
Nor betn‑bet ix dix, majn tajer lebn,
Az du zolst xoč kumen oft cu mir cu gejn.

3. — Viazoj ken ix cu dir gejn,
Viazoj ken ix mit dir redn, oj vej,
Az lib hob ix dix, dem grunt fun majnem harcn,
Nor nemen, dušuńu, konen mir zix nit.

4. — Zog mir dem emes, vos iz geven ba ajx in štub,
Vos dajn mame vil mix nit far kejn šnur, oj vej,
Blind zol zi vern, me zol zi darfn firn,
Az kejn cvejte šnur zol zi far zix nit zen.

5. Dajn tate, dajn tate zol ojx nit kenen gejn,
Un af zajne ojgn zol er ojx nit zen, oj vej,
A nedove, a nedove zol er kumen cu mir betn,
Un ix zol visn, az dos iz er geven.

6. A šejne nedove vel ix im gebn,
   Farvos er hot mir zajn zun nit cugelozt.
   . . . .
   . . . .

7. Dajn švester, dajn švester vinč ix ojx a klole,
   Az se zol ir zajn fil erger fun mir.
   Got zol ir helfn iberajor a libe špiln,
   Un se zol ir ojsgejn aza sof vi mir.

8. — Majn švester, majn švester hostu nit vos cu šeltn,
   Un majne eltern zajnen ojx nit derbaj, oj vej,
   Ix bin ništ kejn kind, ix hob mix batraxt,
   Az du bist an orem mejdele, — ix ken mit dir nit gejn.

9. — Kum nor aher, majn tajer lebn, cu mir,
   Cu vos že hostu zix azoj špet batraxt, oj vej,
   Se iz šojn draj jor cajt, az du tust cu mir in štub arajngejn,
   Un fun der falšer libe lozt zix ojs a tajx...

22. Vos že tojg mir dajn šejner vajngortn

На что мне твой красивый виноградник

1 Vos že tojg mir dajn šej _ ner vajn _ gor _ tn,

az flan _ cn kon ix im nit,

vos že tojg mir mit dir a li _ be špi _ ln,

1.
az ne _ men ko _ nen mir zix nit,

2.
az ne _ men ko _ nen mir zix nit.

2.—Kejn knas _ mol ko _ nen mir nit ma _ xn,

x'hob an el _ te _ re šve _ ster fun mir...

— Kejn tno _ jim ko _ nen mir nit šraj _ bn _

1. 2.
ix' Stej nit on dajn ma _ nen far kejn šnur, šnur.

Вар. 1)

1. – Vos že tojg mir dajn šejner vajngortn,
   Az flancn kon ix im nit,
   Vos že tojg mir init dir a libe špiln, } *2 mol*
   Az nemen konen mir zix nit.

2. Kejn knasmol konen mir nit maxn,
   X'hob an eltere švester fun mir...
   — Kejn tnojim konen mir nit šrajbn —
   Ix štej nit on dajn mamen far kejn šnur. } *2 mol*

3. — Vos že tustu cu šeltn majn mamen,
   C'hot dir majn mame dem veg amol farštelt ?
   Majn mame zogt, az zi vil a šejne mejdele, } *2 mol*
   A šejn mejdele mit nadn a sax gelt...

4. — Vos že zol ix ton, az ix bin nit kejn šejne
   Un ix hob nit kejn nadn mit kejn gelt ?
   Vos že zol ix ton, az ix bin a gemejne, } *2 mol*
   Ci darf ix nit visn fun kejn velt?

5. — Hodi šojn cu vejnen un cu klogn,
   Un nem arop dem šejnem ponem fun mir,
   Un viš zix ojs di trern fun di ojgn, } *2 mol*
   Un af ejbik farblajbstu mit mir...

23. Ver se zogt, az a libe iz a grojs glik

Кто это говорит, что любовь большое счастье

U vu vu vu vu vu vu vu vu...

1. Ver se zogt, az a li_be iz a grojs glik, oj, vej iz mir,

oj, a li_be iz dox an um_glik af der velt, oj, a velt!

a li _ be za va _ re ča _ xot ke,

oj, fun a li _ be ge_jen jun_ge kin_der fun der velt!

U vu vu vu vu vu vu vu vu vu vu vu... D'al

Вар.

2. dajn a _ hin, oj, me zol _ hin, un az

bol_ni_ ce, vet zi nit

U vu vu vu vu vu vu vu vu vu vu vu vu...

1. Ver se zogt, az a libe iz a grojs glik, oj vej iz mir,
   Oj, a libe iz dox an umglik af der velt,   *2 mol*
   A libe z'a vare čaxotke,
   Oj, fun a libe gejen junge kinder fun der velt!

2. Oj, in Vilne iz faran a skore-pomošč, oj vej iz mir,
   Me zol brengen dajn mamelen ahin,   *2 mol*
   Un az me vet zi brengen in bolnice,
   Vet zi nit fodern mer kejn cirung un kejn gelt

3. Oj, in bolnice z'faran cvej vajse klorinke betelex,
   Ejne far dajn mamelen un di andere far dir,   *2 mol*
   Un az me vet ajx brengen in bolnice —
   Zolstu nit zogn, az du host zix ajngelibt in mir.

4. — Majn mame hostu nit vos cu šeltn, oj vej iz mir,
   Ix bin a menč mit an ejgenem farštand,   *2 mol*
   Ix vel nox nemen a ganc fajne mejdele,
   Oj, zi zol nox hobn a remeslo in hant.

U vu vu vu vu vu vu vu vu...

24. Špacirn, špacirn zajnen mir bejde gegangen
Мы вместе пошли гулять

1. Špa _ ci _ rn, špa _ ci _ rn zaj _ nen mir bej _ de ge _ gan _ gen

a _ rum un a _ rum dem bul _ var, var,

uf _ ge _ ge _ sn un ojs _ ge _ trun _ ken

fun a _ ler _ lej cu _ ker _ varg

Вар.

2. —Mu _ ter maj _ ne, mu _ ter ge _ tra _ je...

1. Špacirn, špacirn zajnen mir bejde gegangen
   Arum un arum dem bulvar, *2 mol*
   Ufgegesn un ojsgetrunken ⎱ *2 mol*
   Fun alerlej cukervarg. ⎰

2. —Muter majne, muter getraje,
   Du tu mir nox ejnmol culib, *2 mol*
   Du farleš šojn, farleš šojn dos fajer in majn harcn ⎱ *2 mol*
   Un gi' mir šojn dem, vos ix hob lib. ⎰

3. — Toxter majne, toxter getraje,
   Ajngebn vel ix dir sam,   *2 mol*
   Du host a tatn a nogid, an ojšer —
   Un du vest nemen a nogid far a man. } *2 mol*

4. — Muter majne, muter getraje,
   Mit kejn guts nemt men zix nit iber.   *2 mol*
   Ix hob šojn gezen, fil gresere miljonen.
   Un af kicve kumen zej iber. } *2 mol*

5. — Toxter majne, toxter getraje,
   Mit mir hostu šojn opgeredt,   *2 mol*
   Az du konst šeltn dajn ejgenem foter —
   Nem dir un for mit im avek. } *2 mol*

6. — Griše-duše, Griše-lube,
   Mit majn foter hob ix šojn opgeredt, *2 mol*
   Lomir farnemen dos gelt mit di klejder,
   Un kejn Amerike veln mir avek. } *2 mol*

7. — Kejn Amerike forn, oj, xasene hobn,
   Iz dox an ejdele zax,   *2 mol*
   Her nor ojset, vos ix vel dir zogn,
   Az fun undzer libe zol nit vern kejn tajx. } *2 mol*

8. Texelex, texelex, zej rinen zix ojset,
   Di gribelex blajbn dox lejdik...   *2 mol*
   A dos mejdele, vos zi špilt a falše libe,
   Der šem farblajbt ir af ejbik. } *2 mol*

25. Cu dajn mamen hob ix gornit
Твоей матери не желаю зла

1. Cu dajn ma‿men hob ix gor‿nit, oj vej, gor‿nit, oj vej, gor‿nit,

vajl zi zogt, az zi z'nit šul‿dik in dem.

In di haj‿zer zol zi a‿rum‿ge·‿jn,

zol nox ku‿men be‿tn a šti‿kl brojt cu mir.

In di haj‿zer zol zi a‿rum‿ge‿jn,

zol nox ku‿men be‿tn a šti‿kl brojt cu mir.

Az cu kejn li‿be, ma‿me, zol zi zix nit mi‿šn,

oj vej, col ir, oj, go‿tu‿‿ńu, far mir.

1. Cu dajn mamen hob ix gornit, oj vej, gornit, oj vej, gornit,
   Vajl zi zogt, az zi z'nit šuldik in dem.
   In Ji hajzer zol zi arumgejn,
   Zol nox kumen betn a štikl brojt cu mir. } *2 mol*
   Az cu kejn libe, mame, zol zi zix nit mišn,
   Oj vej, col ir, oj, gotuńu, far mir.

2. Cu dajn tatn hob ix gornit, oj vej, gornit, oj vej, gornit,
   Vajl er zogt, er iz nit šuldik in dem.
   In Kijever špitul zol er lign
   Un zol nit hobn, ver s'zol arajngejn cu im, } *2 mol*
   Az cu kejn libe, tate, zolstu zix nit mišn,
   Oj vej, col im, oj, gotuńu, far mir.

3. Cu dajn bruder hob ix gornit, oj vej, gornit, oj vej, gornit,
   Vajl er zogt, az er iz nit šuldik in dem.
   In Kijever tfise zol er zicn
   Un zol nit zen kejn menčn far zix, } *2 mol*
   Az cu kejn libe, bruder, zolstu zix nit mišn,
   Oj vej, col im, oj, gotuńu, far mir.

4. Cu dain švester hob ix gornit, oj vej, gornit, oj vej, gornit,
   Vajl zi zogt, az zi z'nit šuldik in dem.
   Draj jor zol zi zix mit a libe arumšlepn, } *2 mol*
   S'zol ir ojsgejn aza min sof vi mir.
   Az cu kejn libe, mame, zol zi zix nit mišn,
   Oj vej, col ir, oj, gotuńu, far mir.

26. Aj, du forst avek
Ой, ты уезжаешь

Aj, du forst a- ve- ket, un, aj, du forst a_vek fun mir,

af ve _ men že loz _ tu mix i _ ber?

A _ zoj v'a štejn, a _ zoj v'a bejn, vej z cu ma _ jn le_bn,
Ot heng ix zix, ot štex ix zix, oj, far daj_ne oj_gn,

oj, zec že zix lem mir ejn kap a _ ni _ der.
oj, zec že zix lem mir ejn kap a _ ni _ der.

Aj, du forst avek un, aj, du forst avek fun mir,
Af vemen že loztu mix iber?   *2 mol*
Azoj v'a štejn, azoj v'a bejn, vej z'cu majn lebn,
Oj, zec že zix lem mir ejn kap anider.
Ot heng ix zix, ot štex ix zix, oj, far dajne ojgn,
Oj, zec že zix lem mir ejn kap anider.

27. Fun grojs dosade lejg ix zix, mameńu, šlofn
С большой досады я ложусь спать

1. Fun grojs do _ sa _ de lejg ix zix, ma_me_ńu, šlo _ fn

mit (e) bej _ de hen _ te _ lex cu _ ko _ pn...

Ix špil a li _ be, un ix hob ·xa _ ro _ te

un ken cu_rik šojn ojx nit xa _ pn. Ix xa _ pn.

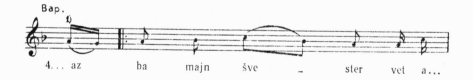

Вар.

4... az ba majn šve _ ster vet a...

5... az majn ge _ lib _ te vet cu dir in...

1. Fun grojs dosade lejg ix zix, mameńu, šloĺn
   Mit bejde hentelex cukopn..
   Ix špil a libe, un ix hob xarote ⎱ *2 mol*
   Un ken curik šojn ojx nit xapn. ⎰

2. Oj, cugebundn bin ix, cugebundn,
   Un cugebundn bin ix mit a štrik...
   In majnem harcn se brent a fajer, ⎱ *2 mol*
   Un lešn ken es, mame, kejner nit. ⎰

3. Di eršte zax vel ix ba dir, mameńu, betn,
   Oj, un di zax zolstu mir ton culib:
   Oj, saj bam esn un saj bam trinken,
   Oj, zol majn nomen nit zajn ba dir in štub. ⎱ *2 mol*

4. Di cvejte zax vel ix ba dir, mameńu, betn,
   Oj, un di zax zolstu mir tun culib:
   Az ba majn švester vet a kind gebojrn,
   Oj, zol majn nomen nit zajn ba dir in štub. ⎱ *2 mol*

5. Di drite zax vel ix ba dir, mameńu, betn,
   Oj, un di zax zolstu ispolńajen:
   Az majn gelibte vet cu dir in štub arajngejn, ⎱ *2 mol*
   Zolstu ir nit abižajen. ⎰

6. Di lecte zax vel ix ba dir, mameńu, betn,
   Az du vest gejn aĺ kejveroves,
   Oj, un di zax zolstu mir tun culib: ⎱ *2 mol*
   Dem erštn kejver zolstu zajn ba mir. ⎰

7. Oj, mit štrik bin ix, mameńu, gebundn,
   Un mit štrik bin ix štark cugebundn...
   Ništo kejn bruder kejn getrajer, ⎱ *2 mol*
   Er zol mir hejln majne vundn. ⎰

28. Fun grojs dosade ver ix anšlofn
С большой досады я засыпаю

1. Fun grojs do - sa - de ver ix an - šlo - fn

mit (e) bej - de hen - te - lex cu - ko - pn,

mit bej - de hen - te - lex cu - ko - pn... Oj, ix

špil a li - be, un ix hob xa - ro - te,

un ke - rik kon ix nit xa - pn.

1. Fun grojs dosade ver ix anšlofn
   Mit bejde hentelex cukopn... *2 mol*
   Oj, ix špil a libe, un ix hob xarote, ⎫
   Un kerik kon ix nit xapn. ⎭ *2 mol*

2. Oj vej, Miše, majn tajerer Miše,
   Vu bistu fun mir antrunen? *2 mol*
   Oj, ix tu dix zuxn in jeder vinkele, ⎫
   Un ix kon dix, Mišeńu, nit gefinen. ⎭ *2 mol*

3. In gospitul štejt a betele,
   Dos betele iz mit vajsn arumgecojgn... *2 mol*
   Un dortn **ligt**, ax, majn tajerer Miše ⎤
   Mit zajne cvej švarce ojgn.   ⎦ *2 mol*

4. Lebn gospitul štejt a bejmele,
   Dos bejmele iz in drajen ajngebojgn... *2 mol*
   Oj, dortn gejt zix majn tajer zis-lebn ⎤
   Mit ire cvej farvejnte ojgn.   ⎦ *2 mol*

5. Lebn jam štejt a šifele,
   Dos šifele iz nit ful un nit lejdik... *2 mol*
   Oj, avelxe mejdele, vos špilt a libe, ⎤
   Farfaln iz zi šojn af ejbik.   ⎦ *2 mol*

29. Oj, di zumerdike naxt
Ой, прекрасная летняя ночь

1. Oj, di zu_mer_di_ke naxt, ma_me, di šej _ ne,

ven a _ le men _ čn, zej tu _ en a _ rum _ gejn...

oj, di le _ vo_ne, zi hot zix šojn der _ vaj _ tert, un di

zun hejbt šojn on a_rojs _ cu _ gejn, oj, di le _ gejn.

2. Oj, af a _ bejn_ke_le zaj_nen mir bej _ de ge _ ze _ sn,

un ge _ ze _ sn zaj_nen mir bej_de tif far _ traxt...

un vi_fl taj_nes mir ho_bn bej_de ajn _ ge _ taj _ net,

un kejn en_de ho_bn mir nox bej_de nit ge _ naxt.

un vi _ fl taj _ nes, oj, mir ho _ bn ajn _ ge _ taj _ net,

un kejn en _ de ho _ bn mir nox bej _ de nit ge - maxt.

1. Oj, di zumerdike **naxt**, mame, di šejne,
   Ven ale menčn, zej **tuen** arumgejn...
   Oj, di levone, zi hot zix šojn dervajtert,
   Un di zun hejbt šojn on arojscugejn. } *2 mol*

2. Oj, af a benkele zajnen mir **bejde** gezesn,
   Un gezesn zajnen mir bejde tif fartraxt...
   Un vifl tajnes mir hobn bejde ajngetajnet,
   Un kejn ende hobn mir nox bejde nit gemaxt. } *2 mol*

3. — Vos že far an ende, oj, vestu mit mir maxn, —
   Ix bin a jingele, vos ix **darf** cum žereb štejn,
   Oj, un kejn knasmol, oj, kon ix mit dir nit maxn, — }
   Bist a klug mejdele, du darfst alejn farštejn. } *2 mol*

4. — Oj, du gi'že mir, lube, s'rexte hentele,
   Oj, du šver mir cu, ci du host mix emes lib,
   Un du šver mir cu, ci du vest mix nit farbajtn, }
   Oje, biskele dem finctern grub. } *2 mol*

5. — Oj, majn hentele ken ix dir gebn,
   Un ix šver dir cu, az ix hob dix emes lib,
   Un ix šver dir cu, az ix vel dix nit farbajtn, }
   Oje, biskele dem finctern grub. } *2 mol*

30. Oj, a kojl, di fajerdike kojl
Ой, пуля, пламенная пуля

1.-Oj, a kojl, di fa _ jer _ di _ ke kojl,

a _ za kojl kon dem men _ čn der _ ši _ sn,

nor ver se hot dix fun mir op _ ge _ redt

far an an_der mej_de_le cu ve _ rn a xo _ sn...

2. Oj, du bist šojn a xo _ sn ge _ vo _ rn,

se zol dir zajn mit ma _ zl un mit glik,

nor ix bin dox nox kejn ka_le nit ge _ vo_rn,

un um_ke_rn ve_stu zix, oj, cu mir ke _ rik.

3. Spa _ ci_rn zaj _ nen mir bej _ de ge - gan_gen,

der šlax iz ge _ ve _ n far undz šmol...

Nor ver se hot dix fun mir op _ ge _ redt,

a rajn zol er in dem vi_stn go_spi _ tol,

nor ver se hot dix fun mir op_ge _ redt,

a rajn zol er in dem vi_stn go _ spi _ tol.

1. — Oj, a kojl, di fajerdike kojl,
   Aza kojl kon dem menčn deršisn,   *2 mol*
   Nor ver se hot dix fun mir opgeredt
   Far an ander mejdele cu vern a xosn...} *2 mol*

2. Oj, du bist šojn a xosn gevorn,
   Se zol dir zajn mit mazl un mit glik,   *2 mol*
   Nor ix bin dox nox kejn kale nit gevorn,
   Oj, umkern vestu zix, oj, cu mir kerik. } *2 mol*

3. Spacirn zajnen mir bejde gegangen,
Der šlax iz geven far undz šmol... *2 mol*
Nor ver se hot dix fun mir opgeredt,} *2 mol*
Arajn zol er in dem vistn gospitol. }

4. Un hajnt, az mir gejen bejde špacirn,
Der šlax iz gevorn far undz brejt... *2 mol*
Nor der zol kejnmol fun kejn guter velt nit visn,} *2 mol*
Ver se hot undzer libe cešejdt... }

5. Cešejdt hot men undz bejde
Azoj vi dem guf mit der nešome... *2 mol*
Nor az dajne sonim veln zix dervisn, }
Derlebn veln zej zix in undz a nekome.} *2 mol*

6. Du forst avek, majn tajer zis-lebn,
Az dajne eltern zoln zix mit mir nit šemen.
. . . .
. . . .

7. — Oj, hodi šojn cu vejnen un cu klogn,
Fun dajne hejse trern vert dajn šejner ponem nas.. *2 mol*
Nor demlt veln mir zix bejde cešejdn, }
Ven a fejgele vet ojstrinken dem kas (! ?).} *2 mol*

31. Di mame t'gezogt „nejn"
Мама мне говорила „не надо"

1. Di ma_me t'ge_zogt „nejn", volt dox ba_darft zajn nejn,

az ix zol mit dem žu _ lik nit gejn,

ix bin mit im ge _ gan_gen, un ix hob mit im far _ braxt,

a til - un _ tel hot er fun mir ge _ maxt.

1. Di mame t'gezogt „nejn", volt dox badarft zajn nejn,
   Az ix zol mit dem žulik nit gejn,
   Ix bin mit im gegangen, un ix hob mit im farbraxt,
   A til-un-tel hot er fun mir gemaxt. } *2 mol*

2. Ci gedenkstu, ci gedenkstu jenem donerštik afdernaxt,
   Ven mir hobn zix getun tun cu derkenen?
   Hajnt, du bośak, dercejlst du dajne gute-brider,
   Az on kejn nadn vilstu mix nit nemen. } *2 mol*

3. Draj voxn noxanand bin ix gelegn krank,
   Un du bist cu mir kejn ejn mol nit gekumen,
   Di beste refue volstu mir geven gebraxt,
   Ven du zolst ejn mol gevezn cu mir kumen. } *2 mol*

4. Oj vej, cores, majne cores, zej ringlen mix arum
   Azoj vi a bonder di fas,
   Hajntike mener — me tor dox zej nit glejbn,
   Azoj vi dem hunt af der gas. } *2 mol*

32. Aj du, du, ruk zix cu
Ой, ты, пододвинься ближе

1. Aj, du, du,   ruk zix cu,   zec zix ne_bn mi _ ir,

ojb du vilst a   li _ be špi_ln, špil že nor mit mi _ ir

1. Aj, du, du, ruk zix cu,
   Zec zix nebn mir.   *2 mol*
   Ojb du vilst a libe špiln, }
   Špil že nor mit mir   } *2 mol*

2. Forst avek, forst avek,
   Lozt zix gornit hern,   *2 mol*
   In majn harcn brent a fajer, }
   Vet dos mir nit dern [?]   } *2 mol*

3. Oj, du parx, oj, du parx,
   Ales iz dox tajer,   *2 mol*
   Aza boxer, vi du bist, }
   Hot di vert a drajer   } *2 mol*

33. Du host dox ongezogt
Ты ведь сказал

Du host dox on - ge - zogt, az du bist a mal - čiš - ke,

far - vos že ho - stu mir ge - drejt a - zoj majn kop?

Du host dox on - ge - vi - zn, konst nit zajn majn xo - sn,

cu vos že ho - stu zix un - ter - ge - xapt?

Ge - ar - bet ho - stu af so - bor - ne plo - ščad,

ge - vojnt le - bn ji - di - šn špi - tol,

du flegst dox durx - gejn a - le tog le - bn maj - ne fen - cter,

kum a - rajn cu mir xoč nox ejn mol.

Ta ra ra ti‿ri‿da ta ta ti‿ri‿da ta ta oj ta ta

Ta ra ra ti‿ri‿da ta ta ti‿ri‿da ta ri ta ta,

ta ra ra ti‿ri‿da ta ta ti‿ri‿da ta ta ta ta,

ta ra ra ra ra ra ra ra ra ra

Du host dox ongezogt, az du bist a malčiške,
Farvos že hostu mir gedrejt azoj majn kop?
Du host dox ongevizn, konst nit zajn majn xosn,
Cu vos že hostu zix untergexapt?

Gearbet hostu af soborne ploščad,
Gevojnt lebn jidišn špitol,
Du flegst dox durxgejn ale tog lebn majne fencter,
Kum arajn cu mir xoč nox ejn mol.

Tarara tirida ta ta . . . .

34. Oj, a xolem hot zix mir gexolemt
Ой, сон мне приснился

1.-Oj, a xo_lem _ hot zix mir ge _ xo _ lemt,

oj, a šlex_ter xo_lem hot zix mir ojs _ ge _ daxt,

az majn ge _ lib _ ter libt šojn a cvejt mej _ de _ le

un fun mir hot er xoj _ zek ge _ maxt.

2.-Oj, in kejn xo _ lem tor men, majn kind, nit glej _ bn,

vajl a šlex_ter xo_lem firt a _ rop fun dem veg,

un mor_gn in der _ fri ve_ln mir cum re _ bn fo _ rn,

un der re _ be t'ojs_lej_gn dem xo _ lem cu gut.

3.-Oj, v'a_zoj že vet mir der re _ be hel _ fn?

Ci (je) ge_bn vet er mir den dem, vos ix hob lib?

1. — Oj, a xolem hot zix mir gexolemt,
   Oj, a šlexter xolem hot zix mir ojsgedaxt,
   Az majn gelibter libt šojn a cvejt mejdele
   Un fun mir hot er xojzek gemaxt.

2. — Oj, in kejn xolem tor men, majn kind, nit glejbn,
   Vajl a šlexter xolem firt arop fun dem veg,
   Un morgn inderfri veln mir cum rebn forn,
   Un der rebe t'ojslejgn dem xolem cu gut.

3. — Oj, v'azoj že vet mir der rebe helfn?
   Ci gebn vet er mir den dem, vos ix hob lib?
   Oj, cu dem, vos ix hob lib, 'el ix zix lozn forn,
   Un kumen vel ix glajx cu im in štub.

4. Ix hob zix šojn gelozt in veg arajn forn,
   Un geforn bin ix dox axt teg durxanand,
   Un in vos far a štetele ix bin arajngeforn,
   Iz mir ojsgekumen ojsštrekn di hant.

5. — Senkt že, menčn, šenkt a nedove,
   ....a šreklexe nojt,
   Un derex a libe bin ix a farfalene,
   Senkt že, menčn, af ajn štikele brojt.

6. — Vos že gejt ir azoj o'gerisn?
   Farvos že šemt ir zix nit ojsštrekn di hant?
   Un ver ir zent un vos ir zent, darf ix dox šojn **visn,**
   Vajl ajer ponem iz mir štark bakant.

7.—Ix alejn bin a gebojrene odeser,
   Ba majne eltern bin ix gevaksn gliklex un rajx,
   Un derex a libe bin ix a farfalene,
   Un a nedove bet ix ba ajx.

8. — Ix hob a froj mit **cvej** kinder,
   Un dos drite darf ot, ot, ot zajn…
   Ix vel farlozn majn froj mit di kinder,
   Un du vest majn gelibte zajn.

9. — Oj, farloz nit dajn froj mti di kinder
   Un leb zix ojs **mit** ir gliklex dajne jor,
   Un derex dir bin ix a farfalene
   Un mučen vel ix zix šojn ale majne jor.

35. Zint ix bin cu majn sejxl gekumen
С тех пор, как я стал понимать вещи

1. Zint ix bin cu majn sej _ xl ge _ ku - men,

oj, a _ zoj bin ix fun der li _ be far _ brent.

In majn har _ cn, oj, brent a he _ liš fa _ jer,

ra _ te _ ven kon mix kej _ ner nit.   nit.

1. Zint ix bin cu majn sejxl gekumen,
   Oj, azoj bin ix fun der libe farbrent.
   In majn harcn, oj, brent a heliš fajer,
   Rateven kon mix kejner nit. } 2 mol

2. Dajne cvej švarcinke ejgeiex
   Mit dajn kepele švarce hor...
   Vi a magnet hostu mix cugecoign}
   Ject kircstu mir majne jor. } 2 mol

3. Vu že nemt men a dokter a gutn,
   Er zol mir gebn a refue cu majn harc,
   Er zol mir gebn a recept, oj vej, a gutn,
   Er zol zajn cu majnem šmarc. } 2 mol

4. M'hot mir geredt kales mit nadn,
   Un mit klejder, un mit a sax gelt.
   Vi a magnet hostu mix cugecojgn,
   Ject gej ix durx dir fun der velt. } 2 mol

36. Ix hob gelibt a mejdele fun axcn jor
Я полюбил девушку восемнадцати лет

1. X'hob ge _ libt a mej _ de _ le fun ax _ cn jor,

un li _ bn lib ix zi šojn cvej--draj jor.

x'hob ge _ libt a mej _ de _ le fun ax _ cn jor,

un li _ bn lib ix zi šojn cvej-draj jor.

2. A _ lejn, a _ lejn iz er a _ vek _ ge-fo _ rn,

un zajn ge _ lib _ te iz krank ge _ vo _ rn.

a _ lejn, a _ lejn iz er a _ vek _ ge _ fo _ rn,

un zajn ge _ lib _ te iz krank ge _ vo _ rn.

1. X'hob gelibt a mejdele fun axcn jor,
Un libn lib ix zi šojn cvej-draj jor. } *2 mol*

2. Alejn, alejn iz er avekgeforn,
Un zajn gelibte iz krank gevorn. } *2 mol*

3. Me hot im avekgešikt a šneln briv,
Az zajn gelibte, krank zi ligt. } *2 mol*

4. Er hot prisiret zajn guts un gelt
Un iz geforn af der frajer velt. } *2 mol*

5. — Gut morgn, gut morgn, gelibte majne,
Vi kumstu in dem švarcn betl zajn? } *2 mol*

6. — Gut jor, gut jor, gelibter knajber,[1)]
Oj, du vest zajn der bagreber majner. } *2 mol*

7. — Oj, nejn, nejn, se kon nit zajn,
Undzer libe vet lenger zajn. } *2 mol*

8. Vi se gekumen nox halber naxt —
Dos trojer-lixtele hot er gebraxt. } *2 mol*

9. Er hot genumen di trojer-lixt
Un hot batraxt ir gezixt. } *2 mol*

10. Vi zi z'geven šejn un roz,
Azoj iz zi gevorn grin vi groz. } *2 mol*

11. Er hot aruntergelejgt di hant untern orem,
Zi iz šojn kalt un ojx nit varem. } *2 mol*

12. Er hot ir ojsgeton dos xupe-klejd
Un hot ir ongeton dos trojer-klejd. } *2 mol*

13. Er hot zi balejt fun štub biz tojer,
Er hot af ir arufgeštelt a švern mojer. } *2 mol*

14. Af dem mojer vet vaksn blumen.
— Cu dir ingixn vel ix kumen. } *2 mol*

15. Se ništ ariber kejn draj frimorgn,
Der junger knajber iz šojn ojx geštorbn. } *2 mol*

16. Oj, oj, s'a jomer un a klog,
Cvej gelibte in ejn axt-tog. } *2 mol*

17. Af der macejve vet zajn gešribn,
Az cvej gelibte iz do farblibn. } *2 mol*

[1)] **Knajber–Knabe** (jingl).

37. Nem mir arojs a ber fun vald
Приведи мне медведя из лесу

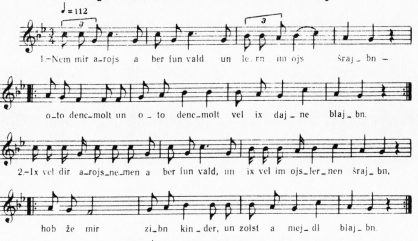

1. — Nem mir arojs a ber fun vald
Un lern im ojs šrajbn —
Oto dencmolt un oto dencmolt ⎱
Vel ix dajne blajbn.   ⎰ *2 mol*

2. — Ix vel dir arojsnemen a ber fun vald,
Un ix vel im ojslernen šrajbn,
Hob že mir zibn kinder,   ⎱
Un zolst a mejdl blajbn.   ⎰ *2 mol*

3. — Ix vel dir hobn zibn kinder
Un a mejdl blajbn,
Max že mir a vigele   ⎱
On hole un on gecajgn.   ⎰ *2 mol*

4 — Ix vel dir maxn a vigele
On hole un on gecajgn,
Nej že mir ojs zibn hemder ⎱
On nodlen un on zajdn.   ⎰ *2 mol*

5. — Ix vel dir ojsnejen zibn hemder
On nodlen un on zajdn,
Xap že mir ojs ale fiš fun jam, ⎱
S'zol kejn ejne nit blajbn.   ⎰ *2 mol*

6. — X'vel dir ojsxapn ale fiš fun jam,
S'zol kejn ejne nit blajbn,
Pregl op zibn fišelex,   ⎱
Zej zoln lebedik blajbn.   ⎰ *2 mol*

7. — Ix vel dir opreglen zibn fišelex,
Zej zoln lebedik blajbn,
Max že mir a lejterl,   ⎱
S'zol cum himl štajgn.   ⎰ *2 mol*

8. — Ix vel dir maxn a lejterl
S'zol cum himl štajgn,
Ix bin a nar, un du a greserer, ⎱
Lomir bejde švajgn.   ⎰ *2 mol*

38. Ix vel dir fun švarce kojln
Из черного угля

1-Ix vel dir fun švar_ce koj_ln ma_xn vaj_se kraj_dn.

un du zolst mir fun ho_ber-štroj Špi_nen vaj_se zaj_dn. zaj_dn

1. — Ix vel dir fun švarce kojln
   Maxn vajse krajdn,
   Un du zolst mir fun hober-štroj }
   Špinen vajse zajdn.　　　　　　} 2 mol

2. — Ix vel dir fun hober-štroj
   Špinen vajse zajdn,
   Nor du zolst mir a lejter šteln, }
   Er zol cum himl štajgn.　　　　} 2 mol

3. — Ix vel dir a lejter šteln,
   Er zol cum himl štajgn,
   Nor du zolst mir zibn kinder hobn }
   Un a mejdl blajbn.　　　　　　　} 2 mol

4. — Ix vel dir zibn kinder hobn
   Un a mejdl blajbn,
   Du zolst mir zibn vign maxn }
   On meser un on gecajgn.　　 } 2 mol

5. — Azoj vi se nit meglex zibn vign maxn
   On meser un on gecajgn,
   Azoj z'nit meglex zibn kinder hobn }
   Un a mejdl blajbn.　　　　　　　 } 2 mol

6. — Azoj vi se nit meglex zibn kinder hobn
   Un a mejdl blajbn,
   Azoj z'nit meglex a lejter šteln, }
   Er zol cum himl štajgn.　　　　　} 2 mol

7. — Azoj vi se nit meglex a lejter šteln,
   Er zol cum himl štajgn,
   Azoj z'nit meglex fun hober-štroj }
   Špinen vajse zajden.　　　　　　} 2 mol

8. — Azoj vi se nit meglex fun hober-štroj
   Špinen vajse zajdn,
   Azoj z'nit meglex fun švarce kojln }
   Maxn vajse krajdn.　　　　　　　} 2 mol

9. — Azoj vi se nit meglex fun švarce kojln
   Maxn vajse krajdn,
   Un ojb du vilst majne zajn — }
   Zolstu ba mir blajbn.　　　　 } 2 mol

39. Zic ix afn štejn
Я сижу на камне

♩=80

1.-Zic ix a᷃ _ fn štejn, plac ix fun ge _ vejn.

a _ le mejd_lex ho _ bn xi _ jes, un ix ej _ ne nejn.

2. Fi _ še _ lex in va _ ser un kre _ pe _ lex in pu _ ter...

Vo _ ser xo _ sn vil nit ne _ men, a ru _ ex in zajn mu _ ter.

1. Zic ix afn štejn,
Plac ix fun gevejn.
Ale mejdlex hobn xijes,
Un ix ejne nejn.

2. Fišelex in vaser
Un krepelex in puter...
Voser xosn vil nit nemen,
A ruex in zajn muter.

40. In hober, in korn
В овсе, во ржи

1. In hober, in korn,
   In hober, in korn
   Hot Roxele dem fartex farlorn,
   Un Jankl hot gefunen,
   Un Jankl hot gefunen,
   Hobn zej six bejde genumen.

2. Oj, Roxl štejt ba dem špigl
   Un kemt arop di herelex,
   Iz engegangen eu n'ir Jankl
   Un hot zi bašotn mit kerelex.

3. Dos vejsn šojn ale,
   Dos vejsn šojn ale,
   Az Roxele iz a kale
   Un Jankl iz der xosn,
   Un Jankl iz der xosn,
   Hobn zej zix bejde gešlosn.

41. Cu der xupe
(Идешь) к венцу

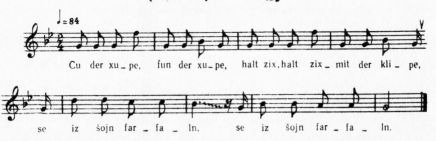

Cu der xupe, fun der xupe,
Halt zix, halt zix mit der klipe,
Se iz šojn farfaln,
Se iz šojn farfaln.

42. Oj, a šejne kale
Ой, красивая невеста

1. — Oj, a šejne kale,
   Šejn iz zi vi gold,
   A simen hot ir ale,
   Az ix hob zi gevolt.

2. — Oj, vos ix' hob gevolt, hob ix ojsgefirt,
   Un lomix azoj lebn,
   Ix hob gevolt a šejne šnur —
   Hot mir got gegebn.

3. — Oj, a šejne šviger,
   Šejn iz zi vi gold,
   A simen hot ir ale,
   Az·ix hob zi gevolt.

43. Ix gej mir cu der xupe
Я иду под венец

Ix gej mir cu der xu _ pe, ix bin dox šejn vi gold,

ix gej mir fun der xu _ pe mit dem, vos x'hob ge _ volt.

Ix gej mir cu der xupe,
Ix bin dox šejn vi gold,
Ix gej mir fun der xupe
Mit dem, vos x'hob gevolt.

44. Cu der xupe gejendik
Жених идет к венду

Cu der xupe gejendik,
Oj, gejt der xosn vejnendik...
—Xosn, xosn, xosn-lebn,
Vos že bistu azoj trojerdik?
— Oj, ix vejn, ix vejn,
Oj, ix vejn, ix vejn,
Ix vil šojn gixer cu der xupe gejn.

45. Špilt že, špilt že, klezmerlex
Играйте, играйте, музыканты

La   la   la   la   la   la,   la   la   la   la

ti di raj ti di raj lam,   ta la la ti ri ta   ta ta ti di

ra ta   ta ra ti ri di ri dam.   Ta   lam   ta da da dam

ti ri da ti ri dam,   špilt že, špilt že,   klez _ mer _ lex,   s'iz šojn take a

plan,   ix hob šojn oj _ xet   xa _ se _ ne,   x'hob šojn ojx a   man.

Ta   la   ti ri la la lam   ra la lam   la la   la la la,

ti ri ra   ti ri   ra   la   la la la la la

la la la la la la   la la la lam   ta la la ri ri ri ram.

Ta   la   la   la   la   la

ti ri dam   ri   daj   dam   S'iz šojn take a

plan,   ix   hob šojn   oj _   xet

xa _ se _ ne,   x'hob šojn   ojx   a   man.

Špilt že, špilt že, klezmerlex,
S'iz šojn take a plan,
Ix hob šojn ojxet xasene,
X'hob šojn ojx a man.

46. Cebajt že mir a finef-un-cvanciker
Разменяйте мне четвертную

1. Ce _ bajt že mir, ce_ bajt že mir a fi _ nef—un--cvan_ci_ker

oj, af go _ le dra _ jer,

ix vel di klez _ mer gut ba _ co _ ln,

zej zo _ ln mir špi _ ln ge _ tra _ ier.

La la la la la la ra ra 'la la la la la la,

la la la la la la ra ra, la la

la la la la la   ra ra,   la la la   la la la,

la la   la   la la la la   la   la

1. Cebajt že mir, cebajt že mir a finef-un-cvanciker
   Oj, af **gole** drajer,
   Ix vel di klezmer gut bacoln,
   Zej zoln mir špiln getraier.

   > La la la la la la ra ra, la la la la la la,
   > La la la la la la ra ra, la la,
   > La la la la la la ra ra, la la la la la la
   > La la la la la la la la laa

2 Cebajt že mir, cebajt že mir a finef-un-cvanciker,
   Oj, af gole cener,
   Ix vel di klezmer gut bacoln,
   Zej zoln špiln šener.

   > La la...

3. Cebajt že mir, cebajt že mir a finef-un-cvanciker,
   Oj, af gole mine,
   Ix vel di klezmer gut bacoln,
   Zej zoln špiln a kinc.

   > La la...

4. Cebajt že mir, cebajt že mir a finef-un-cvanciker,
   Oj, af gole giln,
   Ix vel di klezmer gut bacoln,
   Zej zoln šener špiln.

   > La la...

5. Cebajt že mir, cebajt že mir a finef-un-cvanciker,
   Oj, af gole pozične,[1]
   Ix vel di klezmer gut bacoln.
   Zej zoln nit špiln smutne.

   > La la...

6. Cebajt že mir, cebajt že mir a finef-un-cvanciker,
   Oj, af halbe prialn[2]
   Ix vel di klezmer gut bacoln,
   Zej zoln špiln ale faln.

   > La la...

7. Cebajt že mir, cebajt že mir a finef-un-cvanciker,
   Oj, af gole kareln,
   Ix vel di klezmer gut bacoln,
   Abi mir zol der xosn gefeln.

   > La la...

[1] Pozične — kredit-biletn;
[2] Prialn — imperialn, goldene matbejes. A halber imperial — zibn rubl mit 50 kopkes.

47. Ot azoj un ot azoj
Вот так, вот так

Ot azoj, un ot azoj, un ot azoj, un ot azoj,
Un ot azoj nart men op a xosn.
Me zogt im cu, me zogt im cu, me zogt im cu a sax nadan
Un me git im nit kejn grošn.

48. Oj, šat že, mexutonim ale
Ой, потише, вы, сватья

2. Ci hot zi draj mol dos feld a_rum_tre_tn, ci

hot zi di el_te_rn af der xa_se_ne ge_be_tn,

1. Oj, šat že, mexutonim ale,
   Mir tuen bazecn a jesojme a kale,
   Mir tuen fregn vort ba vort,
   Ci i' zi geven ba ir foter afn hejlikn ort.
   Larara larara larara lara, la ra lara.

2. Ci hot zi draj mol dos feld arumtretn,
   Ci hot zi di eltern af der xasene gebetn,
   La larara larara larara lara, la ra lara.

3. Oj, goteńu, ix štej akegn der levone,
   Er zol nit blajbn kejn almen, un ix kejn almone.
   Larara larara...

4. Oj, šadxn, šadxn, a rux in dir,
   Oj, vos hostu gehat cu mir,
   X'hob dir bacolt far dajne šadxones,
   Un du host mix gekojlet on a raxmones.
   Larara larara...

5. Bagrobn zolstu vern fun got un fun lajt,
   Host mir nazičet a vajb a šlak,
   A vajb a šlak iz dox zejer biter,
   Oj, gi' mir an ejce, viazoj vert men fun ir poter.
   Larara larara larara lara, la ra lara.

6. S'iz avek a jor, un cvej, un draj,
   Un s'iz šojn do a kind derbaj.
   Ix volt zi geget, iz majn kop nit derbaj
   Larara larara larara lara, la ra lara.

49. Oj, Mejlex hot gehejsn
Ой, Мейлех приказал

Oj, Mejlex hot gehejsn xasene špiln, xasene špiln.
Me špilt un me špilt mit grojs gevejn,
Me špilt un me špilt mit grojs gešrej.
Tane-godls toxter vil nit Mejlexs zun,
Tane-godls toxter vil nit Mejlexs zun.

50. Ir fort zix šojn avek
Вы уже уезжаете

1. Ir fort zix šojn a _ vek, ir fort zix šojn a _ vek,

maj _ ne li _ be me _ xu _ to _ nim,

ix gi' dox ajx a _ vek majn tox _ ter far a šnur,

zi zol ba ajx nit on _ ve _ rn dem po _ nem. po _ nem.

2. Ej _ dem maj _ ner, ej _ dem ge _ tra _ jer, dix nem ix

on far an ej _ dem, dix nem ix

on far an ej _ dem, ix gi' dox dir a _

vek   majn   tox _ ter   far   a   vajb,   zi   zol   ba   dir   nit

1. on _ ve _ rn   dem   gej _ der,   **2.** gej _ der.

1. Ir fort zix šojn avek, ir fort zix šojn avek,
   Majne libe mexutonim,
   Ix gi' dox ajx avek majn toxter far a šnur, } 2 mol
   Zi zol ba ajx nit onvern dem ponem.

2. Ejdem majner, ejdem getrajer,
   Dix nem ix on far an ejdem,   2 mol
   Ix gi' dox dir avek majn toxter far a vajb,
   Zi zol ba dir nit onvern dem gejder.   } 2 mol

3. Mexuteneste majne, mexuteneste getraje,
   Ir zolt fun majn kind nit laxn,   2 mol
   Tomer vet ir zen an avle fun majn kind,   }
   Vi an ejgene muter zolt ir es farglajxn.   } 2 mol

4. Mexuteneste maine, mexuteneste getraje,
   Ix for cu ajx in a parikl,   2 mol
   Xoč ix hob gehert, ir hot zix šejne texter,— }
   Ir nemt a šnur, iz zi an antikl.   } 2 mol

51. Šnur, majn šnur
Невестка, моя невестка

1.-Šnur, majn šnu _ ur, zec zix af der fur,

zec zix af der fur un for a _ vek mit mir.

Sojn di fer _ dlex on _ ge _ po _ jet,

šojn dos ve _ ge _ le on _ ge _ stro _ jet,

zec zix af der fur un for a _ vek mit mir.

2.-Vi _ a _ zoj že ken ix fo _ rn, švi _ ger, mit ajx,

az ix hob zix nit ge _ ze _ gnt mit majn ta _ tn glajx.

Zaj ge _ zunt, ta _ te maj _ ner, du host dox mix

uf _ ge _ coj _ gn, mit gold un mit zil _ ber op _ ge _ vojgn,

hajnt for ix a _ vek un varf ajx ale a _ vek.

1. — Šnur, majn šnur,
   Zec zix af der fur,
   Zec zix af der fur
   Un for avek mit mir.
      Sojn di ferdlex ongepojet,
      Sojn dos vegele ongestrojet,
      Zec zix af der fur
      Un for avek mit mir.

2. — Viazoj že ken ix forn,
   Sviger, mit ajx,
   Az ix hob zix nit gezegnt
   Mit majn tatn glajx.
      Zaj gezunt, tate majner,
      Du host dox mix ufgecojgn,
      Mit gold un mit zilber opgevojgn,
      Hajnt for ix avek
      Un varf ajx ale avek.

3. — Šnur, majn šnur,
   Zec zix af der fur,
   Zec zix af der fur
   Un for avek mit mir.
      Sojn di ferdlex ongepojet,
      Sojn dos vegele ongestrojet,
      Zec zix af der fur
      Un for avek mit mir.

4. —Viazoj že ken ix forn,
   Sviger, mit ajx,
   Az ix hob zix nit gezegnt
   Mit majn mamen glajx.
      Zaj gezunt, mame majne,
      Du host dox mix ufgecojgn,
      Mit gold un mit zilber opgevojgn.
      Hajnt for ix avek
      Un varf ajx ale avek.

52. Štejen di karetn
Кареты стоят

1.—Šte_jen di ka _ re _ tn, šte _ jen di ka _ re _ tn

a_rum majn fo _ ters tir. — Sej_ne tox_ter, faj_ne tox_ter,

zec zix, for mit mir. — Vi zol ix zix se_cn fo _ rn mit ajx,

x'ho' zix nit ge_ze_gnt mit majn fo_ter glajx. Zaj ge _ zunt,

fo _ ter maj_ner, bin ix dox ge_ven a tox _ ter daj_ne,

klej_ner_hejt 's'tu mix der_coj_gn, groj_ser_hejt - a _ vek_ge_floj_gn...

Plač, plač, ńe po _ mo _ žet, ko _ xa _ na mo _ ja.
sto _ jat ko _ ni na do' _ ro _ ge,

1. Štejen di karetn, štejen di karetn
Arum majn foters tir...
— Sejne toxter, fajne toxter,
Zec zix, for mit mir.
—- Vi zol ix zix secn forn mit ajx,
X'ho' zix nit gezegnt mit majn foter glajx.
Zaj gezunt, foter majner,
Bin ix dox geven a toxter dajne,
Klejnerhejt 's'tu mix dercojgn,
Grojserhejt — avekgeflojgn...

Plač, plač, ńe pomožet,
Stojat koni na doroge,
Koxana moja.

2. Stejen di karetn, štejen di karetn
Arum majn foters tir...
—Sejne toxter, fajne toxter,
Zec zix, for mit mir.
— Vi zol ix zix zecn forn mit ajx,
X'ho' zix nit gezegnt mit ,majn muter glajx.
Zaj gezunt, muter majne,
Ix bin dox geven a toxter dajne,
Klejnerhejt s'tu mix dercojgn,
Grojserhejt — avekgeflojgn...

Plač, plač, ńe pomožet,
Stojat koni na doroge,
Koxana moja.

53. Šviger, a gut helf ajx
Свекровь, добрый день

1. — Sviger, a gut helf ajx,
Ci di šnur gefelt ajx?
— Gefeln i' zi mir zejer,
A šejne šnur in šlejer.

2. Sejn i' zi vi a kaline,
Zis i' zi vi a maline,
Ram tara ride, ram tara ride,
Ram tara rideram.

54. Vu bistu geven, texterl majne
Где ты была, доченька моя

1. — Vu bistu geven, texterl majne?
   — Ba der bejzer šviger.
   — Vos hostu geton, texterl majne,
   Ba der bejzer šviger?
   — Gevašn tiš un benk,
   Mit trern zej bašvenkt,
   Muter majne gelibte.

2. — Vos hostu gegesn, texterl majne,
   Ba der bejzer šviger?
   — A štikele fiš
   Bam opgedektn tiš,
   Muter majne gelibte.

3. — Vu bistu gešlofn, texterl majne,
   Ba der bejzer šviger?
   — Af a zak mit erd,
   Mitn ponem cu der erd,
   Muter majne gelibte.

55. Di mame hot mix opgegebn
Мама меня выдала (замуж)

1. Di ma_me hot mix op_ge_ge_bn un hot mix a_vek_ge_ge_bn

far cvej un fer_cik majl, majl, un hot mir on_ge_zogt un

on_ge_zogt, az ix zol sojn ba ir kejn_mol nit zajn, zajn.

2. Bin ix nit ge_vezn a jor un cvej, a jor un cvej,

iz dox mir ge_vo_rn ze _ jer vej, ze _ jer vej;

hob ix zix ge_maxt gring vi a fej_ge _ le, gring vi a fej_ge_le,

un bin cu ir ge_floj_gn. 3. Ge floj_gn, ge_floj _ gn der

gol_de_ner foj_gl der gol_de_ner foj _ gl i_ be_rn ge_dix_tn

vald, **vald,** un hot dort far loj_rn dem gol_de_nem fe_der, dem

gol_de_nem fe_der in a frem _ dn land, land.

1. Di mame hot mix opgegebn un hot mix avekgegebn
   Far cvej un fercik majl, majl,
   Un hot mir ongezogt un ongezogt,
   Az ix zol šojn ba ir kejnmol nit zajn, zajn.

2. Bin ix nit gevezn a jor un cvej, a jor un cvej,
   Iz dox mir gevorn zejer vej, zejer vej;
   Hob ix zix gemaxt gring vi a fejgele, gring vi a fejgele,
   Un bin cu ir geflojgn.

3. Geflojgn, geflojgn der goldener fojgl, der goldener fojgl
   Ibern gedixtn vald, vald,
   Un hot dort farlojrn dem goldenem feder, dem goldenem feder
   In a fremdn land, land.

4. Tut dox mir nit azoj bank der goldener feder, der goldener feder,
   Vi di pave alejn, alejn,
   Zint ix bin avek fun majne tate-mame, fun majne tate-mame,
   Zic ix un jomer, un vejn, un vejn...

5. Ba majn mamen — gilderne fingerlex af di finger,
                gilderne fingerlex af di finger,
   Ba majn šviger — geštorbn fun hunger,
                geštorbn fun hunger...

56. Far vemen zol ix šrajen
Кому мне жаловаться

♩ = 69-76

1. Far ve_men zol ix šra_jen, far ve_men zol ix vej_nen,

majn harc ojs_der_ cej_ ln hob ix nit far kej_nem...

Zol ix der _ cej _ ln far majn fo_ter,

zogt er mir, az er iz fun mir po _ ter.

1. Far vemen zol ix šrajen, far vemen zol ix vejnen,
   Majn harc ojsdercejln hob ix nit far kejnem...
   Zol ix dercejln far majn foter,
   Zogt er mir, az er iz fun mir poter. } *2 mol*

2. Far vemen zol ix šrajen, far vemen zol ix vejnen,
   Majn harc ojsdercejln hob ix nit far kejnem...
   Zol ix dercejln far majn muter.
   Zogt zi mir, se iz ir ojx biter. } *2 mol*

3. Far vemen zol ix šrajen, far vemen zol ix vejnen,
   Majn harc ojsdercejln hob ix nit far kejnem...
   Zol ix dercejln far majn bruder,
   Zogt er mir, zajn vajb iz im liber. } *2 mol*

4. Far vemen zol ix šrajen, far vemen zol ix vejnen,
   Majn harc ojsdercejln hob ix nit far kejnem...
   Zol ix dercejln far majn švester,
   Zogt zi, s'iz ir ojx nit beser. } *2 mol*

5. Far vemen zol ix šrajen, far vemen zol ix vejnen,
   Majn harc ojsdercejln hob ix nit far kejnem...
   Zol ix dercejln far majne frajnt —
   Ejner hot mix lib, an anderer fajnt. } *2 mol*

6. Far vemen zol ix šrajen, far vemen zol ix vejnen,
   Majn harc ojsdercejln hob ix nit far kejnem...
   Zol ix dercejln far majne šxejnim —
   Ejner vet laxn, der anderer vet vejnen. } *2 mol*

57. Epelex un barelex
Яблоки и груши

1. Epelex un barelex,
   Vi biter zajnen di kerelex...
   A' der almen nemt di mejdl,
   Bagist zi zix mit trerelex. } *2 mol*

2. A guter vajn n'a šlexter fas,
   Hejbt er on cu zajern...
   A' der almen nemt di mejdl,
   Hejbt zi on cu trojern. } *2 mol*

3. Az der epele iz rojt,
   A vereml derinen...
   A' der almen nemt di mejdl,
   Vert er falš in zajn zinen. } *2 mol*

58. Šlogt der zejger ejns
Часы бьют час

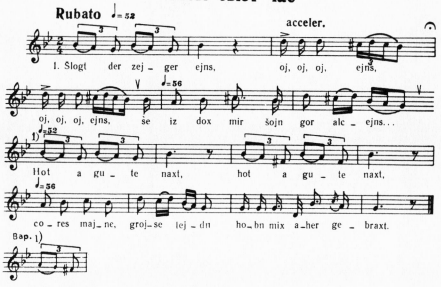

1. Šlogt der zejger ejns,
   Oj, oj, oj, ejns, oj, oj, oj, ejns,
   Se iz dox mir šojn gor alcejns...
       Hot a gute naxt, hot a gute naxt,
       Cores majne, grojse lejdn
       Hobn mix aher gebraxt.

2. Šlogt der zejger cvej,
   Oj, oj, oj, cvej, oj, oj, oj, cvej,
   Se iz šojn mir vind un vej...
       Hot a gute naxt u. az. v.

3. Šlogt der zejger draj,
   Oj, oj, oj, draj, oj, oj, oj, draj,
   Ix bin šojn gevorn farbaj...
       Hot a gute naxt u. az. v.

4. Šlogt der zejger fir.
   Oj, oj, oj, fir, oj, oj, oj, fir.
   Lign zol ix šojn mit di fis cu der tir...
       Hot a gute naxt, hot a gute naxt,
       Cores majne, grojse lejdn
       Hobn mix aher gebraxt...

59. Di zejdes mit di bobes
Дедушки и бабушки

Di zejdes mit di bobes
tuen in drojsn zien
mit di brejte tor — bes,
mit di lan-ge špi — en.
A mej-de-le, vos se vejnt
un vil nit ru — ik zajn,
nemt men un me varft
in tor — beč-ke a — rajn.

Di zejdes mit di bobes
Tuen in drojsn zien
Mit di brejte torbes,
Mit di lange špien.
A mejdele, vos se vejnt
Un vil nit ruik zajn,
Nemt men un me varft
In torbečke arajn.

60. Dem kejsers ojcres
Сокровища царя

1. Dem kej-sers ojc-res mit der gan-cer me-lu-xe
volt ba mir ojx nit ge-ve-zn a-zoj ni-xe,
vi du bist ba mir ta-jer, majn velt, majn šajn,
ix gib af dir a kuk, mejn ix, di velt iz majn.
Šlof, majn kind, šlof, majn kind,
Šlof, majn kind, šlof, majn kind,
zolst mir vak-sn un zajn ge-zunt. zajn ge-zunt.
zolst mir le-bn un zajn ge-zunt. zajn ge-zunt.

Вар. 1)

1. Dem kejsers ojcres mit der gancer meluxe
   Volt ba mir ojx nit gevezn azoj nixe,
   Vi du bist ba mir tajer, majn velt, majn šajn,
   Ix gib af dir a kuk, mejn ix, di velt iz majn.
   Šlof, majn kind, šlof, majn kind,
   Zolst mir vaksn un zajn gezunt.
   Šlof, majn kind, šlof, majn kind,
   Zolst mir lebn un zajn gezunt.

2. Azoj vi di zun gejt avek farnaxt,
   Azoj vestu mir iberšlofn di gance naxt;
   Azoj vi di zun štejt uf inderfri,
   Azoj vestu mir ufštejn fun dajn ru.
   Šlof, majn kind, šlof, majn kind,
   Zolst mir vaksn un zajn gezunt.
   Šlof, majn kind, šlof, majn kind,
   Zolst mir lebn un zajn gezunt.

61. Šlof že, šlof že, kindeńu
Спи, спи, дитя

Slof že, šlof že, kin‿de‿ńu, šlof že, šlof že, ke‿ce‿le...

Slof že, šlof že, kindeńu,
Slof že, šlof že, kecele...

62. Šlof šojn ajn, majn fejgele
Спи, моя птичка

♩ = 69−72

1. Šlof šojn ajn, majn fej-ge-le, far-max dajn gol-dn ej-ge-le un

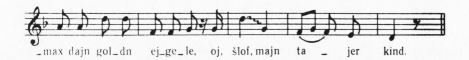

šlof, majn ta - jer kind; šlof šojn ajn, majn fej-ge-le, far-

-max dajn gol-dn ej-ge-le, oj, šlof, majn ta - jer kind.

2. Du vest ojs-vak-sn, zajn grojs, du vest bli-en vi a rojz, dajn

po - nem vet zajn mo-le - xejn; dajn li-pe-le, dajn cejn-de-le, dajn

ej-ge-le, dajn xejn-de-le, af dos vet men mir me-ka-ne zajn.

3. A man vet dix ne - men, a velt vet mit dir še - men, a

ko _ cin, a ke_ner vet ir zajn; kin_der vet ir ho _ bn,

na_xes vet ir klaj _ bn, a ba _ be vet dajn ma_me zajn.

1. Šlof **šojn** ajn, majn fejgele,
   Farmax dajn goldn ejgele
   Un šlof, majn tajer kind;
   Šlof šojn ajn, majn fejgele,
   Farmax dajn goldn ejgele,
   Oj, šlof, majn tajer kind.

2. Du vest ojsvaksn, zajn grojs,
   Du vest blien vi a rojz,
   Dajn ponem vet zajn mole-xejn;
   Dajn lipele, dajn cejndele,
   Dajn ejgele, dajn xejndele,
   Af dos vet men mir mekane zajn.

3. A man vet dix nemen,
   A velt vet mit dir semen,
   A kocin, a kener vet er zajn;
   Kinder vet ir hobn,
   Naxes vet ir klajbn,
   A babe vet dajn mame zajn.

63. Ix zic mir batog in vajngortn
Я сижу днем в винограднике

Rubato ♩=56–69

1. Ix zic mir ba_tog in vajn _ gor _ tn

un špil mit majn xo _ sn in a ta _ le kor _ tn.

Oj, gejt a _ rajn an al _ ter man,

oj, in vaj _ se klej _ der on _ ge _ ton...

Oj, gejt a _ rajn an al _ ter man,

oj, in vaj _ se klej _ der on _ ge _ ton...

2.–A gut-mor _ gn dir, tox _ ter maj _ ne.

–Oj, a gut–jor dir, zej _ de ńu.

- Oj. ix bin nit ge _ ku _ men nox dajn gut -- jor,

ix bin ge _ ku _ men dir kir _ cn di jor.

Oj. ix bin nit ge _ ku _ men nox dajn gut --- jor,

ix bin ge _ ku _ men dir kir _ cn di jor.

3.-Al _ ter zej _ de, loz mix le _ bn,

oj, nit cu _ lib mir, cu _ lib maj _ ne fo _ ter un mu _ ters ve _ gn.

Oj, maj _ ne fo _ ter un mu _ ter, zej ho _ bn mix lib,

zej ve _ ln dir op _ ge _ bn, oj, a _ les fun štub.

1. Ix zic mir batog in vajngortn
   Un špil mit majn xosn in a tale kortn.
   Oj, gejt arajn an alter man, ⎫
   In vajse klejder ongeton... ⎬ *2 mol*

2. — A gut-morgn dir, toxter majne.
   — Oj, a gut-jor dir, zejdeńu.
   — Oj. ix bin nit gekumen nox dajn gut-jor, ⎫
   Ix bin gekumen dir kircn di jor. ⎬ *2 mol*

3. — Alter zejde, loz mix lebn,
   Oj, nit culib mir — culib majne foter un muters vegn.
   Oj, majne foter un muter, zej hobn mix lib, ⎫
   Zej veln dir opgebn, oj, ales fun štub. ⎬ *2 mol*
4. . . . .

   Alcding fun štub loz zix štejn, ⎫
   Un vemen ix ruf — darf er gejn. ⎬ *2 mol*

5. — Alter zejde, loz mix lebn,
   Oj, nit culib mir — culib majne švester un bruders vegn.
   Majne švester un bruder, zej hobn mix lib, ⎫
   Zej veln dir opgebn dos kind fun der vig. ⎬ *2 mol*

6. — Dos kind fun der vig loz zix vign,
   Un ven ix vel es darin — vel ix es ojxet krign.
   . . . .
   . . . .

7. — Ruft mir arajn majn getraje muter,
   Efšer vet mir gringer vern.
   Vi di muter hot geefnt di tir:
   — Majn toxter, vej iz mir far dir.

8. — Ruft mir arajn majn gelibtn xosn,
   Efšer vet mir fort gringer vern.
   Vi der xosn hot geefnt di tir: ⎫
   — Majn getraje kale, mir far dir. ⎬ *2 mol*

9. — Cerajs di tnojim, az vej iz cu mir,
   Majn getrajer xosn, du blajbst on mir.
   Cerajs di tnojim, az vej iz cu mir,
   . . . .

10. — Mame, oj, mame, ix halt es nit ojs,
    Majn gelibte kale — zi gejt šojn ojs.
    Oj, mame, mame, ix halt es nit ojs,
    Majn gelibte kale — zi gejt šojn ojs...

64. A nedove bet ix
Я прошу милостыню

Parlando. Rubato ♩ = 48

1. A ne-do-ve bet ix, oj, an o - re-man a blin - der,

vos ix bin bli - nd fun majn ge - boj - rn,

far - štoj - sn bin ix fun cu zen gots vun - der,

majn lix-ti-ke velt hob ix jun - ger - hejt on-ge-voj - rn.

2. Aj, b - lind bin ix,

oj, ji - di - še kin - der - lex, a - zoj vi fun majn mu - ters bojx.

Cajt ix hob far zix di velt der - šmekt,

o - j vej, oj vej, o rem, o - rem bin ix af majn el - ter ojx,

un mit co - res fil on - ge - zet.

1. A nedove bet ix, oj, an oreman a blinder,
   Vos ix bin blind fun majn gebojrn,
   Farštojsn bin ix fun cu zen gots vunder,
   Majn lixtike velt hob ix jungerhejt ongevojrn.

2. Aj, blind bin ix, oj, jidiše kinderlex,
   Azoj vi fun majn muters bojx.
   Cajt ix hob far zix di velt deršmekt,
   Oj vej, oj vej, orem, orem bin ix af majn elter ojx,
   Un mit cores fil ongezet.

3. Az ix bin geven, jidiše kinderlex, a klejn kind,
   Esn hobn mir majne eltern derlangt.
   Ven majn dernerung, vej iz mir, zol zajn azoj acind,
   Volt ix dir, got in himl, alemol gedankt.

4. Oj, mit trern, oj vej, bet ix ajx,
   Oj, an oremen, a blindn zolt ir bašojnen,
   Nor der got in himl, vos er iz rajx —
   Er vet ajx far ajer nedove balojnen!

5. Ix zic do, oj vej, baštendik un traxt
   Fun a menčns ful zajn der natur /?/.
   Ba mir iz kejn xilek fun tog biskl naxt,
   Cu vos tojg mir majn fincter lebn gor?

65. Elnt bin ix
Я одинок

♩=66

E _ lnt bin ix, op _ ge _ ri _ sn, un der _ cu bin ix on a hant,

un in štub iz ni _ to kejn bi _ sn,

rit.

un far _ tri _ bn bin ix fun majn land.

a tempo

Ci zol ix vej _ nen, ci zol ix šra _ jen,

vos ken mir hel _ fn majn ge _ vejn,

s'a _ zoj ba _ še _ rt min _ ha _ šo _ ma _ jim,

e _ lnt bin   ix   vi   a štejn,

Senkt, ji_di_še kin _ der, a ne_ščast_nem, a blin _ dn, a ka_ li_ ke...

Elnt bin ix, opgerisn,
Un dercu bin ix on a hant,
Un in štub iz nito kejn bisn,
Un fartribn bin ix fun majn land.
Ci zol ix vejnen, ci zol ix šrajen,
Vos ken mir helfn majn gevejn,
S`azoj bašert min-hašomajim,
Elnt bin ix vi a štejn,
    Senkt, jidiše kinder, a neščastnem, a blindn, a kalike...

66. Хапт им, немт им
Ловите его, берите его

Xapt im, nemt im, xapt im, nemt im, xapt im, nemt im

zect im a_rajn, er zol kejn ga _ nev mer nit zajn, a

ga _ nev, a ga _ nev, er hot dox mix ba_

_gan_vet, er hot dox ba mir cu _ ge _ nu _ men

a _ les fun majn štub. Zi _ bn hem_der vi di be_ xer,

draj mit la _ tes, fir mit le _ xer, oj, ge _ vald, a

ga _ nev,   er   hot dox mix ba _ gan _ vet,   er

hot dox ba mir   cu _ ge _ nu _ men   a _ les fun majn štub.

Xapt im, nemt im, xapt im, nemt im,
Xapt im, nemt im, zect im arajn,
Er zol kejn ganev mer nit zajn,

A ganev, a ganev,
Er hot dox mix baganvet,
Er hot dox ba mir cugenumen
Ales fun majn štub.

Zibn hemder vi di bexer,
Draj mit lates, fir mit lexer,

Oj, gevald, a ganev,
Er hot dox mix baganvet,
Er hot dox ba mir cugenumen
Ales fun majn štub.

Zibn lajxter vi di štern,
Draj on fislex, fir on rern,

Oj, gevald, a ganev,
Er hot dox mix baganvet,
Er hot dox ba mir cugenumen
Ales fun majn štub.

67. Hob ix mir a pidžekele
Есть у меня пыджачок

♩=76

1. Hob ix mir a pid_že_ke_le fun na_jem ge_vant,

tra la la la la la la la la, ir megt mir gloj_bn, m'ken s'nit

ne_men in hant, tra_la la la la, la la la la. De_ri_ber

hob ix zix ba_traxt un ix hob fun dem pid_že_ke le a ka_

_pot_ke_le ge_maxt, tra la la la,

tra la la la la tra la la la la la la la.

1. Hob ix mir a pidžekele fun najem gevant,
Tra la la la la, la tra la la,
Ir megt mir glejbn, me ken es nit nemen in hant,
Tra la la la la, la tra la la.
Deriber hob ix zix batraxt
Un ix hob fun dem pidžekele a kapotkele gemaxt,
Tra la la la la, tra la la la la,
Tra la la la la la la la la.

2. Hob ix mir a kapotkele fun najem gevant,
Tra la la la la la, tra la la,
Ir megt mir glejbn, me ken es nit nemen in hant,
Tra la la la la la, tra la la.
Deriber hob ix zix batraxt
Un ix hob fun dem kapotkele a por hejzelex gemaxt,
Tra la la la la la, tra la la la la,
Tra la la la la la la la la.

3. Hob ix mir a por hejzelex fun najem gevant,
   Tra la la la la la u. az. v.
   Deriber hob ix zix batraxt
   Un ix hob fun di hejzelex a kamzojlexl gemaxt,
   Tra la la la la, tra la la la la,
   Tra la la la la la la la la la.

4. Hob ix mir a kamzojlexl fun najem gevant,
   Tra la la la la la u. az. v.
   Deriber hob iz zix batraxt
   Un ix hob fun dem kamzojlexl a žiletkele gemaxt,
   Tra la la la la la, tra la la,
   Tra la la la la la la la la.

5. Hob ix mir a žiletkele fun najem gevant,
   Tar la la la la la, tra la la,
   Ir megt mir glejbn, me ken es nit nemen in hant,
   Tra la la la la la, tra la la...
   Deriber hob ix zix batraxt
   Un hob far dem žiletkele a kestele gemaxt,[1]
   Tra la la la la, tra la la la la,
   tra la la la la la, tra la la...

[1] Cu bagrobn.

68. Gevald, vu nemt men
Гвалд, где мне взять

1. Ge-vald, vu nemt men, vu nemt men, vu nemt men
a lok-šn-bret af ka čen di var-nič-kes,
on hej-vn un on šmalc, un on fe-fer un on zalc,
oj, a lok-šn-bret af ka-čen di var-nič-kes.

1. Gevald, vu nemt men, vu nemt men, vu nemt men
A lokšn-bret af kačen di varničkes,
On hejvn un on šmalc,
Un on fefer un on zalc,
Oj, a lokšn-bret af kačen di varničkes.

2. Gevald, vu nemt men, vu nemt men, vu nemt men
A meser af cu šnajdn di varnickes,
On hejvn un on šmalc,
Un on fefer un on zalc,
Oj, a meser af cu šnajdn di varničkes.

3. Gevald, vu nemt men, vu nemt men, vu nemt men
A tepl af cu koxn di varničkes,
On hejvn un on šmalc,
Un on fefer un on zalc,
Oj, a tepl af cu koxn di varničkes.

4. Gevald, vu nemt men, vu nemt men, vu nemt men
A boxer af cu esn di varničkes,
On hejvn un on šmalc,
Un on fefer un on zalc,
Oj, a boxer af cu esn di varničkes

69. A gut morgn, Fejge-Soše
Доброе утро, Фейге-Соше

1.—A gut _ mor _ gn, Fej_ ge- So _ še,

vos zict ir a_zoj a _ so_ be ne? so _ be _ ne?

—A gut- jor ajx, Faj_ ve_ Jo_še, vajl s'iz mir u _ dob (e)_ ne.

1. — - A gut-morgn, Fejge-Soše,
Vos zict ir azoj asobene?   *2 mol*

— A gut-jor ajx, Fajve-Jośe,
Vajl s'iz mir udobene. } *2 mol*

2.   Efšer vilt ir, Fajve-Jośe,
Farzuxn fun majn prodovolstvie?   *2 mol*

A šabesdikn lokšn-kugl —
S'ara udovolstvie! } *2 mol*

3. Sabes noxn kugl
Bin ix di emese krasavice, *2 mol*
Ojsgepuct un ongeton zix,
Kak ja vam naravitsa? } *2 mol*

4. — Efšer vilt ir, Fejge-Soše,
Mit semečkes ajx ugoščajeven? *2 mol*

— Vajl ba ajx, Fajve-Jośe,
Vel ix prinimajeven. } *2 mol*

5. — Efšer vilt ir, Fejge-Soše,
Gejn mit mir gulajeven? *2 mol*

— Vajl mit ajx, Fajve-Jośe,
Vel ix ispolńajeven. } *2 mol*

70. In Ades, in Ades
В Одессе, в Одессе

In A _ des, in A _ des af der Mal _ da _ van _ ke rit.

x'hob ge _ tanct a po _ lo _ nez mit a šar _ la _ tan _ ke. Fine

Jox _ caj de _ ri _ de _ raj, oj, le _ bn zol A _ des,

Oj, du šej _ ne mej _ dl, oj, lo _ mir bej _ de

fo _ rn kejn A _ des, oj, oj, oj!

D.C. al Fine

In Ades, in Ades
Af der Maldavanke
X'hob getanct a polonez
Mit a šarlatanke.

Joxcaj derideraj,
Oj, lebn zol Ades! } 2 mol

Oj, du šejne mejdl,
Oj, lomir bejde forn kejn Ades, oj, oj, oj!

In Ades, in Ades
Af der Maldavanke
X'hob getanct a polonez
Mit a šarlatanke.

Song Text Translations

1. "If I Had Wings"

(1) If I had wings / I would fly to you / And if I had chains / I would pull you to me.

(2) Oh, on that side of the river, on that side of the bank / The boughs are bent / There, there stands my sweetheart / with tearful eyes.

(3) Oh, stop weeping, stop wailing / You will accomplish nothing with tears / Open up my heart, you'll see it's black / You'll know how I love you.

2. "On the Mountain, Below the Mountain"

(1) On the mountain, below the mountain / Stands Esther the green / Esther stands / Abraham comes / Abraham the patriarch.

(2) If I had a ring / I would wink at you / If I had a goblet / I would drink from it.

(3) If I had strings / I would pull with them / If I had wings / I would fly with them.

3. "On the High Mountain"

(1) On the high mountain, on the green grass / Stand two doves, oh doves / They kiss and pet each other / What ecstasy they feel.

(2) Oh, you are leaving and oh, you are leaving / In whose care are you leaving me / Oh, don't go, don't go, my darling / Come here and sit down.

(3) The coachman has sat down, the coachman has sat down / And tears have come to my eyes / I just saw you, just talked to you / And in one minute you have flown away.

4. "You Are My Heart"

(1) You are my heart, you are my life / Oh, can't you understand that / If I were to give you just one sigh— / But better not, better not.

(2) You have read my sweet letters / Those were hot words on a cold stone / Oh, what was it with you / Better not, better not.

(3) The mother's milk I drank / Sucked out my love / Oh, I'm a bird who has flown the nest / Oh, oh, oh, I've caught nothing.

(4) Every day a limb dies / And the blood stands still / I would be better off in the grave / But better not, better not.

5. "Outside It's Raining"

(1) Outside it's raining / And inside it's damp. I had a true love / Bitter is my lot.

(2) Bitter is my lot / and my birth / I had a true love / And lost her.

(3) I lost her / And can't come to her / Who stands before my eyes / And I can't come to her.

(4) I would have gone to her / But she lives very far away / I would have kissed her / But am ashamed before people.

(5) I'm ashamed before people / That they shouldn't talk about me / Now the time has already come / When we must part.

(6) Parting is no life / It's worse than a divorce / Farewell, my dear / I'm leaving you.

(7) I'm leaving you / Thirty-six miles / I thought my love was eternal / But in the end it's temporary.

6. **"That Night"**

(1) That night we spent together / Until midnight / We sat together a long time / Until we forgot God.

(2) Help me, God, on the water / Help me, God, you alone / I have fled to distant lands / I'm lonely as a stone.

(3) Your eyes are like ink / Your cheeks are finest paper / Your hands are pens / You should write to me often.

7. **"I Pick up My Pen"**

(1) I pick up my pen / My thoughts are melancholy / Where can one find such a good friend / Who can talk away my pain / Where can one find a true person / Who will know what is in my heart / Suffering is in my heart / My suffering is in vain.

(2) Oh, on the high mountain / And on the green grass / We used to walk there / And the flowers' scent reached our noses / Now the path is overgrown / The path of our love's walks / Adieu, adieu my dearest / I cannot marry you.

8. **"Fiery Love"**

(1) Fiery love / Burns in my heart / What use is it for me to love you / When we cannot take each other.

(2) You say you love me / You go into your house / You go off to another girl / And dig my grave.

(3) You dig my grave / And fall in yourself / I have already decided / That you must be mine.

9. **"You Are Leaving"**

(1) You are leaving, my dearest / To whom are you leaving me / Oh, to whom can I say, oh, a word / Except to you, and only, oh, to myself.

(2) Oh, we must already part / Like the body from the soul / Oh, when our enemies find out / They will take great pleasure.

(3) They've already taken great pleasure / I hope to God it's not for long / Do you remember, *vey,* you my dearest / How I used to talk to you as a good old friend.

(4) Oh, whether in a town or a village / Oh, you should write frequent letters / *Oy vey,* you should write frequent letters / So we can remain a couple.

10. **"Kissed and Caressed"**

(1) Kissed and caressed / From the doorway to the train / And when day broke / He was gone as if into the sea.

(2) *Oy vey,* mama, ducks swim / And they splash with their feet / When will my beloved come / Or at least send regards.

(3) *Oy vey,* mama, bears growl / And shake their beards / If love is a swindle / I'll lie under the ground.

11. **"Oy Vey, Mama, Ducks Swim"**

(1) *Oy vey,* mama, ducks swim / When will my beloved come? /—Today or tomorrow / Don't worry so much.

(2) Mama, I'll go to the train / I'll see my beloved there / I'll see my intended there / And kiss as well.

12. **"I Love You"**

(1) I love you, I love you / From the bottom of my heart / Embraced, kissed / Pressed to my heart.

(2) If you say you love me / Well, I'm not against you / If you say you're leaving / I'll leave with you today.

(3) Let him go, let him go / Let him seek his fortune / If you will be my intended / You'll come back.

13. "I Love You"

(1) I love you, I love you / I'll sacrifice myself to you / Embrace me, oh, and give me, oh, a kiss / When no one, no one is looking.

(2) If you go out on the water / Don't drink it / If you see pretty girls / long, long for me.

(3) If you go over a fire / Don't get burned / You will see pretty girls / But you should only know, know me.

14. "Play Me the New Šer"

(1) Play me the new *šer* / Which just came out / I love a girl / But can't get to her.

(2) I would have gone to her house / But she lives very far / I would have kissed her / But I'm shy in front of others.

(3) Not so much for others / As for myself / I'd give anything / To be alone with her.

15. "I Built a Wall"

(1) I built a wall / A wall with six windows / And as many matches as they've proposed to me / You were the most attractive.

(2) I planted a vineyard / The vineyard didn't work out / I lost my young years / Oh, like a card-player loses at cards.

(3) You tied me up hand and foot, hand and foot / And let me swim / A time will come when you'll look for me / And you won't be able to find me.

16. "Oh, a Black Gloom Covered the Sky"

(1) Oh, a black gloom covered the sky / And the clouds spread out / It's been a long time that I've been suffering / And you turned my head.

(2) Let's start, let's start to understand the world / And to grasp that word "love" / It's been a long time that I'm in love / And that you've turned my head.

(3) Oh, I started this love, this love / With zest and spirit / Oh, you led me, oh, from my true path / And have left me in the mud.

(4) You put me, oh, in the mud, the mud / My hands and feet are bound / Oh, there's no doctor, oh, except you in the world / That could heal my wounds.

17. "Paper Is White and Ink Is Black"

(1) Paper is white and ink is black / My heart yearns for you, my beloved / I would like to sit three days in a row / Just to look in your eyes and to stroke your hand.

(2) Yesterday I was at a wedding / I saw a lot of pretty girls / Many pretty girls, but not one compares to you / To your black eyes and your black hair.

(3) Your waist, your carriage, your noble manner / A fire burns in my heart, but can't be seen / There's no one who can see how I'm burning / My life and my death are in your hands.

(4) Your manner, your smile, your noble figure / Oh, tell me, eye, what is it with you / That when you laugh with great joy / A tear falls from you.

18. "I Would Like, Oh, Mama"

(1) I would like, oh, mama, to wander around / And crash at somebody's house / Oh, I beg just one thing, oh, from you, God / That I may take the one I love.

(2) Oh, the one whom I love, oh, I cannot come to him / What use is my life / Since I have mama, no luck / My beauty is ruined.

(3) —Look my daughter, how you've become / How you go around all the time / Oh, go to a doctor, my daughter / He'll tell you what's happened to you.

(4) —Oh, I've already been, mama, to the doctor / I was at the doctor's house / But he just wrote me a prescription / Saying I should take the one I love.

(5) But I can't take the one I love / What use is my life / Since I have, mama, no luck / My charms are ruined.

(6) Do you remember, mama, how you sat with a neighbor / She confided in you and it hurt you as well / And when one is in love with a boy for four years / Can one say that one hates him?

(7) Do you remember, you murderer, how you sat in my house / A fire burned in your heart / And now, as we meet on the same path / You turn your head, you didn't recognize me.

19. "Who's That Knocking so Late at Night?"

(1) Who's that knocking so late at night? /—Berele Kabančik. Open up, open up, Brajndele / I'm your guy.

(2) —How can I open up / I'm afraid of my father /—Oh, open up, open up, Brajndele / It won't hurt you.

(3) —How can I open up / I'm afraid of my mother /—Oh, open up, open up, Brajndele / I won't stay long.

(4) —How can I open up / I'm afraid of my sister /—Open up, open up, Brajndele / To me you're the prettiest.

20. "She Got Wet in the Rain"

(1) She got wet in the rain / She got wet in the rain / Come here, pretty girl / I want to ask you something.

(2) —I don't want to go to you / I'm afraid of my father /—Come on out, pretty girl / I won't hurt you.

21. "Come All Ye Maidens"

(1) Come all ye maidens / You were jealous of my luck, *oy vey* / But now you regret the end of my love / How I remained lonely as a stone.

(2) Oh [missing] / Oh, lonely, mama, oh, lonely as a stone, *oy vey* / I can only implore you, my dearest / To at least come and see me often.

(3) —How can I come to you / How can I talk to you, *oy vey* / When I love you from the bottom of my heart / But, dear, we can't take each other.

(4) —Tell me the truth, what happened in your house / So that your mama doesn't want me as her daughter-in-law, *oy vey* / May she become blind so she has to be led / So she won't see another daughter-in-law.

(5) And your father, may he not be able to walk / And may he not see as well, *oy vey* / May he come beg alms from me / And I would know how he was.

(6) I'll give him good alms / For not letting me have his son. [Missing] / [missing]

(7) I also want your sister, your sister, to have a curse / She should have it worse than me / God grant she falls in love next year / And she should have an end like mine.

(8) —You have no reason to curse my sister / And it has nothing to do with my parents either, *oy vey* / I'm no child, I've thought it over / Since you're a poor girl, I can't go with you.

(9) —Come here, my dearest, to me / Why did you think this over so late, *oy vey* / It's already three years you've been visiting me / And a river of tears has come from this false love.

22. "What Do I Care for Your Pretty Vineyard"

(1) What do I care for your pretty vineyard / When I can't plant it / Why should I fall in love with you / When we can't have each other.

(2) We can't get engaged / Because I have an older sister /—We can't become betrothed / Since I'm no daughter-in-law for your mother.

(3) —Why are you scolding my mother / Has she ever stood in your way / My mother says she wants a pretty girl / A pretty girl with a large dowry and a lot of money.

(4) —What can I do, since I'm not pretty / And I have no dowry with money / What can I do if I'm common / Can't I have a life at all?

(5) —Stop crying and wailing / And turn away that pretty face / And wipe the tears from your eyes / And you'll stay with me forever.

23. "Who Says That Love Is Good Fortune?"

(1) Who says that love is good fortune, oh woe is me / Oh, love is a disaster / Love is a real disease / Oh, young children leave this world for love.

(2) Oh, in Vilna there's an emergency room, oh woe is me / They should bring your mom there / And when they bring her to the hospital / She won't ask for jewelry and money any more.

(3) Oh, in the hospital there are shiny white beds / One for your mom and the other for you / And when they bring you to the hospital / Don't say you're in love with me.

(4) —You've got no reason to scold my mother / I'm my own man / I'll take a quite nice girl / Oh, who already knows a trade.

24. "We Went Walking, Walking"

(1) We went walking, walking / Around and around the boulevard / We ate and drank / All sorts of sweets.

(2) —Mother, dear mother / Do just one thing for me / Put out, put out the fire in my heart / And give me the one I love.

(3) —Daughter, my dear daughter / I'll give you poison / Your father is a magnate, a rich man / And you must have a rich man for your husband.

(4) —Mother, my dear mother / You don't get by on riches / I've seen bigger millionaires / And they end up in debt.

(5) —Daughter, my dear daughter / I've said enough to you / If you want to curse your own father / Take, and go away.

(6) —Griša dear, Griša my love / I've worked things out with my father / Let's take our money and clothes / And go to America.

(7) —To go to America and get married / That's a noble thing / But listen to what I say / Our love will not become a river.

(8) Rivers, rivers, they run dry / And the ditches are empty / And the girl who has a false love / The shame stays with her forever.

25. "I Have Nothing Against Your Mother"

(1) I have nothing against your mother, *oy vey,* nothing / Since she says it's not her fault / May she wander from house to house / And come begging a piece of bread from me / She shouldn't interfere with love / *Oy vey,* pay her, Oh, God, for me.

(2) I have nothing against your father, *oy vey,* nothing / Since he says it's not his fault / May he lie in the Kiev hospital / And have no one to visit him

/ Since, dad, you shouldn't interfere with love / *Oy vey*, pay him, oh, God, for me.

(3) I've got nothing against your brother, *oy vey*, nothing / Since he says it's not his fault / May he lie in the Kiev jail / And not see anyone / Since, brother, you shouldn't interfere with love / *Oy vey*, pay him, oh, God, for me.

(4) I have nothing against your sister, *oy vey*, nothing / Since she says it's not her fault / She should drag around three years with a love / Let her have an end like mine / Since, mama, she shouldn't interfere with love / *Oy vey*, God, pay her for me.

26. "Oh, You're Going Away"

(1) Oh, you're going away, oh, you're going away from me / To whom are you leaving me? / Like a stone, like a bone, woe is me / Oh, sit down next to me / I'll hang myself, I'll stab myself before your eyes / Oh, sit down next to me.

27. "From Great Sorrow, Mama, I Go to Bed"

(1) From great sorrow, mama, I go to bed / With both hands at my head / I am in love, and I am vexed / And cannot retreat.

(2) Oh, I am bound, bound / And I am bound with a rope / A fire burns in my heart / And no one, mama, can put it out.

(3) The first thing I ask of you, mama / Oh, do it for my sake / Oh, while eating and while drinking / Don't mention my name in the house.

(4) The second thing I ask of you, mama, / Oh, do it for my sake / If my sister gives birth to a child / *Oy*, don't mention my name in the house.

(5) The third thing I ask of you, mama / And do this as well / If my beloved comes to your house / Don't offend her.

(6) The last thing I ask of you, mama, / When you go to visit the cemetery / Oh, do it for my sake / Visit my grave first.

(7) Oh, I'm bound, mama, with a rope / I'm strongly bound with a rope / There's no brother, no friend / Who can heal my wounds.

28. "From Great Sorrow I Fall Asleep"

(1) From great sorrow I fall asleep / With both hands at my head / Oh, I'm in love and I'm vexed / And I can't retreat.

(2) *Oy vey*, Miša, my dear Miša / Where have you fled from me / Oh, I look for you in every corner / And I can't find you, Miša.

(3) In the hospital there's a bed / The bed is covered in white / And there lies, *ax*, my dear Miša / With his two dark eyes.

(4) Near the hospital there's a tree / The tree is bent in three / Oh, there goes my dear sweetheart / With his tearful eyes.

(5) Near the sea there's a little ship / The ship is not full and not empty / Oh, a girl who's in love / Is lost forever.

29. "Oh, the Summer Night"

(1) Oh, the summer night, the beautiful, mama / When everyone goes out / Oh, the moon has already faded / And the sun already starts to rise.

(2) Oh, on a bench we sat together / And we sat, both deep in thought / And how many secrets we told each other / And still we didn't come to an end.

(3) —What sort of end are you making, oh, for me / I'm a youth, I must go to the draft / Oh, and no betrothal, oh, can I make with you / You're a smart girl, you must understand yourself.

(4) —Oh, give me, dear, your right hand / Oh, swear that you love me true / And swear, you won't change me for another / Oh, up to the dark grave.

(5) —Oh, I can give you my hand / And I swear I love you true / And I swear I won't change you for another / Oh, up to the dark grave.

30. "Oh, a Coal, a Fiery Coal"

(1) Oh, a coal, a fiery coal / Such a coal can shoot a person / Particularly the one who talked you into / Becoming another girl's groom.

(2) Oh, you're already a groom / May it be with luck and good fortune / But I'm still not a bride / Oh, you'll come back, oh, to me.

(3) We went walking / The road was too narrow / But whoever talked you out of me / Should go into the desolate hospital.

(4) And today, as we go walking / The path has become wide / Only the one who has parted our love / Should know of no good end.

(5) They parted us / Like the body from the soul / When your enemies find out / They'll experience great pleasure.

(6) You're leaving, my dearest / So your parents won't be ashamed of me / [missing] / [missing].

(7) —Oh, stop weeping and wailing / Your pretty face is wet from your hot tears / We'll only part / When a bird will drink up a glassful.

31. "Mama Said 'No'"

(1) Mama said "no," and it should have been no / So I wouldn't go with that rat / I went with him, spent time with him / And he made a ruin of me.

(2) Do you remember, do you remember that Tuesday evening / When we got to know each other / Today, you vagabond, you tell your buddies / That without a dowry you won't take me.

(3) I lay sick three weeks in a row / You didn't come to see me once / You could have brought me the best cure / If you'd have come to see me once.

(4) *Oy vey,* troubles, my troubles, encircle me / Like staves around a barrel / Today's men—you can believe them / Like you'd believe a street dog.

32. "Hey You, You, Come Here"

(1) Hey you, you, come here / Sit down next to me / If you want to fall in love / Do it just with me.

(2) You're leaving, you're leaving / And won't be heard from / A fire burns in my heart / It won't hurt me [unclear].

(3) Oh you scab-head, you scab-head / Everything's expensive / A boy like you / Is worth a nickel.

33. "You Claimed"

(1) You claimed you were quite a guy / Why did you turn my head that way? / You said you can't be my groom / So why did you start?

(2) You worked on the church square / Lived near the Jewish hospital / You used to come past my window every day / Come to me just one more time.

34. "I Had a Dream"

(1) I had a dream / I had a terrible dream / That my beloved loves another girl / And he made fun of me.

(2) —Oh, you can't believe in dreams, my child / Because a bad dream leads you astray / And tomorrow morning we'll go to the rabbi / And he'll interpret your dream for the good.

(3) —Oh, how can the rabbi help me / Will he give me what I love / Oh, I'll go to the one I love / And go straight to his house.

(4) I've gone on my way / And I've traveled eight days straight / And got to some kind of town / And I've had to stretch out my hand.

(5) —Give, give alms, people / [missing] in terrible need / Through love I've fallen / Give me, people, a crust of bread.

(6) —Why are you going around so ragged / Why aren't you ashamed to stretch out your hand / And I ought to know who and what you are, since I know every face.

(7) —I'm from Odessa / Grew up happy and rich in my parents' house / And I've fallen through love / And ask you for alms.

(8) —I have a wife and two children / And the third is almost here / I'll leave my wife and children / And you'll be my beloved.

(9) —Oh, don't leave your wife and children / And live out your years happily with her / Through you I've fallen / And must suffer all my days.

35. "As Long as I Can Remember"

(1) As long as I can remember / Oh, I've been burned by love / An infernal fire burns in my heart / No one can save me.

(2) Your two black eyes / And your head of black hair / You attracted me like a magnet / Now you shorten my years.

(3) Where can one find a good doctor / Who can give me a cure for my heart / He should give me a prescription, *oy vey,* a good one / He should take care of my pain.

(4) They've proposed fiancés with dowries / And with clothes, and a lot of money / You attracted me like a magnet / Now through you I will leave this world.

36. "I Loved a Girl of Eighteen"

(1) I loved a girl of eighteen / And have loved her for two or three years.

(2) He left alone, alone / And his beloved has fallen ill.

(3) They sent him an express letter / To say his beloved lies ill.

(4) He locked up all his goods and money / And traveled into the wide world.

(5) —Good-morning, good-morning, my beloved / How did you get into this black bed?

(6) —Good-day, good-day, dear thief / Oh, you will be my grave digger.

(7) —Oh, no, no, it can't be / Our love will last longer.

(8) When it was midnight / He brought a mourning-candle.

(9) He took the mourning-candle / And looked at her face.

(10) She used to be beautiful and rosy / Now she's green as grass.

(11) He put his hand under her arm / Now she's cold, not warm.

(12) He took off her wedding gown / And dressed her in mourning.

(13) He accompanied her from the room to the gate / And put a heavy wall over her.

(14) On the wall flowers will grow /—I'll come to you quickly.

(15) Three mornings had not passed / Before the young thief died too.

(16) Oh, oh, weeping and wailing / Two lovers in one week.

(17) On the gravestone it will be written: / Two lovers stayed here.

37. "Get Me a Bear from the Woods"

(1) —Get me a bear from the woods / And teach him to write / Only then and only then / Will I be yours.

(2) —I'll get you a bear from the woods / And teach him to write / If you'll make me seven children / And stay a maiden.

(3) —I'll make you seven children / And stay a maiden / If you'll make me a cradle / Without wood and without tools.

(4) —I'll make you a cradle without wood and without tools / If you'll sew me seven shirts / Without needles and without silk.

(5) —I'll sew you seven shirts / Without needles and without silk / If you'll catch me all the fish in the sea / So not even one remains.

(6) —I'll catch you all the fish in the sea / So not even one remains / If you'll fry up seven fish / And have them stay alive.

(7) —I'll fry you up seven fish / And have them stay alive / If you'll make me a ladder / That will reach the sky.

(8) —I'll make you a ladder / That will reach the sky / I'm a fool, and you're a bigger one / Let's both keep quiet.

38. "I Want You to Make White Chalk Out of Black Coal"

(1) I want you to make white chalk / Out of black coal / And to spin white silk / Out of hay.

(2) —I'll spin white silk / Out of hay / But you must put up a ladder / That will reach to the sky.

(3) —I'll put up a ladder / That will reach to the sky / But you must make me seven children / And remain a maiden.

(4) —I'll make you seven children / And remain a maiden / If you'll make me seven cradles / Without a knife and without tools.

(5) —It's just as impossible to make seven cradles / Without a knife and without tools / As it is to have seven children / And remain a maiden.

(6) —It's just as impossible to have seven children / And remain a maiden / As it is to put up a ladder / That will reach to the sky.

(7) —It's just as impossible to put up a ladder / That will reach to the sky / As it is to spin white silk / Out of hay.

(8) —It's just as impossible to spin white silk / Out of hay / As it is to make white chalk / Out of black coals.

(9) —It's just as impossible to make white chalk / Out of black coals / And if you want to be mine / You'll have to stay with me.

39. "I Sit on a Stone"

(1) I sit on a stone / And dissolve into tears / All the girls have luck / Except for me.

(2) Fish in the water / And dumplings in butter / As for a fiancé who won't take me / A curse on his mother.

40. "In Oats, in Rye"

(1) In oats, in rye / In oats and rye / Roxele lost her scarf / And Jankl found it / And Jankl found it / And they took each other.

(2) Oh, Roxl stands by the mirror / And combs her hair / Jankl came up to her / And pelted her with pits.

(3) Everyone knows that / Everyone knows that / Roxl is a bride / And Jankl is the bridegroom / And Jankl is the bridegroom / They decided that.

41. "Going to the Wedding Canopy"

Going to the wedding canopy, from the wedding canopy / The bitch is going / It's all over already / It's all over already.

42. "Oh, a Beautiful Bride"

(1) Oh, a beautiful bride / Beautiful as gold / You should all know / That I wanted her.

(2) —Oh, what I wanted, I got / And let's live that way / I wanted a beautiful daughter-in-law / And God gave me one.

(3) —Oh, a beautiful mother-in-law / Beautiful as gold / You all should know / That I wanted her.

43. **"I Go to the Wedding Canopy"**
    I go to the wedding canopy / I'm as beautiful as gold / I leave the wedding canopy / With the one I wanted.

44. **"Going to the Wedding Canopy"**
    Going to the wedding canopy / Oh, the groom is weeping /—Dear bridegroom / Why are you so sad? /—Oh, I weep, I weep. Oh, I weep, I weep / Because I'd like to go to the wedding canopy faster.

45. **"Play, Play, Musicians"**
    Play, play, musicians / This is the way it is / I too am having a wedding / I too have a man.

46. **"Change Me a Twenty"**
    (1) Change me, change me a twenty / All into singles / I want to pay the musicians well / So they play well.
    (2) Change me, change me a twenty / Into half-dollars / I want to pay the musicians well / So they'll play better.
    (3) Change me, change me a twenty / Into quarters / I want to pay the musicians well / So they'll play real neat.
    (4) Change me, change me a twenty / Into dimes / I want to pay the musicians well / So they'll play better.
    (5) Change me, change me a twenty / Into nickels / I want to pay the musicians well / So they won't play the blues.
    (6) Change me, change me a twenty / Into pennies / I want to pay the musicians well / So they'll play all the tunes.
    (7) Change me, change me a twenty / Into farthings / I want to pay the musicians well / So the bridegroom will please me.

47. **"Like This"**
    Like this, and like this, and like this, and like this / Is how you fool a bridegroom / You promise him, you promise him, you promise him a big dowry / And you don't give him a penny.

48. **"Quieter, All You In-laws"**
    (1) Quieter, all you in-laws / We're seating an orphan bride / We're asking word by word / If she was with her father in the holy place [cemetery— M.S.].
    (2) Whether she went around the field three times / Whether she invited her parents to the wedding.
    (3) Oh, God, I stand opposite the moon / He shouldn't be a widower, nor I a widow.
    (4) Oh, matchmaker, matchmaker, curse you / Oh, what did you have against me / I've paid for your matchmaking / And you've slaughtered me ruthlessly.
    (5) You should be buried by God and man / You got me a bitch for a wife / A bitch-wife is very bitter / Oh, give me advice on how to get rid of her.
    (6) A year, two, three have passed / And there's a child now too / I would divorce her, but my mind isn't on it.

49. **"Oh, Mejlex Said"**
    Oh, Mejlex said we should play at marriage / Play at marriage / We play and we play with great weeping / We play and we play with great shouting / Tane Godl's daughter doesn't want Mejlex's son.

50. "You're All Leaving"

(1) You're all leaving, you're all leaving / My dear in-laws / I give you my daughter as a daughter-in-law / I hope she loses her looks at your place.

(2) My son-in-law, my dear son-in-law / I'm taking you as son-in-law / I give you my daughter as a wife / I hope she won't lose her double chin.

(3) My *maxetejneste* [daughter's mother-in-law—M.S.], my dear *maxetejneste* / Don't laugh at my child / If you see a fault in her / Overlook it as if you were her own mother.

(4) My *maxetejneste*, dear *maxetejneste* / I come to you in a wig / I heard you have beautiful daughters / But you're taking a jewel as a daughter-in-law.

51. "Daughter-in-law, My Daughter-in-law"

(1) Daughter-in-law, my daughter-in-law / Get up on the cart / And go off with me / The horses are already ready / The cart is already set up / Get up on the cart / And go off with me.

(2) How can I go / Father-in-law, with you / Since I haven't said good-bye to my father / Farewell, my father / You brought me up / You weighed me in gold and silver / Now I'm leaving / And am discarding you all.

(3) Daughter-in-law, my daughter-in-law / Get up on the cart / And go off with me / The horses are already ready / The cart is already set up / Get up on the cart / And go off with me.

(4) How can I go, father-in-law, when I haven't said good-bye to my mother / Farewell, my mother / You brought me up / You weighed me in gold and silver / Now I'm leaving / And am discarding you all.

52. "The Carts Stand"

(1) The carts stand, the carts stand / Around my father's door /—Pretty daughter, fine daughter / Seat yourself, ride off with me /—How can I sit down and ride off with you / When I haven't said good-bye to my father / Farewell, my father / I was your daughter / You brought me up since I was small / And now that I'm big—I've flown / [In Russian / Polish:] Cry, cry, it won't help / The horses are on the road / My dear.

(2) [Same, substitute "mother" for "father" in lines 6, 7—M.S.]

53. "Good-day, Father-in-law"

(1) Good-day, father-in-law / Do you like your daughter-in-law? /—I like her a lot / A pretty daughter-in-law in a veil.

(2) Pretty as the snowball bush / Pretty as the strawberry bush / Ram tara, etc.

54. "Where Were You, My Daughter?"

(1) Where were you my daughter /—At the evil father-in-law's /—What did you do, my daughter / At the evil father-in-law's? /—Washed tables and benches / Covered them with tears / My beloved mother.

(2) What did you eat, my daughter / At the evil father-in-law's? /—A piece of fish / At the covered table / My beloved mother.

(3) Where did you sleep, my daughter / At the evil father-in-law's? /—On a sackful of dirt / With my face to the ground / My beloved mother.

55. "Mama Gave Me Up and Gave Me Away"

(1) Mama gave me up and gave me away / Forty-two miles / And told me and told me / That I can't ever visit her.

(2) I didn't for one year and two, one year and two / I began to feel very bad, very bad / I made myself light as a bird, light as a bird / And flew to her.

(3) The golden bird, the golden bird, the golden bird flew, flew / Over dense forests, forests / And lost there a golden feather, a golden feather / In a foreign land, land.

(4) I don't feel so badly about the golden feather, golden feather / As for the peacock itself, itself / Since I left my parents / My parents / I sit and weep and wail, and wail.

(5) At my mother's: golden rings on my fingers, golden rings on my fingers / At my mother-in-law's—dying of hunger, dying of hunger.

56. "To Whom Can I Cry Out"

(1) To whom can I cry out, to whom can I weep / I've poured my heart out to no one / If I can tell my father / He'll tell me he's already rid of me. [First two lines same in all subsequent verses.]

(2) If I tell my mother / She'll tell me things are bitter for her too.

(3) If I tell my brother / He'll tell me he prefers his wife.

(4) If I tell my sister / She'll tell me it's no better for her.

(5) If I tell my friends / One likes me, another hates me.

(6) If I tell my neighbors / One will weep, another will laugh.

57. "Apples and Pears"

(1) Apples and pears / How bitter are the seeds / When a widower takes a young girl / She covers herself in tears.

(2) A good wine in a bad barrel / Begins to go sour / When the widower takes a young girl / She begins to grieve.

(3) When the apple is red / And has a worm / When the widower takes a young girl / He becomes false in his ways.

58. "The Clock Strikes One"

(1) The clock strikes one / Oh, oh, oh, one, oh, oh, oh, one / It's all the same to me / Good-night, good-night / My troubles, great sorrows / Have brought me here.

(2) The clock strikes two / Oh, oh, oh, two, oh, oh, oh, two / It's terrible for me / Good-night [etc.].

(3) The clock strikes three / Oh, oh, oh, three, oh, oh, oh, three / My time has already passed.

(4) The clock strikes four / oh, oh, oh, four, oh, oh, oh, four / I should already lie with my feet toward the door [die].

59. "The Grandpas and Grandmas"

The grandpas and grandmas / Are standing outside / With broad bags / With long ends / A girl who weeps / And won't be quiet / They take and throw / Into the bag.

60. "The Czar's Treasures"

(1) The Czar's treasures and the whole country / Would not please me / As you are dear to me, my world, my beauty / I look at you, and think the world is mine / [Refrain:] sleep my child / sleep my child / Grow and be healthy / Sleep, my child, sleep my child / Live and be healthy.

(2) Like the sun goes down in the evening / You'll sleep through the night / Like the sun rises in the morning / You'll get up from your rest. [Refrain]

61. "Sleep, Sleep, Child"

Sleep, sleep, child / Sleep, sleep, kitten.

62. "Fall Asleep, My Little Bird"

(1) Fall asleep, my little bird / Close your golden eyes / And sleep, my dear child / [repeated].

(2) You'll grow up, get big / You'll blossom like a rose / Your face will be charming / Your lips, your teeth / Your eyes, your dimples / They'll envy me for that.

(3) A man will take you / Your name will be renowned / He'll be a leader, a connoisseur / You'll have children / You'll get satisfaction / Your mama will be a grandma.

63. "I Sit During the Day in the Vineyard"

(1) I sit during the day in the vineyard / And play cards with my fiancé / Oh, in comes an old man / Dressed in white.

(2) —Good-day, my daughter /—Good-day, grandfather /—Oh, I haven't come to say good-day / I've come to shorten your years.

(3) —Old Grandfather, let me live / Not for my sake, but for my mother's and father's sake / Oh my father and mother, they love me / They'll give you everything, oh, in the house.

(4) [First two lines missing] / Forget about everything in the house / Whoever I call, must go.

(5) —Old Grandfather, let me live / Oh, not for my sake, but for my sisters' and brothers' sake / My sisters and brothers love me / They'll give you their children from the cradle.

(6) —Let the child rock in its cradle / And if I need it, I'll take it too [missing] / [missing].

(7) —Call in my dear mother / Maybe I'll feel better / When the mother opened the door /—My daughter, woe unto you.

(8) —Call in my dear fiancé / Maybe I'll feel better / When the fiancé came in /—My dear bride, let it be unto me.

(9) —Tear up the engagement contract, woe unto me / My dear groom, you remain without me / Tear up the engagement contract, woe unto me / [missing].

(10) —Mama, oh, mama, I can't bear it / My dear bride—she's expiring. / Oh, mama, mama, I can't bear it / My dear bride—she's expiring.

64. "I Beg for Alms"

(1) I beg for alms, I'm a poor man, a blind man / Blind from birth / I'm rejected from seeing God's wonders / I lost my bright world young.

(2) Oh, I'm blind, oh, Jewish children / From my mother's womb / Since I tasted the world / *Oy vey, oy vey,* poor, poor am I in my old age too / And full of sorrows.

(3) When I was, Jewish children, a small child / My parents got me my food / If I were nourished / woe is me, like that today / I would thank you constantly, God in heaven.

(4) Oh, I beg you, *oy vey,* with tears / Oh, spare a poor man, a blind man / Only God in heaven, who is rich / Will pay you for your alms.

(5) I sit here / *Oy vey,* always and think / About man's life on earth [unclear]. For me there's no difference between day and night / Of what use is my dark life?

65. "I'm Lonely"

I'm lonely and tattered / And have no hand as well / And there's not a bite in the house / And I've been driven from my country / Should I weep, should I cry out / How would my weeping help me / It's predestined from heaven / I'm lonely as a stone / Give, Jewish children, to an unfortunate man, a blind man, a cripple.

66. "Seize Him"

(1) Seize him, take him, seize him, take him / Seize him, take him, throw him in jail / So he won't be a thief anymore.
[Refrain:] A thief, a thief / Robbed me / He took everything / From my house.

(2) Seven shirts, like goblets / Three with patches, four with holes. [Refrain]

(3) Seven candlesticks like stars / Three without bases, four without tops. [Refrain]

67. "I Have a Jacket"

(1) I have a jacket of new material / You can believe, you can't take it into your hand / I thought it over / And made a cloak out of the jacket.

(2) I have a cloak of new material / You can believe, you can't take it into your hand / I thought it over / And made a pair of pants out of the cloak.

(3) I have a pair of pants of new material / I thought it over, etc. So I made a waistcoat out of it.

(4) So I made a vest out of the waistcoat . . .

(5) So I made a box [to bury it—M.B.] for the vest.

68. "God, Where Can You Find"

(1) God, where can you find, where can you find, where can you find / A noodle board to roll out the *varničkes* [a type of noodle dish—M.S.]. Without yeast and without chicken fat / Without pepper and without salt / oh, a noodle board to roll out the *varničkes.*

(2) A knife to cut the *varničkes* . . .

(3) A pot to cook the *varničkes* . . .

(4) A boy to eat the *varničkes* . . .

69. "Good-Morning, Fejge-Soše"*

(1) —Good-morning, Fejge-Soše / Why are you sitting like that?
—Good-day, Fajve-Yoše / Because it's comfortable.

(2) Maybe you want, Fajve-Yoše / To try my goods? / A sabbath noodle pudding / Such a pleasure.

(3) Saturday after the pudding / I'm a real beauty / Done up and made up / How do you like me?

(4) —Maybe, Fejge-Soše / You'd like some sunflower seeds? /—Since it's you, Fajve-Yoše / I'll try some.

(5) —Maybe you want, Fejge-Soše / To promenade with me? /—Since it's you, Fajve-Yoše, I'll do just that.

70. "In Odessa"

In Odessa, in Odessa, On the Moldavanka / I danced a polonaise / With a false girl / Yippee, derideray / Oh, long live Odessa / Oh, you pretty girl / Oh, let's go to Odessa.

[*The humor of this song lies in the Russian rhyming words at the end of lines 2 and 4 of each verse, giving a "highfalutin" air.—M.S.]

Instrumental Tunes

71. Dobriden
Добрый день

72. Mazltov
Мазлтов

73. Mazltov
Мазлтов

Parlando

lix vojd ha_me_xu_tu [имя......]

a ganc faj-nem ma_ze_tov

Rubato ♩=92

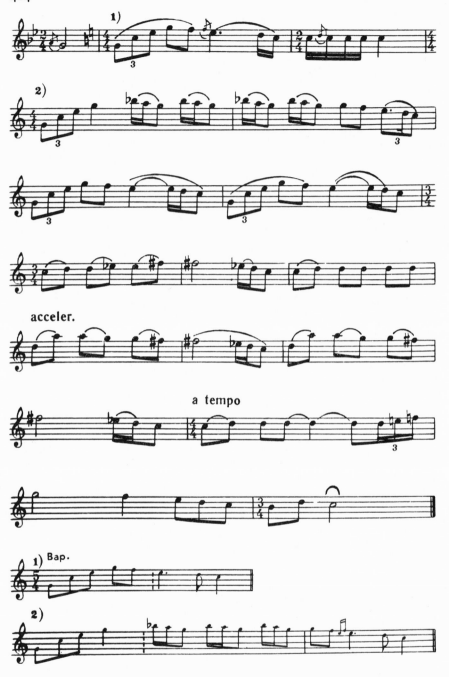

74. Aḥavo rabo
Великая любовь

75. Dojne
Дойна

428

Allegro ♩= 126-138

76. Skočne
Скочна

77. Skočne
Скочна

78. Skočne
Скочна

Andante ♩=96

Fine

Dal %· al Fine

79. Frejlexs
Фрейлехс

80. Skočne
Скочна

Allegretto ♩=120

81. Gas-nign
Уличный напев

82. Gas – nign
Уличный напев

83. Gas-nign
Уличный напев

84. Nign
Напев

85. Zaj gezunt
Прощальная

86. Skočne
Скочна

D'al 𝄋 al Fine

Dal $ al Fine

87. Frejlexs
Фрейлехс

88.Skočne
Скочна

Andantino ♩=76

89. Skočne
Скочна

90. Skočne
Скочна

91. Frejlexs
Фрейлехс

92. Skočne
Скочна

93. Šer
Шер

94. Šer
Шер

95. Šer
Шер

96. Xosid
Хосид

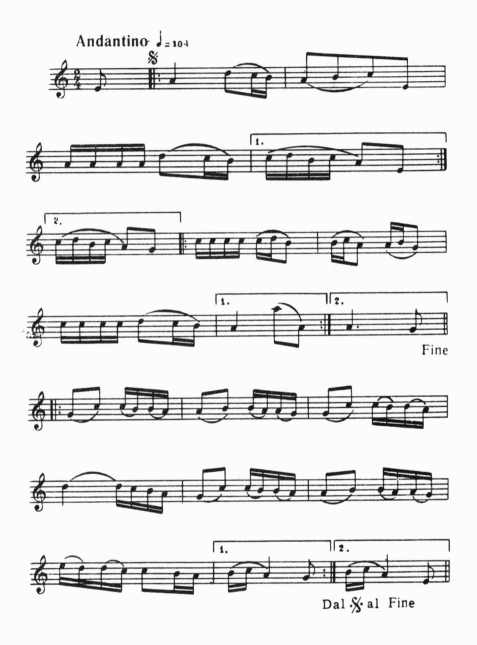

97. Volex
Волах

98. Frejlexs
Фрейлехс

Textless Songs

99.Nign
Напев

Am ba ba bam bam tja ra ra ra ra la ra ra

ra ra na ra ra ra la la la ra ra ri ra ram.

Fine

Dal 𝄋 al Fine

100. Tiš-nign
Застольный напев

101. Nign
Напев

Fine

Dal 𝄋 al Fine

102. Frejlexs
Фрейлехс

103. Tiš-nign
Застольный напев

104. Nign
Напев

454

105. Frejlexs
Фрейлехс

Fine

Da capo al Fine

106. Nign
Напев

Bap.

107. Nign
Напев

108. Nign
Напев

109. Nign
Напев

Bam ba bambambam ba bam ba bam...

110. Tiš-nign
Застольный напев

Fine

Da capo al Fine

111. Frejlexs
Фрейлехс

Am bam bam bam   bababababam

La   ra   la ra   la

ra   la la la   la ra   la la la

112. Nign
Напев

Dal 𝄋 al Fine

113. Frejlexs
Фрейлехс

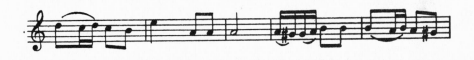

114. Frejlexs
Фрейлехс

115. Nign
Напев

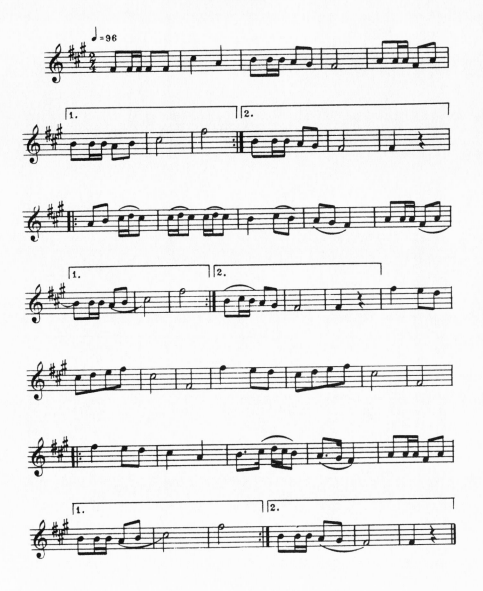

116. Tiš-nign
Застольный напев

117. Tiš-nign
Застольный напев

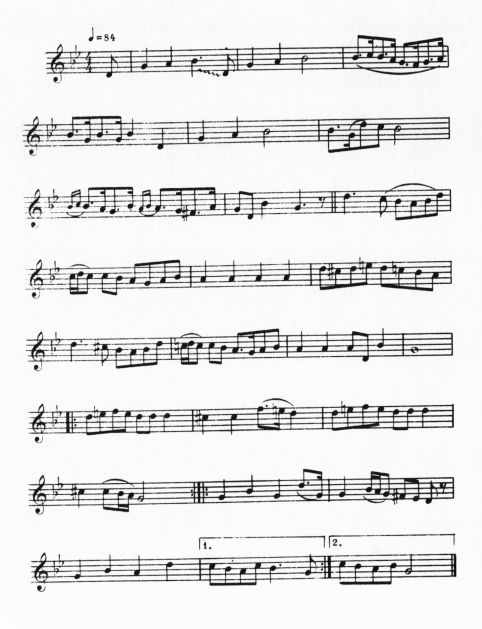

118. Tiš-nign
Застольный напев

119. Tiš-nign
Застольный напев

120. Tiš-nign
Застольный напев

121. Žok
Жок

122. Tiš-nign
Застольный напев

123. Tiš-nign
Застольный напев

124. Tiš-nign
Застольный напев

125. Skočne [1)](#)
Скочна

126. Nign
Напев

127. Nign
Напев

128. Nign
Напев

129. Nign
Напев

130. Nign
Напев

Fine

Dal 𝄋 al Fine

Вар.

131. Nign
Напев

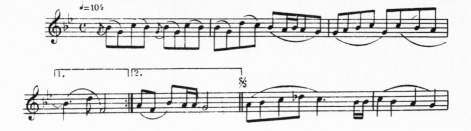

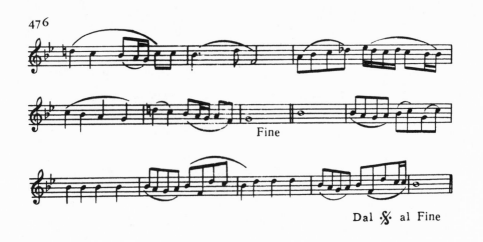

Fine

Dal 𝄋 al Fine

132. Nign
Напев

133. Nign
Напев

134. Frejlexs
Фрейлехс

Fine

Dal 𝄋 al Fine

135. Nign
Напев

136. Nign
Напев

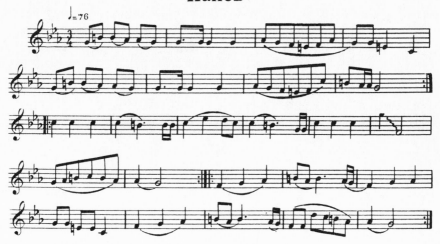

137. Nign
Напев

Fine

Dal 𝄋 al Fine

138. Nign
Напев

Fine

Dal 𝄋 al Fine

139. Nign
Напев

140. Nign
Напев

141. Tiš-nign
Застольный напев

Dal 𝄋 al Fine

142. Nign
Напев

Fine

Da capo al Fine

143. Frejlexs
Фрейлехс

144. Frejlexs
Фрейлехс

145. Nign
Напев

146. Nign
Напев

147. Frejlexs
Фрейлехс

Fine

Dal 𝄋 al Fine

148. Frejlexs
Фрейлехс

Вар.

149. Frejlexs
Фрейлехс

150. Frejlexs
Фрейлехс

Annotations to the Songs and Music

[*Editor's note:* Beregovski's archive numbers are given here for the sake of completeness, though it is not known how much of that archive is in Leningrad at the Institute of Theater, Music, and the Cinema and whether the same numbering system holds true.]

1. FZ-741/4. Transcribed from D. Bergel'son, writer, Kiev (1931). Learned in Bessarabia. Variant in Cahan 1912a: no. 30. The first verse is found in many Jewish songs.

2. FZ-125/1. Transcribed from F. Khenkin, 51, Kiev (1929). Learned in Starodub, Chernigovshchina. Variant in Ginzburg-Marek 1901: no. 134, Cahan 1912a: no. 8, Pinkes 1913: no. 15, all without melodies. For this song with a different melody, see Idelsohn 1932:496. A very old song, close to the love songs. Note the two phrases built on pentachords (D-E-F#-G-A with *e* tonic; lower pentachord of the altered Phrygian E-A with leading tone D). See note to no. 3. Sung parlando. This sort of short tune made of two phrases is rarely found among Jewish songs (outside children's songs, and those lack the augmented second). The two-phrase tune does not match the quatrain stanza of the song.

3. Transcribed by ear from B. Kipnis, 19, art school student, Kiev (1927). Learned in Slovchno, Zhitomir region, from mother, the wife of a leather worker. Variant in Cahan 1912a: no. 46 (with different melody); second stanza found in many Jewish songs. For variant of melody and text, see Cahan 1912a: no. 7.

4. F-122/1. Transcribed from F. Khenkin (see no. 2). Variant of the fourth stanza in Cahan 1928: no. 56, and of the third stanza in Ginzburg-Marek 1901: no. 226 (both without melodies).

5. FT-799/2. Transcribed from L. Vinokur, 20, worker (female) in Belaia Tserkov', Kiev district (1933). Variant text and melody in Kipnis 1918:19–20; analogous in Cahan 1912a: no. 16. Variant in Cabinet FE/227 (1), transcribed in 1912–14 from Proskurov, Kamenets-Podol'sk *gubernia*.

6. FZ-409/2. Transcribed from I. Barash in Zhitomir, Volynsk *gubernia* (1912–14). Variant Leman 1928: no. 11. Recruit songs were sung to this tune (nos. 128, 129); see pp. 473, 474. Third stanza found in many Jewish songs. Variant of several stanzas: Kipnis 1918:31 (with different melody).

7. FZ-360/1. Transcribed from F. Shnaider, 20, and Sh. Kiperman, 22, workers in a candy factory in Dubno, Volynsk *gubernia* (1913). Kiselhof recording. Variant in Cahan 1912a: no. 20. The second half of the song was sung a half step higher.

8. FZ-44/3. Transcribed from P. Zaiats in Berditchev, Kiev *gubernia* (1912–14). Variant of melody and first stanza in Leman 1928: no. 281, Cahan 1912a: no. 5, text in Ginzburg-Marek 1901: no. 175, *Tsaytshrift* 1928: no. 8. Variant in Cabinet (F3-364[1]), transcribed in Korets, Volynsk Province (1912–14). This variant has the altered Phrygian (Ex. 5).

9. FZ-67. Transcribed from G. London, 17, shoemaker, in Belaia Tserkov' (1929). This song was transcribed from the singer twice in a space of three weeks. The singer gave the strong impression of an immediate, striking folksinger, largely of lyric-dramatic songs. Returning to Belaia Tserkov', I decided to record several songs again. I came to be convinced that at each new performance of the same song he introduced more or less significant changes. The impression was a kind of framework of melody to which new artistic formulation was given at every performance. It was necessary to note, in comparing both variants, that the more stable part of the melody lay in its character (lyricism in this case), tempo, meter,

Example 5

and scale. Musical phrases of a melismatic character (e.g., opening of the third phrase) were often sung differently. Example 6 shows one verse of the second transcription (FE-43/4).

10. FZ-62/1. Transcribed from Leby, 30, worker, Kiev (1929). Learned in Telesht, Bessarabia, where he lived. Text transcribed from cylinder. Variant in Cahan 1912a: no. 1.

11. FZ-249/2. Transcribed from G. Gertsberg, 28, actress, Odessa J. Theatre, Odessa (1930). Variant of first stanza in Cahan 1928: no. 46, as a children's song, without words.

12. FZ-950/4. Transcribed from L. Fishman, 26, worker, in L'vovo, Kalinindorf district, Nikolaev region (1936).

Example 6

13. FZ-248. G. Gertsberg (cf. no. 11). Performer (female) learned in Kremenchug, Poltava region, from working girls.

14. FZ-951/4. Transcribed from Z. Nitikman, 29, student of agronomy school in L'vovo, Kalinindorf district, Nikolaev region (1936). Variant text in Cahan 1912a: no. 10 (different melody); Cahan 1928: no. 84; Pinkes 1913: no. 20; Bastomski 1913: no. 9, last three without melody. The melody of this version was taken from the popular wedding dance the *šer.* Cf. the transcription of Shalyt and Kopyt, *Jewish Folk Songs* (St. Petersburg, n.d.), no. 24. For discussion of the *šer,* see note to no. 93, below.

15. FZ-208/4. Transcribed from D. Levina, 21, student at Odessa school of education, Odessa (1930). Variant melody and text in Cahan 1912a: no. 24; stanzas 4–5. Same text, different melody in Idelsohn 1932: no. 271.

16. FZ-197. Transcribed from F. Reshetnikova, 30, worker in textile factory in Odessa (1930). Learned in Bendery, Bessarabia, from (female) tailor. Variant of first stanza in Cahan 1928: no. 35 (there also as love song, without melody).

17. FZ-57/1. Transcribed from L. Rom, actress Moscow Jewish Theater, Kiev (1929). Variant in Cahan 1912a: no. 47; variant of second stanza in Pinkes 1913: no. 11. In the Cabinet are two variants, one close to no. 17 here, transcribed in Kiev (1928) from Kh. Gitelman, student of Kiev Jewish Pedogogical Technicum. Learned in Berdichev, where she lived. In Gitelman's version the melody is more even; it lacks the dotted eighths and sixteenths of no. 17. The second variant in the archive (transcribed by ear) of A. Khabenski is interesting because the first musical phrase is taken from a widespread Ukrainian song, "Stoit gora

visokaia" (Ex. 7). Transcribed by ear from F. Mazur, 20, Ushomir, Zhitomir region (1929). As we can see, the first phrase almost completely corresponds to a Ukrainian melody. This was undoubtedly the beginning stage, when the original had preserved all its distinctiveness. Beginning with the second phrase, the singer sings the melody as no. 17.

18. FZ-430/2. Transcribed by Z. Bernshtein, Zhitomir (1912–14). Variants in Leman 1923: no. 14 and Idelsohn 1932: no. 589. The texts of the first two stanzas are taken from the recording; remaining stanzas are taken from the version transcribed from the teacher M. Shpolianskii in Chernikhov, Zhitomir region (1927), in which the fifth verse is repeated after the sixth verse. We collected an interesting variant of the second and third stanzas in Odessa in 1930 from R. Polonoer, a (female) student of the Odessa Institute of Mass Education, who learned it in Liubar, Zhitomir region. The first stanza is different. Example 8 shows the melody of the first stanza (FZ-169/3).

19. FZ-170/2. Transcribed from three students of Odessa Institute of National Education (1930). This has a rare occurrence of the introduction of elements of two-part singing in the performance of a group of singers of an old Jewish song. Once a lower third to the penultimate pitch of the second phrase appeared, the first phrase was sung in thirds; see Example 9 text variant and melody in Kipnis 1918:21–22 (fuller text).

20. Transcribed by ear from B. Gutianskii, writer, Kiev (1929). Learned in Bershadi, Vinnitska region.

21. FZ-334/1. Transcribed from I. Libershtein in Polonna, Kamanets-Podol'sk *gubernia* (1912–14).

22. FZ-86/1. Transcribed from X. Alper, 20, worker (female) in Belaia Tserkov' (1929). Variant of first stanza in Cahan 1928: no. 2 (different context).

Example 7

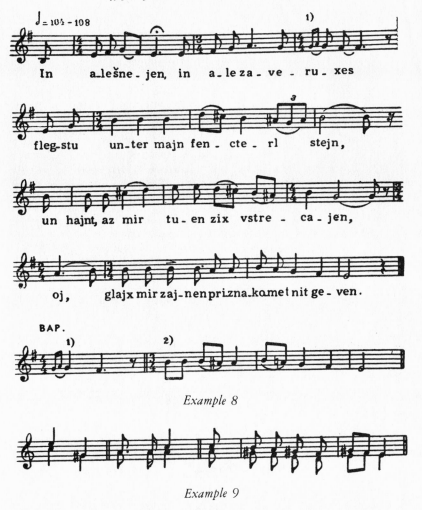

In a.lešne.jen, in a.le za.ve.ru.xes

fleg.stu un.ter majn fen.cte.rl stejn,

un hajnt, az mir tu.en zix vstre.ca.jen,

oj, glajx mir zaj.nen prizna.kamet nit ge.ven.

BAP.

Example 8

Example 9

This stanza can be found in a series of Jewish folk songs (cf. Cahan 1928, note to no. 26). Idelsohn 1932 (no. 128) has this song with a different melody.

23. FZ-57/2. Transcribed from L. Rom (cf. note to no. 17). Learned in Meyshagol, Vilensk *gubernia* in 1910. Variant in Kipnis 1918:7–8; Leman 1923: no. 20. Variant of first stanza (different context) in Cahan 1912a: no. 17. In the Cabinet variant, the first and last phrases are sung to the syllable *ay* instead of to the *U vu vu* of no. 23.

24. FZ-102/2. Transcribed from Z. Kashtylian, 33, tailor, in Belaia Tserkov' (1929). Variant of eighth stanza in Cahan 1928: nos. 24, 37, both without melodies.

25. FZ/2. Transcribed from Kh. Ḡitelman, 21, student (female) of the Jewish Pedagogical School in Kiev (1929), who learned the song in Berdichev, where she had lived.

26. FZ-796/2. Transcribed from D. Vinokur, 24, worker (female) in Belaia Tserkov' (1933).

27. FZ-185. Transcribed from A. Mil'on, 38, worker in Odessa (1930). Cf. note to no. 28.

28. FZ-387/1. Transcribed from B. Ainbinder, 13, in Kovele, Volynsk *gubernia* (1913). Recorded by Kiselhof. Variant for nos. 27 and 28 in Leman 1923: variant of no. 42 (without melody); Cahan 1912a: no. 39 (different melody); Pinkes 1913: no. 4. For variant of first stanza, see Cahan 1928: no. 23, second stanza (in different context, with different melody). In the Cabinet there is a close variant to no. 28 (FZ-76/2) transcribed from P. Flaks, 15, Belaia Tserkov' (1929). The first verse is shown in Example 10.

29. FZ-181. Transcribed from A. Perlshtein, 29, worker (female), Odessa (1930). Variant text in Cahan 1928:44a (different melody); variant of first stanza there in nos. 44–46, first stanza. For variant of second stanza, see Leman 1923: no. 7, second stanza (different context and melody); Pinkes 1913: no. 16.

30. FZ-70/1. Transcribed from R. Kleiman, 18, worker (female), Belaia Tserkov' (1929). In the Cabinet archive there are two more variants. One of them (FZ-285/1) was transcribed in Dubno, Volynsk *gubernia* in 1913, while the second (FZ-390) was transcribed in Medzhibozh, Kamanets-Podol'sk *gubernia* in 1912–14. The first variant is similar to no. 30 (see Ex. 11). Though many details differ, it is still close to no. 30. The unusually beautiful analogies to individual images of this song can be found in a very old Yiddish song: These lines were first

Example 10

printed in a book quite popular in its day, Zeligman of Ulm's *Der zukhtshpigl* (1st ed. 1610, later eds. 1678, 1691, 1716). Cf. Dr. I. Tsinberg 1943:300–301.

31. Transcribed from Kh. Gitelman (cf. note to no. 25). Variant to fourth stanza in Cahan 1912a: no. 1 and Kipnis 1918:78. There is another variant in the Cabinet, transcribed in Zhitomir and Belaia Tserkov'.

32. FZ-60/4. Transcribed from L. Vinogradov, 30, worker, Kiev (1929). Learned in Teleneshty (Bessarabia) where he lived.

33. FZ-240/2. Transcribed from R. Pesina, 40, dressmaker, Odessa (1930). Melody taken from the popular wedding dance, *šer.*

34. FZ-164. Transcribed from D. Leshner, 35, worker (female) in a bristle factory, Odessa (1930).

35. Transcribed by ear by A. Khabenski, from M. Volordarska, 34, housewife, Ushomir, Zhitomir region (1929).

36. FZ-50/3. Transcribed from three working girls in Belaia Tserkov' (1929). In the Cabinet archive there is another variant of this ballad (FZ-701/2), transcribed from B. Sitsh, 18, a textile worker in Uman' (1939). For variant of text, see Prilutski nos. 168, 169; Cahan 1912a: no. 10 (first three stanzas only with different melody); Pinkes 1913: no. 5; Bastomski 1913: nos. 5, 9; Graubard 1914: no. 9; Landoy 1926: columns 18–19. All these without melodies.

37. FZ-809/1. Transcribed from Z. Skuditskii, scientific worker, learned from someone in Gomel'. Text transcribed from a student (female) of the Kiev Jewish Pedagogical School. T. Muchnik, in 1927. See note to no. 38.

38. FZ-808/3. Transcribed from R. Tsianovska, 48, Kiev (1933). In the Cabinet there are four variants of this song: (1) schoolboy in Belaia Tserkov' (transcribed by ear, 1928); (2) in the Frayleon Kolkhoz, Kaliningrad district, Nikolaev region (942/2) (1936); (3) Belaia Tserkov' (1930) (FZ-856/1); (4) by ear from D. Kipnis, Kiev (1927), who learned it from his mother in Slovochno, Zhitomir region. The mother was a housewife, 50, wife of a leather worker. The Kipnis variant differs considerably from all the published and unpublished variants. In all the variants it is presented as a joke, for fun. The boy and girl pose each other problems, knowing they cannot be fulfilled. In the Kipnis variant we find a bad reaction on the part of the man, and threats toward the woman. Kipnis' first two stanzas are close melodically to our no. 38. However, the special tension and arrangement of the Kipnis variant allowed the anonymous author to introduce significant melodic changes. Our no. 38 is in major, whereas the first two stanzas of the Kipnis variant are in minor. The tempo is slower and the melody lacks the "mazurka" grace of no. 38. Beginning with the third stanza, the Kipnis variant changes. The melody of the third stanza (also used for the fifth and seventh, where the man speaks) changes to the altered Dorian scale. This scale is further developed in the fourth and sixth stanzas (the woman's reply).

39. FZ-752/3. Transcribed from L. Cherniak, 30, teacher (female), Kiev (1933). Learned in Khotimsky, Mogilev region. Variant of first stanza in Ginzburg-Marek 1901: nos. 243, 245, 249.

Oj, a kojl, oj, a fa.jer.di - ke kojl...

Example 11

40. FZ-249/1. Transcribed from G. Gertsberg (see note to no. 11), learned in Kremenchug, Poltava region. For variant of text, see Cahan 1912b: no. 23 (different melody). Variant of first stanza in Pinkes 1913: no. 20, Pinkes 1922: no. 9, Cahan 1928:84—all without melodies.

41. Transcribed by ear from Birgerzon, 23, student of Jewish Pedagogical School, Kiev (1928). This is a variant of a Mikhl Gordon song, "Fun der xupe cu der sude"; see Gordon 1889:84–92. Learned at a wedding in a Jewish agricultural colony (Khersonshchina) from settlers from Uman'. They sang only the stanza given. In the Cabinet there is a variant transcription in Zhitomir in 1912–14 (Z3-429/2, male voice).

42. FZ-925/5. Transcribed from M. Oziyarnski, 20, collective farm worker, Bobrovy-kut Colony, Kalinindorf district, Nikolaev region (1936). Šer melody.

43. Transcribed by ear, Kiev (1935).

44. FZ-971/1. Transcribed from I. Goldenberg, 30, worker in a mill in Belaia Tserkov' (1935), learned from his mother in Tetieva, Kiev region. For text variant, see Cahan 1912b: no. 21, which has fuller text and different melody; compare it to his no. 20.

45. FZ-241/1. Transcribed from R. Pesina (cf. no. 33). Šer melody.

46. FZ-858/1. Transcribed from R. Yaroslavsaia, 30, teacher in Belaia Tserkov' (1935). Learned from father, 62, former teacher; he remembered all the songs I recorded in the Yaroslav family included here (nos. 51, 55, 56, 58), which he remembered from his childhood (1880s) in Antonovo near Skviry, Kiev region.

47. Transcribed by ear from Z. Skudnitski, scientific worker. Text variant in Ginzburg-Marek 1901:238, Cahan 1912b: no. 22, both without melodies.

48. FZ-74/1. Transcribed from T. Pavlovskaya, 22, worker in Belaia Tserkov' (1929). This is a parody of the *gramen zogn* of the badxn, performed at the *bazecn*. The song imitates playing on the fiddle, which accompanied the badxn. Similar stanzas in Cahan 1928: no. 109, Ginzburg-Marek 1901: nos. 279, 280, both without melodies. Here the stanza is a couplet, with paired rhyme. The melody is a period consisting of two parts (four musical phrases). The intro has been changed and simplified compared to what would have been performed at a wedding. Usually this "riff" *(otygrysh)*, performed by the solo fiddler, was in the altered Phrygian scale. The recitation of the badxn was in natural minor. The singer of this version did not sing all verses in the same form. The first verse consists of four phrases—*abcd* —but without the introduction; the second verse has a first, second and fourth phrase (the last somewhat altered); the fourth phrase was sung to the syllable *la,* replacing the "riff"; the fourth and fifth verses consist of all four phrases plus the "riff."

49. This is a fragment of a very old song with unclear content. *Mejlax* is a man's name, but it also means "king"; *Tane-godl* means "great secret." Transcribed by ear from Sh. Dobin, scientific worker, Kiev (1928), who learned it around 1875 from his grandmother, who was then sixty, in Bober (Belorussia). He remembered only this verse.

50. FZ-102/1. Transcribed from Z. Kashtylian (see no. 24). The Cabinet has two more variants of this song, the first transcribed in Odessa in 1930 (FZ-234/2) and the second in Belaia Tserkov' in 1933 (FZ-719/4). Variant of text in Pinkes 1922: no. 10.

51. FZ-858/2. Transcribed from R. Yaroslavski (see no. 46).

52. FZ-121/2. Transcribed from F. Khenkina (see no. 2). Variant of text in Cahan 1928: no. 111 and Pinkes 1922: no. 7, both without melodies.

53. FZ-947/1. Transcribed from A. Kaneveski, 64, collective farm worker in the Sholom Aleichem Colony, Kalinindorf district, Nikolaev region (1936). Text in Ginzburg-Marek 1901: no. 257.

54. FZ-946/4. Transcribed from Kh. Kutsenok, 25 (female) collective farm worker, "Fraylebn," Kalinindorf district, Nikolaev region (1936). Text variant in Cahan 1928: no. 113. Fuller text in Ginzburg-Marek 1901: nos. 267, 268.

55. FZ-870/2. Transcribed from Kh. Yaroslavski (see no. 46). Variant melody and text in Beregovski 1934: no. 97.

56. FZ-858/3. Transcribed from R. Yaroslavsaia (see no. 46).

57. FZ-121/3. Transcribed from F. Khenkina (see no. 2). Text variant in *Tsaytshrift* 1928: no. 13. Similar stanzas in Ginzburg-Marek 1901: no. 283, and Pinkes 1913: no. 8, all without melodies. Close parallel to the third stanza in the Isaac Waliho manuscript (1605), which reads:

> Es ist kein Apfel so rosenrot
> Es steckt ein Wurm darin,
> Es ist kein Meidlein so hübsch un' fein
> Es furth kein falschen Sinn.

Incidentally, we can note that we find stanzas close to the second and third stanzas of no. 57 in a German folk song of the sixteenth century printed in Erk and Böhme 1893–94:

> 8. Wenn der best Win in alten Fass war
> Darin muss er ersauren;
> So wenn ein jungs Maidlein ein alten Mann nimmt
> Ihr junges Herz muss trauren.
> 11. Und war der Apfel noch so roth
> So findt man ein Wurmlein drinnen
> So welch Jungfräulein sauberlich sein
> Di konnen viel falschen sinen.

These verses coincide with the Jewish folk song both textually and in form (quatrain, *abcd* rhyme, etc.).

58. FZ-895/4. Transcribed from S. Yaroslavski (see no. 46). For a similar orphan song (with different melody), see Cahan 1912b: no. 18. Our version is fragmentary.

59. FZ-56/1. Transcribed from L. Rom (see no. 17), learned from her father in Meishagol, Vilensk *gubernia* (1910). Variant of text in Ginzburg-Marek 1901: no. 69, third stanza; no. 63, fourth stanza. Both have a fuller text. Text and melody variant in Idelsohn 1932: no. 60.

60. FZ-173/3. Transcribed from R. Pesina. Variant text and melody in Kiselhof 1912: no. 36. Text variant in Cahan 1912b: no. 5.

61. Transcribed by ear from B. Gutyanski, writer, Kiev (1928), learned from his mother in Sobolevka, Vinnitska region. This song never had a fixed text. Rocking the child, the mother improvised the text each time. The informant said his mother learned it from her grandmother and great-grandmother, usually being sung while rocking children.

62. FZ-755/1. Transcribed from S. Fibikh, actress and performer of Jewish folk songs; learned in Dvinsk. Text variant in Ginzburg-Marek 1901: no. 71; no. 70 has a variant of our third stanza; see also Ginzburg-Marek 1901: no. 79.

63. FZ-41/1. Transcribed from G. London (see no. 9). Text transcribed by Sh. Kupershmid as dictated by the singer. The first three stanzas are recorded by me from the same singer. The text was corrected according to the recorded version. The other stanzas, transcribed by ear, are more schematic, at times deformed. Text variant in Kipnis n.d.:nos. 44–47 (different melody) and Prilutski 1913: nos. 106–8, all without melodies. Songs about death have long been widespread among Jews. In the Isaac Waliho manuscript cited in note to no. 57 there are three songs about death. Similar songs can be seen in various *purimšpils,* some of which have parodies of this type of song.

64. FZ/3. Transcribed from E. Weissman, 82, blind beggar, Kiev (1929), who often sang songs on the streets of Kiev, where he lived since 1915. For more details of this singular and, in his manner, striking singer, see no. 88, p. 273. He sang very expressively, usually in a free recitative. Text variant in Idelsohn 1932:-698, with different melody.

65. FZ-250/1. Transcribed from Hoffman, 28, actress, Odessa (1930).

66. FZ-822/4. Transcribed from B. Gutianski and Z. Skudnitski, Kiev (1934). Text variant in Cahan 1912b:12, different melody.

67. FZ-169/1. Transcribed from I. Entin, 20, student Institute of National Education, Odessa (1930).

68. FZ-156/1. Transcribed from V. Beker (see no. 65), Odessa (1930). Text variant in Cahan 1928:171 (without melody).

69. FZ-208/2. Transcribed from I. Entin (see no. 67). Melody variant in Cahan 1912a:1 and Leman: no 31. Both have different texts. The song belongs to the broad and varied category of Jewish macaronic songs. See Beregovski 1930.

70. FZ-208/1. Transcribed from I. Gendler, Odessa (1930).

71. Transcribed from G. Barkagan, clarinetist, leader of a klezmer band in the Kalinindorf colony (1936). *Dobriden, dobranoč, mazltov*—these are the names of pieces performed by the wedding band to greet the guests. These were performed for individual guests at the table. The *dobranoč* was performed to greet the guests arriving for the banquet at the home of the bride's parents and should not be confused with the *Dobranoč (a gute naxt);* the latter was performed at the departure of the guests after the meal, while they parted with the hosts. They played more solemn, large works for more honored guests, and smaller pieces for the rest. After the performance of such a piece they played a *frejlaxs.* No. 73 begins with a recitation of the *badxn:* "Lekoved hamexuten (his name), a ganc fajnem mazltov!"

72. Transcribed from A. E. Makonovetskii, violinist, former bandleader, in Khabnoe, Korosten' (1928).

73. FZ-111. Transcribed from I. Triplika, 58, flutist and barber, Slavuta (1929).

74. FZ-465. Transcribed from M. Steingart, fiddler. Bogopol, Kamenets-Poldolsk *gubernia* (1913). Variant of this table song in Beregovski and Fefer 1938: nos. 482–83. *Ahavo rabo* is one of the terms for the altered Phrygian scale used by cantors and klezmorim. Cf. Bernstein 1927:xviii and P. Minkovskii's entry "Khazanut" in the encyclopaedia "Otsar yisroel."

75. FZ-837/2. Transcribed from Z. Gulerman, 43, flutist and barber in Kiev (1935), from Makarov, Kiev region, where he learned to play the flute from local klezmorim. He has lived since the beginning of the 1920s in Kiev, where he plays in various klezmer collectives and is invited to weddings, parties, and so on. Jewish wedding musicians played the doina as a table song. The doina played by Gulerman is built on the first phrase of a humorous anti-Hasidic song, "Vos farlangt der rebe," while the second part is a *frejlaxs.*

76. FZ-867/2. Transcribed from B. Cherniavskii (1936), clarinetist in Belaia Tserkov'. There are dances with similar names among several Slavic peoples. In the Ukrainian dance repertoire we find a dance entitled "Skochni, doskochni, doskochisti" (Kvitka 1973:41). One finds the *skoczek* among Polish dances (Stracewski 1901:717), and in the Czech repertoire there is a *skočna* (ibid.:673). According to many klezmorim, the *skočna* was not a special dance among Jews. Usually is was a *frejlaxs* somewhat more technically developed and played for listening, and not for dancing. However, it is not uncommon to find klezmorim calling *frejlaxs* "*skočna.*" One can also find the term applied to textless tunes (see no. 125).

77. Transcribed from D. Rotenberg, Moscow (1926); learned from a Belorussian klezmer.

78. Transcribed from A. E. Makonovetskii (see no. 72). This variant was in the manuscript notes of B. Sakhinovski, an amateur fiddler in Makarov, Kiev region. Sakhinovski learned the fiddle from local klezmorim in the 1890s, when he made the transcriptions. There are two sections to this tune. In the late nineteenth century, all klezmorim played from notes. There is evidence that bands of small shtetls often copied out music from bands of larger towns and cities. Undoubtedly this included small pieces and dance tunes (*frejlaxs, skočna, šer,* etc.). As soon as they learned these new pieces, they became "overgrown" with new elements, ornaments, and turns of phrase. This probably explains the rare coincidence of sections of tunes from among various klezmorim. As a rule, one can say that there will be as many variants as klezmorim who copied one tune (or as many klezmorim as have been able to collect the same tune). For a good instance, a variant for no. 78 is shown in Example 12.

79. Transcribed from A. E. Makonovetskii (see no. 72). The *frejlaxs* (literally: "happy") is a general dance with any number of dancers who take each other by the hands or around the shoulders and dance in a circle. In the case of a great number of dancers, a smaller inner circle is formed. Often one or more dancers go out into the center of the circle; these may be particularly light and graceful, or they may do grotesque figures. The *frejlaxs* had various names: *hopke, redl* (circle), *karahod* (from Russian *khorovod,* round dance), *drejdl* (top), *kajlexiks* (circle), *rikudl* (dance), and so on. The *frejlaxs'* tempo varied, from moderate to very quick. It was usually moderately quick for round dances. Naturally, the character of the tune changes with the tempo. *Frejlaxs* were in duple meter. They are most often in two short sections, rarely reaching eight- or sixteen-measure periods, or in a complex three-part form. The *frejlaxs* is not only a dance but also a tune or lyric piece; in such cases the term *frejlaxs* indicates the mood.

80. Taken from Kiselhof's notations of anonymous klezmorim, date and place unknown.

81. Transcribed from G. Gershfeld, fiddler and composer in Tiraspol (1937). The literal translation of *gas-nign* is "street tune." This is what the klezmorim called the pieces they played on the street while accompanying guests home at night after the wedding feast or the following day after a solemn meal. The most important trait distinguishing these pieces from the wedding repertoire is the triple meter. It is not known how this tradition of playing the *gas-nign* in triple time began. It is also not clear whether this is typical of the *gas-nign* only in the Ukraine.

82. FZ-863. Transcribed from F. Beliavskii, 45, in 1935, a clarinetist in Belaia Tserkov'.

83. FZ-833/4. Transcribed from I. Karlik, 24, weaver, in Jelal, Crimea (1937). Learned from klezmorim in Boguslav, Kiev region, where he lived.

Example 12

84. Transcribed from M. G. Komendant in Krements, Volynsk *gubernia* (1885). From the archive of the Society for Jewish Music in St. Petersburg.

85. Transcribed G. Barkagan (see no. 71). This sort of piece was played toward the end of the wedding ceremony, when the guests were leaving. After the farewell tune, as after all lyric pieces, they played a *frejlaxs*. A. M. Bernstein (1927:243) says these pieces were played also in Lithuania. On leaving, the matchmakers cried, after which the musicians played a *frejlaxs* and everyone danced in a circle.

86. FZ-831/2. Transcribed from M. Slobodskii, 49, clarinetist playing in a band in Brusilov, Kiev region.

87. Transcribed from G. Hershfeld (see no. 81).

88. Transcribed from A. E. Makonovetski (see no. 72).

89. Transcribed from Ziserman, musician, Vinnitsa (1932).

90. FZ-845/1. Transcribed from B. Dunlitski, 60, clarinetist, Kiev (1935). Since childhood he had played in many klezmer bands in the Kiev area.

91. FZ-862/2. Transcribed from B. Cherniavski, clarinetist (see no. 76).

92. FZ-861/1. Transcribed from B. Cherniavski, clarinetist (see no. 76).

93. Transcribed from M. Mesman, fiddler. From the manuscript collection of the Society for Jewish Music, St. Petersburg (1912). Place not given. The *šer* is a couple dance, danced by four or eight couples. From the music and its character it is very hard to distinguish the *šer* from the *frejlaxs*, if the latter is in a moderate

tempo. The tempo of the *šer* is more or less always the same: allegro. In practice, the klezmorim never played the same piece for both a *frejlaxs* and a *šer*. Each band had several pieces which it played for the *šer*. Collecting materials from klezmorim of various regions, we often found the same piece used as a *šer* in one region and a *frejlaxs* in another.

94. Transcribed from G. Barkagan (see no. 71).

95. Transcribed from B. Knayfl, 60, bass player, Vinnits (1937). The *xosid* is a grotesque solo dance imitating a dancing Hasid. In her book *Memoiren einer Grossmutter* (Berlin, 1908), p. 174, Paulina Wengerow describes the wedding of her sister in Brest-Litovsk in 1848. Among the dances performed, she remembers a *xosid* accompanied by lively music (fanfares and tambourines).

97. Transcribed from G. Barkagan (see no. 71).

98. From manuscript notation of an unknown klezmer.

99. FZ-22/1. Transcribed from N. Louria, writer, Kiev (1929). In the archives of the Cabinet there is a variant (FZ-812/4) sung by L. Limpan, 23, who learned the tune from his father in Troyanovka, Zhitomir region; transcribed in Kiev in 1934. In the Engel archives there is a notebook with transcriptions of Jewish folk songs and tunes done in Moscow in 1898 from various performers. Example 13 is a variant of no. 99, transcribed by Engel.

100. FZ-1015/1. Transcribed from M. Yanovski, 60, bookkeeper and musically gifted man who knew many tunes and folk songs which he sang expressively.

Example 13

Yanovski composed tunes and songs (both texts and melodies, though more often just melodies to the texts of Jewish Soviet poets). He taught himself to read music and wrote down his pieces, folk songs, and tunes without the help of an instrument. He lived in Kherson; the transcription was made in Kharkov in 1938.

101. Transcribed in Kiev from a group of artisans (1927).

102. Transcribed from Sh. Dobin, Kiev (1916).

103. Transcribed by Kiselhof from I. Shteinschneider (1913), place unknown.

104. FZ-294/1. Transcribed from A. Rozmarin in Luts (1913). There is a variant by A. Khabenski (Ushomir, 1929) in the Cabinet.

105. Transcribed by ear from Sh. Dobin, Kiev (1916).

106. FZ-28/1. Transcribed from National Artist of the U.S.S.R., S. M. Mikhoels, Kiev (1929).

107, 108. Transcribed by me from cylinders made by Sh. An-ski. Kh.N. Bialik, the poet, sang. Date not indicated. Kiev (1920).

109. Transcribed by ear in Kiev (1927), from A. Tversky, learned in Makarov, Kiev *gubernia* (1900–1903).

110. Transcribed by ear from the singer V. Khirge, Kiev (1940).

111. FZ-877/4. Transcribed from a group of the Moscow Jewish Theater. Kiev (1935).

112. FZ-30. Transcribed from P. Paz, 51, Kovele, Volynsk *gubernia* (1913).

113. FZ-116/1. Transcribed from Sh. Halperin, 50, in Slavuta (1929).

114. Transcribed by ear from Sh. Dobin, Kiev (1916). Variant transcribed from B. Lantsman, 60, bookkeeper, Kiev (1945).

115. Transcribed by ear in Kiev in 1920. The singer learned it around 1900 in Makarov, Kiev *gubernia.* We have two variants of this tune recorded from instrumentalists. In 1945 I transcribed a version from B. Lantsman (see no. 114). According to the latter, cantor Yosef of Tolna was the author of the tune, from whom he learned it in the mid-1890's. Comparing the four variants cited, it appears that Lantsman's version is not authentic and scarcely conforms to the original version. It lacks the second section, which all three of the other variants have (the fourth variant lacks the third section). It also differs in terms of melodic line.

116. Transcribed by ear in Kiev in 1920. The performer learned it around 1900 in Makarov, Kiev *gubernia.* There is a variant in the manuscript of an unknown klezmer or amateur fiddler from Ivankov, Kiev *gubernia* and from an unknown klezmer from Romno, Poltava *gubernia.*

117. FZ-270. Transcribed from A. Perelman in Petersburg (1913).

118. Transcribed by ear in Kiev (1920). The performer learned it around 1900 in Makarov, Kiev *gubernia.*

119. Transcribed by ear from A. Tversky in Kiev (1928), who learned it in Makarov around 1902. According to Tversky, the author of the tune is Yosl Tolner.

120. Transcribed by ear from Sh. Glazman, Kiev (1937). According to the performer the tune was written by the cantor Yakov-Shmuel Morgovski, who was very popular in his day (known as Zeydl Rovner) and from whom he learned it in 1904.

121. FZ-990/2. Transcribed from a collective farm worker in the Gorki Colony, Novozlatopolskii district, Dnepropetrovsk region, 1937.

122. FZ-986/1. Transcribed from N. Azriel, collective farm worker, same time and place as no. 121.

123. Transcribed by ear from the klezmer M. Komediant in Kremenets, Volynsk *gubernia* (1913).

124. FZ-311. Transcribed from D. Petreshki, 42, cantor in Olyk, Volynsk *gubernia* (1913).

125. Transcribed by ear in Kiev (1928). The variant is a transcription by ear of Kiselhof from G. Mitink from Sadagora (Bukovina) (1913).

126. From the manuscript of an unknown klezmer.

127. Transcribed by ear from K. Lantsman (see no. 114) in Kiev (1945); learned from Yosl Tolner. Sung on the last day of Succoth (ca. 1895).

128. FZ-348/2. Male voice. Oster (1913).

129. FZ-368/2. Transcribed from Sh. Kulish in Liudmir (1913). There is a variant transcribed by ear by Kiselhof from A. I. Berdichevskii in Bogonole, Podolsk *gubernia*, 1913; Berdichevskii called it a skočna.

130. FZ-369/1. Transcribed from a group of Hasidim, adherents of the tsadik Nachman of Bratslav, Berdichev (1913). The variant comes from repetitions of the same performance.

131. From the manuscript of an unknown klezmer.

132. FZ-342/2. Transcribed from Kh.-I. Beytsman, Berdichev (1913).

133. FZ-751/1. Transcribed from M. Diamant, Kiev (1932), learned in Poland, where he lived since childhood. Example 14 is the variant Kiselhof transcribed in Dubrovno, Mogilev *gubernia* (1913).

Example 14

134. FZ-315/2. Transcribed from a group of men in Kremenets, Volynsk *gubernia* (1913). There is a variant done by ear from S. Gutenmakher, 56, a slaughterer in Bershadi, Vinnitska region (1945). The tune belongs to the Bratslav Hasidim.

135. Transcribed by ear in 1929. There is a Kiselhof variant done by ear from L. Hochberg in Dubno (1913).

136–137. Transcribed by ear from M. Yanovski (see no. 100) in Kherson (1938). He learned it in the 1880s.

138. FZ-118/2. Transcribed from B. Robert in Slavuta in 1929. The variant was done by ear from A. Krugliak, student of the Jewish Pedagogical School, Kiev (1920); he learned it in Boguslav in 1910.

139. FZ-118/2. Transcribed from Robert B. in Slavuta (1929). Variant transcribed by ear from A. Krugliak, student of the Jewish Pedagogical School, Kiev (1920). Learned in Boguslav in 1910.

140. From the manuscript of an anonymous cantor.

Example 15

141. FZ-291/1. Transcribed from I. Berman, 52, cantor, in Olyk, Volynsk *gubernia* (1913). Variant transcribed in Kovele, Volynsk *gubernia,* 1913.

142. Transcribed by ear from I. Weissman, journalist, Kiev (1933). Learned in Podobranki. Variant FZ-327/2 transcribed from L. Melamed in Derazhan, Podol'sk *gubernia,* 1913; there is also a variant by ear of Kiselhof from M. Koiler, 53, synagogue servant, Oly, Volynsk *gubernia,* 1913.

143. FZ (number lost). Transcribed from Manusevich, teacher in Krements, Volynsk *gubernia,* 1913.

144. FZ-478/1. Transcribed from E. Lerner, 47, cantor, in Krements, 1913.

145. Transcribed by ear in Kiev (1928). Learned in 1900 in Makarov. Variant done by ear in Bar, Vinnitska region, 1940.

146. Transcribed by ear from M. Timianski, 74, tailor in Bershadi, Vinnitska region, 1945; Bratslav Hasidic tune.

147. FZ-350. Sung by a male voice, transcribed in 1912–14. The manner of performance lends it a grotesque character. This is aided by the unusual syllables used by the singer (xo-ca-ca, xo-ca-ca, oy-ca da ri da ray, etc.). A variant of this tune (FZ-374, male voice) sounds like a lyric-dramatic tune without the slightest trace of grotesque. The syncopations are rarer in the variant shown in Example 15.

148. FZ-268. Transcribed from Sh. Kulish, 24, tradesman in Luidmir, July 17, 1913. Variant by ear of Kiselhof from A. I. Berdichevskii, 43, dentist in Bogopol, Podol'sk *gubernia,* 1913. Berdichevskii learned it from a clarinetist, who played it as a skočna.

149. FZ-535/2. Male voice. Transcribed in Medzhibozh, Podol'sk *gubernia,* 1913.

150. Transcribed by ear from Sh. Gutemakher, 56, butcher, in Bershadi, Vinnitska region, 1945. Bratslav Hasidic.

Works Cited

Bastomski, Sh.
   1923   *Baym kval.* Vilna: Naye Yidishe Folksshul.
Beregovski, M., and Fefer, I.
   1938   *Evreiskie narodnye pesni.* Kiev: Ukrnatsmenizdat.
Bernstein, A. M.
   1927   *Muzikalisher pinkes: Nigunim-zamlung fun yidishn folks-oytser.*
Braun, J.
   1978   *Jews and Jewish Elements in Soviet Music.* Tel Aviv: Israeli Music Publications.
Cahan, Y. L.
   1912a   *Yidishe folkslider oys dem folks-moyl, gezamlt fun Y. L. Cahan,* vol. 1. New York and Warsaw: Internatsyonale Bibliotek Farlag.
   1912b   Ibid., vol. 2.
   1928   "Yidishe folkslider: naye zamlung fun Y. L. Kahan." *Pinkes,* pp. 65–128, 321–68. New York: YIVO.
   1938   *Yidisher folklor.* Vilna: YIVO.
Dobrushin, I. M., and Iuditskii, A. D.
   1947   *Evreskie narodnye pesni.* Moscow: Ogiz.

Engel, J.
n.d.   Song arrangements, in Addenda to *Trudy muzykal'no-etnograficheskoi komissi imperatorskogo obshchestva liubitelei estestvoznaniia, antropologii, i etnografi*, vol. 1. St. Petersburg.
1909   *Evreiskie narodnye pesni v muzykal'noi obrabotke Y. Engelia*, vol. 1. Moscow.
1912   Ibid., vol. 2.
1930   *Evreiskie narodnye pesni dlia fortepiano v 2 ruki.* Moscow: Muzsektor gosizdat.

Erk, L., and Böhme, F. M.
1893   *Deutscher Liederhort.* Leipzig: Britekopf und Härtel.
1894

Ginzburg, S. M., and Marek, P. S.
1901   *Evreiskie narodnye pesni v Rossii.* St. Petersburg: Voskhod.

Gniessin, M. F.
1956   *Mysli i vospominaniia o Rimskom-Korsakove.* Moscow: Gosmuzizdat.

Golomb, G. E.
1887   *Koil Jehudo: Sobranie evreiskikh pesen i p'es dlia fortep'iano.* Vilna.

Gordon, Mikhl
1889   *Yidishe lider fun Mikhl Gordon.* Warsaw.

Graubard, ?
1914   "Folkslider fun Graubards zamlung." In *Frishmans yubileum-bukh.* Warsaw.

Gudemann, M.
1922   *Yidishe kultur-geshikhte in mitlalter.* Berlin: Klal-Verlag.

Idelsohn, A. Z.
1932   *Der Volksgesang der Osteuropäischen Juden*, vol. 11 of *Hebräisch-orientalischer Melodienschatz.* Berlin: Friedrich Hofmeister.

Karpenko, Stepan
1864   *Vasil'kovskii solovei kievskoi ukrainy: slavianorusskii al'bom dlia odnogo golosa s akkompanementom fortep'iano sostavlennyi iz 115 malorossiskikh i nekotorykh russkikh, pol'skikh, chernorusskikh, bolgarskikh i moldavskikh pesen, dum i romansov, s prisovokupleniem malorossiskikh i evreiskikh tantsev.* St. Petersburg.

Kipnis, M.
1918   *60 folkslider fun M. Kipnis un Z. Zeligfelds kontsert-repertuar.* Warsaw: Gitlin.
n.d.   *80 folkslider fun Z. Zeligfelds un M. Kipnis kontsert-repertuar.* Warsaw: Gitlin.

Kiselhof, Z.
1912   *Lider-zamlbukh far der yidisher shul un familie.* St. Petersburg and Berlin.

Kvitka, K.
1973   "Professional'nye narodnye pevtsy i muzykanty na Ukraine." In *Izbrannye trudy*, vol. 2, ed. P. Bogatyrev, pp. 279–324.

Landoy, A.
1926   "Dr. A. Landoy-bamerkungen tsum yidishn folklor." In *Landoy-bukh.* Vilna.

Leman, Sh.
1923   "Di kinder-velt: Gramen, lidlekh, hamtsoes un shpiln." In *Ba undz yidn*, ed. M. Vanvild, pp. 113–49. Warsaw.

1928   *Ganovim-lider mit melodies.* Warsaw: Graubard.

Nef, K.
1938   *Istoriia zapadnoevropeiskoi muzyki,* trans. and ed. B. Asaf'ev. 2d ed. Moscow: Gosmuzizdat.

Olgin, M.
1927   *My village in the Ukraine* (in Yiddish). New York.

Pinkes
1913   *Der pinkes: Yorbukh far der geshikhte fun der yidisher literatur un shprakh, far folklor, kritik un bibliografie,* ed. Sh. Niger. Vilna: Kletskin.
1922   *Pinkes far der geshikhte fun Vilne in di yorn fun milkhome un okupatsie,* ed. Z. Reyzn. Vilna.

Prilutski, N.
1913   *Yidishe folkslider, gezamlt, erklert un aroysgegebn fun N. Prilutski.* Warsaw.

Prytucki, N.
1911   *Yidishe folkslider.* Warsaw: Ferlag Bikher-far-ale.
1913

Raduga
1922   *Raduga: Al'manakh pushkinskogo doma.* St. Petersburg.

Rimski-Korsakov, N.
1926   *Letopis' moei muzykal'noi zhizni.* Moscow.

Rosenberg, F.
1888   "Über eine Sammlung deutscher Volk-und Gesellschafts-Lieder in hebräischen Lettern." *Zeitschrift für die Geschichte der Juden in Deutschland.*

Saminsky, L.
1914   *Ob evreiskoi muzyke.* St. Petersburg.

Straczewski, F.
1901   "Die polnische Tänze." *Sammelbände der internationalen Musikgesellschaft* 4.

Tsaytshrift
1928   *Tsaytshrift far yidisher geshikhte, demografie, un ekonomik literaturforshung, shprakh-visnshaft un etnografie,* vols. 2–3. Minsk: Izdanie Instituta Belorusskoi Kul'tury.

Tsinberg, I.
1943   *History of Jewish literature* (in Yiddish). New York: Shklyarsky.

PART TWO

ESSAYS

3

THE INTERACTION OF UKRAINIAN
AND JEWISH FOLK MUSIC
(1935)

In Jewish and Ukrainian folk music we find a series of similarities in melody and means of expression. We cannot say who borrowed from whom in all cases, although we can ascertain the Ukrainian or Jewish derivation of some melodies. We can list a fair number of older Yiddish folk songs which have been sung to melodies of popular Ukrainian songs, for example, "U susida khata bila," "Gop moi grechaniki," "Petrus," and "Stroit gora visokaia." In the older Yiddish folk song repertoire there is a large number of melodies which we could positively state were borrowed from Ukrainian folklore, although we cannot establish exactly from which Ukrainian song they were adopted (e.g., "Mama majne, ci bin ix nit a toxter dajne"). However, there are also common elements that do not come from Yiddish or Ukrainian folk music. These elements may have been adopted from a third source.

One can also see the impact of Ukrainian folklore in the texts of Yiddish folk songs, for many Yiddish song texts are translations or adaptations of Ukrainian songs. This does not mean that in all cases of song text similarity we are dealing with direct translation or adaptation from the Ukrainian. There are cases where both the Jewish and the Ukrainian folk

Originally published as "Kegnzaytike Virkungen tsvishn dem ukraynishn un yidishn Muzik-Folklor," in *Visnshaft un Revolutsye* (Kiev) 6 (1935):79–101.

artist have adopted a given motif (of literary origin) from a third source (e.g., Polish, German, Rumanian). Adopted Ukrainian texts have usually been given different melodies among the Jews, just as borrowed Ukrainian melodies (barring exceptional cases) have been adapted to a new song text. We will not take up the separate question of borrowed Ukrainian song texts. Here we want to introduce several Ukrainian and Jewish melodies that have many traits in common.

The first phrase of "Di gildene pave" (Ex. 16) is very close to the first phrase of a Ukrainian song.[1]

The first phrases of both melodies coincide almost note for note. The further development of each tune is quite different. In the first two lines of the Ukrainian song (first melodic phrase) the heroine tries to decide whether she should love this idler *("ledashche")*. In the last two lines she decides categorically that she doesn't need him. To a certain extent, the musical formulation of the song corresponds to the content. The even motion of the first phrase moves to a dotted, sharp rhythm, as if the

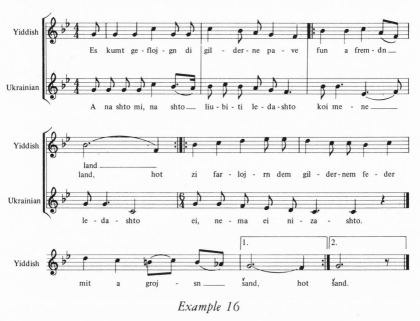

Example 16

1. Yiddish song: Kiselhof 1912: no. 33; Ukrainian song: Narodni 1929: no. 137. Both songs have been transposed. In Ex. 16 and below, similar musical phrases are marked with common bar-lines. Incidentally, the first stanza of "Di gildene pave" coincides with the first verse of the Ukrainian song (Narodni 1929: no. 530) "Letila pava, letila, zlote perechko tratila." We find this verse in a number of Ukrainian songs, but not one of the songs with this text is similar melodically to "Di gildene pave."

heroine wanted to push something away. The interval leaps in the second half (B-flat–E-flat, G–C) are also characteristic. The melody returns to G and moves decisively down to the tonic (last measure, in 6/4).[2]

We have an entirely different development of the melody in "Di gildene pave." The heroine complains in heartfelt words about her bitter fate in a strange house—"boarding with the in-laws." However, her complaints do not swell to a protest. A passive mood dominates the song. This lyric tone coincides to a certain extent with the even rhythm (quarters and eighths) in which the whole melody is contained. In the last phrase the melody subsides, featuring an augmented second between the second and third steps.

We also have a close parallel in Ukrainian to the Yiddish song "Zayt gezunterheyt mayne libe eltern" (Ex. 17)[3]. In these two melodies we are struck by the first and last musical phrases. The stanza in the Ukrainian song is a two-liner, while in the Yiddish song it is a quatrain. The first phrase of the Ukrainian song is close to the Yiddish song, and the second is similar to the last (the fourth) of the Yiddish song. The Ukrainian song is a *vesnianka* [spring song—M.S.]. The second line is a refrain that recurs in all subsequent verses. In the lyric form of this song we notice the contours of a love motif. The Yiddish song is one of parting and conveys a heavy mood.[4] The Yiddish stanza is a quatrain. Corresponding to this broader form, the melody is also broader than that of the Ukrainian song.

The Ukrainian song seems to be in embryonic form; the musical theme

2. I do not mean to say that the melody of a song in strophic form always exactly illustrates the whole text-content of the song, musically throughout. In fitting the melody to the text, the folk artist orients himself to the general mood of the text and melody and cannot always musically "translate" the text. This would be impossible if only because the whole song, that is, a large number of stanzas, is sung to exactly the same melody. In dialogue songs, stanzas of completely different content and character are sung to one and the same tune. The character of the melody is determined not so much by the content of the individual words, sentences, and dialogue as by the author's relationship to the persona of the song.

3. Ukrainian: *Ukrainski* 1922: no. 24. Yiddish: Engel n.d.: no. 2. Idelsohn (1932:viii) writes that this melody type with the augmented second between second and third steps does not exist in Slavic (he means Ukrainian) song. This does not correspond to reality. There are a great many melodies with this melody type in Ukrainian folk music. The Ukrainian folklorist on whom Idelsohn relies does not distinguish this melody type from the other one, which has the augmented second between three and four, considering them to be the same melody type.

4. Ginzburg and Marek (1901: nos. 261, 263) have three variants of this song text. The first two are fragments, the third is a fuller variant. It is hard to tell from the text where the hero is going (to the army, to be a wandering journeyman, emigrating?). We find the melody to this song in the wedding repertoire of klezmorim. It's played as a *zajt gezunt* (good-night piece). From this we can infer that the song was a parting song of the child from the parents after the wedding. S. Aynhorn (n.d.) also remarks on this song. He describes it as a parting song after the wedding.

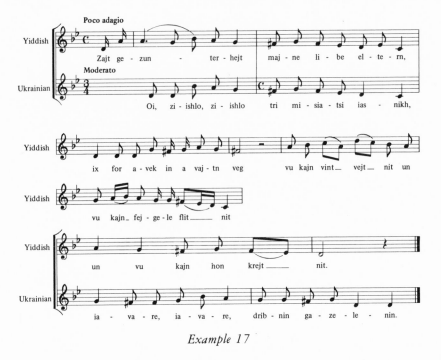

Example 17

is given in sparing strokes, while in the Yiddish song it is broadly developed. As in the earlier Yiddish song, the highest point is in the third phrase. The range of both the emotion and the musical means of expression has been considerably widened.

Using the same melody type (with augmented second between steps two and three), we have another Ukrainian song with a melody close to the Yiddish song "Oy du forst avek" (Ex. 18).[5] Here again the Ukrainian verse is a two-liner. The first melodic phrase is similar to that of the Yiddish song and the second to the last (fourth, the Yiddish verse being a quatrain) of the Yiddish song. The character of the songs is different. The Ukrainian song is lyric (the collector, Konoshchenko, marked it *andante cantabile*), while the tempo is more restrained. The Yiddish song has the element of irony. The performer has the tendency to accelerate the tempo, which corresponds to the character of the song.[6]

5. Yiddish: Beregovski n.d.: no. 11; Ukrainian: Konoshchenko 1909: no. 79.
6. There are also certain ironic elements in the song text, especially in the quick transition to the words "ot heng ix zix, ot štex ix zix far dajne ojgn" ("I'll hang myself, I'll stab myself before your very eyes").

Example 18

The examples just cited illustrate how the Yiddish and Ukrainian songs can handle the same musical theme in different ways, corresponding somewhat to the varied content and verse structures of the songs. We have not set ourselves the task of assigning "priority": did the Jewish composer adopt the musical theme in question from a Ukrainian, or vice versa? However, it is hard to deny, given the musical formulation of the Yiddish songs, that the Jewish melodies were adopted from Ukrainian folklore. On the other hand, we have no firm grounds for deciding that the Ukrainian folk artist actually borrowed the melodies from Jewish folklore. It is possible that such melodies penetrated both Ukrainian and Jewish folklore from a third, common source. It is important for us to establish that in both the Ukrainian and the Yiddish case the melody is adopted not mechanically but rather creatively, as we have seen. In the Yiddish song, the author broadened and developed the musical material; one can say that it has been artistically accomplished and, to a certain extent, that it corresponds to the character of the song.

Even in cases where the Jewish author has not artistically developed the material, he has not mechanically adopted the tune. For example, there is a very close Ukrainian variant of the tune to "Amol iz geven a majse" (Ex. 19).[7] The Ukrainian coincides with the Yiddish song almost note for note, except for such details as the cadence of the first phrase (G-F#-D in the Ukrainian and G-F in the Yiddish version). The G-F#-D cadence is typical of Ukrainian folk music, where we find it often. It is found much less frequently in Jewish folk music.[8]

The Yiddish singer could not adopt the melody in question with its unfamiliar musical turns of phrase, which were not in the "arsenal" of his musical means of expression. In the Yiddish song the cadence in question

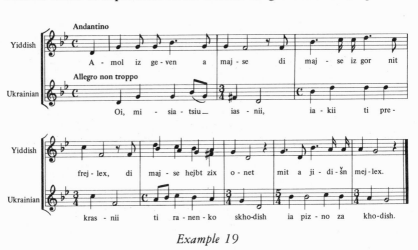

Example 19

7. Yiddish: Kipnis 1918: no. 17; Ukrainian: Konoshchenko 1909: no. 483. Kipnis gives the song in 2/4. The note values are half as long there. We have not included the refrain, "Lyulinke majn kind." There was also a drinking song, "Ayeh toldot noax" (Idelsohn 1932: no. 32; Cahan 1912: no. 154) with the same melody, in which the melody has been structured for parody. In our Example 19 the smaller notes belong to Idelsohn's variant.

8. In Jewish folk music this cadence is often altered as follows:

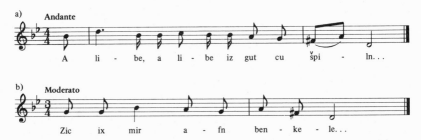

Sometimes we find it in Yiddish folk music in the same form as in Ukrainian; cf. Idelsohn 1932: nos. 298, 391, 414, 433, 636.

is altered according to the style of Yiddish songs of this type.[9] The penultimate phrase is also altered in the Yiddish song.

As for the time-signature changes in the Ukrainian song, which do not exist in the Yiddish version, I do not see them as being specifically tailored to the Ukrainian song in this case. The time-signature changes do not come from constructive variation of the melody. The 4/4 time moves to 3/4 only at the end of the musical phrase. One finds the abbreviation or lengthening of a musical phrase toward its end often in recorded Jewish songs; there are many examples of this in Beregovski 1934 and works in manuscript. In this case the Ukrainian song is merely better notated than the Yiddish. This is true also of the penultimate measure; in the Ukrainian it is 5/4, and 4/4 in the Yiddish with a fermata over the third beat.

We will allow ourselves one more example of the similarity between a Jewish and a Ukrainian melody. The Ukrainian tune is a close variant of the song "Ix gej arojs ojfn ganikl"(Ex. 20).[10] These two melodies are close not just in melodic and metric structure but also in mood. There are, however, particular moments where the two diverge (starting in the seventh measure). These divergences are different from those we have seen in earlier songs. In the previous songs, we encountered a difference in formulation through divergent means of expression. Particular musical turns of phrase, as in Example 19, may differ in Jewish and Ukrainian folklore. Before we can examine the last example in detail, we must briefly review the various lengths of musical phrases in the Ukrainian song. The proportion is as follows: $4 + 3 + 4 + 1$, where the numbers refer to the number of measures in each phrase. I think, however, that the proportions must originally have been $4 + 4 + 4 + 1$; the fourth and fifth measures of the second phrase have been collapsed into one measure. The resulting fragment might have looked like Example 21.

It seems that the singer himself felt that something was missing and compensated by dragging the tempo. The song was basically in one tempo, allegretto, but the measure in question is in andante, after which tempo primo recurs.

If we accept that the abbreviation is an accidental result of the singer and that it would be possible to make two measures of the section, as in Example 21, then the divergence between the Yiddish and Ukrainian

9. We find F-sharp in the Yiddish variant, but in a different context: at the end of the third phrase, where it goes back to G. It would have been possible for a Ukrainian singer to hear such a cadence in the first phrase as well; it is common in both song traditions.

10. Cf. also Idelsohn 1932: no. 142 (two variants) and a variant with some differences in Cahan 1912: no. 231.

Example 20

Example 21

variants lies only within the same melodic scheme; both would look like
Example 22.[11]

Example 22

As noted above, Jewish songs are usually built on a quatrain stanza in
which the last two lines are repeated. This scheme is less widely spread
in Ukrainian folk songs. In the examples just cited the Jewish songs have
repetitions of the third and fourth lines. In the Ukrainian song there is the re-
petition of an added measure (adagio) instead, which ends the melody.[12]

11. The last musical phrase (adagio measure) has certainly been shortened in Example
22. Originally it must have consisted of two measures, and the pitches were probably the
following: G (on the syllable *se,* a quarter note) and B (on *lo-sti,* both eighths). This ends
the first measure. The second measure then consisted of the last two notes: A (a quarter or
an eighth) and G (two quarters, or two quarters and an eighth). Unfortunately, I could not
find another variant of this Ukrainian song. If we had other variants, the metrorhythmic
scheme of the melody would be clearer as well.
12. In the introduction to vol. 9 (1932), Idelsohn states quite categorically that the
melody to the song "Ix gej arojs afn ganikl" has been adopted from the Slovak hymn "Nad

Example 23

In all the Ukrainian and Yiddish examples just cited, the melody type has not changed. However, there are also examples in which the common Ukrainian-Jewish melodic material may be formulated in differing melody types. Example 23 shows a variant of a very popular lullaby, "Untern kinds vigele." The melody consists of two musical motives (see

Tartu." (He even includes the music of the hymn.) There is scarcely any evidence for such a statement. The first phrase of the Slovak tune does bear some resemblance to the Yiddish song; however, this is insufficient evidence for claiming that the Yiddish song is derived from the Slovak hymn. For one, the Slovak song has a marchlike character, while the Yiddish song is in 3/4 and is lyric. The melodic formulation of the songs also gives little substance for such assertions. The scheme of the hymn is: first phrase in minor (two measures), second phrase (measures three to four) repeats the first phrase a third higher, in the relative major. The last three bars have a return to minor and a final cadence. This is a widespread scheme that can be found in songs with completely different emotional content.

It should be noted that the Ukrainian counterpart song of Ex. 22 has the main caesura on the fourth scale degree, as does the Yiddish song. This is a phenomenon which Idelsohn thinks is typical for Jewish folk song; however it is frequently found in Ukrainian folklore as well.

Example 24

Example 25

Ex. 24).[13] These motives appear in sequence. The singer may begin the song with the first motif or with the second. The transition from one motive to another is not tied to the overall construction of the melody.

Example 25 is a Ukrainian lullaby,[14] the melody of which consists of three motifs, shown in Example 26. Comparing the motifs of the Ukrainian lullaby with those of the Yiddish one, we soon see that motif *a* is exactly the same in both songs. Motif *b* is also very similar in both, but it is altered in the Yiddish song according to the melody type with augmented second between steps two and three. Motif *c* is not in the Yiddish song. We do find it partially in another variant of the same song (Kiselhof 1912: no. 44), shown in Example 27. The last phrase of this variant is close

13. I recorded this example in Belaia Tserkov' from L. Vinokur, age 21, a worker in a tailoring shop (1933), cylinder 799/5.
14. Konoshchenko 1909: no. 323. His no. 567 is also a lullaby in which the middle phrase is built on motive *b,* as in Example 25.

Example 26

Example 27

to motif *c* of the Ukrainian song but is also altered according to melody type (as in the previous example).[15]

One must imagine that a certain melody type is always adopted together with the whole melodic material. However, when a certain melody type has penetrated a certain milieu, it can also influence melodies which were created and disseminated in another melody type. We often find cases in which the same melodies (sometimes even with the same song

15. Various colleagues have informed me that they have heard such lullabies with Yiddish or Ukrainian texts sung by Jewish women in various locales (Zhitomir, Belaia Tserkov', Bershad, etc.). There is also a considerable parallel to Ukrainian folk music in the lullaby "Lyu-lyu lyulinke" published by Liov (1917). Cf. Konoshchenko 1909: no. 166, where there is another verse of text. This appears to be a love song. Both the Yiddish and Ukrainian songs are quatrains, and the melody consists of four musical lines. All the lines of music of both songs nearly coincide, except for details which we cannot discuss here. The Ukrainian song is in 3/4, the Yiddish song in 4/4. However, it is not hard to see that the 4/4 of the Yiddish song derives from a prolonging of the final syllable in nearly all measures. Here as well the borrowing has not been mechanical, but creative. It is noteworthy that in well-to-do and middle-class Jewish families there were often Ukrainian female servants (maids, nannies). One can imagine that these girls brought Ukrainian melodies into Jewish circles (and song texts), and perhaps vice versa: they may have transmitted Jewish melodies and songs to the Ukrainian milieu.

text) are sung at times in major and at times in minor (such a phenomenon is noticeable not just in Jewish folk music); or even in the melody type with the augmented second between second and third scale degrees. Melodies in minor may be altered to have an augmented second between second and third, or third and fourth, scale degrees.

It is worth establishing that all the examples cited, whether Ukrainian or Yiddish, are typical of the genres of their respective musics. None of the songs has specific means of expression that would lead the researcher to posit borrowing. We noted earlier that in the case of the first three Yiddish songs it is difficult to tell if they are in fact borrowed from the Ukrainian. The second and third songs (in the melody type with augmented second between steps two and three) are typical enough of either Jewish or Ukrainian folk music. Ukrainian folklorists hold that these melodies have been adopted from several ethnic groups, especially from the Turkic peoples (Crimean Tatars, etc.).

We can speak most easily of a large number of melodies with particular musical means of expression (not just limited to the first three examples above) which have been adopted from somewhere outside into both Jewish and Ukrainian folk musics and have been adapted in particular ways.

In the succeeding Jewish examples cited above, we can easily see that they have been adapted from Ukrainian folk music. However, they have been creatively adapted to fit the concrete expressive demands of the Jewish folksinger. Such adopted melodies, or especially melodic fragments, rarely remain unchanged. These "borrowed" melodies are particularly quick to lose those specific national details that are not appropriate to the expressive means of the new user. Sometimes, however, certain melodies are deliberately adopted as extraethnic. In Jewish folk music we have a certain number of melodies adopted from the Ukrainian (e.g., the very widespread dance tune *kozačok*) and a great number of folk songs sung to the melodies of popular Ukrainian songs. The aims of such borrowing might be diverse. Sometimes it reflects the close and intimate relationship between similar social strata of various ethnic groups, while at other times the borrowings are made for the sake of "exoticism," or for good-humored parody or not-so-friendly satire. In the latter cases the songs are usually exaggerated and charged with typical extraethnic features and manner of performance.

When we find similar song-texts in Yiddish and Ukrainian songs, we can establish in the majority of cases that the Jewish singer has adopted

and reworked the songs from the Ukrainian. The small-town Jewish population stood in a close relationship to peasants and knew the Ukrainian language to a certain extent. It was even closer for those Jewish
families who lived in or spent considerable time in villages (e.g., black-
smiths, millers, innkeepers, wandering journeymen, traveling sales-
men).

There are also a large number of known cases in which Ukrainians
adopted Yiddish songs. The singers of my no. 108 (see p. 455, this
volume) told us that the song had been taken over by a Ukrainian in
Tshernigov. Song no. 183 (Beregovski, unpublished ms) was learned
from a Ukrainian peasant who had worked in a Jewish family.[16] We know
of cases in which Ukrainian villagers adopted songs from Jewish villagers.
It is easy to imagine how a Ukrainian peasant who had learned a Jewish
song could put a Ukrainian song-text to it or might weave together particular melodic and rhythmic usages of the Yiddish song which reflect, to a
certain extent, his expressive needs.

Jewish and Ukrainian instrumental musicians had no small role in
mutual borrowing.[17]

Jewish musicians used to play frequently at non-Jewish weddings and
festivities where they undoubtedly played Jewish tunes in addition to the
Ukrainian dance-repertoire. In the same way they brought their Ukrainian
repertoire to Jewish weddings (e.g., *kozačkes, skočnas*).[18] Non-Jews often
played in Jewish bands.[19] V. Kharkov, administrator of the Cabinet, told
me that in 1927 he transcribed a whole series of *frejlaxs*, which they called
frejlik, from Ukrainian peasants in the village of Bondashevke; Example

16. Kipnis 1918: no. 23 was transcribed from a Polish girl in Radom.
17. Y. Aksenfeld (1931: no. 168), in his work "The First Jewish Recruit," describes
how Nakhman of Bratslav sang his song to a tune played by a Ukrainian musician in a tavern
on Sunday; here we have a good example of how a Ukrainian tune was adopted into the
Jewish milieu.
18. A klezmer (G. Rizitski, 57, clarinetist) told me that in the 1890s he played in a band
in Brusilov (Kiev area), which used to play for Ukrainian artisans (at that time there was
a great number of shoemakers in Brusilov who made boots and sold them in Brusilov and
other towns) at their weddings and celebrations, to which they invited Jewish musicians. The
Ukrainian youth there danced the *šer* as well.
19. In the summer of 1933 I transcribed tunes from a fiddler who played Jewish
dance-tunes in the courtyards of Kiev. I transcribed several tunes of his repertoire, then saw
that he was not a Jew, but a Pole (Felix Svitelski, age 31). As he told me, he had played
with Jewish musicians for fifteen years in the town of Korostishev (Kiev region). He picked
up the klezmer manner of playing so accurately that I was sure I had a typical small-town
klezmer before me. Joel Engel mentions a similar fact. In his report on the An-ski expedition
of 1912, he tells of how a non-Jew (a Russian or Moldavian) was at the head of the klezmer
band in Ruzhina. This musician even composed his own pieces for the band. "He tried to
get me to buy a sparkling 'majafes' which he wrote himself," writes Engel (Engel n.d.:11;
this report, in Russian, is in typescript and is in the archive of the Cabinet).

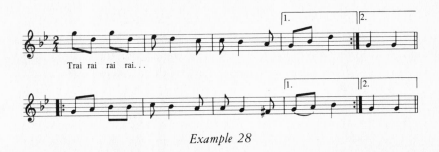

Example 28

28 is one. Such *frejlaxs* are very popular in that village and are sung for dancing. Bystanders who are not dancing clap their hands. The musicians also play *frejlaxs* at weddings, sometimes accompanied by singing.

There are also Ukrainian songs with melodies adopted from Yiddish folk music. In the same village, Kharkov transcribed the song shown in Example 29.[20] The second section (performed without words) is especially typical, as is the syncopated rhythm. This sort of thing is typical of the Jewish *frejlaxs* and does not occur in Ukrainian folk music.

The possibility that such songs (e.g., *frejlaxs*) were sung in other Ukrainian villages cannot be ruled out. Just because they have not been noted down does not mean that they did not exist.[21] The bourgeois nationalist folklorists did not notate such melodies—their whole attention

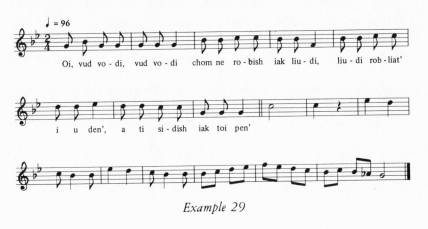

Example 29

20. The last two examples are taken from the Cabinet archive (nos. 2379, 2575). I would like to take this opportunity to thank the administrator for his information.

21. In a Ukrainian song anthology of the 1860s (Karpenko 1894), we find Jewish dances alongside Ukrainian dances. In this anthology three Ukrainian and three Jewish dances are published, including an older, a newer, and a women's dance. The anthology was intended for a user in the city (but non-Jewish), showing that Jewish dances were popular in some urban non-Jewish circles.

was directed to those parts of folk music which, according to their defini-
tion, were specifically national. The bourgeois nationalist folklorist always
prefers to notate the "authentic" and "indigenous" in folklore and tries
to avoid elements that indicate mutual influence of ethnic milieus. It is
sufficient to remember that the nationalist music-folklorists did not collect
the Ukrainian revolutionary songs of the 1905 period and of the Civil
War. They simply doubted the existence of such songs, although many of
us still remember the tens of revolutionary songs which were sung at that
time in the Ukraine both in cities and in the countryside. More recent
collecting has shown that in fact a great number of revolutionary folk
songs were created in Ukrainian in the period of the Civil War.

As stated earlier, we have not set ourselves the task of exhausting the
problem of mutual influences between Jewish and Ukrainian folk music.
With the examples cited we tried only to indicate some of the characteristic moments. We are far from definitive solutions; serious research is
demanded. It must be added that the study of mutual influence cannot be
limited to examples in which the extraethnic impact or borrowing is
apparent at first glance (as is very often the case, e.g., the *kozačke*). The
research must be expanded to the most "national-typical" pieces, since in
the most typical Jewish folk music we find not a little that is analogous to,
or borrowed from, other ethnic groups. The semantic significance of such
common melodic complexes must also be discovered.

The important result to be gleaned from the materials adduced here
is that the musical creativity of the Jewish folk masses, with all their
differences and isolation, has not remained isolated and is often influenced
by the folk music of other peoples, in this case by the Ukrainian. On the
other hand, one must also establish that Ukrainian folk music has freely
borrowed from Jewish folk music.

Works Cited

Aksenfeld, Y.
  1931   *Works*, ed. M. Viner, vol. 1. Kiev.
Cahan, Y. L.
  1912   *Yidishe folkslider mit melodyen, oys dem folksmoyl.* New York and War-
          saw: Internatsyonale Bibliotek Farlag.
Engel, J.
  n.d.   "Evreiskaia narodnaia pesnia." In *Etnograficheskaia poezdka letom
          1912 g.* N.p.
Ginzburg, S., and Marek, P.
  1901   *Evreiskie narodnye pesni v Rossii.* St. Petersburg: Voskhod.

Idelsohn, A. Z.
  1932   *Der Volksgesang der osteuropäischen Juden,* vol. 9 of *Hebräisch-orientalischer Melodienschatz.* Berlin: Friedrich Hofmeister.
Karpenko, S.
  1894   *Vasil'kovskii solovei kievskoi Ukrainy.* St. Petersburg: Bernard.
Kipnis, M.
  1918   *60 folkslider fun M. Kipnis un Z. Zeligfelds kontsert-repertuar.* Warsaw: Gitlin.
Kiselhof, Z.
  1912   *Lider-zamlbukh far der yidisher shul un familie.* St. Petersburg and Berlin.
Konoshchenko, A.
  1909   *Ukrainski pisni z notami.* Odessa.
Liov, L.
  1917   *Viglid far khor un piano, aranzhirt fun Leo Liov.* Warsaw: Nigun.
Narodni
  1929   *Narodni pisni z Galitskoi Lemkivshchini.* Lvov.
Ukrainski
  1922   *Ukrainski narodni melodi,* vol. 2 of *Etnografichnii zbirnik.* Kiev: Slovo.

4

⌒⌒∧∧⌒

JEWISH INSTRUMENTAL FOLK MUSIC
(1937)

We have already done some work on the Jewish folk song in the U.S.S.R. The Folklore Section of the Cabinet of Jewish Literature, Language, and Folklore of the Academy of Sciences of the Ukrainian S.S.R. now has a nice archive consisting of several thousand folklore items (songs, tales, proverbs, sayings, etc.). The *phonoteque* (phonograph archive) of the Folklore Section now [January 1, 1937] consists of 980 cylinders, on which are recorded (sung or played) more than 2,500 items of folk music (songs, tunes, instrumental works, etc.).

Much of this material has already been researched and part of it published [see pp. 19–284 and projected vol. 2, cf. p. 3—M.S.].[1] The work of researching continues at the present time. There is, however, one area of Jewish folk art which has scarcely been touched by the researcher or the collector: Jewish instrumental (klezmer) folk music. Only a few items of the hundreds of klezmer musical numbers cited above have been published to date. If we want to find out, for example, how the klezmer trained himself, how and where he learned to play, or how he acquired the necessary repertoire, we know scarcely anything!

Originally published as *Yidishe instrumentale folks-muzik* (*Program tsu forshn di muzikalishe tetikayt fun di yidishe klezmer*). Kiev: Kabinet far derlernen di yidishe sovetishe literatur, shprakh un folklor, folklor-sektsye, 1937.
    1. See also a series of Jewish folk songs in the volume *Tvorchestvo narodov* in the series Dve Piatiletki (Moscow: Pravda publishers, n.d.).

If we know little about the average klezmer, are there perhaps descriptions of the talented, gifted ones? Also scarcely any! Can we perhaps say that klezmer music has not been taken up because it is too trifling to be interesting for purposes of collection and study? Because the mass of klezmorim was so gray and untalented, so artistically poor and untalented, so artistically poor and uninteresting, because we won't find any talented and interesting personalities among them? No! Even superficial acquaintance with the art of the klezmer and with the tens of talented artists produced by the mass of klezmorim is enough to convince us that it is worth taking up this neglected and overlooked area. The music researcher as well as the music historian have much to do based on klezmer art and the talented folk artists, those who grew out of the mass of klezmorim. We could pose, and study, many problems that are important for the history of Jewish music.

Klezmer music used to be played almost exclusively at weddings. But one need not think that this music has only a cultural historical value. The best klezmer pieces could easily be taken into the Soviet musical repertoire (especially Jewish folk dances). In addition, Soviet composers could borrow from klezmer music.

The goal of the present work is to draw the attention of the Soviet musician (especially the Jewish Soviet composers), as well as amateurs, to the folk art of klezmer music. First we must undertake a great collection of the musical works of the klezmer repertoire, and it is also necessary to gather the associated descriptions of the musical works and of the klezmorim themselves. Through this we can lift out the best and most beautiful of klezmer music, adopt it, and pour it into our new Soviet folk art.

We know from available evidence that klezmorim have been part of the Jewish way of life for centuries. We can locate klezmer ensembles over a very long period in nearly all cities with a significant Jewish population. It is literally impossible to imagine a wedding without klezmorim, and that is typical not just for the nineteenth century but for earlier centuries as well. Thus, for example, it is well known that when the various German Jewish communities met (in the fifteenth century) they would forbid music-making for various reasons (e.g., a death in a royal family). In those locales, weddings had to be celebrated outside the town borders in order to have music at the wedding (Gudemann 1922:89; Glantz 1939:80). A certain amount of material has been gathered on Jewish klezmorim and klezmer bands in Western Europe (Wolf 1908–9; Nettl 1923, 1927). This material sheds light only to a certain extent on the klezmer way of life or the material and social condition of klezmer bands.

We know nothing of the music the klezmorim played, not to mention the fact that there are no manuscripts or published works of the older klezmorim; we are missing the most essential part. There is no doubt that many traces of the older klezmer repertoire existed in the nineteenth century. Unfortunately, we must state that nowhere (at least to our knowledge) has anyone been interested in collecting the works of and data on the klezmorim in all the lands inhabited by Jews, where there were klezmorim in the nineteenth century and even, to a great extent, still today.

Is it still possible to accomplish this? Certainly! It is still relatively easy to establish the klezmer repertoire of the late nineteenth century. One can find a great many klezmorim in their fifties and sixties (and, not rarely, in their seventies and eighties) everywhere. These klezmorim know many pieces: dances, instrumental works played at the table, street tunes (accompanying the march to the *xupe* [wedding canopy], leading the in-laws, etc.) which they learned from their fathers, grandfathers, and older klezmorim. Sometimes among the older klezmorim (and amateurs) we find handwritten notations that have been passed down from fathers and grandfathers. These collections can give us a more or less complete picture of the klezmer repertoire, beginning in the late nineteenth century. Of course, from such private collections we cannot track down all the remains of the klezmer repertoire of past times. That would be much easier if we were to have at hand a greater collection of materials gathered in a whole series of countries and regions (U.S.S.R.: Ukraine, Belorussia, Moldavia, Jewish Autonomous Region [Birobidzhan, in Siberia—M.S.]; abroad: Lithuania, Poland, Galicia, Rumania, Czechoslovakia, America, etc.). First, this would give us a rich and complete picture of Jewish instrumental folk music in the late nineteenth century; second, we might indeed be able to trace the older klezmer repertoire which may have remained in the repertoire up to the present, albeit in altered form and with many local modifications. I would like to emphasize here that we can do a thorough study of Jewish instrumental folk music only when we have the requisite materials from a whole series of countries and regions. It would be superficial, and not sufficiently fruitful, to pose and work on problems based only on local materials when data from other lands and countries are totally unknown. We will often face phenomena whose historical roots are not clear or are entirely hidden; purely local data will not help us illuminate these phenomena.

Let us give an example of how hard it is to uncover the historical roots of particular phenomena in klezmer music based on limited local materials. Gathering data on Jewish folk dances,[2] and especially on the widespread *frejlaxs* and *šer,* we stumbled on the fact that the *šer* was never mentioned in Jewish literature, either in belles lettres or in memoirs. We copied out a whole series of descriptions of Jewish weddings, among them some which were very precise, with many details, for example, the wedding description in Ettinger's song "Di lixt." Various dances are mentioned in all these descriptions, but never the *šer.*

It is worth noting that for the most part, the descriptions of weddings date from the nineteenth century, and at that time men did not participate in couple dances. The *šer* and other couple dances were done by women (or girls) alone. In all the descriptions of weddings no special women's dances or the *šer* are mentioned. There is evidence that in earlier centuries women did indeed dance together with men; however, it is never indicated what sort of dances were performed (*Istoriia evreev v Rossii* vol. 1, pp. 346–47).

In L. Levanda's article "Starinnye evereiskie svadebnye obichai (*Perezhitoe* 3), the author lists the dances done by girls with the bride at the preliminaries including: polka, waltz, mazurka, quadrille, and lancers. The *šer* is not mentioned there. I imagine this happened because Levanda wrote the article in Russian and did not try to include dances other than those generally known; thus, it is typical that the *frejlaxs* is also not cited. Most of the dances Levanda mentioned were spread among the masses only in the second half of the nineteenth century. As is known, the polka was created only around 1830 (in Czechoslovakia) and the quadrille in the early nineteenth century (Parisian), and the lancers was first performed in the Berlin ballet only in 1857. There is no question of the "Old Jewish wedding customs" of the title of Levanda's article.

Except for isolated references, the *šer* is also mentioned very rarely in folk songs. These folk songs are all from the Ukraine (cf. Cahan 1912a:18 from Tshemirovits, Podoliya; Cahan 1912b:47 from Uman'; Beregovski 1962, from the Kalindorf and Kherson regions).

Was the *šer* known only to Ukrainian Jews? Certainly not. Although we have no data from the literature, according to information from a whole series of informants we do know that the *šer* was widespread in

2. While the music of the folk dances was foremost in our minds, in the process we learned that it was impossible to take up this topic without the question of how the dances were performed. By itself, the musical form cannot always indicate the difference between various dances.

Belorussia, Lithuania, and Poland. Even if we do not find this dance in other regions and countries in recent times (perhaps even in the last half of the nineteenth century), it does not mean that it was not known there previously. The Jews could not have adopted the dance from the Ukrainians (or in general from the Slavs), since they have no such dance, and whenever Ukrainians do dance the *šer,* they have adopted it from the Jews (see chapter 3 of the present volume).

In Böhme 1886:56 we find a dance named "Der Scherer oder Schartanz." In Schünemann 1923:275 we find as subtitle to no. 158 "Scher-lied oder Tanz," and the same for no. 339. In the note to no. 339, Schünemann writes: "This is a popular dance-song which consists at the beginning of incomprehensible word constructions as we find in children's and counting songs" (Schünemann 1923:413). This is all we could find in the German dance repertoire that has anything in common with our *šer.* We can approach the music to such dances very carefully for comparison with the *šer.* The melody of Böhme's "Scherer" dates to the year 1562. The *sher-lieder* were transcribed by Schünemann at the time of World War I. In terms of melodic structure, the two tunes are quite different. "Der Scherer" is in 2/4 time and consists of several sections, while Schünemann's examples are both in 3/8 with a melody in one section (four musical phrases corresponding to the four lines of the verse).

We know Jewish *šers* that have been written down in recent years. Many of these *šers* are in the klezmer repertoire of the late nineteenth century. They have features in common with the older German "Scherer" and not with the "Scherlieder." The Jewish *šer* is always in 2/4 and consists of several sections (usually two, less often three). We must again state, however, that in speaking of the "Jewish *šer*" we have before us only a few examples collected and transcribed in the Ukraine. It is impossible to say whether these *šers* are similar in music and dance style to the *šer* in Poland, Czechoslovakia, or Galicia, Rumania, and so on.[3] To date we have no publications and no data bearing on this question, and it may well be that nothing has been collected either. This is not the place to describe the *šer* in more detail. However, we can advance the hypothesis that this particular dance was adopted by Jews in Germany several centuries ago and that it was "Jewishized" to a great extent (at least musically).[4] A

---

3. Here I do not mean melodic variation of one or another *šer* but of the very style of the melodies itself. The Ukrainian *šers* are in general very close to the *frejlaxs.* Is this a local or universal phenomenon?

4. I deal with this matter more fully in a work "Jewish Folk Dances" [unpublished—M.S.].

broader, more definitive statement can be made only when we have the Jewish material from a series of countries.

Let us introduce another example, a dance such as the *kozak (kozačok)*, which was and still is widespread among Ukrainian Jews (and also in Poland).[5] There can be no doubt about the Ukrainian origin of this dance. It is important to note the spread of this dance among Jews outside the Ukraine (in Poland) and to determine those features introduced by the Jews; we find such features in the music.

There are also cases in which the name of a Jewish dance is not Jewish but Ukrainian, yet it is hard to ascertain that the dance has been adopted from the Ukrainian surroundings. The klezmorim used to play *skočnes* at Jewish weddings. According to their style and character, *skočnes* were almost the same as *frejlaxs,* and melodically they have no non-Jewish traits. In Ukrainian we find a dance named *skochni, doskochni, doskochisti* (Kvitka 1924:41), and in Polish we find a dance called *skoczek* (Straczewski 1901: 717). We find the same name, *skočna,* in the Czech dance repertoire. From what many klezmorim tell us, the *skočna* among Jews was not a separate dance-type. Usually they called a tune *skočna* if it was a *frejlaxs* (or, more precisely, a piece in a form similar to a *frejlaxs*) which boasted a certain technical elaboration. This could not have been adopted from the Ukrainian folk music, since there were far fewer professionally trained Ukrainian folk musicians than Jewish ones.

It can also happen that a dance has a Yiddish name and the melody for the dance is borrowed from another people. Thus, a polonaise might always be played for a *košer-tanc.* Many klezmorim, when we asked them for such a dance, played Aginski's popular polonaise "Les adieux à la patrie."

We could multiply such examples. We could show not only that one runs into difficulties trying to establish the roots of the Jewish dance-repertoire, but also that the task is no easier in terms of what is played for listening. We feel we have convincingly demonstrated through the examples cited that we can do little on the basis of local materials to shed light on the roots of Jewish klezmer folk music.

We have already noted that there are wedding pieces for listening in the klezmer repertoire as well as dances: *bazecns, dobridzen, dobranoč,* pieces

5. It is noteworthy that in both belles lettres and folklore the *kozačok* is mentioned much more frequently than the *šer.* Is this perhaps because the *kozačok* was a male dance (though also a female dance) that was performed at the wedding in the presence of all the guests? The *kozačok* was basically a solo dance in which the more talented dancers could distinguish themselves.

at table, *zaj gezunt,* playing out the in-laws, and so on. The gifted folk artist, the talented klezmer, could always find the path to the aesthetic feeling of the listeners. And we can say that among village musicians there were always richly talented personalities, true artists, who touched and moved the broad masses with their art. We have many descriptions of such folk artists in the literature. Folk tales and legends were told about them. It is enough just to recall with what love one used to speak of such folk artists as Pedotser (Aron-moyshe Kholodenko), Stempenyu (Yosele Druker), Alter Tshudnover (Alter Goyzman), Mitsi (Avrom-Yitskhok Berezovski), and others. "His fiddle speaks," "His fiddle speaks words" —those folk expressions convey the enthusiasm of a good player. The Jewish masses were not the only ones who recognized talented klezmorim; there is evidence that many non-Jews were enthused by the playing of Jewish klezmorim too. Thus, for example, Y. Kotik tells us about a klezmer named Shepsl who headed the Kobrin klezmorim (a city in Grodner *gubernia*, mid-nineteenth century). Shepsl could not read music, but he was the most outstanding fiddler and was well known in the whole region.

Writes Kotik (n.d.:37–38) "Shepsl was so well known that his name reached as far as Poskewicz, the Polish landowner. He sent for him to play, and Shepsl played alone on his fiddle. Poskewicz was amazed. . . . He used to invite distinguished guests every evening and Shepsl played at midday dinner for two or three hours. . . . He gave him a thousand rubles and a diploma on which it was written that Shepsl has divine musical talent, though he is untutored."

Another landowner (Sikhovski, himself a pianist) was enraptured by Shepsl and his playing and told him that he never heard such fine playing in his life (Kotik n.d.:233). When such a klezmer accidentally had the opportunity of displaying his art to the best musicians, he evoked enthusiasm for his abilities and his art. We have only to remember that wonderful talent, Mikhoel-Yosef Guzikov (1809–37), who, with his simple klezmer folk art, playing on a cymbalom, aroused wonder and excitement in many cities of Europe and in the greatest centers of musical art. Mikhoel-Yosef Guzikov was born in Shklov (Mogilev *gubernia*) into a klezmer family that had been producing good flutists for centuries. Mikhoel-Yosef also played flute, like his father, grandfather, and great-grandfather. However, early on he showed signs of tuberculosis and had to abandon the flute, so he took up the cymbalom. He constructed his own instrument made of wooden boards spread on a bed of straw. The sound of this cymbalom was very weak, but he captivated his listeners with his rich and restrained tone.

We do not know how he began to concertize. It is known that in 1832 he appeared at a concert in Kiev, where he was heard by the then-famous violinist Lipinsky. Lipinsky was amazed at Guzikov's playing. After his appearance in Odessa (the same year), a concert tour across Europe was arranged for him (Vienna, Germany, France). He had colossal success everywhere. He started back to Russia from Brussels, but did not make it home. In Aachen he died in a theater, at a concert, with his cymbalom in his hands. Guzikov could not read music, so he played from his klezmer repertoire (Schlesinger 1836; Fetis 1834). Felix Mendelssohn-Bartholdy, who heard Guzikov along with the famous violinist David in Leipzig, wrote to his mother on February 18, 1836:

I am curious if Gusikov has pleased you as much as me. He is a true phenomenon, a wonder, who takes second place to no virtuoso of the world in performance and preparation and who therefore gave me more enjoyment on his wood and straw instrument than many do on their pianos, just because it's more thankless. . . . Moreover I have not enjoyed myself so much at a concert in a long time as at this one, simply because he's a true genius. (Quoted in Wolf 1909:156)

This evaluation applies not just to Mikhoel-Yosef Guzikov, the wonderful cymbalist, who was heard by and who amazed the best musicians of his times, but also to a considerable extent to tens of Guzikovs, who stayed in villages and who delighted just the masses of Jewish folk and of whom no trace or account has remained.

However, we need not think that in collecting data on klezmorim we must be interested only in the most talented and that the ordinary klezmer does not merit attention. That would not be right. The most talented klezmorim grew up among a mass of klezmorim and absorbed what was best and most beautiful of klezmer music. In studying the klezmorim and their music as a whole, we will perforce more fully treat the best and most interesting of the artists and works.

While there is a certain amount of literature about the Jewish klezmorim in Western Europe, almost nothing is known of the klezmorim in the former Russian lands (including Poland and Lithuania). Only a laughable amount of data are available on the klezmer bands, especially talented klezmorim, and so on. Little has also been collected of the klezmer repertoire—and all this at the time when there was scarcely a large village in Russia that did not have a klezmer. In cities like Berdichev there were over fifty klezmorim in the late nineteenth century, making up three large bands—Pedotser's, Stempenyu's, and Moyshe-Abe's—with several smaller ones. In the second half of the nineteenth century there were a couple of thousand klezmorim in the Ukraine alone, among them tens of talented artists, including performers and composers.

It is quite some time now that we have been more or less systematically collecting klezmer pieces, various accounts, documents, and other sources concerning the klezmorim. At the present time the Folklore Section has six hundred klezmer pieces (concertos, marches, *dobridzens, dobranoč,* dances, etc.), mostly written by klezmorim of the Ukraine. We have also collected data about various klezmorim and klezmer bands, including photographs. We are now preparing a large work on Jewish instrumental folk music for publication, to present the better items of the klezmer repertoire. However, the materials gathered to date are not sufficient for a large work, so we plan a more intensive subdivision of the field. It is clear that by itself the small number of researchers of the Folklore Section (just two people) is not in the position of executing the necessary work of collecting in this area, as is the case for all the other areas of Jewish folklore. Without the active help of a larger number of correspondents and amateurs of Jewish folk art, we can do little with our limited energy. Something of value can be contributed by every teacher, administrator of libraries and clubs, cultural activists in cities and in the country, every worker and farm worker. Write down what you remember about klezmorim, about dances that were done at Jewish weddings and festivities; ask older people and write down their information in this area, or ask the local klezmorim. Help us locate klezmorim and get in touch with them to transcribe their musical repertoire—all this is a relatively simple task that anyone can do easily. All told, what we will get from a large number of correspondents will yield a great deal of material.

Schools and independent groups (choruses, orchestras, drama circles, etc.) can be particularly active in this work. We have met children in the upper grades who show great interest in folk art. In such schools, children's folklore circles have been established (under the guidance of a teacher). Such circles have sent us valuable data that they collected. It is not hard to assign a special group of children to gather data on local klezmorim, to interview and collect from mother, grandmother, and so on, about the dance repertoire at Jewish weddings, or to learn themselves how to do the most popular dances (e.g., *šer, frejlaxs*), and describe how they are danced. Local musicians (teachers, the klezmorim themselves) can help transcribe the dance tunes.

It is to be hoped that the data collected about the klezmorim and klezmer music be systematized, so that this beautiful branch of Jewish folk art can be illuminated in as full and many-sided a way as possible. To this end we have attached a special questionnaire (program) according to which data should be gathered. The program is divided into four headings: (1) the klezmer, (2) klezmer bands, (3) the klezmer repertoire and dances, and (4) amateur musicians.

Under the first heading we aim at obtaining the necessary data about individual klezmorim, principally the more talented ones. However, it is important to collect data about some average klezmorim in order to get a true picture of this type of typical klezmer. Older klezmer families deserve special attention. The collector should describe such families as fully as possible, going back to the oldest representative and continuing the description down to the last generation.

The second heading is devoted to klezmer bands. Here it is important to shed light on the artistic level of the given band, which depends on the particular klezmorim included. One or two talented klezmorim lend it brilliance. One must remember that the division into headings is conditional and that only taken as a whole will the material give a true and comprehensive picture of klezmer activity. We have tried to distinguish the activity of the individual klezmer from that of the group in their locale and society.

The third section aims at shedding light on the klezmer repertoire. We would hope that collectors might give the repertoire historically. It is easy to write down what was played, but it is necessary to think about the evolution of the repertoire. The klezmorim in their seventies to nineties still remember when *taksims* (a type of free improvised form which has a great deal of scale and other passage-work which embellished the main theme of the piece; after such improvisations comes a frejlaxs in 2/4) were played. The younger klezmorim don't even recognize the concept of *taksim;* they have played doinas instead of *taksims* since the beginning of the twentieth century; in addition to the fiddler, the clarinet or flute used to play solos at table.

It is particularly important to describe the Jewish wedding dances. First, it is necessary to transcribe the specifically Jewish dances such as the Kosher-dance, bride-dance, *šer,* and *frejlaxs.* Widely known dances like the waltz, lancers, and quadrille should be indicated but not described. Sometimes dances are mentioned in the literature for which we have not been able to gather data, although they were danced in the late nineteenth century. For example, a folk song (Ginzburg-Marek 1901: no. 254) mentions a dance called *semene* (Moliver, Vilna, Kovno *gubernias*):

> Gave a tree / took it back
> Play a *semel* for an aunt.

In another folk song the dance is called *semele* instead of *semene* (Cahan 1914: no. 106):

Špilt mir a semene	Play me a *semene*
Nit kejn kozacke	Not a *kozacke*
Ix bin an oreme	I'm poor
Ober a xvacke.	But I'm some guy
Nat ajx a pajem	Here's a *payem* (?)
Špilt mir a semele	Play me a *semele*
Xanele xosele	*Xanele xosele*
Ruft men Avremele.	Is what they call Avremele

Cahan 1931 has a little information on this dance. There he cites all the folk songs that mention the *semene/semele* dance. Cahan introduces some German folk songs as well as Jewish ones in which we find a similar dance. However, the material is too limited to allow the possibility of saying anything definitive about the dance in question. At the moment I can think of another song in which we meet the same dance: Zunser's "fun xejdr zog men nit ojs" (Zunser 1895:30):

> Vajberlex, pačt! Ir hot naxes derlebt
> Bejde maxetejnestes a šemele tancn.
>
> Women, clap! You've gotten satisfaction:
> Both mothers-in-law dancing a *šemele*.

This song has great value for us. First, we can be sure that the *semene/semele/šemele* dance was a solo dance (both mothers-in-law) and that, second, it was well known in the 1870s and 1880s (at least in the Vilna area). The name might well have remained in folk songs after the dance itself was forgotten, but Zunser, who sang his songs for wedding guests, would certainly not have needed to mention a long-forgotten dance. From this it is clear that through some effort one could still find living people who remember how it was danced. Old klezmorim from the appropriate regions could tell about this dance and give the melody. Perhaps this is not the only dance which has been forgotten. One must establish as far as possible everything that relates to the late nineteenth century, and that is not too difficult to accomplish.

Jewish klezmorim often played at non-Jewish weddings, festivities, entertainments, and so on. Here it is interesting to establish whether non-Jews adopted Jewish dances. We know of cases in which Ukrainian peasants took up Yiddish *frejlaxs* and *šers* (cf. chapter 3 of the present volume). The *šer* is also widespread in Moldavia among the non-Jewish village population (they call the tune *šrayer*). We would need to collect more data to understand how widespread this phenomenon was. Sometimes non-Jewish musicians would play at Jewish weddings. For example, Mendele Mokher-Sforim tells us that at a wedding in Kapulye (Belorussia) the Jewish klezmer Faytel played on weekdays and Kondrat would play on the Sabbath at the bride's for the preliminaries (at Shloyme Reb Khaym's wedding). It is important to find out from those who remember such weddings what the non-Jewish musicians played, the repertoire that non-Jewish musicians would play, and especially the specifically Jewish works of their repertoire. At times, non-Jewish musicians would come to play for local Jews on various holidays. Here one should establish what things these musicians would play in such cases.

It is superfluous to mention the importance of collecting photographs of individual talented klezmorim and bands, as well as manuscripts of klezmer pieces.

In the hitherto published collections of Yiddish sayings, we find a certain number of proverbs about klezmorim and klezmer ways. The number of such sayings is very small (about twelve to fifteen). One can imagine that one could collect new, as yet unknown, proverbs on this topic. It would be particularly good to ask for this, since often these short but pointed expressions portray the klezmer and the klezmer lifestyle.[6]

In working out our research program, I basically relied on the materials in our archive. Our data have been gathered from klezmorim them-

---

6. Here are some of the proverbs about klezmorim [with their translations—M.S.]:
1. Vos far a klezmer, aza xasene.
2. Az me cejlt sfire, kumt af di klezmer a pegire.
3. Nojsn becimbl; hojlex betencl.
4. Az cvej klezmorim gejen tancn, cerajsn zix ba di klezmer di strunes.
5. A levaje on gevejn iz vi a xasene on klezmer.
6. A badxn maxt di gance štub frejlax un alejn hot in der hejm cores (or: alejn ligt er in der erd).
7. Draj mencn af der velt zingn far cores: a xazn, a betler, un a maršelek.

1. The type of klezmer means that quality of wedding.
2. When they count the *sfire* (a forty-day period in which music is not allowed) the klezmer can drop dead.
3. Nathan's at the cimbalom—let's dance.
4. When two klezmorim go dancing, they break the klezmer's strings (since they don't want to pay they make up all sorts of excuses).
5. A funeral without wailing is like a wedding without a klezmer.
6. A *badxn* makes the whole house merry, and has trouble at home himself (or: he himself is in bad shape).
7. Three people in the world sing out of need (i.e., for money): a cantor, a beggar, and a *badxn* (wedding entertainer).

selves (in the Ukraine). However, we have to a certain extent used published sources which have no direct bearing on the Ukraine.

We hope that this work will also interest comrades in other republics of the Soviet Union, especially in the Jewish Autonomous Region. There, much can be done in this field, as in other areas of folklore. In the various towns, villages, and settlements of the Jewish Autonomous Region, one can find immigrants from all the republics and also from abroad. Our work could also be done if people abroad were interested (e.g., from Poland, Lithuania, Rumania, Czechoslovakia, Galicia), and much could be accomplished in America, where there are immigrants from many countries of Eastern Europe.

Our research program consists of approximately one hundred questions. However, one cannot just go around with this program as if it were an ordinary questionnaire with yes or no answers. The task of the collector is to extract as much information as possible from what is asked and to make short but clear write-ups. Our questions are only points of departure for the collector and should help him to know where to concentrate while interviewing.

The program contains questions directed at the professional musician. If the collector does not have the requisite musical training, it is hoped that he will read the questions through with the interviewee and write down the latter's answers. It is clear that it would be best if the musician himself were to answer the questions.

We also thought it necessary to add a category about amateur musicians. Klezmorim were the professional musicians who played only at weddings, more rarely on other occasions. Among the broad Jewish masses there was a strong drive to music; they wanted to hear music more often and to make music themselves. Amateur musicians—who perhaps learned to play an instrument to become professionals, but more likely out of a drive for music in general—are a common enough phenomenon in Jewish life.

"Do you want to know how many men there are in a house? Look on the walls! As many fiddles as hang there—that's how many men" (Vilt ir visn vifl manslajt es gehert cun a štub? Kukt af di vent! Vifl es hengen fidelex azojfil manslajt!; Perets: "A gilgl fun a nign"). It is worthwhile to collect a certain amount of data to shed light on this phenomenon. Here it is important to make clear how large the number of amateur musicians in towns, villages, and settlements was, what instruments they usually played, what works made up their repertoire, from whom they learned to play, whether they played from music or by ear, and which social strata most often learned to play.

One can imagine that it is better to work out one part of the program thoroughly and write down everything related to that part than to answer all the questions superficially.

The smallest bit of work that any individual collector can do in this area has a certain value for us. The total of all such smaller collections that arise from a large number of collectors is significant. It will be useful for the history of folk art, for science, and even for the broad masses of people.

Research Program

I. THE KLEZMER

1. Name
2. Age
3. Present place of residence
4. Earlier place of residence
5. Instruments played (past and present)
6. How long have you been involved with music?
7. Were your forebears or relatives klezmorim (e.g., father, grand-father, brothers)?
8. From whom and for how long did you learn to play?
9. How did you learn?
   A. Systematically, following a playing-school (using music?), or using written "lessons"? Did you play special exercises, studies, pieces, concertos, etc.? Cite a few.
   B. Did you learn to play by yourself, from a father, brother, or friend, by ear?
10. Where did you get the instrument when you learned to play? Did they sell instruments in small towns? Who sold them? What sort of instruments?
11. When did you begin to play in a band? As an apprentice or as a paid member?
12. Was music your vocation or avocation? With what did you occupy yourself besides music?
13. What was the pay in the band? If you were on shares, how much did you get for a season or a year?
14. Did you compose your own things (concertos, dances, etc.)?
15. From whom did you learn, or copy down, your repertoire? How often did you learn (or introduce) new works?
16. Did you give lessons on your instrument?
17. Who learned to play from you?
18. Did you know the klezmer argot?
19. Are your children involved with music?

II. KLEZMER BANDS

1. What did you used to call a band: *kompaniye, kapele, orkestr, klezmer*?
2. How many bands were there in your city, town, or village? How many musicians made up the band? What instruments?
3. How did you create your band? When did it begin?
4. Regions in which the band used to play.
5. Were there occasions when the band took on weddings not in its own region?
6. How did the band that usually played in that area react?
7. Did an intruding band pay off the local band?
8. Would it be possible for a second band to develop in a town that already had a band?
9. Did the band have to get permission from someone to play (the Jewish community, the state rabbi, police, etc.)?
10. Who used to determine the question of adopting a new musician into the band?
11. Were rookie players auditioned? What did they play at an audition?
12. Did a young klezmer who had just joined have to treat the older klezmorim respectfully?
13. Did a new band member get paid right away, or did he serve as unpaid apprentice for a while? How long?
14. Did children play in the band at weddings?
15. Did nonklezmer families give their children to klezmer bands?
16. How did band members get paid? According to shares or evenly? How large was each musician's share, or how much was he paid (per job, per week)?
17. At table the first violinist usually played. Did other musicians (clarinetist, flutist) also play solo at times?
18. Which instruments accompanied the soloist?
19. How was the fiddle tuned, besides the usual way, for various pieces?
20. Did klezmorim (fiddlers and others) sometimes use tricks (holding the fiddle behind the back, upside down, etc.)?
21. Do you remember if a cimbalom was played in the band?
22. When the klezmorim played in the street (going to the *xupe*, accompanying the in-laws) did the bass fiddle play?
23. Did the first violinist sit with the other musicians or play standing?
24. Did the first violinist play dances?
25. Where and in what order did the band sit while playing at the wedding (a) for dance, (b) at table?
26. In what order did the band proceed along the street?
27. Did the musicians come to the wedding in weekday clothes or did they change?
28. Did they honor the klezmorim at the dinner?
29. When did the klezmorim eat the dinner? After the guests? Who served them? Did they get the same dishes as the guests, or leftovers?

30. Was there a particular *badxn* in your band, or did someone in the band fill the role of *badxn* (saying rhymes, presiding at gift-giving, etc.)?
31. If the *badxn* did not play an instrument, did he sit with the guests?
32. Did they pay separately for every dance or for the whole wedding? Which of the musicians would gather the money for the dances? Was there a special cashbox (or violin case)? Who kept track of the amount?
33. If a musical work especially pleased, how did the audience show it?
34. Were there times when the guest (father of the bride) was unhappy with the music played for him? How did he express his dissatisfaction?
35. Did they sing along with the band at weddings?
36. Did the klezmorim themselves sometimes sing along while playing (*"Oy,* a beautiful bride, good-night, mazel tov, they're dancing well,"* etc.)?
37. How often did you rehearse?
38. Who gave directions at a rehearsal?
39. Did you learn dances from music or by ear? Who indicated the bass, second part, etc., and what notes or chords should be used?
40. Were larger works played from music or also by ear?
41. Did your band play at rich folks' weddings? Was the number of musicians increased for such weddings? What instruments did you add?
42. How many klezmorim usually played at poor weddings?
43. Was there a difference in repertoire for weddings of varying classes?
44. How did the musicians relate to different classes?
45. Did your band play at non-Jewish festivities: (a) peasant weddings; (b) upper-class balls and festivities?
46. How were the musicians paid at non-Jewish festivities—for the evening, for the whole time played, or per dance?
47. What dances (and other pieces) did you play for peasant weddings? (Write down the names as exactly as possible.)
48. What sorts of things did you play at non-Jewish upper-class occasions?
49. Did the klezmorim sometimes play Jewish dances or other Jewish things at non-Jewish weddings? What sort of dances?
50. Did the upper-class non-Jews sometimes ask for Jewish pieces or dances?
51. If so, did they take the pieces seriously, with interest, or ironically to mock them?
52. Did non-Jews come to hear klezmorim at Jewish weddings (outside the windows)?
53. How did non-Jews (Ukrainians, Belorussians, Moldavians, Poles, peasants, middle class) relate to Jewish music and dances? Seriously, with interest, or ironically.
54. Did non-Jewish musicians play in your band at times? Did you ever hear of such a thing happening in other bands? Which instruments would they have normally played?

55. Would non-Jewish musicians play on the Sabbath at the preliminaries?
56. Who played at the klezmorim's own weddings?
57. Did klezmorim play at affluent houses at Chanukah and Purim time?
58. Did klezmorim accompany the singing of *purimšpilers?*
59. Did klezmorim play at home for the family or guests? Under what circumstances? What would they play?
60. Were klezmorim ever invited to friends' houses to play gratis?
61. What did klezmorim call the instruments and parts of instruments?
62. Did all klezmorim know the klezmer argot?
63. Were various klezmorim given nicknames according to their instruments (e.g., Benci Clarinet, Šaya Bas) or were everyday names used with the addition of "klezmer"?
64. Were there craftsmen in small towns that produced instruments (fiddle, cello, strings, etc.), or did klezmorim and amateur musicians buy ready-made instruments and equipment?
65. Do you know any tales, legends, anecdotes, jokes, songs, etc., about klezmorim? If so, write some down.

III. THE KLEZMER REPERTOIRE AND DANCES

1. With what sort of piece did the musicians start a wedding (*mazltov, dobranoč*)?
2. What sort of dance did the preliminaries start with and what was the melody?
3. What sort of dance was done with the bride for *badekns?*
4. What did the musicians play for *bazen di kale?* Do you remember the words?
5. How did one make way?
6. What did you play for leading the groom to the *xupe?* The bride? Leading from the *xupe?*
7. What was played at table?
8. What sort of cheers do you remember?
9. How did the *micva-tanc* or the *košer-tanc* go, and what was the tune?
10. What collective figure-dances were done?
11. How are the *šer,* the *barojges,* the *bejgele,* and other dances done?
12. How was the bride's "golden dance" done, and what was the tune?
13. Was the *frejlaxs* known under different names in various locales: *frejlaxs, hopke, skočne, karahod, redl, drejdl, kajlexikes, rikudl,* etc.? What did they call it in your area?
14. *Was the frejlaxs* simply done in a circle, or were there other figures (e.g., snake)?
15. Was there a circle within a circle for the *frejlaxs?* Did various dancers or couples go into the circle?
16. In the circle, did they dance? (a) holding hands, (b) hands on shoulders, or (c) some other way?
17. Was the *frejlaxs* a mixed dance or segregated?

18. Do you know the *semene* or *semele* dance? How was it danced and to what tune?

IV. AMATEUR MUSICIANS

1. In your town (or in other towns you knew) were there amateur musicians who learned to play an instrument without becoming professional musicians?
2. What instruments might they have played?
3. What social background did they belong to?
4. Did they learn from a local klezmer or by themselves? From music or by ear?
5. What works did they have in their repertoire (*frejlaxs*, religious songs, operetta numbers, dances, etc.)?
6. At what occasions would they play (*mlave-malke*, Friday night festivities)?
7. Would such a musician play at a wedding with klezmorim? For money or gratis?
8. Would several amateurs get together and play? What pieces would they play?

Works Cited

Böhme, Friederich
    1886   *Geschichte des Tanzes in Deutschland.* Leipzig.
Cahan, Y. L.
    1912a   *Yidishe folkslider oys dem folks-moyl, gezamlt fun Y. L. Cahan,* vol. 1. New York and Warsaw: Internatsyonale Bibliotek Farlag.
    1912b   Ibid., vol. 2.
    1931   "Tsum ufkum fun yidishn tants-lid." *Yivo-bleter* 1.
Fétis, F.-J.
    1834   *Biographie universelle des musiciens.* Paris.
Ginzburg, S. M., and Marek, P. S.
    1901   *Evreiskie narodnye pesni v Rossii.* St. Petersburg: Voskhod.
Glantz, R.
    1930   "A barikht fun a ben-dor vegn der fayerlikher protsesie fun di prager yidn." In *Arkhiv far geshikhte fun yidishn teater un drama,* 80– . Vilna and New York.
Gudemann, M.
    1922   *Yidishe kultur-geshikhte in mitlalter.* Berlin: Klal-Verlag.
Kotik, Y.
    n.d.   *Mayne zikhrones,* vol. 1. N.p.
Kvitka, K.
    1924   *Profesionalni nar. spivtsi i muzikanti na Ukraini.* Kiev: UAN.
Nettl, P.
    1923   *Alte jüdische Spielleute und Musiker.* Prag.
    1927   "Die Prager Judenspielleutezunft." In *Beiträge zur böhmischen und mährischen Musikgeschichte.* Brünn.

Schlesinger
1836   *Über Gusikow.* Vienna.
Schünemann, G.
1923   *Das Lied der deutschen Koloniosten in Russland.* Munich: Dreimasken-
        verlag.
Straczewski, F.
1901   "Die Polnische Tänze." *Sammelbände der internationalen Musikgesell-
        schaft,* vol. 4.
Wolf, L.
1908–9 "Fahrende Leute bei den Juden." *Mitteilungen zur jüdischen Volk-
        skunde.*
Zunser, E.
1895   *Shiri Am: dray naye lider tsum zingen mit melodien.* Vilna.

5

THE ALTERED DORIAN SCALE IN JEWISH FOLK MUSIC (ON THE QUESTION OF THE SEMANTIC CHARACTERISTICS OF SCALES) (1946)

The question of the semantics of the expressive means of music remains neglected. However, it can be said that no single element of a musical language, taken in isolation, has a permanent hold on the particular expressive quality with which it is associated. Each separate element has a specific semantic characteristic, depending on the context and on its conjunction with other elements. Consequently, such an element can serve as the expressive means for many, sometimes completely contradictory, emotions.

A scale, after all, is just one of the elements of a musical language. Of course, the scale is not merely an equal among the other musical elements of a piece; it creates the coherence and logic of the musical language in

Originally published as "Izmenennyi doriiskii lad v evreiskom muzykal'nom fol'klore (k voprosu o semanticheskikh svoistvakh lada)," in I. I. Zemtsovskii, ed., *Problemy muzykal'nogo fol'klora narodov SSSR.* (Moscow: Muzyka, 1973), pp. 367–82. Zemstovskii edited the article without precise indications of how he did so.

general and of each melodic line in particular. However, it cannot be demonstrated that the scale structure alone determines the conceptual-emotional content of a piece of music. No contemporary musicologist is ready to repeat Plato's theses on the helpful and harmful scales (in terms of their action), nor will he try to classify precisely the conceptual-emotional content of basic scales and rhythmic types, as did Aristotle and other philosophers and musicians of antiquity.

The present work attempts to pose the question of the semantic characteristics of the scale on a different plane. It seems that in the folk musics of various peoples we find a whole series of different scales. We will not touch on the question of the origin of a particular scale in any given music. We are interested in the situation of the folk music of a given people when the various scales have become, to a considerable extent, traditional. What guides the folk artist in his choice of scale while forming a new melody? Does he hit on this scale or that, or does he calculatedly select, search out, and adapt to certain characteristics of a given scale?

The importance and strength of tradition in folk art is a well-known fact. However, the creative work of the folk artist (both the original author of a new work and the subsequent talented performer/co-authors) is not a mechanical act of combining canonized poetic and musical elements. In addition, the folk artist does not always stay within the bounds of the traditional means of expression; he does not always use the old, but also creates the new. The process of using an artistic tradition is in itself a creative act. It entails selecting from the storehouse of folk art precisely those elements which are useful and suitable to the artist for the expression of his emotions and ideas, and for the embodiment in artistic form of what he wishes to say with his new composition.

Suppose we compare the degree of feasibility of conscious choice between poetic (oral) and musical elements. At first glance it might appear that in relationship to the latter, the folk artist is nearly devoid of opportunities of making deliberate choices. It is evident that the discussion is not about theoretical realization, but about an intuitive and practical ability to comprehend the expressive characteristic of artistic elements and their suitability for embodying what the artist seeks. Naturally, poetic means are more accessible and understandable than musical means. However, a deeper study of the question assures us that musical elements are chosen not accidentally but with a fixed understanding of the strength and degree of their expressivity and effectiveness.

The melodic elements of folk songs are not identical in their accessibility to conscious choice. Some of them are more available, not just to intuitive action but to deliberate selection as well. For example, elements of melody such as tempo, basic character, and expression are chosen by folk artists with complete awareness. It may be said that even the outlines of the musical picture as a whole do not escape the consciousness of the creator and the audience. Scale structure is one of the most difficult elements for real awareness. The widespread conceptions of major and minor, at least among urban listeners with no special musical education, are often confused, depending on the tempo, character, expression, and other factors.

Because of the underresearched nature of the question at hand, we have decided to begin with less-widely-distributed scales, found in Jewish folklore, first and foremost the so-called altered Dorian scale. This scale is not specific to Jewish folk music. It has a certain place in Ukrainian folk music as well. Almost all the *dumy* [Ukrainian epic songs—M.S.] are sung in the altered Dorian scale. Quite a number of other Ukrainian songs are also built on this scale. This scale is also found in other folk musics (e.g., Moldavian, Rumanian). Thus we feel that the conclusions reached on the basis of researching the Jewish materials will be confirmed in the folk music of other peoples.

Still another factor stimulated us to study this question. The altered Dorian scale is found in all the basic genres of Jewish folk music: in songs, instrumental works, and textless songs [Yiddish *nign*—M.S.]. However, the place the scale occupies in different genres is variable. In songs and instrumental folklore, melodies in the altered Dorian scale make up 4 to 5 percent. It is worth noting that in the Jewish songs created in the Soviet period this scale has completely disappeared. It is found again in the songs created during the German occupation in the camps and ghettos of the so-called Transnistria. Hoping to discover the cause of this occurrence, I began to work on the role of the given scale in Jewish folklore, to find a key for explaining this fact, which interested me.

The pitches of the altered Dorian scale are shown in Example 30. The term "altered Dorian" needs to be precisely understood. This scale has more traits in common with contemporary scales than with ancient scales. Its tonic basis is a minor triad (G–B-flat–D); the fourth above tonic is raised, the sixth is major, and the seventh minor. F# is used below the tonic, not F as in the upper octave. C# and C-natural often alternate in a single melody. Most often the C-natural is used in the third part of the melody (corresponding to the third line of a quatrain). This calmer melodic line, like a short breathing space, very sharply sets into relief the foregoing and subsequent tense melodic line C#–D, C#–B-flat. Many

Example 30

tunes built completely on another scale (usually the natural minor) include the altered Dorian as an episode. Sometimes, having begun a song in natural minor, the performer changes over to the altered Dorian as early as the second half of the first line, maintaining it for all the succeeding lines. Yet another characteristic of the melodies under question should be noted: They seem to be accompanied by a drone on the tonic. Jewish folk songs are exclusively monophonically performed among the folk, without any instrumental accompaniment. The given songs are often accompanied by a drone or an ostinato bass, consisting of tonic and dominant; it is not performed, but implied. The drone, realized or implied, makes one think that these melodies were performed or accompanied at some time by instruments with a continuous bass sound, like the bagpipe, or the Ukrainian *lira* [a hurdy-gurdy—M.S.].

Let us get acquainted with the content and character of the songs whose melodies are built on the altered Dorian scale. Example 31 is a song that tells of a young worker who was injured by a fragment while working on a motor. The fellow is taken to a hospital, but the doctors determine that he cannot be saved, and he dies [see p. 139 in present volume—M.S.]. The author vents the feelings that grip him in connection with the misfortune described. He is moved to the depths of his soul and is in a state in which he can respond only through lamenting. Alongside the nature of the scale, the sharply lamenting character of the melody is determined by a whole series of other elements, such as: the broad ambit (a twelfth, D–G), the breathing, the high point reached at the opening of the song, the rubato delivery at a generally slow tempo, and the cadences. If the scale structure were maintained and any of the other factors left out, the character of the melody would undoubtedly vanish to a certain extent.

Let us look at the song "Far vemen zol iz šrajen" (Ex. 32). A young woman given into marriage endures many hardships. "To whom can I complain, before whom can I weep; I have no one to pour out my grief to. I would tell my father, but he says that I'm no longer his concern, and mother says that it's bad for her too, while brother says that his wife is dearer to him than his sister, and that it's no better for her," etc. [see p. 385 in present volume—M.S.]. It is easy to see that this melody is quite

Example 31

similar to the previous one (Ex. 31) both in melodic line and in many details. However, it is free of that sharpness of expression which characterized Example 31. How did this happen? It seems to us that the cause is the even note-values of the pitches and the short breaths of the first two lines, divided here by a caesura. Staying on the tonic (and not on the fifth, as in Ex. 31) at the end of the first two lines also robs it of sharpness. We will take up this occurrence later. Still, the character of this melody remains that of lamentation, and the discussion is only of a greater or lesser degree of sharpness of expression.

Let us look at the song "Vos vejst ir menčn" (Ex. 33) (Beregovski: unpublished ms). The song tells of a young man who has run away from his wife, "not writing her letters or sending her money." He has left his wife a bird to amuse her. The wife grieves. The bird has flown over high forests, up to the gates of the outlaw (husband). The bird tells him that his young wife is pining away for him. He declares that the abandoned wife is of no use to him. The bird has him write a letter to his wife. The

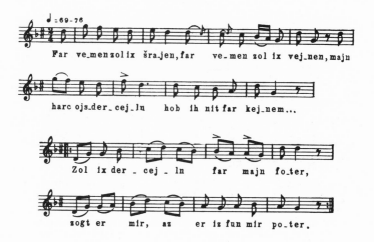

Example 32

bird flies home and gives the wife the "bitter tidings." "When she took the letter into her hand, she lay with her face to the wall." (She died.) Having much in common with what has gone before, the melody is distinctive in having the high point transferred to the second line, while the first prepares it.

We have the same type of melody in the song "Ix zic mir ongešpart ojf dem elntn bojmele" (Ex. 34). It also tells of an abandoned wife. She sits by a lonely tree, weeping rivers of tears. She has gone to seek her husband, "on all the steamboats until she reached the railway." She has asked everyone about her husband—all in vain. "It would be better if he had sent a divorce," she cries, "than to leave me in such a situation." She longs for her husband, for the father of her children. While this melody has many traits in common with the preceding songs, it differs in a number of ways. Of its four lines, three end on the tonic, and only one on D; this D can be taken as being somewhat different in this song than the others. There the melodic line B-flat–C#–D, though it did not actually reflect active protest against what happened, it nevertheless sounded like a firm demand for an answer to cruel and unjust actions—how could something like this happen? In Example 34 there are no imploringly demanding melodic turns. The abandoned wife, in whose name the song is sung, has had her strength beaten down. Every phrase of the melody, even if the breaths are broad, returns to the tonic after a significant rise, as if falling, exhausted.

I must qualify what I say here. While considering that the folk artist

Example 33

Example 34

intuitively chooses his musical expressive means knowing the strength of their efficacy, I do not mean to say that one could relate this approach to all the individual details of the melody. Of course the discussion is only about general tendencies, of a trend toward seeking and choosing a melody of this or that type. The melody in Example 34 portrays many details which give the spiritual state of an abandoned wife who has spent her strength in search of her husband. However, it is easy to see that in the melodies of other variants of the same song, while the general lamenting tone is preserved, many details of our variant may not appear.

Let us introduce another melody (Ex. 35). It is interesting in that in its formulation we see how the altered Dorian gradually takes the place of the natural minor, which disappears altogether in the second couplet. "They separated us, as a body from a soul." "Let a bullet strike the one," she says, "who separated you and me and persuaded you to become the groom of another girl." The first line of the first couplet in no way hints at the altered Dorian. Without avoiding the character of this phrase, it could be performed as well as in Example 36. The E-flat is sung without any tension, since this phrase is still in natural minor. The second line has a deviation to D minor. It does not contain the typical traits of the altered Dorian. And it would not have kept the melody from going back to G minor in subsequent lines; we see that possibility occurring in variants of the song in question, in which the tune stays in G minor to the end. It is only in the third line that the altered Dorian is established; it then remains in the subsequent couplet, completely pushing out the natural minor.

Finally, let us introduce yet another melody (Ex. 37) where the first line is in the natural minor and all the others in altered Dorian. In contrast to Example 36, the first line here remains unchanged in subsequent verses. The content of the song: A girl is ready for great suffering (wandering out in the world, living in strange houses), just to marry her beloved [see p. 325 in this volume—M.S.]. Example 37 has many points in common with Example 35, but it is more expressive and more goal-oriented than the latter. Example 37 unfolds gradually; its range and emotional content grow continually, reaching tension at the high point (measure 8), after which it gradually subsides after an insignificant rise in the last line.

Example 35 is less goal-oriented; it is repetitive. In the first line the pitch C is found three times. Despite the fact that the C is accented differently at each occurrence, the manifold return to the same pitch blunts its effectiveness. The pitch G in the first, and especially the third, line is even more weakly introduced; the double appearance of the high point dulls the expression somewhat. All indications point to the fact that in the

Example 35

Example 36

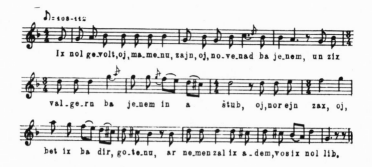

Ix nol ge·volt, oj, ma·me·nu, zajn, oj, no·ve·nad ba je·nem, un zix

val·ge·rn ba je·nem in a štub, oj, nor ejn zax, oj,

bet ix ba dir, go·te·nu, ar ne·men zal ix a·dem, vos ix nol lib.

Example 37

first verse the performer of Example 35 did not find the appropriate concentrated artistic form and corrected that only in the second verse.

The examples just cited give one a sense of the basic group of songs whose melodies are built on the altered Dorian scale and of those in which the scale occupies an important place. We turn now to another group: instrumental music.

In instrumental music the altered Dorian scale is most often found in works built in the form of the Moldavian and Rumanian doina. Such works consist of two parts. The first is in a slow tempo, and the melody is presented with much passage-work, decoration, and other melismatic ornamentation, while the second part is in duple meter, built on the musical material of the first part. Outside the doina itself (performed at the wedding feast, principally at table), there are also other works in the doina style.

Example 38 is an excerpt of the instrumental work "Dobranoč," performed in honor of individual guests at weddings. Without going into

Example 38

details of the Jewish wedding ceremony, in which pieces of a lyric and lamenting character had their place (at *bazecn,* etc.) let us note that such works were played especially often when the bride was an orphan. The meeting of relatives with the bride evoked memories of her deceased parents, and the musicians in such situations played works of a sad or lamenting character. We can also note that the progression of pitches of the tonic six-four chord in descending order is typical of many songs in this scale as well.

In the performance of the Jewish klezmorim, the "plot" of the doina was usually presented in the following way: A shepherd has lost a sheep (or sheep). Weeping, he goes in search of it. He asks every passerby about the lost sheep, but no one can tell him where it is. Finally he finds the sheep and pours out his joy in a jolly dance tune.

There are also so-called *"taksim"* works in the doina form. The *taksim* and the doina are of different origin. The klezmorim were able to identify them.[1] Example 39 is an excerpt from the first section of a *taksim*. A section of the *frejlaxs* (a round-dance with an unlimited number of partici-pants—I.Z.) for the *taksim* of Example 39 is shown in Example 40. An excerpt of the first part of a doina is found in Example 41. Example 42 shows an excerpt from the *frejlaxs* section of the same doina. One can sharply feel, it seems to us, the greater or lesser degree of lamentation in the first part of the doinas just cited. However, at the same time we have hit upon a new occurrence: *a frejlaxs,* a work of jolly character, in the same altered Dorian scale. It should be noted that such *frejlaxs* are basically found only in doinas and *taksims,* that is, in works meant for hearing. It is extremely rare to find such *frejlaxs* performed for dance. Their character might be described as laughter through tears. The deep sorrow brought on by the first part of the doina is somewhat cleared up. The heaviness, which weighs upon the soul, is somewhat dispersed, but the tears evoked by the narration about what has been endured have not yet dried up; we feel their aftertaste even in the *frejlaxs.* We can sense—as we perceive it —a distinct irony. The irony is directed not to the events described but at itself, at its readiness to make a transition to a lighter mood, to take part in merriment after we were so deeply moved by hearing the tale of some deep sorrow.

---

1. See the introduction to volume 3 of "Evreiskii muzykal'nyi fol'klor," in manuscript (there is a copy in the library of the Moscow Conservatory). At present this manuscript is part of the Beregovski archive in the Leningrad State Institute of Theater, Music, and Cinematography [—I.Z.]. [A copy of this unpublished work is also housed in the archives of the YIVO Institute for Jewish Research, New York—M.S.]

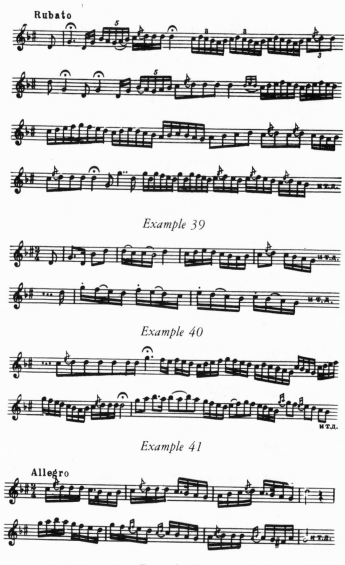

Example 39

Example 40

Example 41

Example 42

It remains to become briefly acquainted with how the altered Dorian is used in Jewish textless songs. We have already noted that the altered Dorian occupies a smaller role in this genre. Example 43 shows a short song. The melodic line of measure two, especially the second half, asks, demands, something and contains in itself both repose and the knowledge of inevitability. Among all our transcriptions (about eight hundred tunes) and all the printed corpus of textless songs, this is the only example of a

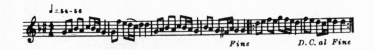

Example 43

melody built entirely on the altered Dorian. Basically, in these songs the altered Dorian scale expresses not lamentation, but rather a more or less solid demand for an answer to what arouses the folk artist. For example, in Example 44, the emotional tension grows gradually, leading to a high point in the opening of the third part. The culmination is long and solid. A typical rhythmic formula enters, and only with the fifth measure of the third part is there a preparation for release. Outside the common rhythmic formula of the whole piece (Ex. 45) one cadential passage (measures 7–8) concludes all three parts of the tune.

We have an even greater expression of tension in the song shown in Example 46. The scheme of the song is *abcb.* The first and second sections have many elements in common: the second part is built on the second phrase of the first part, and in addition both parts have the same cadence

Example 44

Example 45

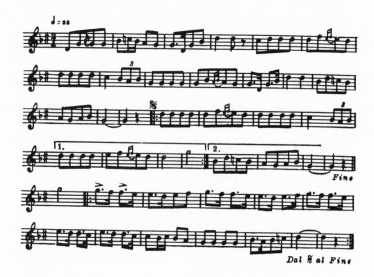

Example 46

(last four beats of the first part and second ending of the second part). The high point of the song is located in the third part. It is long, beginning with the first outcry of the section, and it begins to fall off only in the fifth measure, after a repeat of the opening of the section. The dotted rhythm and devices of this section strengthen the solid demand for an answer to the uneasy question of the author. The second section is heard again after the third. The author finds no response to his uneasy question and seems to make peace with it. The second section now sounds, after the third, much softer, less demanding.

The examples just cited (and their number could be multiplied), indicate eloquently that in Jewish folk music the altered Dorian scale is mainly used to express the grief of lamentation and complaint. However, we are not able to ascertain to what extent this scale is known by the folk artist to be a means of expressing the given emotions. We know many songs in Jewish folk music of a lamenting type whose melodies do not use the altered Dorian. A clear example is the published variant of the song about the worker (Ex. 31), in which the melody is built on the minor scale. Finally, the melodic lines of Jewish women's lament for the dead also lacks the characteristic elements of the altered Dorian. Doubtless the melodic line of the lament for the dead is considerably older and more widespread in Jewish life than the altered Dorian, which seems to be an occurrence of later date and more local distribution in Jewish folk music. The particularly sharp melodic lines of the altered Dorian, in comparison to the natural minor, could not help but attract the attention of the folk artist, and he always turned to it when seeking means to match his expression. We can confirm the deliberateness of the choice as we familiarize ourselves with how the scale in question is used in humorous songs. Whenever an author wants to create the impression of lamentation for humorous purposes he turns to the altered Dorian scale.

Example 47 shows a widespread humorous song [see pp. 400–401 in this volume—M.S.]. The song begins with a refrain (first fourteen measures). The text of the refrain and its melodic formulation create the impression that we are really dealing with someone who has suffered a burglary. He calls for help: "Catch him, hold him . . . put him in prison . . . he robbed me, he stole everything that was in my house." The melodic line is weeping, imploring. The range of the melody broadens in the song proper, where the victim begins to enumerate the stolen items. The more we become aware of what was stolen, the more it is clear that the robbery was made up, that the thief did not find such rich goods—the hero of the song is just sarcastically mocking his own bitter poverty: "Seven new shirts, three with patches, four with holes, seven candle sticks, like stars: three without bases and four without tops." He wanted not to complain to us but to confuse us.

We can find a hint of the use of the altered Dorian for parody of the

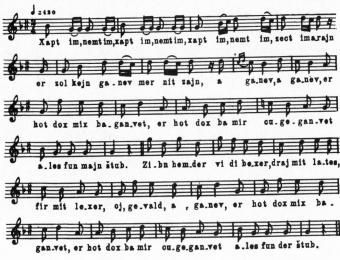

Example 47

melodic lines of lamentation in the song "Oj vej, majn vajb iz krank" (Ex. 48). The melody is built in the confines of a perfect fifth, and the C# here is the only sign of the altered Dorian. The C# is only used in the first half of the melody. By using the melodic line D–C#–B-flat the author wanted to create the impression that the husband in whose name the song is sung was sympathizing with his wife's illness. But as soon as it is clear that he is sorry not about his wife but about the money he has to spend on the doctor, which he would rather use for playing cards, the complaining melodic line is no longer necessary, and C-natural appears in the place of C#.

For an even clearer use of the altered Dorian for humorous purposes, let us look at the popular song "Varničkes" (Ex. 49). The broken descending line of the first four measures, the rhythm, and the content of the text of the first lines lead one to expect a story about some great grief. But we have been led on by a false lamentation. The girl in whose name the song is sung needs many things for her dumplings: a board for rolling out the dough, and, in subsequent verses, a knife to cut the dough, a pot to cook the *varničkes,* and, finally, a boy to eat them. As soon as the author has accomplished his goal of having the lamenting tone make you sympathize,

Example 48

Example 49

the altered Dorian is no longer needed, and he continues the melody in natural minor.

This use of the altered Dorian in humorous songs serves as a striking illustration of the fact that the folk artist used the scale completely consciously to express various degrees of sharpness of complaint, up to the point of lament, when he gives reign to his feelings. This is the basic semantic *dominanta* which the altered Dorian scale had in Jewish folk music. This also explains the variable percentage of melodies in the given scale in one or another branch of Jewish folk music.

Can we conclude that the altered Dorian scale is capable of expressing only feelings of a lamenting character? No. True, this scale has ample means of expression for reflecting such emotions: three minor seconds and one augmented second, an augmented fourth above the tonic, and finally, a major second, which sounds tense enough alongside the various minor tonic triads. In folk art, where melody is the basic, and often the only, means of expression, the expressive possibilities of the given scale could not help being noticed and used by the folk artist.[2]

Let us examine one more example (Ex. 50), a textless song. The scheme of the song is *abca*. The *c* is in the altered Dorian. Here there can be no question of lamenting emotions. It is more like sweet joy, or crooning of some sort, which contrasts very well with the major of the first and second sections of the song.

Finally, let us introduce one more song, a lullaby in the form of a verse and refrain (Ex. 51). The first eight measures are the refrain, repeated after every verse. In scalar terms this is a hybrid, where D minor and G minor alternate with episodes in the altered Dorian. Here, as well as in Example 50, there can be no question of reflecting lamentation, but rather of dreaminess, joy, caressing, and crooning. It can be noted that in its emotional content this is the only song of its kind in Jewish folklore, or at least in our archives and the available printed sources.

---

2. There is another scale with highly expressive elements in Jewish folk music, the so-called *frigiš*, or altered Phrygian, with the following scale:

We cannot spend time on its role. Let us just note that in the *frigiš* scale the tension is only in the lower tetrachord; the upper has no special characteristics that contrast with the natural minor. It is different in the altered Dorian; not only does the lower pentachord have a tense melodic line, but the upper tetrachord is tense due to the major sixth above the tonic, which sounds like, or implies, a drone in this scale.

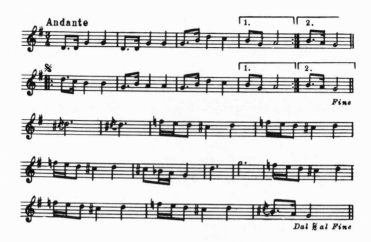

Example 50

What conclusions can we draw?

First, it must be said that the altered Dorian scale is used in Jewish folk music only to correspond to the semantic *dominanta* found in folk art, principally as a means of expressing various degrees of lamentation and complaint.

However, a certain number of songs and musical works on a non-lamenting character indicate that the semantic characteristics of this scale in folklore are not limited to those just cited.

Finally, it is worth noting that this scale can enrich the palette both of the folk artist and of the contemporary composer.

Example 51

APPENDIX A:

*Selected Bibliography on the Music Culture of the
Eastern European Jews
(Materials Published Since World War II)*

The following bibliography does not pretend to be comprehensive, since it is
meant to provide the reader with a selective list of writings on topics addressed
by Beregovski that have appeared since he completed his work in the early 1940s.
It is remarkable how little has been written on the subject of traditional music
among the Jews of Eastern Europe, despite the extensive literature on other aspects
of their culture, particularly the Yiddish language.

For basic orientation, the reader is advised to consult two encyclopedia entries
that introduce the general topic of Jewish music as well as provide bibliographical
listings: "Music," in the *Encyclopaedia Judaica* (Jerusalem: Keter, 1971); and "Jewish Music," in *The New Grove Dictionary of Music and Musicians* (London: Macmil-
lan, 1980).

Avenary, Hanoch. "The Concept of Mode in European Synagogue Chant." In
Yuval, edited by A. Shiloah, vol. 1, pp. 11–22. Jerusalem: Hebrew University, 1971.

———. "The Musical Vocabulary of Ashkenazic Hazanim." In *Studies in Biblical
and Jewish Folk-Lore,* edited by R. Patai et al., pp. 187–98. Bloomington:
Indiana University Press, 1960.

Cahan, Y. L. *Shtudies vegn yidisher folksshafung.* Edited by M. Weinreich. New
York: YIVO Institute for Jewish Research, 1952.

———. *Yidishe folkslider mit melodies.* Edited and with an introduction by M.
Weinrich. New York: YIVO Institute for Jewish Research, 1957.

Hrushovski, Benjamin. "On Free Rhythms in Yiddish Poetry." In *The Field of Yiddish,* edited by U. Weinreich, pp. 219–66. New York: Linguistic Circle of New York, 1954.

Mazor, Yaacov, and Hajdu, Andre. "The Hasidic Dance-Niggun: A Study Collection and Its Classificatory Analysis." In *Yuval,* edited by I. Adler and B. Bayer, vol. 3, pp. 136–266. Jerusalem: Hebrew University, 1974.

Mlotek, Eleanor Gordon. "America in East European Yiddish Folksong." In *The Field of Yiddish,* edited by U. Weinreich, pp. 179–95. New York: Linguistic Circle of New York, 1954.

———. "A gilgul fun mikhl gordons di bord," *YIVO-bleter* 25 (1951):299–311.

———. "International Motifs in the Yiddish Ballad." In *For Max Weinreich on His Seventieth Birthday.* The Hague: Mouton, 1964. Pp. 209–28.

———. *Mir trogn a gezang.* New York: Workmen's Circle, 1974.

———. "Soviet-Yiddish Folklore Scholarship." *Musica Judaica* 2, no. 1 (1977–78):73–90.

———. "Traces of Ballad Motifs in Yiddish Folk Song." In *The Field of Yiddish, Second Collection.* The Hague: Mouton, 1965. Pp. 232–52.

Mlotek, Eleanor Gordon, and Mlotek, J. *Perl fun der yidisher poezie.* Tel-Aviv: Peretz, 1974.

Noy, Dov. "Dos meydl un der royber." *Yorbukh fun literatur un kinst* 5 (1969): 177–224.

Pipe, Sh. Z. *Yiddish Folksongs from Galicia: The Folklorization of David Edelshtat's Song 'Der Arbeter'; Letters.* Edited by Dov Noy and Meir Noy. Folklore Research Center Studies 2. Jerusalem: Hebrew University, 1972.

Rubin, Ruth. "A Comparative Approach to a Yiddish Song of Protest." *Studies in Ethnomusicology* 2 (1965):54–74.

———. "Slavic Influences in Yiddish Folksong." In *Folklore and Society: Essays in Honor of Ben Botkin,* edited by B. Jackson, pp. 131–52. Hatboro, Pa.: Folklore Associates, 1964.

———. *Voices of a People.* 2d ed. New York: McGraw-Hill, 1973.

Sekulets, Emil. *Yidishe folkslider fun rumenie.* Tel-Aviv, 1970.

Sendrey, Alfred. *Bibliography of Jewish Music.* New York: Columbia University Press, 1951.

Slobin, Mark. *Tenement Songs: The Popular Music of the Jewish Immigrants.* Urbana: University of Illinois Press, 1982.

———. "The Evolution of a Musical Symbol in Yiddish Culture." In *Studies in Jewish Folklore,* edited by F. Talmage, pp. 313–30. Cambridge, Mass.: Association for Jewish Studies, 1980.

———. "The Uses of Printed Versions in Studying the Song Repertoire of Eastern European Jews: First Findings." In *The Field of Yiddish, Fourth Collection,* edited by M. Herzog et al., pp. 329–70. Philadelphia: ISHI, 1980.

Slotnick, Susan. "The Contributions of the Soviet Yiddish Folklorists." *Working Papers in Yiddish and East European Jewish Studies* 20. New York: YIVO Institute for Jewish Research, 1976.

Soifer, Paul. "Soviet Jewish Folkloristics and Ethnography: An Institutional History, 1918–1948." *Working Papers in Yiddish and East European Jewish Studies* 30. New York: YIVO Institute for Jewish Research, 1978.

Stutschevsky, J. *Folklor muzikali shel Yehudey mizrakh Europa.* Tel-Aviv: Bialik, 1958.

Suliteanu, Ghisela. "The Traditional System of Melopeic Prose of the Funeral Songs Recited by the Jewish Women of the Socialist Republic of Rumania." In *Folklore Research Center Studies,* edited by D. Noy, vol. 3, pp. 291–349. Jerusalem: Hebrew University 1971.

Weinreich, U. "Di forshung fun 'mishshprakhike' yidishe folkslider." *YIVO-bleter* 34 (1950):282–88.

Weisser, Albert. *A Bibliography of Publications and Other Resources on Jewish Music.* New York: Jewish Music Council, 1969.

Werner, Eric. *A Voice Still Heard . . . : The Sacred Songs of the Ashkenazic Jews.* University Park: Pennsylvania State University Press, 1976.

Wohlberg, Max. "The Music of the Synagogue as a Source of the Yiddish Folksong." *Musica Judaica* 2, no. 1 (1978):21–50.

APPENDIX B:

Archival Resources for the Study of Eastern European Jewish Folk Music

A wide variety of potential research materials is housed in various private collections and institutional archives in the United States and Israel. It would be impossible at this time to furnish a comprehensive listing, as the initial survey work remains to be done. What follows is a small sample designed to indicate the range of resources; the order is random.

PERSONAL COLLECTIONS

1. Meir Noy's personal archive, Tel-Aviv. Meir Noy has privately collected and comprehensively cataloged an extensive library of songs and secondary sources relating to Jewish song in Yiddish and Hebrew. His holdings also include a number of valuable studies he has written, which remain in manuscript form.

2. Eleanor Gordon Mlotek's personal archive, New York. Mlotek, like Noy, has assembled an impressive body of materials on songs in Yiddish.

3. Ruth Rubin's archive. Rubin was a pioneer in the United States in initiating fieldwork among post–World War II immigrants. Her collection of 132 tapes is deposited at the Archive of Song of the Library of Congress and at YIVO in New York. It covers a broad range of materials, from children's songs through folksingers to theater and art songs by a wide variety of performers.

INSTITUTIONAL HOLDINGS

1. U.S. Library of Congress. In addition to the Rubin tapes just mentioned, the Library of Congress also has the somewhat analogous, smaller Stonehill collection, as well as sheet music editions of Yiddish songs.

2. The Phonoteque of the National Sound Archives, at Hebrew University, Jerusalem. Along with materials of the Jewish Music Research Center of Hebrew

University, this comprises a large body of materials relating to the Eastern European Jewish heritage as preserved in Israel.

3. YIVO Institute for Jewish Research, New York. YIVO's holdings encompass a wide variety of manuscript and printed materials that include both primary and secondary sources. Just to include basic categories, there are field tapes based on oral tradition, virtually all the available published song anthologies, memoirs and historical records of important collectors, scholars, and scholarly organizations, and 78 rpm recordings of Jewish folk and popular folk-based music.

Two special collections deserve particular mention: (A) the tapes and transcripts of the YIVO Jewish Folksong Project, directed by Barbara Kirshenblatt-Gimblett. This represents several hundred hours of interviews and well over a thousand songs, the work being done in the early 1970s and funded by the National Endowment for the Humanities; (B) the recently (1981) discovered 1938 song anthology by Beregovski cited in the Introduction to the present volume. This extremely significant item is unique and merits some description. It represents the final preprint copy of author's proofs set in type, of the entire volume, minus (unfortunately) the actual music notation of the songs. Included are: (1) the introduction; (2) the entire collection of 240 song texts; (3) the annotations to the songs, and (4) the detailed list of informants.

The 1938 volume was meant to be the "folk song" anthology, as opposed to the largely worker and revolutionary orientation of the 1934 volume included in the present edition. It consisted of ten sections, only the last of which had Soviet-topic songs: love songs, way-of-life songs, humorous songs, recruit and army songs, songs of street singers, songs about death, riddle songs, lullabies, children's songs, folk songs of the Soviet period. Virtually all seventy of the songs in the posthumous 1962 song anthology (included in the present volume) are found in this 1938 unpublished book. According to Eleanor Gordon Mlotek, who has surveyed the volumes, there are some differences in text between the versions in the 1938 book and the 1962 book.

Index of First Lines of Songs in the Song Collections

575

Index of Instrumental Tunes

Publications of the American Folklore Society
New Series
General Editor, MARTA WEIGLE